BEYOND BASKETBALL

Mike Krzyzewski

ALSO BY MIKE KRZYZEWSKI

Five-Point Play
Leading with the Heart

BEYOND BASKETBALL

COACH K'S KEYWORDS FOR SUCCESS

MIKE KRZYZEWSKI

with JAMIE K. SPATOLA

Published by Warner Books

NEW YORK   BOSTON

Warner Business Books
Hachette Book Group USA
1271 Avenue of the Americas
New York, NY 10020
Visit our Web site at www.HachetteBookGroupUSA.com.

Warner Business Books is an imprint of Warner Books, Inc. Warner Business Books is a trademark of Time Warner Inc. or an affiliated company. Used under license by Hachette Book Group USA, which is not affiliated with Time Warner Inc.

Printed in the United States of America

First Edition: October 2006
10 9 8 7 6 5 4 3 2 1

Library of Congress Control Number: 2006928991
ISBN-13: 978-0-446-58049-6
ISBN-10: 0-446-58049-X

Dedicated to Captain Chris Spatola, who goes
above and beyond in so many ways.
—M.K. and J.K.S.

ACKNOWLEDGMENT

Intimate experiences are precious in life. I have enjoyed one of the most intimate in writing this book with my daughter Jamie. We have spent a lot of time together on airplanes, in gyms, sharing meals, talking on the phone, and I have loved every second of it.

Since she was a little girl, Jamie has loved to write and I have known that she has a gift. I have used her gift to help me share some of my life stories with you and she made it easy for me. I often say that two is better than one if two can act as one. Jamie and I truly acted as one and grew together during this project. I thank her as I love her—with all of my heart.

—Mike Krzyzewski
June 2006

CONTENTS

Introduction / xi

Adaptability / 1

Adversity / 4

Balance / 9

Belief / 14

Care / 19

Challenges / 23

Collective Responsibility / 26

Commitment / 30

Communication / 33

Courage / 38

Crisis Management / 43

Culture / 48

Dependability / 51

Empathy / 54

Enthusiasm / 57

Excellence / 62

Failure / 66

Family / 71

Friendship / 77

Fundamentals / 81

Giving Back / 85

Guidance / 89

Imagination / 92

Integrity / 97

Learning / 101

Love / 105

Motivation / 108

Next Play / 112

Ownership / 117

Passion / 121

Poise / 126

Pressure / 130

Pride / 135

Respect / 140

Selflessness / 145

Standards / 149

Talent / 152

Trust / 157

Will / 162

Work / 165

Conclusion: The Fist / 169

INTRODUCTION

I am a believer in the power of words.

Before many of our team's practices and games, I will write a single word or two on the whiteboard of our locker room. To me, these solitary words speak more than any lengthy speech. I want to have each player picture himself doing these words: having *passion*, striving for *excellence*, playing with *poise*. When my players take the court and momentarily lose sight of our team's goal for that game, they can think back on that one word. They regain focus and they can look around at their teammates and know that that word resonates in their minds as well. They may even repeat that word in a huddle, or I may say it on the bench during one of our time-outs. It keeps us together and committed to a common goal, even in the heat of the game.

When you read this book, I want you to ask

yourself an important question: how do our brains assign meaning to a particular word? Many of you would respond by reciting a dictionary definition: what the word signifies, its pronunciation, its etymology, and what it means to us today. If you have a good dictionary, you may even be offered the word in the context of a sentence. The dictionary is a great thing to study if you want to learn how to use words in sentences, paragraphs, in speeches and novels. Remember, however, that you are only borrowing these words.

This book is not about merely USING or BORROWING words; it is about OWNING them.

To incorporate these words into your own life, or to teach them to your own team, your business, or your children, merely memorizing a definition is insufficient. Anyone, through enough practice and repetition, can recite the definitions to countless words. But for these words to become instinct, part of the person you are, requires understanding.

So, in addition to an explanation of meaning, I would like to offer you a story from my own life to accompany each word. For me, these stories encapsulate not only a definition but a moment in my life in which the word's true meaning became abundantly clear. I want you to imagine yourself in those stories and try to get a grasp of how that word played a key role in my life, the life of my family or my teams. I am honored to lend you our stories.

But my ultimate goal in writing this book is for you to have your own stories, for you to look into your past and pay attention to your present so that your image of the word will become a story from your own life experiences. I truly feel that we all should be able to write this book.

Then, when your son or daughter, your player or employee asks you what the word means, you won't recite them a definition; you will tell them a story. When you talk about life's most vital and beautiful words, you are not merely borrowing them from a dictionary or from someone else's life experiences, they are yours. Those words belong to you.

I hope that you find these words as powerful as I do, that you will believe in them, and, most of all, that they become your own.

BEYOND BASKETBALL

Adaptability

As a point guard at West Point, I had the privilege of playing for the legendary Bob Knight, a tough coach and probably the best of all time. There was one particular drill, called "Zig Zag," that we did in practice every single day. It was a defensive drill that was difficult and physically exhausting. Though it's a great and effective drill, my teammates and I dreaded it, but we always knew it was coming.

Five years later, after the completion of my service in the United States Army, I was able to reunite with Coach Knight as a graduate assistant coach at Indiana for the 1974–75 season. It was an unbelievable start for a coaching career, because not only did I have the opportunity to work under the best in the business, but he also had the number one team in the country that year with such standout players as Scott May, Kent Benson, and Quinn Buckner.

At our very first practice of the season, I was so excited just to be there. But I couldn't help but notice that we did not do the "Zig Zag" drill. In the locker room after practice, I was thinking about saying something to Coach Knight about it, but I thought better of it, and didn't say anything. Surely we would do the drill tomorrow.

The next day, we had a great practice, but again, no "Zig Zag." That day, Coach Knight seemed like he was in a pretty good mood and I was feeling sure of myself.

"Coach," I said, to get his attention.

"What?" he responded. I was already thinking that this was a mistake, but at this point I had to say it.

"Well, at Army, we did the 'Zig Zag' drill every single day, often multiple times. How come we haven't done it with this team?"

Coach Knight walked calmly over to me, put his hand on my shoulder, and said, "Michael, there is a big difference between you and Quinn Buckner."

He was right. Drills like "Zig Zag" that are a necessity for some teams may not be appropriate for others. You have to adapt what you do based on who you are. A drill that Mike Krzyzewski needs to do every day, Quinn Buckner may never have to do or may only have to do infrequently. Every player is different, every team is different, and to merely apply a formula is not fair to those players or those teams.

You can always learn something from great teachers. I had the privilege to learn from one of the best coaches of all time. From Coach Knight, I learned passion, commitment, persistence, and intensity. But I also learned adaptability.

That lesson is the reason why I have written a different practice plan for every single practice of my career. In teaching, you must remember that no group or individual is the same as who you taught the day before, the year before, or the decade before. Your plan has to suit who you and your team are *right now*. And you must always be willing to adapt. When you do, you and your team will be even more successful.

Adversity

What I believe separates good teams and individuals from great ones is the manner in which they handle adversity. Do you let it beat you or do you use it to make you better?

Adversity can teach you more about yourself than any success, and overcoming an obstacle can sometimes feel even better than achieving an easy victory. Additionally, you can discover things about your endurance, your ability to turn a negative into a positive, and your personal strength of heart.

One of the greatest comments I ever heard about adversity came from the current Duke University president, Richard Brodhead. He said to me, "You outlive your darkest day." In other words, failure can never be your destination. In adverse circumstances, you must remind yourself that this day is not your last. You will get through it, but can you use it to get better? Improvement comes as the result of adversity; it comes from learning about limits and how to break those limits. Whenever I face adversity, I look *at* the problem and then *beyond* the problem. I look for the solution and then I look for the positive impact it will have on me, my team, or my family.

In the summer of 2003, after doing a speaking engagement in Colorado Springs, I heard on television the frightening news that my former Duke point guard Jason Williams had been in a horrific motorcycle accident. I immediately made calls to find out about Jason and learned that he was in serious condition and had been taken to a trauma center in Chicago. The initial prognosis was that he had a chance of losing his leg and never being able to walk again. I immediately changed my original schedule and flew to Chicago to be with him.

On the flight, I thought about Jason's current condition and all that he had already accomplished in his young life: he was a Duke University graduate, a National Champion, a two-time National Player of the Year, and he had his jersey retired and hanging from the rafters in Cameron Indoor Stadium.

One thing that had always blown me away about Jason is that he was never afraid to make mistakes. In the 2001 National Championship game, Jason had hit only one three-pointer in ten attempts, but going into the last few minutes of the game, I called a play for him to shoot another three. He was not afraid to take that next shot. And he hit the three that proved to be the biggest shot in the last few minutes of the game. As a result, we all became National Champions. Jason was fearless because he grew up with great parents, knowing that he had their unconditional love and support and that a mistake was never the end-all. I tried to offer him the same type of support during his college career. His fearlessness made him one of the best players I have ever coached.

I will always remember walking into Jason's hospital room, seeing him in that condition, and hugging his crying mother and father. As I bent over and kissed him on his forehead, Jason said to me, "Coach, thanks for being here."

I then proceeded to talk to Jason in positive terms about the fact that he would not only walk again but also would be in the NBA again. I gave him a holy saint's medal of mine that I had carried with me for years. Every time he looked at the medal, I wanted him to look beyond the adversity he was currently facing and to remember that those who love him will be behind him throughout his recovery and the rest of his life. I wanted to give him *a destination beyond the devastation.* I said to him,

"Jason, this medal is very special to me, but I want to lend it to you. You have to promise to give it back to me the day that you play in your next NBA game. And you can be sure that I will be there."

The doctors would talk about the solution to Jason's medical problems, but I wanted to be sure that, mentally and emotionally, he was looking beyond the problem and that his destination was not adversity, but success.

I have always known that Jason has the heart of a champion and with him it is best to let him follow his instincts. Winners expect to win. And Jason expects that he will come out a champion yet again. His limits have been tested in a very serious way. But he is approaching this scary situation and his arduous recovery with the same fearlessness with which he played every game of basketball. He has taken his recovery time to develop as a student of the game, attending as many games as possible, asking questions of other players and coaches, and even doing television commentary during some games. Because I know Jason has a winner's heart, it doesn't surprise me to watch as he has gone from not knowing whether or not he will walk again to having the opportunity to begin playing basketball.

The adversity did not beat him. Rather, he has used it as an opportunity to grow as a person and to learn a great deal about what a strong man he is, mentally, emotionally, and physically. Jason looked at his adversity and beyond, and his champion heart has him running and jumping again, less than three years later. What a winner!

Balance

Drive, passion, and intensity: these are all good things. They are elemental to finding success in your life and career. But just as important to life as all of these things is balance. Being motivated in your career is important, but you must be cautious not to become one-dimensional. If there is no balance between the time and energy spent on your career, your family, your religion, your friendships, and community service, you can become unbalanced internally.

I was reminded of the need for balance by my then eleven-year-old daughter, Jamie, after a heartbreaking loss in 1993. Our team had won back-to-back NCAA National Championships in 1991 and 1992, but California had just beaten us to end our pursuit of a third title in a row.

On the jet going back to North Carolina that

night, the mood was very somber. I walked down the aisle of the plane thanking our cheerleaders and band members for all that they had done as a part of our team. At the same time, I was watching my players, and particularly my seniors, to see if any of them needed my friendship or assistance during this difficult time. I heard Jamie's voice whispering, "Dad, come here." At first I tried not to pay attention to her because I was focused on my team. But she was persistent. When I went over to her, she said, "Dad, can we have a family meeting tomorrow?"

We had not had a family meeting in a number of months, and there I was, worried about my team, and my eleven-year-old wanted to call one. However, always wanting to give my children the time and attention they deserve, I agreed to a meeting the next evening at six o'clock.

That next morning, Jamie came into our bedroom with clipboard and pen in hand. She asked me to rank my level of happiness on a scale of one to five: one being the lowest, and five being the highest. Because of the loss and the mood I was in, I wanted to tell her it was a zero. But, because she was eleven, I told her it was a three: a very mediocre response.

"Okay," she said, taking note of my answer, "now, how would you rate your happiness level if we were to get a dog?"

I could see where this was going but I responded anyway. "Four."

At 6:00 p.m. sharp, we all gathered in the family room. Jamie had the entire family in front of her, and behind her two posters. The first sign read, in large letters, "Issue #1: A Dog," and below it had the action statement, "Act Now." Next to it, the second sign read, "Issue #2: Family Vacation," and below that, "Badly Needed." With a pointer, she indicated the first topic and began to plead her case. She even revealed a bar graph she had drawn displaying the family level of happiness without a dog and the projected level of happiness should we decide to get a family pet. The graph showed that the family happiness level would go from 60 percent to 80 percent. A shocking 20 percent increase in overall family happiness! She then used her pointer to indicate the action statement as she read aloud the words, "Act Now."

During the next twenty minutes, the discussion turned into the typical family debate over whether or not to get a pet. Who would train the puppy? Who would take the time to walk and exercise him? Who would clean up his messes? After the unconvincing responses that my daughters would take care of all of those things, we told Jamie that it was not going to happen. Jamie cried. The meeting was over. We never even got to issue number two.

The next day I left for a recruiting trip. When I returned the following day, I opened the door, and to my surprise, we had a dog: a beautiful black Lab puppy that we named Defense.

In that situation, Jamie proved to be wrong. She said the happiness would increase by 20 percent; it actually went up 40 percent, because now we were 100 percent happy. Defense turned out to be an amazing addition. And, a year later, we added another dog to our family, a chocolate Lab named Cameron. "D" and "Cammy" have brought joy, comfort, and unconditional love into our everyday lives. When I come home from a long trip or a hard practice, there is nothing I love to do more than get down on the floor and spend time with our dogs.

After getting to know Defense for a couple of days, I left town again to work for CBS during the 1993 Final Four. I was gone for seven days. When I returned home, I was exhausted and emotionally drained but was scheduled to leave the next day for a five-day recruiting trip. As I was sitting in the family room, I looked up and Jamie's signs were still there. I stared hard at the sign that read, "Family Vacation: Badly Needed." After thinking momentarily, I canceled the recruiting trip and took that time to go to the beach with my family.

While at the beach, I was able to spend some

one-on-one time with my middle daughter, Lindy, who was going through a very difficult teenage crisis. After a long walk on the beach and a great discussion, we together had come up with a solution to the crisis. Our family happiness increased yet again. All because my eleven-year-old daughter persisted in making sure that I keep balance in my life.

As a leader and a career-oriented individual, you must take care not to allow one aspect of your life to so consume you that you neglect the others. Your family and friends are there to remind you when you need to "act now" on regaining some balance and when getting back on the right and healthy track is "badly needed." At a time in my life when my career had stirred up some very intense emotions, I was reminded to put time into the other parts of my life, and it ended up changing all of us for the better. Balance can put things in perspective, can bring you joy even when you are down, and can allow you to be at your best in all aspects of your life.

Belief

Those three magic words "I love you" are words that are important and meaningful in any culture. But there are four words that are not said nearly enough by families interacting with kids or people interacting in a team environment.

In all forms of leadership, whether you are a coach, a CEO, or a parent, there are four words that, when said, can bring out the best in your team, your employees, and your family.

"I believe in you."

Those four words can mean the difference between a fear of failure and the courage to try. When you look someone in the eyes and tell them, "I believe in you," you are letting them know, "You are not going to take this journey alone. I'm not going to allow you to." When someone believes in you, it helps you to overcome the anxiety that comes as a result of feeling alone. Belief raises your confidence level and allows you to try things that are impossible to do by yourself.

On a team or in a family, belief makes each individual stronger and also fortifies the group as a whole. You know that there is somebody there to catch you if you fall, and someone to give you that extra push when you need it to overcome an obstacle.

When a group shares belief you share the brunt of any defeat, making it easier to turn a mistake into a positive. Likewise, successes feel even better because you share the rewards. You have all been a part of the success. In an atmosphere of belief, both wins and losses are shared.

Belief does not occur naturally; you have to work for it, earn it, and continue to deserve it. The basis of belief is in individual relationships. If I lie to you, I create a breach in that relationship, and it becomes more difficult for you to believe what I say. As powerful as belief can make you and your team, it is also fragile. You have to take care of it.

BELIEF IN ACTION

When I think about belief, the first person that comes to mind is my associate head coach, Johnny Dawkins. My first couple of years at Duke were difficult times. In two seasons, I had a 27–30 record, and many critics were anxious to see me fired. In our first couple of seasons, my staff and I had tried to recruit a large number of kids and had fallen short on most of them; we had cast our net too wide. So we changed our strategy. We decided that we were going to be much more focused in our recruiting effort, giving us a chance to form meaningful relationships with the few kids we were trying to bring in.

Johnny Dawkins was a highly touted high school standout from Washington, D.C. I can remember spending time with him and his family in the living room of their home and I remember his spending time with my family at ours. My four-year-old daughter, Lindy, even handed him a note asking him if he was coming to Duke, providing "yes" and "no" boxes for him to check. Johnny and I bonded instantly. I knew he was something special.

Recruiting in those days was more difficult for me because I had no résumé to show. I didn't have a winning record and we had not won any championships. So, in recruiting Johnny Dawkins, who was being pursued by all of the top schools, I was really asking him to believe in me, even though I didn't have any tangible reasons to offer as to why he should.

He was our first major recruit, our first major talent, and our first McDonald's All-America. I can never emphasize enough what Johnny's commitment to me and to Duke meant to our future success. As much as a great player needs a start, needs someone to believe in his ability, a coach needs a start too. I did not always win at Duke. There was a time when we were nowhere near the top of the college basketball ranks. *I needed someone to believe in me. Johnny did that and I am so thankful that he did.*

After coming to Duke and having an incredible career, scoring more than 2,500 points and being named National Player of the Year, Johnny was a lottery pick in the draft and had a long and successful career in the NBA. And, as much as Johnny showed belief in me, I always believed in him as well. If he missed four or five shots in a row, I would remind him to keep shooting, to treat every shot like it was his first. Because we both exhibited mutual belief, we developed an amazing bond as a coach and a player. Following the example set by him, we have continued to have success in recruiting some of the top high school players.

As if he hadn't already done enough, Johnny came back to Duke as a coach, and our bond continued to develop as head coach and associate head coach. And there is no one more qualified to pass on our shared belief to others than Johnny Dawkins, whose power to believe got this whole thing started.

Johnny was a trailblazer. His commitment to Duke and our mutual belief stands as the foundation of the tradition we have established for our program: a foundation of strong belief. My assistants and I continue to go into the living rooms of talented young men and tell them that we believe in them and ask if they, too, will believe in us. And, thanks to Johnny Dawkins, the example has been set. When those youngsters agree to believe in us and we commit to believing in them, great teams, players, and traditions are born.

Care

When you care about someone or something you show genuine concern for that person or thing, in good times and bad.

In the development of our basketball teams, care is as crucial an aspect as any. You want to care about one another as individuals, have empathy and compassion. And you also want to care about each other's performances on the court. When you care about one another *and* about your purpose, you are compelled to put your feelings into action.

Care is so important to a team because, if you want to change limits, there are going to be times when members of the team make mistakes. When you make a mistake, and you know it, you become very vulnerable. The immediate responses of those on your team, those you trust the most, will determine how you perceive your mistake. It can make you feel fearful of making that mistake again. Or you can feel that you put yourself on the line, and even though you did not succeed, you know that your teammates care about you and you will not hesitate to step up again. You never want to let a mistake be the last time an individual dares to try. Care makes you more confident. You know that you have someone's unconditional support. It creates an atmosphere that breeds success and gives you the confidence to try again.

Care is developed by fostering individual relationships. This means not only caring about how the team does on the basketball court but caring about their lives off the court and taking the time to get to know who they really are as a person, not only as a basketball player. Several times a year, my wife, Mickie, and I will have the team over to the house for an afternoon. We will serve a casual meal, put football games on the television, and allow the guys to relax and be themselves. Additionally, I will often meet with the players one-on-one and ask them questions about their lives: their families, their girlfriends, their classes. These are all opportunities to show my team that they are not merely basketball players to me. I genuinely care for each and every one of them, and after our time together while they are at Duke, I will continue to care about them. I absolutely love when my former players call me to ask for my input or advice, or even just to catch up. It is the ultimate proof that I have been successful in showing that I do care for them.

CARE IN ACTION

After our 1999 season in which we played in the National Championship game, I was at home recuperating from hip replacement surgery. Our great player and leader Trajan Langdon had graduated, and three of our players had decided to leave the program early to pursue a career in the NBA. One player transferred to another school. From a team that was one of the best in the nation and won 37 games, we now had only three veteran players returning. In many ways, I began to feel down and alone. Chris Carrawell, Nate James, and Shane Battier, who would become our team captains for the following season, came to visit me. They set up three chairs next to my bed and we sat there and had a long discussion about what was to come. The first thing they said to me was, "Coach, how are you doing?" Such a simple question but, for me, it carried so much meaning. They were asking how I was doing after my operation but also how I was doing in coping with the loss of so much of the team. My answer was a completely honest one. "I am okay now that you guys are here."

These three guys had taken the initiative to

come to my house and show me that they cared. While I was experiencing much doubt about the upcoming season, this meeting revived me. By the time they left, we were all talking about where we were headed that year, and because they had shown such care for me, I was able to tell them confidently that I thought we were going to have a great team and a great season. I looked at them and said that we were going to be good and then asked them, "Do you believe it?"

The response I received from Chris Carrawell is one of the greatest things a player has ever said to me. He said, *"Coach, if you say it, I believe it."*

The next season, we finished 29–5 overall, were ACC regular season champions with a 15–1 record, and ACC Tournament champions. The following year, Shane Battier and Nate James were leaders on our 2001 National Championship team. After a difficult time for me and the Duke program, those three players showed me that they truly cared. It gave me the foundation of support I needed to move on positively and develop my team to the highest level. All because they cared.

Challenges

After meeting with some success, it is often difficult for a leader to maintain a high level of passion. One way to avoid getting into a rut is to ensure that you are not doing the same thing over and over each year. I try to see each season as a new challenge because I have a new team to work with, new opponents to encounter, and often new ideas and theories to try. Approaching each season in this manner helps keep me fresh.

I think it is important not to get into a personal comfort zone. To avoid this, I try to constantly take on new challenges, to test limits, and, often, to discover that those limits were never really there. Approaching the same challenges with fresh eyes and taking on entirely new challenges isn't easy, but it can help you discover things about yourself that you may have never known, even at fifty-nine years old!

Over recent years, I have taken on such challenges as motivational speaking, the building of the Emily Krzyzewski Family Life Center, and an XM Satellite Radio show. And in the fall of 2005 I accepted one of the greatest challenges of my career.

It was a great honor when Jerry Colangelo, managing director of USA Basketball, offered me the position of United States National Team coach for three years, culminating with the 2008 Summer Olympics in Beijing. However, there were some personal issues within my family that needed to be discussed before I accepted the honor. My wife, daughters, and their husbands, while realizing the magnitude of this opportunity, were concerned that such a large undertaking would make my already busy schedule simply impossible. Additionally, they brought up health concerns that often accompany being overworked and exhausted: legitimate concerns, considering that sickness and exhaustion kept me from coaching my team the second half of the season in 1994–95.

At a dinner with my entire family, each raised their worries about the undertaking, and the discussion was at times contentious and emotional. But I explained how I feel about challenges, how they keep me fresh, young, and hungry. When everyone understood that I saw this position as an incredible honor, a chance to serve our great country, and a new personal challenge, they all took a deep breath and understood. When approaching new challenges, it is imperative that you have the support of those who love you most. Now that I know their support is there, I can throw myself into this experience knowing that, even if I fail, my family will have my back.

No matter how successful you believe yourself to be, you can never feel as if you've reached the absolute pinnacle. There are always new and wonderful challenges out there, and part of maintaining success is knowing when you need to accept them. I am rejuvenated, I am nervous, I am eager, and I am so excited to discover what amazing things I will learn as a result of taking on this new challenge.

Collective
Responsibility

W̲e win and we lose together.

The best way I can describe collective responsibility is to point to a scoreboard. At any point in the game, when you look up there, there is no one individual's name. Instead, it shows the team name: Duke, the Chicago Bulls, the USA. This means that in no way does a single individual win or lose a game. Each game, and indeed each moment within a game, is the responsibility of the entire team.

On a team that wins and loses together, there is no such thing as blame. Blame is a destructive force within a group and has no place in the locker room of a true team. *When somebody does something well, we all do it well. When somebody makes a mistake, we all make the mistake.* Outsiders, like opposing fans and the media, can say what they will: Christian's missed free throws lost the game for Duke, or Sean's last-second three-pointer is the reason we won. But behind closed doors, we know beyond any doubt that this is not true. If we won, we did it together. If we lost, that responsibility belongs to all of us as well.

Handling the responsibility for wins and losses together removes the burden from one individual's shoulders and distributes it among each member of the team. Sometimes a load is too heavy for one to carry alone. Just imagine: *what could you do if you believed you could not fail?* Being on a team that embraces collective responsibility puts you in that position. You, individually, cannot fail. That atmosphere is conducive to high-level performance and places you and your team in the position to be bold and unafraid, and if you should lose, you are not alone.

One concept I have always tried to instill in my teams is the idea that you play for the name on the front of your jersey and not the name on the back. In other words, you play as a member of the Duke team, not for the name that appears across the back of your jersey. When your team embraces that concept, then *we* competed in a game and *we* either won or lost.

J.J. Redick is the all-time leading scorer in Duke Basketball history, the leading scorer in Atlantic Coast Conference history, and the NCAA's leader in three-point shooting. He was a great player for us, the National Player of the Year. In our 2005–06 season, the media focused an incredible amount of attention on the young man, tracing how many points he needed to hit his next milestone, praising him when he had scored 30 or more points in 14 games (a Duke record), and chastising him when he had an off shooting night.

Because of the incredible amount of personal pressure placed on J.J. to score points for us and the added pressure of chasing and breaking so many records, it was often difficult for him to remember that the fate of our team and our season did not rest squarely on his shoulders.

In J.J.'s final game at Duke, we played Louisiana State University in the Sweet Sixteen. He had his worst game of the season, going 3 for 18 shooting. We lost. When J.J. came out of the game with nine seconds left, he was completely distraught. In his own mind, he took full responsibility for the loss and knew that there would not be another game to make amends. His teammates and coaches tried to console him, but it was to no avail. It really took a couple of weeks before J.J. was able to believe that it was not his fault. We had to remind him that if it were not for his performance throughout the season, we never would have been in the Sweet Sixteen. J.J. had allowed our entire team to take collective responsibility for all 32 of our wins during the season, and this time he needed to allow us, as his teammates, to help take responsibility for the LSU loss.

Earlier in the season, J.J. was able to pass the lesson of collective responsibility on to one of the younger members of our team. He embraced being a part of a team and, though he was very hard on himself, he knew the importance of collective responsibility. Our first loss of the season was to Georgetown in late January by a narrow three-point margin. With six and a half seconds left on the clock, we had a chance to tie, but our freshman point guard, Greg Paulus, dribbled into a bad situation and was unable to get the ball to J.J. for a shot. When the buzzer sounded, J.J. walked off the court with his arm around Greg. "I told him it's okay," he said afterward. *We win together, we lose together.*" Moments like that make me proud to be a coach.

J.J.'s reaffirmation of our team philosophy of collective responsibility was a reminder to Greg that his play did not decide the game for us. We lost that one together. But because we all maintained responsibility, we were able to win many more games together, finishing with a 32–4 record and becoming both the outright ACC regular season and ACC Tournament champions. We were collectively responsible for a great season.

Commitment

Aside from the vows I took with my wife, Mickie, thirty-seven years ago, the most life-altering commitment of my life came from my first athletic director at Duke, Tom Butters.

In 2004, representatives from the Los Angeles Lakers came into my living room and offered me $40 million to become their coach. In the days that followed, my family and I did our best to evaluate who we were and where we were going. In that time of self-analysis, I called my former AD.

"Mike, what are you calling me for?" he asked, surprised to hear my voice.

"Well, whenever I need good advice, I always come to you. And right now I need some good advice. Tom, someone just came into my house and offered me $40 million to coach their team. Now, when I first signed on at Duke in 1980, my starting salary was $40,000. We've come a long way since then."

Tom jokingly replied, "Well, I think I deserve a 10 percent finder's fee."

"Sounds fair," I responded. "I'll send you a check for $4,000!"

We both laughed and enjoyed the moment before delving into the more serious aspects of my situation. When it comes time to make important decisions, I always seek Tom's advice. His commitment to me, even after my first three seasons with a 38–47 record, is why I was able to get things going at Duke. I never doubted his support. And because he was committed to me and never doubted me, *I never doubted me.* His commitment made me better because I was never afraid of losing my job. It is easy to be committed to someone or something during good times, because when you are winning, your commitment is never challenged. But loyalty and dedication during more difficult times can be tough. Tom never wavered, and when commitment doesn't waver, that's when you have the greatest chance of winning. And we did win!

During the seventeen years that he was my boss, he always told me to follow my instincts. Even when we had losing records, he never interfered, he only asked me that I ensure our student-athletes were a good representation of Duke both on and off the court.

When I think back on his decision to hire me, I am amazed. He told me years later, that, following my job interview in 1980, he simply couldn't get me out of his mind. He tried to convince himself that I was not the right one for the job. But when it came down to it, he just had to follow his heart. From that day forward, we were on the same team.

Tom gave me the same advice on that summer day in 2004 that he always had. He told me to be myself, to make sure that I continue to do what I love, and to follow my instincts. The decision became easy. Because of Tom's commitment to me, I developed a commitment to Duke that I knew I could never give up. Not only that, but he taught me to be committed to myself and to follow my heart. As long as I am coaching, I will give my Duke teams the very same commitment that Tom Butters gave me.

Communication

Effective teamwork begins and ends with communication. The word, of course, means to convey a message. In order to communicate with your teammates, coworkers, or family, you must ask yourself and one another two critical questions:

- How do we talk to one another?
- How do we listen?

However, communication does not always occur naturally, even among a tight-knit group of individuals. Communication must be *taught* and *practiced* in order to bring everyone together as one.

My team has one rule regarding communication: *when you talk to one another, you look each other in the eye.* Eye contact is an important act of mutual respect but also enforces the most crucial element of communicating: telling the truth. Lying and quibbling are unnecessary impediments to working as a team. Face-to-face communication and truth should serve as the basis of all team communication.

In our team's preparation, there are three systems that I and my coaching staff try to instill. Of course, there is an offensive system and a defensive system consisting of basketball "x's and o's," but there is also a communication system. In our locker room conversations, tape sessions, and individual meetings, I encourage my players to look me in the eye and to be honest and forthright, never feeling afraid to express themselves. In these meetings we establish a system of communication steeped in honesty. By eliminating counterproductive quibbling, we establish our basis for collective communication among all members of the team, top to bottom.

On the basketball court, there is very little time to get your message across. In the heat of a game, a basketball team speaks a different language; it is not a language based on long sentences, but it is a language nonetheless. To acclimate our team to speaking this language, we do not merely drill defensive stances and positioning in our practices, we drill talking. When you talk, your body reacts, your hands get ready, and your mind becomes prepared to respond, even under pressure.

On our Duke Basketball teams, I never want to be the only communicator. In order for a message to get across, it must be echoed by every member of the group. I constantly look for members of my team who can help convey the message. It starts with my staff. Currently my coaching staff consists of three of my former players. I like having my former players as assistants because they have already been a part of the culture we instill in our young men. Often my assistants are better equipped to communicate a particular message to the team because they can present the same message in their own words or provide more current examples. It is difficult for me to believe that I am now forty years older than my players—I never thought I'd be forty years older than anybody! So my staff often helps to bridge the communication gap that can exist between generations.

The bottom line on communication is that everyone on a team should feel comfortable expressing themselves. The freedom to express oneself to other members of a team, business, or family breeds a sense of ownership. And, most importantly, each member of the team knows that when we look each other in the eye and communicate, we are honest. That type of communication can help to turn a group of individuals into a true team.

COMMUNICATION IN ACTION

I remember a few years ago I gave my team a motivational speech in our locker room before practice. At the time, I thought it was a great speech, one that would surely inspire an energetic and passionate practice. So as we left the locker room to take the court, I was proud of myself. I thought to myself, as far as speeches go, there's King, there's Lincoln, and there's me. But as we stepped onto the court, there was no pat on the back from my assistants or surge of excitement from the team. They calmly jogged out on the court and not a word was spoken.

As we took the court for practice, I asked my assistants, searching for a compliment, "How do you think it went?" Instead of the praise I had expected, my assistant Steve Wojciechowski said to me, "Coach, I don't think they understood anything you said." At first I was angry with that response because it was not what I expected. However, it was honest and made me realize that my message did not get across to my team.

I asked the team to come and sit on the bleachers and listen. When they were all gathered in front of me I asked if they had understood what I said to them in the locker room. Shane Battier, one of our team captains, stepped up and said, "No, Coach, we didn't understand."

"Well, here's what I was trying to say." I proceeded to sum up in about thirty seconds the message that I had previously tried to convey in a fifteen-minute speech. I then told Shane that if that ever happened again, I needed to know right away that my message was not received. I needed immediate communication. Shane said, "I got it, Coach. Let's start practice."

That is the type of communication I want on my team, the type where everybody can express themselves and no one feels stifled. I want the type of communication where, even if your head coach believes he has delivered the basketball equivalent of the Gettysburg Address, you can tell him that his message has not resonated. That rare but essential brand of communication turns a group of individuals with different backgrounds, talents, and ideas into a unit that can effectively talk and listen, both on and off the court.

Courage

I often share with my Duke Basketball teams a Winston Churchill quote: *"Courage is the first of human qualities because it is the quality which guarantees all the others."*

In other words, you can possess countless good qualities as an individual, but if you don't have the courage to proceed, you may never see those qualities come to fruition. It takes courage to put what you believe to be the best of you on the line, to test it, and to see how far it takes you. Courage means daring to do what you imagine.

For the most part, people do not attempt things because they fear the consequences. But the greatest consequence of all comes in not attempting to do the things that you believe you can. Having courage means boldly pursuing your dreams, no matter what the consequences may be.

Sometimes in basketball games, I will bring my players into a huddle and see fear in their eyes. Maybe a particular player has missed several shots in a row, or perhaps the opposing team has made a run and put us back on our heels. My job as a leader is to show them a face of courage. That is what a team is all about. When one individual gets down or afraid, they will look to their teammates and their leader, in particular, to bring them out of it. I want my face to tell them, "Let's all get together and let's do those things that we imagined and prepared for in practice. Let's have the courage to do the actions necessary to reach our goals." I want to take them past the hurdle of fear and help them in times of both individual and collective doubt. All of a sudden, we walk away from that huddle and, together, we are going to go after it. We are going to have a chance.

I can remember a time of extreme doubt in my life when I was offered the chance to attend the United States Military Academy and to play basketball there. At first there was no way I was going to go. I was too afraid and too full of self-doubt. But I received the encouragement I needed from my parents, my greatest supporters.

My father, in particular, was not a man of many words, but when it came to ensuring that his son did not turn down a great opportunity because of simple fear, he was vocal and emphatic. Thanks to him and my mom, I was able to find the inner courage to make the right decision, one that shaped who I would become as an adult. Just look at the word "encouragement" and you will see that it means helping another find courage. *Always surround yourself with individuals who will help to enable your courage when it is lacking from within.*

The most courageous player I ever coached was Bobby Hurley. Even when I myself felt stifled by moments of doubt, I could look into Bobby's eyes and find the confidence to proceed. My job in coaching him was to give him the freedom to boldly follow his instincts.

In the 1991 NCAA semifinal game against the University of Nevada–Las Vegas, we were a considerable underdog. UNLV had won 45 games in a row, including the National Championship game from the previous year when they beat us by 30 points, 103–73. Unlike the year before, this year's game was hard-fought, close, and incredibly exciting. Throughout the course of the game, usually only one basket separated the two teams' scores.

With under two and a half minutes remaining, UNLV jumped to a five-point lead and it seemed the momentum was going their way. When Bobby brought the ball down the court, I recognized that UNLV had changed from man-to-man defense to a matchup zone. I jumped up off the bench to tell Bobby to run a certain play against this new defense. Just as I got to my feet, Bobby took a three-point shot and knocked it down. He did not need my instruction, he needed to courageously follow his instincts. As a result of that play, the momentum shifted back and we were put in the position to win the game in the last few seconds. Bobby's three-pointer was as big a shot as any Duke player has ever hit. After we beat UNLV, we won our first National Championship by beating Kansas 72–65. Many people think of game-winning shots as last-second shots. This is not always the case. Bobby's courageous shot in the UNLV game is the perfect example.

The following year, we again found ourselves in the national semifinal game, this time matched up against Indiana. The Hoosiers played an amazing first half and really should have blown us right out of the gym. However, Bobby hit four three-point shots in that half to keep us within striking distance. We played well and together in the second half and won, eventually beating Michigan for our second straight National Championship. Neither of those championships would be ours unless Bobby had the courage to follow his instincts.

Courage is the capacity to confront what can be imagined. We all have the capacity to imagine

amazing things, but you need courage to take those
often frightening steps toward making your dreams
a reality. Your time will come. As President John F.
Kennedy once said, *"Courage is an opportunity that
sooner or later is presented to all of us."*

Crisis Management

As a leader, and particularly a leader in sport, I am often asked about how to act and lead your team in a time of crisis. My response is that, once you find yourself in that crisis moment, it may already be too late. If you have not developed your team properly, members of that team will not feel the sense of ownership your group needs in this type of moment.

Crises are not handled in the instant they occur but are prepared for in all of the moments that you and your team spend leading up to that one. You prepare for the crisis well ahead of time by establishing trusting relationships among all members of your team. For me, every team meeting, every practice, every individual conversation that occurs throughout the season establishes who we will collectively be when a crisis occurs. If you plan to manage a crisis when the time comes, it is already too late to establish the communication and trust that should already exist among the members of your team.

Crisis causes people to think and act as individuals rather than as part of a team. In difficult situations, it is human nature to feel alone, and you may start worrying about your personal plight as opposed to the unit as a whole. A leader's goal during these times must be to refocus every individual's attention on the group, the entity that you have created, which is far stronger than each separate individual. When you truly trust and rely on one another, you find strength in your unity and can face challenges with the courage and confidence that comes with knowing you are not in it alone.

In any profession, a crisis presents a situation in which it is the leader's job to find a way to win. Of course, my version of a crisis as a basketball coach is minimal when put into perspective. A crisis for me is being down by one point with only a few seconds on the clock, while others face terminal illness, being sent to war, and other life-or-death situations. No matter how strongly you feel about what you are doing, it is important that you keep a sense of perspective about the "crises" you face.

If you have a trusting team, business, or family, a crisis becomes an opportunity to shine. You relish the predicament because it is a chance to prove to yourselves and to show others the strength you have developed as a unit during the course of your time together. A well-prepared team embraces crises as defining moments and overcomes those crises together, as one.

CRISIS MANAGEMENT IN ACTION

One of the great basketball stories during my time at Duke was the 1992 NCAA regional championship game against the University of Kentucky. The winners would earn a trip to the Final Four and the losers would find themselves at their season's end. Many still refer to it as the greatest college basketball game ever played. Everyone who has seen the game recognizes the incredible passion and heart with which both our and the Kentucky kids played. It was truly a beautiful game.

The Kentucky game serves as a perfect illustration of team crisis management. With a trip to the Final Four on the line, I and my team found ourselves in overtime, down by one point with 2.1 seconds remaining on the clock. We had possession of the ball on one end of the court and had to score on the opposite basket, 94 feet away.

I had some great players and amazing young men on my team that year, including All-Americas Christian Laettner, Bobby Hurley, and Grant Hill.

As they came to the bench for that last timeout, I could see a look of defeat in their eyes. The first thing I said to them as they sat down in our huddle was, "We are going to win." Whether they believed this seemingly ridiculous claim or not, it had the effect of immediately focusing everyone's attention on our collective goal instead of thinking about blame, regret, fear, or what beach they would be going to next week instead of the Final Four.

Then I looked Grant Hill in the eye and asked him if he could pass the ball 75 feet to Christian Laettner, who would be waiting to receive the pass at the opposite free throw line. He responded that, yes, he could do that. I then turned to Christian, looked him in the eye, and asked him if he could catch the ball and get a shot off in the very short 2.1 seconds that remained in the game. He said to me, "Coach, if Grant throws a good pass, I'll catch it."

Both players said that they could and, more importantly, that they *would* accomplish their assigned tasks. They both made positive statements. I loved Hill's and Laettner's responses, because in their voices we heard confidence, and that confidence was felt throughout the entire team. It is so vital in a group for each member to hear the team message echoed by more than one voice. Christian and Grant both exuded confidence in themselves and in our team, and as a result, we left that huddle all feeling like we would be winners.

It all went according to plan. Grant threw the ball to Christian, as promised, and Christian caught the ball, dribbled once, turned around, and took our team's shot. The ball left his hand and, while it seemed to hang in the air forever, the clock expired. It went in. Pandemonium.

A lot of people say that we were lucky that day. I say, luck favors those who have spent their preparation time building effective systems of communication and trust in one another. That way, when a crisis occurs for you, within your family, your team, or your business, it can turn into an opportunity to shine.

Culture

Making shots counts—but not as much as the people who make them.

Developing a culture means having a tradition that maintains the standards you want to define your program. A common mistake among those who work in sport is spending a disproportional amount of time on "x's and o's" as compared to time spent learning about people. Culture is established by the people who compose your team and is carried on through those people. In other words, culture can only exist through the relationships among the people who make up your group, those in the back offices and on the front lines. A successful development of culture means that you hear different voices echoing the same message throughout the organization—now, through the history of your program, and into its future. But you cannot merely expect culture to be a natural occurrence; it has to be taught and made a part of your everyday routine.

Culture is a continuum. This means that it is not merely a matter of creating a culture, but perpetuating it. Those who have been in the organization for the greatest amount of time pass on the values and the message of the organization to those who are just entering. A recent trend in college basketball has seen many players leaving college early or forgoing their college career entirely to enter the NBA. While this has become virtually unavoidable, it does have a significant effect on the culture of individual programs and college basketball as a whole.

Recruiting is a key aspect of growing a culture. When my staff and I decide which kids to recruit, we don't merely look at the youngster's athletic ability, statistics, and grades, we look at how they treat their parents, how they interact with their classmates, and what other ways they contribute to their communities. One of my favorite things is when we go for a home visit and the player has his best friend with him, a friend who may not even play basketball. This shows that, at a young age, he understands that it's not all about him and he is willing to share his life with those close to him: an indication that he is willing to look beyond himself and become a part of something greater.

Culture is passing on the values and teaching

the standards that you have learned as an upper-classman to the young players on the team. I can remember many practices during the 1986 season when my starting backcourt of Johnny Dawkins, a senior, and Tommy Amaker, a junior, would completely dominate our second team.

Quin Snyder was a freshman on that second unit and would leave a number of practices feeling down and defeated. Johnny and Tommy would take Quin off to the side and tell him about when they had gone through those experiences as well. It was all a part of developing as an individual player and as a part of the Duke Basketball culture. They reminded Quin to keep working hard and keep listening to the coaching staff and that eventually it would all work out. Quin became a starter the next season and was one of our captains and major contributors on the 1989 Final Four team. He, in turn, spent time passing the lessons he learned on to Christian Laettner, who was a freshman on that 1989 team. Teaching culture is not just a leader's task; everyone on the team is responsible for passing the values, standards, and traditions on to the next generation. Christian passed it on to Grant Hill, Grant Hill to Jeff Capel, Jeff Capel to Trajan Langdon. And so on. And so on.

Dependability

Dependability is the ability to be relied upon. To always be there trying to do your best.

I have always admired Cal Ripken. Playing in a record 2,632 straight games, he earned a reputation as baseball's "Iron Man." What that means to me is that Cal played when he was sick, injured, tired: times when many other people would not have. It would be amazing to be Cal Ripken's teammate; you knew you could always depend on him. He was always there, giving his all. I try to encourage in my teams the importance of showing up and being at your best each and every day. Being able to depend on one another gives us the greatest chance of collectively achieving our goals.

Just like Cal Ripken was for the Baltimore Orioles, my brother, Bill Krzyzewski, is the Iron Man of our family. He retired recently as a captain in the

Chicago Fire Department, after thirty-seven years of service. In all of those thirty-seven years, my brother never missed one day of work. Whether it was a small fire or a terrible one, you could count on his being there and doing whatever was necessary to get the job done. Whenever I would go to the firehouse for a visit, some of Bill's men would take me aside and tell me how lucky I am that he is my brother. "He is always there for us," they would say. "We would follow him anywhere."

Bill is three and a half years older than I and we didn't really "run in the same circles" growing up. Our interests and talents were different and so were our friends, but we were always brothers. I could always count on that. If there was a problem, Bill would take care of it. He would handle it in the best possible fashion and he would never, ever say, "You owe me." He didn't do it because he wanted anything in return, he did it because he was my older brother and he loved me, and that is what older brothers are supposed to do. We all need heroes. My brother is my hero.

Dependability is not only about being there physically, but being there at your best. It is about loyalty and commitment, about being someone on whom your teammates can count. You don't have to have a master's degree to teach dependability; you teach it by example. I learned it from Bill.

I have often told my brother, "I could never be as good a brother to you as you have been to me. You are the guy I have counted on and looked up to for my whole life."

My greatest honor is when my hero, my Iron Man, looks back at me and tells me, "I love who you've become." Knowing that my brother was always there for me has helped me immensely. I tell Bill, "I love who *we* have become." All this would not have happened unless Bill was there.

Empathy

Empathy: the ability to walk in another person's shoes.

As a coach, a parent, or a leader of any kind, one of the most important things that you can feel for one of your "teammates" is empathy. If someone believes that you can identify with their situation and understand their feelings, they are more apt to trust you, which leads to faster responses to situations and better conclusions.

Empathy is important not only in coaching man-to-man defense, but in helping to soothe a daughter with a broken heart. In either situation, though the feelings involved are completely different, empathy means having the ability to, most literally, feel what the other person is feeling. Then they will never feel alone.

Showing empathy for someone can help them

to develop empathy for others. My oldest daughter, Debbie, who is now an incredible mother to her four children, told me an amazing thing. She told me that I taught her how to empathize. And I remember just the moment she was talking about.

She had come home from Duke after a rough breakup with a longtime boyfriend and was completely heartbroken. She cried and talked to my wife, Mickie, for hours. Finally, emotionally exhausted, she fell asleep lying across her bed. She said that the first thing she remembers after that is waking up with me sitting on the bed next to her and gently patting her back. When she turned to look at me, I was crying too. "Dad, what's wrong?" she asked. I replied, "I just feel so sad for you." It was true. Her heartbreak was my heartbreak too; that's what makes us a family and the greatest of teams. For a person to know that someone else understands their feelings really validates those feelings. Once acknowledged or validated, the person has a greater chance of moving on to something better, instead of being a prisoner of that particular feeling.

Part of being on any team, and a family team in particular, is trying to truly understand what each of your teammates is going through. If you feel true empathy, it can be a beautiful thing. Their difficult times become your difficult times and, likewise, their successes become your successes. Either way, your collective moments become better, less sad, or more celebratory. Someone else feels what you feel. It is not about each of us individually but, rather, all of us together. Empathy brings your group closer together by allowing all members of the group to feel as if all of their feelings are truly a shared experience.

Enthusiasm

Enthusiasm is a great interest or excitement. When you are enthusiastic, you are a catalyst to those around you. Your unabashed love and emotion for what you are doing is contagious.

As a coach, many people may think that my job is about giving: giving instruction, giving advice, giving encouragement. But when I look into the eyes of someone like Chris Collins, it is hard to explain how much I receive in return. Chris was the captain of the 1996 team and is now one of my assistant coaches. When he was a player, I saw the enthusiasm written across his face, and it fueled me. I was lucky to coach him and now am fortunate to have him on my staff, where he can share his enthusiasm for the game of basketball with our current players.

Chris Collins was the embodiment of enthusiasm. He loved to get the crowd into the game; he loved to slap the floor; he loved to get excited. Quite simply, he loved to play basketball. But my favorite part about Chris's enthusiasm is that it was not singular. It was plural. He would be even more excited about a great play made by a teammate than one he made himself.

Chris was a part of our Duke teams during a very difficult stretch, one in which we went from having a 28–6 season in 1994 to being 13–18 the following year. This was the year in which I was forced to take off the majority of the season due to my health, and it created a time of great concern for the future of the program. Let's just say it was a difficult time to be enthusiastic.

When I returned to coaching in 1996, Chris's senior year, we had a great group of young men, but the talent level was not as high as other Duke teams I've coached. In January, we headed to North Carolina State for a conference road game. We had lost four games in a row and our record in the Atlantic Coast Conference was 0–4. Since we had placed last in the ACC the previous year, many feared we were headed in that same direction. In many ways, it felt as if the direction of not just our season but our program hung in the balance of that game. We could win and be rejuvenated or lose and have our morale further decreased.

In a hard-fought battle, Chris's unwavering enthusiasm served as the emotional backbone for the rest of our team. N.C. State was ahead 68–63 with 1:30 to go in the game. Jeff Capel drove to the basket and had his shot blocked and the ball began to go out of bounds near half-court. Chris chased down the ball and dove over the scorer's table to send it back inbounds to Ricky Price. But Chris did not stop there. He immediately got up and ran back onto the court, receiving a pass from Ricky and hitting a three-point shot to cut State's lead to two. With the short amount of time left on the clock, we made the strategic decision to foul and send N.C. State to the free throw line. After they hit both of their free throws, Jeff Capel drove and quickly scored on the offensive end, putting us within two points once again. With 16 seconds left, we fouled again, and this time the State player missed the front end of a one-and-one free throw opportunity.

On our last possession of the game, Chris dribbled up the court to where we had drawn up a play for him to hand the ball off to Ricky Price. However, instead of handing the ball off, Chris's instincts told him to shoot. With six seconds left on the clock, he fired up a three-pointer and, after spending what felt like forever bouncing on the rim, the ball fell through the net. We won 71–70.

Chris remained our leader for the rest of the season, in which we finished 18–13 overall and 8–8 in conference play. The N.C. State game had been a springboard for Chris and the rest of our team. During the last month of the season, Chris was not only our emotional leader, he was our best player, averaging close to 27 points a game. His contagious enthusiasm led us to the NCAA tournament in a year we were not expected to make it. The following year, and in fact the next five seasons in a row, we won the conference regular season championship.

Chris Collins's undying enthusiasm set the program back on the right path. Despite the difficult times, Chris never allowed his spirit to be defeated, and as a result he was the catalyst for getting the Duke program back on the path to success. Being excited about playing and being a part of a team is easy to do when you are winning 30 games a year and contending for championships. But it becomes more difficult when you are losing, when fans and the media are taking shots at you, and when it feels as if nothing is working. Chris's enthusiasm was particularly impressive because he showed it at a very high level even when it was difficult to do so.

I often refer to Chris as "the bridge." He is the guy that led us over a difficult season and connected the success of the 1994 Final Four team with the future success of Duke Basketball. In 2000, Chris returned to Duke as an assistant coach. That 2000–01 season, we won our third National Championship. I was so happy to share that with Chris Collins, who deserved it as much as any kid I have ever coached.

Of his time at Duke, Chris has said, "If there's one thing that I would like to be remembered for when I leave Duke, it's that that kid just really loved to play the game." And Duke fans *will* never forget the enthusiasm of Chris Collins.

Excellence

When I sign autographs for kids, I almost always put the same message: "Always try your best." If they get nothing else from meeting me, I want them to remember these words.

Excellence is not measured the same way for everyone. A .500 season may be a perfect standard of success for one team, while a National Championship is the standard for another. Define your own success and failure; only *you* know whether or not you have given it your all. The persistent pursuit of excellence determines winners, not the score of the game.

To be excellent, you must be yourself. Do the very best that you can do. In giving your best every day, improvement will come naturally. Giving your all makes you better; it's that simple. Remember that there is a vital distinction between excellence and perfection. If you ask a young person to be excellent, he or she may think, "Oh, man, I have to be perfect? I can't do that." But if you ask him or her to just give their personal best, anybody can do that.

In the context of a team, there are many times when you are not the best individual on the team in a particular activity. You can sometimes have the tendency to look at the best person and say that he or she is excellent and you are not. This is a big mistake. Each person can be excellent, but one person may have more ability or expertise at a given time and in a given situation. This happens every year on a basketball team. What I tell my players is, "You have to *run your own race* individually while we are running our collective race as a team."

In 1998, Elton Brand and Shane Battier were both freshmen and starters for us at Duke. Elton became one of the best players in the country his first year and was National Player of the Year the next. Shane was not at that level of play immediately, but still played excellent basketball. He was a starter and was named National Defensive Player of the Year as a sophomore. Shane averaged only about 9 points a game that season, far fewer than Elton's 17. However, he always had a high opinion of his accomplishments and he was never jealous. He never felt frustrated about his efforts because he did not compare them to Elton's. Elton left Duke before his junior year and was the number one pick in the NBA draft. Shane stayed and became an all-conference player, and in his senior year was the National Player of the Year, just like Elton had been. They both ran different races, and achieved equal excellence.

Another part of seeking and maintaining excellence is always surrounding yourself with others who have high personal standards. Sometimes, when you are not at your best, someone else will be, and they can help raise you to that level.

I learned about excellence from my college coach, Bob Knight. I was the point guard for Coach Knight at West Point for three years. During that time, I learned what it meant to pursue excellence. Coach demanded that from us every day and it was a great lesson for me to learn. Coach Knight is one of the best leaders I have ever known.

After I graduated from West Point and finished my five-year service commitment to the United States Army, I was presented with the opportunity to join Coach Knight's Indiana University staff as a graduate assistant. This was another great chance for me to be around him and his team. During this experience, I met some other excellent coaches, most notably Hall of Fame coaches Henry Iba and Pete Newell. Both of these legendary coaches told me that I had an incredible opportunity to learn from the best in Coach Knight. And they gave me some advice that I will never forget. They told me to learn absolutely everything I could from Coach, to soak up his theories and philosophies, his genius for the game, and his ability to motivate. But they also told me not to try to *be* Coach Knight or anyone else, but to take everything that I learned from him and fit it into who I am as a person, a leader, and a coach. Essentially, they told me to be myself.

It is overwhelming to tell someone that they have to be Michael Jordan or Grant Hill or Ernest Hemingway or Albert Einstein. They will think it impossible. Our goal should not be to *be* our heroes, but rather to *learn* from them and then do the best possible job of being ourselves. That is how I define excellence.

Failure

Winning does not define who I am. Don't get me wrong—I am competitive and I love to win, but it does not define me.

Growing up, I knew what I was good at and I stuck to it. As a result, I became captain of my high school basketball team, a member of the national honor society, and vice president of my class. But going to school, playing basketball, and leading— these were all things that came naturally to me. I played it safe and I didn't venture beyond what was comfortable and easy for me.

My first real experience with failure came when I went to West Point. There, failure was a common occurrence for me. I didn't know how to tie a knot, I didn't know how to swim, and, growing up in inner-city Chicago, I had never had much experience with the great outdoors. At West Point, you were expected either to already know these things or learn them *very* quickly.

I learned so much at West Point both as an individual and as a member of a team. A major part of this learning process was stepping out of the realm of what came naturally, attempting new things, and, sometimes, failing at those things. I learned from West Point, and have tried to pass the message along to my teams, that progress is impossible if you only attempt to do the things that you have always done.

As an individual at West Point, I experienced my first failure when I did not pass my fall semester physical education requirement. For an all-state basketball player and someone who was considered a better than average athlete, this was the ultimate failure. The two PE courses I had that semester were swimming and gymnastics. I knew from the beginning that this would be problematic. I did not know how to swim and I had never tried gymnastics, nor any athletic endeavor that required flexibility. Everything was completely foreign to me. Though I was able to pass gymnastics by a very slim margin, I failed the swimming class and had to join a remedial swimming course until I passed the survival swimming test. The test consisted of being handed a ten-pound brick and being told to swim as far as I could, with the brick, in a seven-foot-deep pool. After I pushed away from the side, the brick went to the bottom of the pool and so did I. It was not surprising that my grade sunk as well.

The inability to pass this test the first time around and the resulting failing grade in physical education forced me to take a test with a number of other cadets to prove that I was physically capable of staying at the Academy. That test did not include swimming or gymnastics and I was able to pass with flying colors. Failing initially, but working hard to learn enough about swimming to pass the swimming test as well led me to understand that I could eventually do things that I had never done before.

My failures at the Academy were not limited to individual endeavors; I met with group failure as well. As freshmen, our platoon was asked at times to change from one uniform to another in a very short period of time. We would be told to dismiss from a formation, go back to our rooms, change to a different uniform, and be back in the same formation within three minutes. To me, this was impossible. The first time around, everyone panicked and tried to accomplish this feat completely on their own. I remember my two roommates and I ran into each other, pushed one another, and all of us were late in coming back out to formation. The upperclassman in charge of the formation asked us why we were late. The only permissible answer was, "No excuse, sir."

"That's right. There is no excuse," he said. "All of you should be out here on time." The next time we were put in this situation, one of my roommates miraculously made it out in time, but my other roommate and I were late. The upperclassman then yelled at all three of us, saying, "Either all of you are going to be late or you will all be on time." After many such situations, we made the realization that we would need to employ teamwork to be ready in time. When we worked together to be ready, we finally all made it on time to the formation. In that situation, failure forced us to find a way to help one another succeed.

Changing limits is not easy. If it was, everyone would do it without a second thought. One of the biggest lessons I have learned in my life is that failure is a natural result of breaking out of your comfort zone. At West Point, I learned to view each failure not as its own entity but as a stepping-stone on a path to something greater. It was never a destination, but I had to pass through failure to be successful at what I was attempting to do. In order to change what you believe to be your limits, you have to try new things or raise your old limits to a new level.

I had to recall this lesson throughout my life

and career because, like most people, I have failed time and time again. I can remember my third season at Duke. The group of freshmen I had that year was one of my top recruiting classes in all my years of coaching: Mark Alarie, Jay Bilas, Johnny Dawkins, David Henderson, and Weldon Williams. We had an incredible amount of talent that year but not much experience. When we ended the season with 11 wins and 17 losses, I had to teach my team that what happened was part of a process. We used that season as a learning experience and were able to look to the future: a future that we all expected would be bright. As Johnny Dawkins put it twenty years later, "We knew we were better than that, but that is where our journey began."

And because we saw that 1982–83 season as a stepping-stone on the way to something greater, the rest of our journey was incredible. The next three seasons, we had an 84–21 record, and in 1986 we won 37 games, which is still the most ever won by a college basketball team in a single season.

No one can be perfect. When you break out of your comfort zone and try new things, you will probably experience some form of failure. Failure cannot be your final destination; rather, you can use it to shatter limits. It is merely a stepping-stone on your journey to greatness.

Family

No matter how involved you are in what you do, no matter how many hours a week you devote to your career pursuits, you must always remember that your family is your primary team.

Most likely due to the fact that I have been a basketball coach for so many years, my family has always thought of itself as parallel to a basketball team. Our nucleus includes five people: myself, my wife, and our three daughters, like the five players on the basketball court at any given time. While each of us has a life and interests that are our own, we gather strength from that nucleus. We're in this together.

Over the years, each of our daughters has married and we have been blessed with five grandchildren, who call me "Poppy." We have never seen it as our children leaving, but rather as expanding our strong core. There come times in our lives when any one of us may need to "circle the wagons." In other words, when key decisions need to be made, when there is a crisis, when one of us is sick or needs help, we bring our core group together, we try to ignore other influences, and we rely on one another as teammates to develop a collective resolution.

A huge part of ensuring that your core is strong is allowing the members of your team to be a part of what you do. I always wanted my wife, my girls, and now my sons-in-law and grandchildren to be a part of what I am doing at Duke. They are not merely invited to practices, games, and team trips; I encourage them to be there if they can. I tell them about things I am trying with my team, ask for their advice on any problems, and watch game tapes with them. My girls grew up watching game film and tapes with me in our home, whether it was to analyze our team's practices and games to see how we could improve, or to scout our upcoming opponents' strengths and weaknesses. I remember when my girls were young, they would love when a reel of film would be over and there would be a white light shining from the projector onto the wall. For the next few minutes, we would do shadow puppets together. I'm not sure that they liked analyzing the film at that age, but I know they liked the shadow puppets. They were a welcome break for me as well.

Because my family has always felt like a part of Duke Basketball too, it was easier when I had to be away for long periods of time on road trips and recruiting. I never compartmentalized my career and my family. They are both a part of who I am, and being good in one can help tremendously with the other.

Additionally, when you allow those closest to you to be involved, they will be better able to support you in your times of need. And you have to let them. I remember a specific moment of family support following a tough season-ending loss to Kansas in the 2003 NCAA tournament. After the game, my family joined me in the locker room area, including my two young grandsons, Joey and Michael, who were three and a half and two years old, respectively. As we stood there in the coach's locker room, with several adults around me, Joey came confidently up to me, tugged gently on my pants leg, looked me in the eye, and said, "Don't be sad, Poppy. Your boys played really hard." It brought a smile to my face and set me at ease, and, what's more, he was right. My boys had played really hard. That's the kind of support you can get from your family, even a three-year-old member of that family, if you can allow them to be a part of your entire life.

While allowing my daughters to be a part of my career, my wife was always adamant that there be things devoted strictly to family. In fact, when the girls were growing up, there was nothing related to Duke Basketball put on display in our home: no trophies, photos, or memorabilia. We always believed that a home is about family, so we surrounded our home with family photos and items reflecting the accomplishments of our children. Your children must always believe that what they are doing and what you do as a family is the top priority.

A person is never more comfortable than when they are with their family, which is why I try to create a family atmosphere with my team and encourage people in other businesses to do the same with their employees and organization. When you are with your family, you are yourself, and when you are yourself, you are at your very best.

FAMILY IN ACTION

In 1994, we were in Charlotte, North Carolina, where Duke was playing in the Final Four. We were set to play the University of Florida in the Saturday night game in order to advance to the National Championship game. My middle daughter, Lindy, was still in high school and was going to finish out the school week before joining us for the games that weekend. One afternoon after school, she had gone to a local shopping center to run some errands. As she was getting out of her car, she was carjacked by a man with a gun. Luckily, Lindy was not injured and was able to get away and run to a police substation in the mall. Needless to say, it was a frightening incident, especially for a seventeen-year-old kid whose parents were out of town!

We asked Assistant Coach Tommy Amaker's wife, Stephanie, a successful area psychologist, and a part of our extended Duke Basketball family, to bring Lindy to Charlotte right away. After hugging her and telling her how happy we were that she was safe, my wife and I sat down with her and began to ask her a barrage of questions. How are you feeling? What did he say to you? Did you see the weapon? How did you get away? Did you see his face?

After answering a lot of questions, Lindy became exhausted, and, in reality, she was also beginning to move on from that moment and feel excited to be at the Final Four. Even so, my wife asked her, "What was he wearing?"

"A black shirt, jeans, and a baseball cap."

"Was there anything on the cap?" I asked.

With a look of exasperation and an obvious desire to move past the topic, Lindy looked me in the eye and said, "Yeah . . . Florida!"

While his hat, obviously, did not really say Florida, this was Lindy's way of telling me that she appreciated our concern but, enough about her, it was time for me to focus on why we were there: on beating Florida. What an amazing gesture of support from my daughter. While still concerned for her well-being, I could focus on the task at hand, knowing that I had her full support. We beat Florida and had the opportunity to play in the National Championship game. That kind of support is what family is all about.

Friendship

There is nothing more valuable than a true friend. They remind you of who you were, who you are now, and who you are going to be. They keep you both grounded and going in the right direction. Sometimes listening to a friend is like listening to yourself. They can be your conscience and your memory.

My very best friend is named Dennis Mlynski, but I have always called him "Moe" since we were boys growing up in Chicago. And to him and my other boyhood buddies, I will always be "Mick." He has been one of my greatest supporters throughout my life and career. Moe is the gold standard of friends. He is a better friend to me than I am to anyone, and I consider myself a good friend.

Every success that I have ever felt, Moe has felt

it too. Every failure I have experienced, he has put into perspective for me. He has been there every step of my journey, and I have been there for his. We have never been alone because we always know we have each other.

Specifically, this past year, after our season-ending loss to Louisiana State University in the Sweet Sixteen, Moe came to my hotel room along with my family. Long after everyone else had gone to bed, Moe, my wife, Mickie, and I were still talking. At the end of every season, I struggle with what I could have done differently, how I could have done better, and I reevaluate where I am in my life and career.

Feeling as down as I could be, I found myself wondering if coaching was still what I wanted to be doing, contemplating what was next for me. "Mick," Moe said to me, and even just hearing the name from my youth brought me back to earth. "You have always loved to lead." He put it so simply that I couldn't help but realize that he was right. I started that evening feeling down and wondering if I wanted to continue coaching. Thanks to Moe and his friendship, we ended our conversation at 5:30 in the morning with my being incredibly excited about the next season. That is what a friend does. He or she will listen to your ramblings, and because they know you so well and you can trust them to be honest and genuine, they help you clarify those ramblings.

As you grow and change, your true friends become friends to your family as well. I learned from my son-in-law about how Moe's friendship transcends generations. Chris Spatola, who is married to my youngest daughter, was an Army captain on a yearlong tour in Baghdad, Iraq. He told me that he had received several packages from Moe, including some long and wonderful letters. Chris, like me, had played basketball for the United States Military Academy at West Point. Moe also included in his packages to Chris several game programs and newspaper clippings about me and my teams from when I played at West Point. I couldn't believe it. Not only had Moe been there for so many of those games, not only had he saved those programs and clippings for more than thirty-five years, but he thought enough about me and my family to know that Chris would appreciate those things. My family feels lucky that Moe has become a part of their lives too.

True friends are with you for life, they remind you of the things that you need to know at the points in your life when you need to know them most. They care for you and try to clarify things for you during difficult times. And, most amazingly, friends like Moe never ask for anything in return. In life, there are not many absolutes, but when you have a great friend, that is an absolute. And Moe is *absolutely* the best friend in the world.

Fundamentals

When you have been in a particular business for a long time or, for me, when you have been through a long season of basketball, you can find yourself getting caught up in the complexities of what you are doing and forget about the fundamentals. It is important to remind yourself and your team of the essential building blocks of the game and to ensure that you continue to practice and improve on these. These building blocks are like the soil from which your skills grow. Practice will help keep that soil fertile.

At a dinner in the beautiful Wynn Las Vegas resort, I was reminded of the importance of fundamentals by a most unexpected source. My friend Steve Wynn, who, along with his wife, Elaine, has built some of the most phenomenal resorts in the

world, told me the profoundly simple concept behind their most recent masterpiece.

He told me that when approaching the building of his new hotel and casino, the first to bear the
Wynn name, he just went back to the basics. After
building such amazing places such as the Mirage
and Bellagio, it had become clear to him that there
was little "new" he could do in the hotel business.

Instead, Steve returned to the fundamentals.
The guiding thought behind the building of the
Wynn resort was, as Steve put it, "*doing the basics, better.*" Steve and Elaine spent the next several years
doing a multitude of basics better, such as ensuring
that the sheets were of the best quality, that each
room be a manageable distance from the elevators,
and that each area of the hotel had a pleasant and
welcoming scent. And, having been a guest at the
Wynn, I can assure you that the basics there are absolutely the best.

It is the same in basketball, or in any business.
I sometimes find myself devising complicated
schemes, trying to be more creative. Because I have
been coaching for so many years, I sometimes forget that a team, even a veteran team, needs a solid
foundation. Steve Wynn is right, I need to remind
myself that you can be the best in the business by
merely doing the basics, better.

To help turn fundamentals into habit requires

intensive, intelligent, and repetitive action. If any one of these elements is missing, something will be missing from the foundation of your team. This is why, in every practice, even late in the season, I always have my team continue to work on fundamental drills. It is vital that the athletes actually drill these basics. I constantly remind myself of the most basic formula of teaching: you hear, you forget; you see, you remember; you do, you understand. And when you truly understand, that is when the basics become habitual.

Every summer, we host a basketball camp at Duke for youngsters ages eight to eighteen who come from all over the world to learn from me and my staff how we do the fundamentals. One of the campers' mothers came up to me at registration and told me that her son would be attending two of the three sessions. I thought to myself, "This is great, she really understands the importance of learning how to drill the fundamentals." But then she asked me what her son would be doing differently in his second week of camp. I explained to her that the second week would be more of the same. There would be different coaches and different competition, but the focus would continue to be on the basics of basketball. I explained to her about fundamentals becoming habits and how the drills we do in camp are a step toward that. What's more,

I told her that her son would be in even better shape if he continued to work on the drills when he returned home after his two weeks at camp. If you want to strive for excellence, you must embrace continual work on fundamentals.

I think it's amazing that everyone—from a young kid going to summer camp to someone as successful as Steve Wynn—can always remember that *with intensive, intelligent, and repetitive work, we can all do the basics, better.*

Giving Back

I t is not all about winning games. There are much greater battles to fight. As I have grown older and experienced some success, I have learned that when you use your success to have a positive impact in these other battles, it adds depth to your life. Having a positive influence on people, helping others: that's winning.

For someone to be a total human being, they must realize that something happened before them, something is happening now, and something will happen after they leave. As I have become involved with more community service, I have felt more complete. The feeling of winning a basketball game, or even a National Championship, is much deeper when it leads to the feeling that comes with raising money for the Duke Children's Hospital, building the Emily Krzyzewski Family Life Center, and the feeling that will come when doctors and scientists discover a cure for cancer.

Many people give money to charities. This is a great thing to do, as many of these organizations and foundations need these funds in order to pursue their mission. However, not everyone has the ability to give financially. One thing we can all give is *time*. And this is absolutely the most valuable thing you can give to another person, a group, or a charitable organization. When you spend time with someone in need or contribute to a cause, you really become a part of that person or a part of that endeavor. The feeling you have is addictive. It is a unique feeling knowing that you have gotten outside of yourself and made a positive impact on someone else.

I always remind myself that I came from somewhere. Where did I start? I was not a Hall of Fame coach or a public figure my whole life. Who helped me? I know I did not get here alone. There were people who helped me along the way. Everyone needs people like that. This is why I am a strong advocate of mentorship programs. Such programs give children a chance to be around and learn from positive influences. Often the impact you have on these youngsters will lead them to have a similar impact on someone else. Giving back breeds giving back. It is simply the right thing to do.

I also try to keep in perspective how lucky my family and I have been to have our health. Some people are not so lucky and they need others to help boost their morale and help them heal mentally and emotionally, as well as great doctors to help them get well physically. Cancer has had an impact on nearly everyone. In my life, it took my mom and my friend Jim Valvano. As a member of the board of the Jimmy V Foundation for Cancer Research, I believe that, through the hard work of the doctors and scientists who research the disease, as well as other foundations like the Jimmy V, we will eventually win this battle. I have always been amazed at how many courageous people I have met through these endeavors. These friendships are cherished by me and my family.

Sometimes in life you need people to remind you of the necessity to move outside yourself and give back to the people and community around you. P.J. Carlesimo, one of my friends and an assistant coach for the San Antonio Spurs, often serves as that reminder for me. He will call me up and say, "Hey, One-Way." This is his way of reminding me not to be a "one-way" type of guy. In life, I have been given a lot, but it is not a one-way street. I must remember to give back, to be a two-way person. Utilizing the success I have achieved to have a positive impact on people is what makes my life fulfilling. Usually whatever I have given, I get back more.

No matter who you are or what you have achieved, you are incomplete until you find a way to use the blessings you have experienced in your life to have a positive effect on others. For me, it is not all about winning games but, rather, how we can use the success that we achieve on the court to contribute to the greater good.

Guidance

Guidance is help. We all need it. How do we get it? And how do we give it?

When someone you care about asks for guidance, it is often difficult to know exactly what to say. After all, it is their life, not yours, and they know more about the entirety of the situation than you do. But because you care for them, often you will try to put yourself in their shoes and to help in any way you can. As a leader and, more importantly, as a teacher, it is crucial to know how to properly offer guidance. It is something that is very difficult to do and something at which very few people are good.

Father Rog, a geometry teacher at my high school, Weber, knew exactly how to give guidance. I grew up in a very strict Catholic family and attended Catholic boys' school all my life. My faith was important to me but there were many things about it that I did not completely understand. When I was a teenager, I had many questions, but, because of my upbringing, these were difficult to ask. At times, I really did not know how to put them into words. And at other times, I just didn't want to ask because I might appear foolish. Fear of looking foolish is a common impediment in the lives of teenagers.

Because Father Rog had been my teacher and had worked a lot with the athletes at Weber, I had grown to trust him. He knew me well enough to see when I was troubled by something. One day, he asked me to sit down with him in an empty cafeteria after one of our basketball practices. He said, "I know you have some things on your mind. Why don't you tell me about them." Then he did the best thing you can possibly do for a troubled youngster: *he listened.* He did it intently and he did not interrupt. Then he tried to help me clarify what I was really asking. And finally, in offering his counsel, he didn't simply provide me with an answer. Rather, he led me down a path where the solution would be mine to discover. I finally got answers to questions that I either did not know how or was too afraid to ask.

I have continued to seek Father Rog's counsel and wisdom throughout my life. And each time, he has reminded me about what it means to offer guidance. You do just that: you *guide.* You can go to someone you trust and respect to point out a path, but remember: *solutions are personal.* They are yours. You must take ownership of them.

As a college basketball coach, I work with young men who are experiencing a great deal of change in their lives. The transition from high school to college is a giant mental and emotional leap. I am a part of their lives during this impressionable time. And, again, I am their coach, friend, and advocate as they make the equally great transition from college to the real world.

During these tenuous times, I recognize that these young men are likely experiencing the same sort of feelings and questions that I had when I first sought the counsel of Father Rog. I know that I cannot merely give them the answer that worked for me back then, or even answers that have worked for my other players in the past. Just because the resolution I came to worked for me does not mean it will work for them. My job is to point them to a path where they can discover their own solution. Then the solution is *theirs* and they are more apt to stick by it and even be proud of it. In offering a path as opposed to an answer, you put people in the position to follow that path again and again when new and different problems arise throughout their lives.

Imagination

Everybody has the ability to imagine. However, this gift is often underutilized by today's youth. In a world of video games and mp3 players, too often youngsters are entertained by someone imagining for them.

I can remember playing basketball, all alone, in a Chicago schoolyard as a kid. I would take jump shots, drive to the hoop for layups, shoot free throws, all the while verbalizing a running commentary of the game that I was playing in my head. "Down by one . . . 79–78 . . . six seconds on the clock . . . Krzyzewski dribbling down the court, crosses over . . . 3 . . . 2 . . . 1 . . ."

As I took that final shot, I felt like I was really there, that the game was really on the line, and that I had the chance to be a hero. If the shot went in, the final buzzer sounded and I celebrated the victory. If I missed, there was, of course, a foul on the play and the game continued as I stood at the free throw line with no time on the clock. Though I enacted a broad range of imaginary scenarios throughout my youth, one thing remained the same: when I imagined, I always won!

Imagination gives you a destination. When you dream, and you feel what it is like to be inside that dream, you feel inspired to make that dream a reality. You begin a process, a journey, toward making real those feelings that you first found in your imagination.

In my career as a basketball coach, I have been in countless end-of-game pressure situations that can bring about nerves and anxiety. But because I imagined myself in these positions as a kid, I have always felt like I've been there before. The mind is so powerful. If you commit to utilizing your imagination to envision positive things, you will come to truly believe those things.

In early 2006, we opened a community center in downtown Durham, North Carolina, for children from low socioeconomic backgrounds. I am so proud that the center was named in honor of my late mother, whose hard work and commitment to family provided me and my brother with opportunities to imagine. The Emily Krzyzewski Family Life Center's motto is "Dream, Do, Achieve." In other words, the center and its programs strive to inspire youngsters to dream of a better future, provide them with opportunities to develop their fundamental skills, and, ultimately, promote achievement through the development of character, capability, and confidence. The foundation of this pathway toward achievement is in dreams, in imagination.

The greatest gift a coach can give a player, a teacher can give a student, and a parent can give to their child is the opportunity to imagine great things. These dreams in childhood pave the way for future successes.

IMAGINATION IN ACTION

Following the 1999 season in which we lost to the University of Connecticut in the National Championship game, several of our players decided to leave school early, either entering the NBA draft or transferring to another school. Shane Battier was one of the players who would return for two more seasons. Though he was a key player and starter on the team, Shane had averaged only about eight points a game and contributed to the team more as a role player than a star.

My staff and I knew that in order for us to be successful in the coming seasons, Shane was going to need to maximize his potential and become our star. The only problem was that he had never thought of himself as a star; he had never imagined it. He was much too humble. I told Shane after that 1999 season that he was going to have to spend the off-season imagining himself in a starring role.

That summer, as a follow-up to that conversation, I called Shane and asked him, "Shane, this morning while you were shaving, did you look in the mirror and imagine that you were looking at next year's conference player of the year?"

He chuckled and began to respond, "Coach, c'mon, I didn't . . ."

Click. I hung up the phone.

The next day, I called him again and this time asked, "When you were on your way to your internship this morning, did you picture yourself going for 30 points against Virginia?"

Again, Shane responded with a cautious laugh.

I hung up on him again.

A few seconds later, my phone rang and it was Shane. "Coach, don't hang up on me!"

"I won't hang up on you if *you* won't hang up on you. We made a deal that you would imagine those things." Shane needed to imagine because, by doing so, when the time came and he actually found himself in those situations, he would feel as if he had already been there.

That next season, Shane averaged nearly 18 points and six rebounds a game and was first team

All–Atlantic Coast Conference. A year later, in his senior season, he earned National Player of the Year and National Defensive Player of the Year honors and led our team to the 2001 National Championship.

He always possessed the tools necessary to be a star and a great leader, and he was always incredibly talented and smart, but Shane only fully realized his potential when he allowed himself to imagine great things. As a result, his teammates and I were able to go along for the ride as all of Shane Battier's dreams came true.

Integrity

Integrity means doing what is right whether you are alone or with a group, doing the right thing no matter what the rewards or the consequences may be. It means putting your base of ethics into action.

It takes strength of character to have integrity. Imagine yourself in a group of four kids. One is urging the rest of you to do something that you know is not right. Peer pressure is a powerful thing and can cause people to do things that are completely against their personal code. By saying no and not allowing yourself to fall victim to the pressure, you may be providing the other two individuals with the strength they need to say no as well. Perhaps they, too, knew it was wrong but simply were not strong enough to take a stand. You can walk away from the situation feeling proud that you stood your ground and that maybe you helped someone else find the strength to do so as well.

I learned about integrity in the simplest possible way; my parents told me to do the right thing. So it was no surprise for me when I wound up at West Point, which operates under a strict code of ethics. The honor code states, "A cadet will not lie, cheat, steal, or tolerate those who do." If you have integrity, and you can count on the others around you, your teammates, to be ethical as well, imagine the strength that you can form as a team: an entire group of individuals committed to simply doing the right thing.

I have always told my teams and my three daughters that getting a D on a test, or even in a course, is far from the worst thing one can do. You can recover from that. You can study harder for the next test, you can get a tutor, you can even retake the course. The only bad thing would be if you were to cheat. *Cheating means you are giving up on yourself.* You lose a piece of yourself each time you violate your personal sense of what is right and what is wrong.

Giving up on your integrity is a dangerous thing. One slip can lead to another, and before you know it, you may forget your ethics completely. With each violation, it becomes easier, and you feel less and less like what you are doing is wrong. However, if you stand by your code of ethics no matter what, your foundation becomes stronger and it becomes increasingly easy to follow your code through even the most trying times.

INTEGRITY IN ACTION

When I was a kid, I remember my father used to carry a lot of change in his pants pocket; you could hear it as he walked down the hall. Each day when he came home from work, he would hang his work pants over the back of a chair in his bedroom. One afternoon, knowing that he was in another room, I sneaked into their bedroom and took a small amount of change from his pants pocket. Surely there was so much of it that he would never notice. I took the coins, bought some candy that I had wanted, and enjoyed it.

The next day, my father called me into his room and asked me if I had taken the change from his pocket. I was scared that I would certainly be in trouble, so I lied and told him that I had not. As it turns out, one of the coins I had taken happened to have some sentimental value to my father; it was his lucky coin. It seemed pretty unlucky to me.

Now I realize how lucky that coin really was. My dad told me that he was very disappointed. Not only did I steal, but also I followed that up with a lie. One unethical thing led to another.

I remember how I felt that afternoon. I had disappointed my dad, but, even worse, I had let myself down. I am glad I got caught that day. It set me on a path where I knew I never wanted to feel that way again. From that point on, I have tried to live my whole life with integrity. Doing the right thing becomes easier with time and repetition. Eventually, your integrity becomes an integral part of who you are and your ethics serve as a moral guide in all of life's decisions.

Learning

To me, living *is* learning. Once you stop learning, you are no longer living.

Even as someone who considers himself a teacher, one of the most important things I always try to recognize is that I never stop learning. Of course, I have learned an incredible amount from my parents, my wife, and my teachers and coaches throughout my life. But you do not merely learn from these traditional teaching sources. As a teacher, you can learn from your students. As a CEO, from your employees. As a parent, from your children. The key to learning is *listening.* I try to make it a habit to listen to everyone.

Tommy Amaker is the first great point guard that I ever had at Duke. He had tremendous poise. He came to Duke already prepared to play at the ACC level as a freshman. He had incredible instincts about the game, particularly on the defensive end. In his first two practices as a freshman, I remember teaching a defensive stance, specifically used when putting pressure on the opponent with the ball. I was in my ninth year as a head coach and I had been taught that the proper way to guard the ball was with your palms up. Tommy was playing pressure defense and he had his palms down, but he was doing a great job!

Regardless, I stopped the drill and told Tommy that he needed to have his palms up when guarding the ball. When Tommy asked me why, I was stumped. It was the manner in which I was always taught to play defense and I never really thought about why it was done that way. Tommy made me think. "Well," I said, "I suppose it is because, with your palms up, you have less of a chance of being called for a reaching foul."

"Coach," Tommy responded, "I won't reach." Tommy had better balance with his palms down. He had a tremendous knack for stopping the dribbler and, therefore, became a National Defensive Player of the Year and the best on-the-ball defender Duke has ever had. He instinctively did not reach where others may have had a tendency to do so. So why not let him do what was more natural to him? As a result, I examined with more scrutiny the way I taught other parts of the game. The lesson I learned was that, with great players, it pays to be flexible. There isn't just one way to do things.

Six years later, I had another great defender on my team named Grant Hill. He was the most graceful player I have ever coached. He had a great career at Duke, was an All-America, and the National Defensive Player of the Year. After graduating, he became the third overall pick in the 1994 NBA draft.

Grant had a different way of denying the ball to the player he was guarding. Though I had always taught that this should be done with a fully extended arm, Grant did not completely extend his. I asked him why, and he said that he felt more comfortable doing it that way. He was great at denying the ball, and if he felt more comfortable doing it that way, then that's the way he should do it. He got the job done, and he got it done extremely well.

From that day at practice with Tommy in 1983, I learned that the things you teach do not necessarily apply to everyone in every situation. And it was a lesson I had learned from an eighteen-year-old freshman point guard! Learning from your students is something a teacher in class may be able to do by asking them questions and allowing them to participate. Interaction between the coach and the player, the teacher and the student, or the parent and the child is the best way for both parties to learn.

I always remind myself that you learn forever and from everyone. That is why, with everyone I meet, I try to listen with an open mind and the willingness to learn. You never know when or from whom your next great lesson will come!

Love

In 1974, when I was twenty-seven, my wife, Mickie, and I took a big chance and gave up the steady income and benefits of my being an Army captain with five years of experience to pursue a career as a basketball coaching family.

The situation was a difficult one for a young family. With our four-year-old daughter, Debbie, we moved to Bloomington, Indiana, where I become a graduate assistant at Indiana University. In addition to attending classes and studying, a graduate assistant's duties were the same as a full-time assistant, including going on the road to recruit. As a result, I was away from home literally every weekend. Mickie had a job at a local bank in order to supplement our income and was also working hard raising Debbie. It was difficult for us to find time to spend as a family, and

many times we felt very distant from one another.

One evening when I returned home after a
recruiting trip, my wife and I began a discussion
about *us*. "What is going on? What is this about?"
she asked, in reference to our current situation.
"We are always apart. You don't spend time with us.
Why are we even married? Why are we doing this?"
she said. Her questions really bothered me, and,
distraught, I put my head in my hands.

"I don't know," I responded. "It must be love."

After a slight pause, Mickie burst out with
laughter and I burst out with relief. I had given the
right answer, the only answer. Then the two of us
laughed together. "I think you're right," she said.

For me, that story is a reminder that love does
not always make sense, nor is it always convenient.
Even when circumstances were seemingly against
us, Mickie and I always told ourselves and each
other that we had to work hard to keep love strong
and to nurture it. We believe that love and marriage is, above all else, about making each other
better.

The two of us have spent thirty-seven years together, and as our family increased to include three
daughters, we learned that love grows as our family
does. As our girls have grown older, each of them
has fallen in love and married. In their choice of

spouses, my wife and I have asked them only one question. Do you make each other better? In all three cases, they responded with an enthusiastic "Yes!" And they were right. All three of my sons-in-law have made my daughters better, and in turn, my daughters have made them better, the same way Mickie and I have always done.

As your family becomes larger, showing love may become less convenient because of the many responsibilities and often conflicting schedules. But we have always sought ways to express our love for one another, whether those means are conventional or out of the ordinary.

Because Mickie and I have that foundation of love and the love has grown to include our daughters and their families, we are able to extend our love to a larger group, the Duke Basketball family. I love each of my assistants and players, and so do my wife and daughters. With them, just like with my wife and family, we have to work on our relationships and find ways to express our love for one another. When times are difficult, when I experience setbacks, and when I want to ask why I am even doing this, I tell myself *it must be love.*

Motivation

Motivation: the extra push needed to reach a goal.

You can't just write out a game plan of how to motivate people, you have to do it by feel. You have to know your people.

One of the best ways to motivate is to be sure that you have surrounded yourself with great teammates. I think my mom explained it the best. As I was walking out the door of our inner-city Chicago home on my first day of high school, she told me, *"Mike, be sure that you get on the right bus."*

"Mom, I know what bus to take. Damen to Armitage or Division to Grand—"

"No, that's not what I mean," she said. She went on to explain that I was starting high school and that I would meet many people and learn many new things. She wanted me to make sure that I chose the right people to get on my figurative bus. And she did not want me to get on the bus of anyone who would lead me in the wrong direction. In other words, she meant for me to be on great teams.

I have been lucky to be on some tremendous teams in my life: the United States Army, Duke University, my church, and my family. I have found that great teams serve to motivate me as an individual.

When you are on a bus with good people, you and those people are mutually motivated simply by being around one another. There is an atmosphere and an attitude conducive to winning.

Once you feel confident that you are on the right bus, the next step is establishing great relationships with the people around you. For my team, this begins in the recruiting process. We do not over-recruit and are very choosy when offering a scholarship. In fact, in all of my twenty-six seasons at Duke, we have never once utilized our full allotment of scholarships. Sometimes by adding more in terms of quantity, you actually get less in terms of team cohesiveness and the ability to form relationships. We seek young men who have talent, of course, but also those who possess the values and qualities necessary to be part of a team, young men who we believe will share in our vision. Young men of character.

The development of these relationships takes

time. There is time spent working on the fundamentals of basketball and teaching them our team
offensive and defensive concepts, but there is also
time spent talking to one another, goofing with one
another, and sharing moments off the court. People tell you things in different ways and a leader's
job is to learn that where one individual may sit
down and say, "Coach, I am really down right now,"
another may say it with a facial expression, their
body language, or merely with their eyes. There are
countless different ways of communicating. And I
have to learn to respond to each. One of the most
fascinating things about leading is figuring out how
different people communicate their emotions. My
goal is to learn, for each kid and for the team as a
whole, how to recognize what they are attempting
to communicate. I get better as a coach as I learn to
respond in a quicker and more effective manner.

Once you come to know and understand the
people on your bus as individuals, you will also
come to realize that everyone needs to be motivated differently. There is no specific formula. I
motivate by feel. There are times for patting on the
back, times for hugging, and times for yelling. I
don't give my teams an inspirational *Braveheart*-like
speech in the locker room before every single game.
Sometimes you can look in their eyes and see that
they are already prepared to play. In other words,

motivating people must be a flexible and versatile process. And you have to know the people on your bus well enough to see which tactics to apply at what times. I follow my heart in these situations. I instinctively react to the needs of the individual or the team.

Even as a coach and a leader, I will not always drive the bus. At times, I have to let others take the wheel. Maybe there is nothing I can say to my team before a game that will get them in the right frame of mind, but there may be something that Steve Wojciechowski can say as an assistant coach, or something that Chris Duhon can say as a team captain. No one person can be the sole source of a team's motivation. Everybody on the bus feeds off one another's excitement, belief, and commitment to the team.

Over the years I have been motivated by what a player says or the look on his face. In the locker room before a game, I might be nervous as I walk in to talk to my team. When I see David, Billy, Tommy, Danny, Tony, Trajan, Chris, and countless others sitting at the edge of their chairs in great anticipation of competing, it always motivates me to be a better leader. *When we motivate each other, our bus usually ends up at a great destination.*

Next Play

In basketball and in life, I have always maintained the philosophy of "next play." Essentially, what it means is that *whatever you have just done is not nearly as important as what you are doing right now.*

The "next play" philosophy emphasizes the fact that the most important play of the game or life moment on which you should always focus is the next one. It is not about the turnover I committed last time down the court, it's not even about the three-pointer I hit to tie the game, it is about what's next. To waste time lamenting a mistake or celebrating a success is distracting and can leave you and your team unprepared for what you are about to face. It robs you of the ability to do your best at that moment and to give your full concentration. It's why I love basketball. Plays happen with rapidity and there may be no stop-action. Basketball is a game that favors the quick thinker and the person who can go on to the next play the fastest.

It is the same in life. If one of my daughters brought home a bad grade on a report card, of course my wife and I would be concerned and feel compelled to take action. However, it is fruitless to continue to harp on what she should have done last semester to raise her grade. That is all in the past. The grade is what it is and will remain as such. However, it becomes imperative to focus on what's next: the next homework assignment, the next study session she can attend, the next test. These upcoming events grant the opportunity for improvement, that the next report card could show an A. If we work together to focus on this next play, we will all feel good that we have addressed the problem and not merely bemoaned what we should or could have done in the past.

In our basketball season, the ultimate moment for "next play" is March Madness, tournament time. At this point, I always tell my team, "Okay, as of right now, we are 0–0," meaning all of our wins and losses, any praise or criticism we have received, all individual performances and honors mean nothing now. All that matters is the journey on which we are about to embark.

This past 2006 season, before the Atlantic Coast Conference and NCAA tournaments, my staff and I needed to find an impactful way to emphasize our collective need to move on to the next play. We had a great regular season and ended up 27–3, we were No. 3 in the national polls, and were the ACC regular season champs. Additionally, two of our players, J.J. Redick and Shelden Williams, had tremendous seasons in which they broke numerous individual records and were given constant media attention as two of the best players in the country. However, we had just come off two of the worst weeks of basketball that we had played all year, with back-to-back conference losses against Florida State and North Carolina. We were very distracted.

The first part of our plan was to change venues, to get out of the locker room and the gym and meet somewhere comfortable, intimate, and, most importantly, different. We scheduled our team meal and meeting in one of the banquet rooms at the nearby Washington Duke Inn. After our meal, we conducted a thorough analysis of the tape of our last game against UNC. We got out a chalkboard and created two columns: good plays and bad plays. The motivation behind this was that we wanted to get a really good look at who we were as a team at that particular time. Once we finished reviewing the tape, our managers brought out two large cardboard boxes, one labeled "Preseason NIT," and the other "Regular Season."

I told my team that we were going to fill the boxes with everything that had come before this moment in time. At the beginning of the season, our team had won the NIT championship. So in that box we put the trophy from that tournament, all-tournament team and MVP plaques of our individual players, and the tapes of the games. In the "Regular Season" box we did the same, filling it with scouting reports and game tapes from our regular season games. I then asked each member of the team to write down on a piece of paper anything that they wanted to include: memories and frustrations from the season to that point, individual honors they had received, anything that they felt should be included relating to their personal experiences in our season. The personal statements were sealed in envelopes marked with each player's name and placed in the box.

"Okay," I said, "when we close these boxes, we are 0–0. We have had a great season to this point and have many things to be proud of. But that is not for right now. At the end of our season, we will open these boxes, return your envelopes to each of you, and collectively remember and recognize all that we have done together. But for right now, it's on to the next play."

We won the ACC Tournament, another out-standing team accomplishment, especially consid-ering that only five teams in the past twenty years have won both the outright regular season champi-onship and the ACC Tournament championship. They have all been Duke teams. Again, something to celebrate. But not now. After we returned to Durham and the brackets for the NCAA tourna-ment were revealed, our staff brought out another box labeled "ACC Tournament." We filled that box, sealed it, and put it away.

Bringing out a final empty box, this one labeled "NCAA Tournament," I asked my team to imagine the things that we could put into this box. The next day, we would begin preparing for our first NCAA tournament game against Southern University. Next play.

Ownership

Whatever we have, let's take care of it.

My mom was a person of modest means. But everything she had, she valued. One day, getting off of a city bus in Chicago, she was attacked by three young men who tried to take her purse away from her. They knocked her down and pulled at her purse but she never surrendered it. The young men, seeing other people approaching, ran away. Afterward, my brother and I asked my mom, "Why didn't you just give them the purse? They could have hurt you." Her only response was, "It's my purse. It didn't belong to them."

I learned about ownership from both my mom and the neighborhood in which I grew up. It was not affluent or ritzy, but it was a great place to grow up because everyone took the time and effort to take care of it. Every day, I would see people planting flowers or sweeping the sidewalks, doing whatever they could to improve the community because they felt ownership of it. Watching the adults around me care for our neighborhood established a great foundation for me. I learned that if something belongs to me, I should take good care of it.

At Duke, my staff and I try to create a climate where everyone believes it is theirs. When our players, managers, and staff feel ownership they feel empowered and proud. But, most importantly, they feel inspired to take care of the program, uphold its standards, and defend its beliefs.

Often a leader feels as if he has to be in control of everything taking place on his or her team. I want my philosophy of leadership to create a much greater sense of ownership among all members of the team.

Picture your team as a wagon wheel and you, the leader, as its hub. The spokes of the wheel run from the people on the outer rim to the leader at the center, representing the relationships that the leader forms with each member of the team. If this is how your team is modeled, imagine what happens to the wheel when the hub is removed. Without the leader, the entire team will collapse.

Because I believe in making my teams stronger than any one individual, including myself as the leader, I have learned to operate in a different and much more effective way. Instead of having all relationships run directly to me, I have placed an emphasis on forming bonds among *all* members of the team. Now the spokes do not merely run from player to head coach but rather from player to player, assistant to player, manager to assistant, and so on. These relationships will sustain the wheel even if its hub is removed. The wheel is sustained by mutual ownership, not by a single individual serving as the wheel's hub. We all do a better job of taking care of what's ours when we feel as if the ownership is distributed equally.

The team belongs to all of us and it is the responsibility of all of us to sustain it and to defend its values, purely because they are ours.

OWNERSHIP IN ACTION

One of my favorite cheers performed by our students and the rest of the "Cameron Crazies" in our home arena, Cameron Indoor Stadium, is a simple chant in which they merely repeat, "Our house . . . our house . . . our house!!!" Many students even have T-shirts that state this simple message.

Our students actually feel like they are part of the team. They are not entertained by the team, they are on the team, it's theirs. They are truly our "sixth man." The message, "Our House," is that we need to protect what is ours. Our players, our staff, and our students have an obligation to Duke University to do whatever we do with the utmost pride and intensity. The chant is a reminder that in our house, under our collective roof, we need to defend what belongs to us.

I want to create an atmosphere in which everyone feels a part of the team and knows that they are important. They are! When everyone has this feeling of ownership, our wheel will never collapse.

Passion

When I have speaking engagements, I often tell my audience how lucky I am to have never had a job. After some confused laughter, I explain that, because I have always done what I love to do, I have never considered my work a job. I have merely been pursuing my passion and loving every minute of it.

I define passion as extreme emotion. When you are passionate, you always have your destination in sight and you are not distracted by obstacles. Because you love what you are pursuing, things like rejection and setbacks will not hinder you in your pursuit. You believe that nothing can stop you!

A key question in leading, and particularly in parenting, is: how do I discover what my child is passionate about? My advice would be to allow a young person to try as many things as they can: science, history, sports, music, art, writing. Allow them to attempt a number of things and then simply watch for their eyes to light up. I knew my daughter Lindy had a passion for theater from looking into her eyes after her first play, just like I knew Steve Wojciechowski's passion for leadership after watching him in one of his high school games. It is vital that you allow people to discover their own passions.

My passion has been for teaching and coaching, from the days when I organized my buddies into teams in a Chicago schoolyard, to acting as a player-coach on a post basketball team while serving in the Army, to having the opportunity to coach some of the world's elite athletes as the United States National Team coach. One of the reasons I have been able to achieve some of these things is that I never kept my passion to myself. I told my parents what I loved to do early on in life, and as a result, they were supportive of the decisions I made, even when they did not completely understand. Additionally, I have always shared my goals with my wife, Mickie, and she has been my most important teammate throughout our marriage and career. Sharing your passion with those who love you can provide you with the support you need to overcome obstacles along the way. Likewise, it is vital that you be supportive of the passions of those whom you love, particularly your spouse and children.

Additionally, in putting together a team, it is important that the leader not be the sole passion-provider for that team. You have to find others who feel the same way you do. This is one reason I surround myself with assistant coaches who are equally motivated. During videotape sessions and scouting reports that often last all night, my assistants and I continually find strength and inspiration in each other's drive toward our common goal. Surrounding yourself with other passionate people can help keep you motivated and driven.

PASSION IN ACTION

No one who has heard one of his broadcasts can deny Dick Vitale's passion for the game of basketball. I was surprised when I learned that Dick had begun his career as an accountant following his graduation from Seton Hall with a business degree. But for him, accounting was his job, not his passion. So he took a great risk in pursuing a coaching career and was initially met with many letters of rejection. However, because he never stopped listening to his passion and had the support of his family, Dick eventually landed a coaching spot at an elementary school. His passion continued to lead him to the high school coaching ranks, then to college, and even to the NBA before he became a broadcaster with ESPN. Dick has indicated to me that the reason behind his success in broadcasting is the fact that he's never really felt like a broadcaster. He approaches the game with the passion of a player and a coach, and as a result he feels the necessary empathy for those he discusses on television. His contagious passion, quite frankly, is why he is the best in the business.

My friend Jim Valvano was one of the most passionate people I have ever known. College basketball fans may remember his celebratory run, arms extended, across the court after North Carolina State's last-second victory to win the National Championship in 1983. But Jimmy's legacy extends well beyond the boundary lines of the basketball court.

When Jimmy was diagnosed with incurable cancer in 1992, he started his passionate crusade to discover a cure for the disease. Jimmy knew that he could not be saved, but he was not stymied by this fact. His passion became to beat cancer, even though he knew the victory would come after his death. He enlisted the help of many of his good friends, including myself and Dick Vitale, and he acted on his passion along with the passions of his teammates by starting the Jimmy V Foundation for Cancer Research. To date, the foundation has raised over $50 million and is now fully endowed. Jimmy V's legacy is a legacy of passion. And now it is up to those of us on the foundation board, contributors, and those doctors and scientists who are passionate about what they do to finish what Jimmy started.

Anytime I need to put in perspective what passion is really all about, I watch the tape of Jimmy's speech at the 1993 ESPY Awards. When he finishes with the amazing words, *"Don't give up, don't ever give up,"* I get chills remembering what true passion can empower someone to do.

Poise

Poise: keeping your composure in spite of the circumstances.

Poise requires maturity. It's about remaining mentally and emotionally balanced all the time, no matter what is taking place around you.

In competition, the element of poise can make you appear much stronger in the eyes of your opponent than can your talent alone. I tell my players that you never want to show your opponent a weakness through your words, facial expressions, or body language. No matter what they are saying to you, no matter what the crowd is chanting, if you can show poise, you demonstrate to your opponent that they cannot rattle you. Just keep your mind on what you're doing and maintain that inner balance. Act like you have been there before and that you expect to do well.

When one of our bigger players is positioned on the offensive end of the court, near the basket, we say that he is "in the post." Many times when this player receives the ball, he is instantly guarded by two defenders who are trying to double-team him. Being double-teamed creates quite a challenge and it is hard to keep your wits about you. On our teams, we continually use the expression with our post players that they must show "poise in the post." This means that if you get double-teamed, you must remain composed. Remember your training and make a choice. Ask yourself: What do I do? Do I pass the ball out to a teammate? Do I make a move to the basket? Do not panic. Make a play.

The opposite of poise is panic, and if your opponent sees that, they will double-team you time and time again. If you can maintain composure, though, your opponent's best efforts are foiled. They will see that they have not succeeded in robbing you of your poise and they will know that they cannot dictate your reaction.

Likewise, as a guard, you can find yourself facing full-court pressure defense, or being trapped by defenders in one of the corners of the court. Do you let panic set in and turn the ball over? Again, remember your training and make a choice. Do you call timeout? Or can you see past the trap to an open teammate who is prepared to score?

In moments of doubt, I tell my players to listen to that voice inside their head and to be sure that the voice is always positive. It's the one that says things like, "I'm good" and "I can do this." Tune out the voice that says things like, "Oh no" and "I'm really in trouble, here." If you make a habit of this, that negative voice will eventually disappear entirely.

When you are able to show poise as an individual, you set an example for others of how to handle a tough situation. This is why, even in stressful game situations, I try to never let my team see fear or defeat on my face. I want to show them, through my own actions, the path to success. I want to show them that I've been there before.

There come times when it is necessary for you and your team to show poise together. When the game is on the line and one play will decide whether you win or lose, the team that exhibits maturity and poise has the greatest chance of coming out victorious.

I believe that sport is a tremendous venue in which young people can develop poise. The value of sport is in using the lessons learned on the court or the playing field to help you in other aspects of your life. Poise is not about winning and losing—you can show poise and still lose a game. However, you will have a much better chance of winning if you learn how to keep your composure in spite of the circumstances.

Pressure

Pressure is a compelling influence. It can be suffocating, stifling, and can cause individuals to resort to negative action or no action at all.

When you are attempting to deal with pressure, there are some things that you can do to ensure that it does not overwhelm you and that you become better as a result of the experience.

The ability to handle pressure is all in how you look at it. I look at being put under pressure as an opportunity to show how strong and capable you and your team really are.

Preparation is key if you hope to operate well under pressure. Hopefully, during the course of your training, you have done enough thinking about what it is like to feel pressure. If you think about the potential for pressure in advance, you can use repetitions and simulations in practice to help you feel as if you have been in that spot before.

Another way to help cope with pressure is segmenting. I try to divide the situation into manageable steps rather than considering the imposing big picture. It seems much more simplistic. When it becomes a task-by-task process, the big picture will not cause overwhelming pressure. When one of my basketball teams goes into the NCAA Tournament, we do just that. If I went into the locker room and said, "Okay, here is what we need to do. We need to win six games and become National Champions," that would put an undue amount of pressure on the team. Instead, I tell them to focus on one game at a time and to segment the NCAAs into three two-game tournaments. If we win our first two games, we go to the Sweet Sixteen, if we win our next two, we go to the Final Four, and if we win the next two, we are National Champions. Each of those segments becomes a four-team tournament that we have to win in order to advance, and that is much less intimidating.

In addition, if you have built a great support group around you, you know that the pressure is not yours to deal with on your own. Therefore, another part of segmenting is dividing up responsibility among members of your team. This past year, we had an end-of-game pressure situation on our home court against Virginia Tech. With 1.6 seconds left on the clock, we were down by one point and needed to go full-court and score in order to win the game. Josh McRoberts's responsibility was to get the ball inbounds. Sean Dockery's part was to catch the ball and shoot. Our staff had put the play together. The players on the bench and students in the stands needed to provide support and keep the level of intensity high. That way, each member of the team was able to focus on a specific task rather than on the big picture, which was: we had a heck of a lot to do in a very short amount of time in order to win. But everyone maintained the understanding that we are a part of a team, and in this pressure situation each player just had to do his part and trust that the others would do the same. As a result of this segmenting of responsibility, Sean Dockery was able to hit a three-pointer from just across half-court and we won the game 77–75!

Ultimately, having pressure on you is a healthy thing. If you are never put in pressure situations, you are not testing your limits and you will never see how far you can go. You are just playing it safe. And remember, for those times you do not succeed under the pressure, if you do not hit that last-second shot, you should never consider yourself a failure. You should feel proud that you have done your very best in a tough situation. Even when it feels like the pressure is on, *never fear the result of your best effort.* Just concentrate on making the play.

PRESSURE IN ACTION

In all my years of coaching, no player has handled pressure more gracefully than Christian Laettner. A two-time National Champion, one of the only players in history to play in four Final Fours, 1992 National Player of the Year, and the all-time NCAA Tournament leader in points scored, Christian hit more pressure shots than anyone I have ever coached: a last-second shot against Connecticut his sophomore year to send us to the 1990 Final Four, two free throws against UNLV his junior season that led us to the 1991 National Championship, and the incredible last-second shot versus Kentucky in the 1992 East Regional final that will live forever in the memories of basketball fans.

Christian thrived under pressure. He loved it. And now, years later, talking to him about those shots reminds me of how I must continue to coach my future teams to operate under pressure. When I asked him how he was able to handle pressure so well, he said to me, "Because I had a responsibility to the people around me to do my best. I always knew that the only people I had to answer to were the people in the locker room. That was my responsibility and that is why I wanted to succeed." He told me that the staff at Duke had taught him that he could be successful if he gave of himself to be a part of the team. His team was his primary motivation when he was, what he called "blessed," to be put in those pressure situations.

I marvel when I listen to Christian, because what seems so plainly simple to him is nearly impossible for others to see. But if more players can look at it the way Christian did, perhaps they can find enough strength in those around them, in their team, and in their preparation to realize that these situations really are blessings. Then they can confidently give their all and never, ever fear the result.

Pride

Pride can come from many sources, but ultimately it can be defined as self-respect and a feeling of satisfaction over an accomplishment. It can also be a feeling you get from being a part of something bigger than you.

There is a dignity that comes from doing something well or being a part of a group that does something well. Pride means having an understanding that you put your signature on everything that you do and ensuring then that what you do is done in the best manner possible.

The first person to ever teach me about pride was my mom. She told me, "Michael, everything you do has your personal signature on it. You should take pride in it because it's yours." As I have grown older, I have come to develop a better and deeper understanding of what she meant. You do not have pride in something because it earns you accolades or because someone gives you a trophy or tells you it's great. The pride comes not in the recognition you receive for something, but merely in *doing that thing to the best of your ability.* Whether you are playing a basketball game, painting a portrait, or cleaning your house, you should take deliberate pride in it because it is a reflection of you. It will always carry your signature.

But my mom didn't merely teach me pride by telling me what it means, she taught me by being an example of pride in everything she did, right down to the way she made chocolate chip cookies. No matter what day it was or who the cookies were for, she always made them the exact same way: the very best way she could. She put the utmost care and paid such attention to detail that each cookie would have an equal number of chocolate chips. When we couldn't afford much, there were three chips. Later, there were four. But they were always the same because they were *always* the best chocolate chip cookies she could make. After all, they were *hers.* Anything that Emily Krzyzewski did was going to be the best.

That type of pride is individual pride and it is vital to have in every aspect of your life. But the greatest pride of all comes from being a part of something that you could never do alone—being a part of a team. Players on a basketball team, members of a great family, troops serving in the military: those people have the potential to feel the greatest pride of all. Then, in everything you do, not only do you sign it with your personal signature, but with that of the group as a whole: Duke, the Krzyzewskis, the United States of America.

One of the proudest days of my life was when I was inducted into the Naismith Basketball Hall of Fame in 2001. While standing at the podium that day, I could not help but think of my dad. When my parents were young, times were difficult for an immigrant family with a distinctly Polish name. In order to avoid the inevitable ethnic discrimination he would experience, my dad actually shortened his name to the more acceptable William Kross. This helped him in applying for jobs and when he served as a private in the United States Army during World War II. The pride I felt at my induction was multiplied by the pride I knew my father would feel were he still living. Now the name Krzyzewski would join some of the greatest names in basketball: Erving, Russell, Knight, Smith.

To think that at one point my dad had to change his name, and now—his real name, our family name, the name we are all proud of—would be looked upon with honor and distinction. What an amazing moment!

It was the concept of collective pride that inspired my staff and me to bring our team together the evening prior to a home conference game in 2006. Typically, we all meet in the locker room for our standard pre-game meeting. This time, however, I asked them to join me on the Cameron court where the center circle is painted with the large "D" that is our Duke Basketball logo. We vowed that the next day, each of us was going to do our very best to represent ourselves with pride as individuals, the Duke team, and as defenders of our home court. Giving each member of the staff and each player a permanent marker, we all signed the "D" at center court, thus agreeing to the terms we, as a team, had established.

In signing the court that evening, we symbolized how everything we did on that court, as members of this team and as individuals, was going to be done with pride. And now it, most literally, had our signature on it. We were going to hold ourselves accountable to take care of what was ours. Nobody had the right to come into our gymnasium and take away our pride. Our house, our tradition, our Duke name meant too much to us. We would play to the best of our ability, we would uphold our standard of excellence, and we would do it together. We won that night, and in his post-game interview, Duke senior guard Sean Dockery said, "It was something where you look down there and it's your house. *Today I saw my own signature down there and said, 'Come on, you have to play hard.'* "

Pride means ensuring that anything that you do, anything that has your name on it, is done right. So for my team, anything that Duke does should be done to the highest level. I want myself, my players, and my staff to have as much pride as my mom and dad did. Remember, the effort that you use to do this is rewarded tenfold by the feeling you get from your actions.

Respect

When I hear the word "respect," I think of treating everyone the same.

I had the great privilege of being an assistant on the 1992 Olympic team, known as the "Dream Team." It consisted of some of the greatest players of all time, such as Michael Jordan, Magic Johnson, and Larry Bird. As a part of that team, I learned a lot about the game, but I also relearned a lesson about respect.

After a team practice, I stood by myself on the sidelines drinking a Diet Coke. Michael Jordan walked over to me and said, "Coach K, I would like to do about a half hour of individual work and I was wondering if you could please work with me." So there I was, faced with a very difficult decision: working with the greatest basketball player of all time or continuing to drink my Diet Coke. I think I made the right decision.

After our workout, Michael shook my hand and said, "Thanks, Coach."

Michael Jordan had just called me "Coach," and he had said "please" and "thank you." This was at a time when he was at the very top of his game and was one of the most recognizable faces not only in sport but throughout the world. Michael Jordan had earned global recognition as a symbol of excellence. That day, I learned that everyone on Michael Jordan's team is treated with respect.

I have said many times that my mother was the greatest person in my life. She had an eighth-grade education and cleaned floors at the Chicago Athletic Club for a living. So I had the benefit of learning at an early age that some of the greatest people in the world clean floors for a living. When you value everyone and treat everyone with respect, you may just be amazed at how they can make you better.

One of my very best friends at Duke was a custodian named D.C. Williams. He and I had a tremendous relationship. Many people think that I was merely being kind talking to D.C. and spending time with him, when in reality I valued his friendship and advice as much as anyone in my life.

D.C. was responsible for the cleanliness and upkeep of our locker room area at Duke. But in addition to taking care of his responsibilities, he maintained a spirit that permeated through everyone in our program. You knew when D.C. was around because there would be gospel music playing and he would be diligently at work with his ever-positive attitude.

D.C. did his job with obvious pride. Because his standards were so high for his own work, it raised everyone else's standards as well. Our players wouldn't want to drop something on the floor knowing that D.C. would have to pick it up. D.C. helped to create an atmosphere conducive to success, one with the bar set high and drenched in pride.

During his eighteen years at Duke, it was D.C.'s locker room, not Coach K's locker room, or Grant Hill's locker room, or Shane Battier's locker room. D.C. took ownership and everyone benefited as a result. Often he would offer insight into the mood of the team or a particular player based on his observations. "Coach, something is not right with Nate," or "I think the team is really down this week." I would always listen. And he was always right.

We have had a great winning percentage on our home court during the past couple of decades.

When I walk off the court at the completion of each home game, I do not stop to talk or shake hands with anyone; I am focused on getting to my team in the locker room. But after every home game for eighteen years, the person that I did shake hands with was D.C. He was always in the same spot waiting for me. Win or lose, D.C. was my true friend. And, like any true friend, he made me better.

I spoke at D.C.'s funeral in 2005 and had the privilege of meeting some of his family and friends. I was told over and over about how proud D.C. was to be a part of Duke. Additionally, I was instantly validated in the eyes of everyone there, because D.C. had had respect for me as well. Imagine all we would have missed out on if we had not initially shown respect for one another.

Too often, people will miss out on meaningful relationships with amazing people because they quickly pass judgment based on what that person does for a living, the clothes they wear, what kind of car they drive. D.C. Williams was a great man. I miss him terribly. But I was lucky to have known him and to have benefited from our eighteen-year friendship. I would never have received all of those benefits had I not initially treated him with respect and understood how important it is to value everyone. The simple act of showing respect can allow you to meet people like D.C. Williams, to let them come into your life, and to make you a better person.

Selflessness

Selflessness means that you will do what is best for the team. Jimmy Valvano once told me, *"A person does not become whole until he or she becomes a part of something bigger than himself or herself."* It is the best and most simple description of being a member of a team and its rewards that I have ever heard.

Being a part of something bigger than yourself requires selflessness and an understanding that there will be personal sacrifice for the good of the team. And most people desire to be a part of something bigger and to feel as if their actions are for the greater good.

Non-scholarship players, known as "walk-ons," have always been an important part of our program, serving as an ideal illustration of selflessness. They receive minimal playing time and virtually no media attention but are expected to work just as hard as any All-America. One of the greatest walk-on stories of my career came in the 2004–05 season after back-to-back losses to Maryland and Virginia Tech. I was furious with my starters and a statement needed to be made.

In a brief meeting following those losses, I announced to our team that those who had exhibited the best work ethic would be rewarded with starting positions against our upcoming opponent, Wake Forest. My staff and I thought it would be a key moment in our season, a turning point, and that it would send a message to the entire team. But what happened, thanks to the selflessness of former team manager and junior walk-on Ross Perkins, turned what we thought would be a good moment into a great one.

At our next practice, I put the names of four of our five starters on the board; they were all walk-ons. I then told my team that whoever played the hardest in practice that day would be given the fifth spot. At the end of practice, the lineup was set: four walk-ons and J.J. Redick.

A walk-on can expect to see only a few minutes of playing time throughout the course of a season, and so for a walk-on to start in a conference game has the potential to be one of the greatest days of that individual's life. After our lineup announcement, Ross Perkins asked if he could come by my

office and speak with me privately. "Of course," I
replied.

When Ross came in twenty minutes later, we sat
down and began a great discussion. "Coach," Ross
said, "when you put my name on that board, it was
the proudest moment of my life."

"Ross, you deserve it. You are going to start
against Wake Forest tomorrow."

What happened then changed the course of our
season.

Ross looked me in the eye and said, "Coach,
thank you so much for the opportunity and for having confidence in me, but I think it would be better
for the team if Shelden starts tomorrow . . ." Here
was a kid who truly wanted what was best for the
team and was willing to give up what could have
been a very memorable personal moment in order
for us, together, to be successful. Amazing!

I was completely taken aback. Now the moment
was no longer about my disappointment in our
team's play for the past two games. Now it was about
the incredible selflessness of this kid and his sacrifice of individual glory for the good of the team.
Ross's actions remind us all of what it means to be
a part of something bigger than you, and I will talk
about Ross Perkins and his selflessness for the rest
of my career.

Shelden did start against Wake Forest and we

were victorious in what was a tightly fought game. Ross was the first player I went to hug afterward. Ironically, he never played a second in that game, but his selflessness is the reason we won.

Standards

Standards: a level of excellence that we consider our norm.

After a particularly frustrating conference road loss in 2004, our second in a row, my team and I were riding back to Durham on our team bus. Typically after a loss, I have some idea of the next steps that our team needs to take. I often have a direction in mind—maybe not a solution, but at least a direction. For the first two and a half hours of the three-hour bus trip, I went through many options in my mind regarding the appropriate action to take. I finally came to the conclusion that, on this occasion, I was lost.

I said to my staff, "I have never told you this before and it may be a little scary, but I have no feelings or intuition on this one. My instincts have escaped me." I looked to my associate head coach and longtime friend, Johnny Dawkins, and told him that I simply did not know what to do. He touched me on the arm and spoke some incredible words.

"Coach," he said, in his typical calm but commanding and dependable tone, "*it's all about standards.*"

Johnny was absolutely right. All of a sudden, my coaching instincts came back to me, and, along with my staff, we developed a plan of attack. As the bus stopped at Cameron Indoor Stadium, I asked the team to come to the locker room for a quick meeting. I repeated to them what Johnny had just told me. It is not about losses; it is about standards. We needed to be playing at the level that Duke teams play. We were simply not doing that. As a team, we had allowed our standards to slip. It had become acceptable to not play every defensive possession with the utmost intensity, to allow offensive rebounds, and to play as individuals on offense. We thought that we could do less and still receive the same rewards.

Standards define what is and is not acceptable for an individual or a team. When you allow your standards to slip, you are saying, "We do not have to be this good all the time," and as a result your level of success will decrease right alongside your team effort, work ethic, and sense of pride. We made sure that we got back to the standards we had set for ourselves.

After a very disappointing NCAA tournament loss, a close friend of mine, Steve Delmont, sent me a Jean Giraudoux quote, *"Only the mediocre are always at their best."* If your standards are low, it is easy to meet those standards every single day, every single year. But if your standard is to be the best, there will be days when you fall short of that goal. It is okay to not win every game. The only problem would be if you allow a loss or a failure to change your standards. Keep your standards intact, keep the bar set high, and continue to try your very best every day to meet those standards. If you do that, you can always be proud of the work that you do.

I am lucky to have teammates like Johnny and friends like Steve to remind me that, when it comes down to it, it's all about standards.

Talent

Talent is natural ability. It is important but it isn't everything.

A team is a collection of individuals with varying levels of talent. When you talk about talent in the context of a team, you can talk about it both individually and collectively. The more talent you and your team have, the more room for error. I often employ the analogy that talent is really the difference between taking a superhighway and having to take side streets to reach a destination. In other words, if you have a lot of talent, the road is wider, it is easier. You can get to your destination faster if you do it the right way. But even if you do not have a lot of talent, you can still reach your destination. There are more obstacles, and therefore I refer to operating with less talent as taking side streets. The lanes are not as wide. You may have to be more creative and innovative, and it probably will take more time and effort.

One of the key things to remember about talent is that it has to be developed. When you've got it, it's like having amazing raw materials. But those raw materials do not become anything of substance unless they are honed through hard work and learning. Developing your talents makes you strong. If you only use your raw talent, it can eventually make you weak by allowing you to merely "get by." You can even lose your talent because it has not been developed. The road can come to an abrupt end.

The maturing process is a key factor in the development of talent, and education is a major part of becoming a mature adult: education in the classroom, on the court, and in life. That is why school is a great venue for the development of talent. In school, an individual is educated in all facets of life. They are tested in every way. Places like Duke are amazing because you are around excellence all the time, and being around excellence makes you strive to be better.

Chris Carrawell is a great example of talent development. When he came to Duke from inner-city St. Louis, he was intelligent and very street-wise. In basketball, he was not the most gifted athlete, but he understood the game and how to work with his teammates to produce positive results. He was never the most talented player on my teams at Duke but he used his abilities to fit in with our star players. As a result, he kept getting better. And in his senior year, he was named the ACC Conference Player of the Year, even though he was not as physically gifted as some others in our conference. He traveled on side streets wisely and creatively to reach a destination others in the league could not reach even though they were on superhighways.

There will be times in basketball when you are matched up against an opponent with considerably less talent than you. For instance, in the first round of the NCAA Tournament, many of college basketball's best teams are matched up against teams that are simply not as talented. Our goal in those games is not just to win, but to work harder and to outplay that team. What we are trying to do is to keep developing as a basketball team. We are trying to get better so that we do not lose the talents that we have as individuals and as a team.

Many people are confused when my team has won a game by a large margin and I am still upset and disappointed by our performance. I feel that way because many times we have only won the game because of our talent. If that is the case, then we have not gotten any better as a team by playing in that game. We coasted. And getting by on talent alone is not acceptable. If we continue to rely on our talent to win games, eventually someone will be better than we are. When two equally talented teams are matched up against each other, most often the team that works harder and works together will be victorious. But never fear the talent of your opponent. You can find yourself in the position to beat a more talented team if you make up for the difference in talent with hard work and the development of a cohesive unit.

Championship teams are not always a collection of the most talented individuals. In other words, you do not need three leading actors to have a great movie, you need supporting actors as well. Our teams often have several role players who complement our most talented players. These players may not score the most points but their contribution to our team's success is not measured by statistics, it is measured in the wins and losses we achieve as a team. Often, with time and maturity, those supporting actors, like Chris Carrawell, develop into stars themselves.

Talent is a natural gift and it is a wonderful thing to have. The ability to develop your talent is a talent in itself. Whether we get to our destination on a superhighway or a side street is not the issue. The people who reach their destinations are the ones who develop their talents fully and effectively. *A talent is a blessing,* and it is our responsibility to develop it.

Trust

Trust is an enormous word if you want to live a happy, fulfilling, and productive life. As much as it means to relationships, trust should be an eighteen-syllable word. But that one syllable, those five letters, represent the foundation upon which relationships must be based, whether those relationships be one-on-one, with a team, in a business, or in a family.

Trust is developed through open and honest communication and, once established, creates a shared vision for a common goal. Established trust among a group of individuals bolsters a feeling of confidence that only comes in knowing that you are not alone. In basketball, if you are defending an offensive player on the wing and that player is able to drive past you, you have two choices: one, you can foul that player, or two, you can trust that your teammate will be there to help play defense. On our teams, we prefer the latter. As a result of this trust, you play defense with tenacious abandon. Trust brings you together and makes everyone more confident.

Trusting relationships serve as a reminder that you are not doing it alone, that someone else believes in you and that you can believe in them. If you are wondering whether or not you can "get it done" and someone you trust tells you that they believe in you—that is a powerful thing. Will you always get it done? No, but you certainly have a better chance when you possess the confidence that comes with knowing that you are not doing it alone.

Part of building trusting relationships is confrontation. I do not define confrontation as something negative; it simply means meeting the truth, head-on. In my relationships, I want you to believe me when I tell you that you are great *and* I want you to believe me when I tell you that you are not working hard enough. Both of these are confrontations, but, because we trust each other, we know that our confrontations are truthful. No time is wasted trying to decipher meaning or understand motive. The confrontation, whether the subject is positive or negative, can immediately inspire action producing a positive result.

At least once a season, I turn to one of my players in the locker room and ask them, "Son, are two better than one?" He'll look back at me, afraid to give the simple answer, thinking I will use the opportunity to goof on him. "Come on," I say, "it's a simple question. Are two better than one?" Begrudgingly, he will eventually respond, "Yes, Coach, of course two is better than one." "Not necessarily," I reply. "Two are better than one only if two can act as one." Establishing trust among a team allows you to act as one.

Trust is a confident belief in your team, a person in your life, or a member of your family. Essentially, it means, "I have your back." I have yours and I believe that you have mine. Trust builds confidence, and with confidence, you and your team have a much greater chance of achieving at a high level.

TRUST IN ACTION

Elton Brand is a Los Angeles Clipper, an NBA All-Star, and a member of the United States National Team. In 1998, he had just completed his freshman year at Duke, in which we had had a great season, losing in the NCAA Regional championship game to the University of Kentucky. At the end of each season, many of the great players in college basketball are pursued by the NBA to forgo the rest of their college career and enter their name in the NBA draft.

In discussing his predicted position in the draft, Elton and I came to the conclusion that it would be better for him to come back for his sophomore year, continue his education, become a better player, and improve his position for the 1999 draft.

On the last day that an undergraduate was permitted to turn in his name for the draft, I received a phone call from Elton. Because the school year had ended, he was already at home in New York. Through his tears, he explained to me that he was being pressured by many around him to enter the NBA draft and that, based on our previous discussion, this was not what he wanted to do. Instead of faltering under the pressure, Elton trusted me enough to let me know that he was feeling pulled in another direction and to ask for my guidance. In the face of a personal crisis, he came to me because we had established a basis of trust and he knew that I wanted what was best for him. Should he do what other people were asking him to do or should he do what he believed was right for him?

By the end of the day, Elton Brand was still a Duke Blue Devil. He felt strong enough to say no to the NBA. To me, he just said, "Thanks, Coach."

That summer, Elton became a key member of the United States Goodwill Basketball Team, enhancing both his skills and his reputation. Before the start of the 1998–99 season, it was predicted by many that he would be selected as the National Player of the Year.

Elton started the year playing fairly well, but not to the level that both he and I knew he could. I asked him to meet with me individually in my office, and we had a very serious talk in which I told him that he would not be in the starting lineup for our next two games. The morning after our conversation, Elton knocked on my office door, stuck his head in, and said, "Coach, you're right. And we won't have to have this talk in the future." Again, he trusted me.

At the end of the 1999 season, Elton *was* named National Player of the Year and our team had the opportunity to play in the National Championship game. This time, after the season, he and I, together with his mother, made the decision that it was the right time for him to put his name into the NBA draft. Elton became the number one overall pick in the 1999 NBA draft. He is now the go-to guy for the Los Angeles Clippers and is financially secure for the rest of his life. If you asked Elton Brand, he would tell you: *trust pays off.*

Will

E ven after reviewing the stat sheet and seeing that he had scored only one point, I knew that Wojo had won the game; *he willed it.*

Steve Wojciechowski, nicknamed Wojo, was our captain and senior point guard for the 1997–98 season. It was our final home game and we were playing our archrivals, the University of North Carolina. The winner would be the Atlantic Coast Conference regular season champions. By our standards, the Duke program had been down the past couple of seasons and we were just beginning to get back on track. Since 1993, we were 1–9 against Carolina and they had a very talented team again this year. Needless to say, we wanted this one badly, especially Wojo. This was his last game in Cameron Indoor Stadium and he was determined that his senior class would go out as winners.

In fact, the team wanted to win so badly that it seemed to make us play tight in the first half. We were not playing to win, we were playing not to lose, and as a result we were down by 13 at the half. At halftime, I was very emotional with my team in the locker room; I asked if they were scared and why we weren't fighting. I knew, looking into Wojo's eyes, we would play a tremendous second half, and that the outcome of the game would rely on this kid's will.

The tide began to shift at around the 12-minute mark of the second half, and by the time there were eight minutes left in the game, it felt as if the momentum had swung in our direction. It was the loudest (and the hottest) that I can remember Cameron Indoor Stadium ever being. The crowd was exceptional, Elton Brand and Roshown McLeod had begun to hit shots, and our defense had begun to slow Carolina down. It was as if our community had come together to win this game; we had to win this game. In the middle of it was Wojo; he was the maestro of it all. His job was to ensure that all of us sustained that level of intensity for the remainder of the game.

According to him, "It was one of those games where you'd rather die than lose." When you invest in something at such a high level, you will do anything to make it happen. To Wojo, there was only one possible outcome of that game. And to achieve that outcome, someone had to have the will to lead our entire community for those final eight minutes.

Will begins with a foundation of character, values, and standards. As a leader or parent, you cannot merely look at a kid and order him or her to have willpower. You have to begin by establishing a core set of values that will make up his or her character. The definition of will, then, is a refusal to give up those values. Will can only be displayed when it is tested by challenging circumstances. Wojo had the will, and the UNC game that year gave him the platform on which to exhibit that will. We came back from a 17-point deficit in the second half to win 77–75, in one of the most dramatic comebacks ever in Cameron Indoor Stadium.

Many people have seen the conclusion of that game when Wojo runs across the court to me and we hug. That hug was one of the great moments of both of our careers. The reason why the two of us instinctively came together at that moment was because we both knew why we had won: he knew it and I knew it and, chances are, no one else did. We won because of Wojo's will.

Work

Ambition alone is not enough. That ambition must be coupled with hard work for success to be achieved.

I love hard work. It is a staple of all that I do and all that I ask of my teams. A lot of people hear the words "hard work" and say, "Oh, no. I don't want to do that." I want to coach kids who hear that they are going to have to work hard and then get excited about how much they will improve as a result.

I grew up in an environment of hard work. My father was an elevator operator in Chicago and my mother scrubbed floors at night at the Chicago Athletic Club. Even if they were sick or tired, they always went to work and worked hard. They truly believed that there was a dignity in their work. I attended Catholic schools my whole life, and then

West Point, where the lesson was reinforced by my teachers and coaches.

Work is a necessity if you want to improve. It is the road you have to follow to become better. Throughout my time as a coach, it is no coincidence that my best players have been the hardest workers. When I had the opportunity to serve as an assistant coach for the 1992 Olympic "Dream Team," I noticed that even these individuals, some of the greatest athletes in the world, always put forth extra effort. Players like David Robinson, Karl Malone, and Chris Mullin always had a daily routine that they did in addition to our normal practice session. They would lift weights early in the morning, work on their endurance, or stay after practice to get in extra shooting. They embraced work as the process that you go through to become exceptional.

I often give my players quotes about a certain word or topic in order to help them better understand and remember its meaning. One of my favorite quotes about hard work was said by one of the greatest coaches of all time, John Wooden. He said, "*Nothing will work unless you do.*" In other words, you can have the best plans, the most perfect offensive and defensive schemes, and even a great amount of talent. But if you and your team are not willing to put in hard work, your plans will never be realized.

Another quote I often share with my players was by NBA legend Jerry West. He said, "*You don't get much done if you only work on the days that you feel good.*" Hard work cannot be sporadic. It cannot take place only on the sunny days. If you want your best to become a habit, you must engage in intensive, intelligent, and persistent practice. I believe you play like you practice, so when you practice hard every day, playing hard will seem natural when the game is on the line.

A final quote about work that I share with my teams is Roger Staubach's: "*Spectacular achievements are always preceded by unspectacular preparation.*" Hard work is not pretty, or glamorous, or even fun. But, as I learned from my coach Bob Knight, winners prepare to win. Of course, everybody would like to win. But real winners put forth the time and effort to make it happen. And, in fact, by putting in the work, you make yourself worthy of winning. And I truly believe that you will not win consistently unless you are worthy.

I have been blessed to coach some extremely hardworking young men over the years. When I coached Bobby Hurley, he would work incredibly hard throughout practice, and afterward he would get on a StairMaster and work out at least an additional half hour. He never wanted his body to tell his mind that he was tired.

Shelden Williams and J.J. Redick are the two most recent examples of what you can become by working hard all the time. Each of them never missed a practice and would never substitute themselves out of a drill. They wanted to be in every play. They also worked after practice each day to get better. Although they were ambitious, they knew that ambition alone would not do it for them. *Hard work had to form a partnership with ambition* for them to achieve the success they desired.

Conclusion

The Fist

You should never stop learning to own words. There are always more words, deeper meanings, and more stories to go with those words. Each time I witness one of these words in action, I come to own it more completely. In this book, I have offered you a beginning: forty words, explanations, and stories that are important in my life.

Coming to understand and own each individual word is a great beginning. But just as words come together to form sentences, paragraphs, and entire books, the concepts behind the words come together to form an individual's character or the collective character of a team, business, or family. For many years, I have used the analogy of The Fist to describe how five vital words come together and help to create teamwork. The Fist is a teaming of words and concepts in order to form one single powerful entity.

Five fingers held together in a tight formation, a fist, is far more effective and powerful than five fingers held outstretched and alone.

In basketball, the five individuals on the court must act as one, as a fist, in order to achieve the success that they could not find acting as five independent players.

Each separate finger that makes up The Fist symbolizes a fundamental quality that renders a team great. For my teams, we emphasize five words, all of which appear in this book: communication, trust, collective responsibility, care, and pride. I believe that any of these traits alone is important. But all five together are tough to beat. In reality, those five fingers can represent any five words that one wishes to emphasize with their team, business, or family. What unites you? What are your common purposes? And what methods do you plan to use in bringing your team together? What words comprise your Fist?

My goal, when I teach The Fist, is five people playing together for one purpose. In our pre-game and pre-practice huddles, we do not say, "Defense!" or "Win!" Instead, in unison, we say, "Together!" And we intend to play that way. The Fist serves as a symbol of how we can achieve that togetherness.

Instead of giving high fives or patting one another on the back, my teams put their fists together. When I show them my fist and they show me theirs, we remind one another of the five words that will bring us together and allow us to be the strongest that we can be.

Everyone should be able to write a book like this, illustrating the words that are important to who we are using stories from our own lives. Actually, this book does not have an ending. There are always more words, more stories and examples, and heightened understanding. There are words that others could teach me that I do not yet own myself. My goal is to never stop learning and understanding keywords. As I grow to understand these things more and more, I know I have more to offer my teams, my friends, and my family. I know that, as my treasury of words grows, I continue to grow and develop as a person, a family man, a coach, and a leader.

ABOUT THE AUTHORS

MIKE KRZYZEWSKI is the *New York Times* bestselling author of *Leading with the Heart: Coach K's Successful Strategies for Basketball, Business, and Life.* He has been the head basketball coach at Duke University since the 1980–81 season, leading the Blue Devils to ten Atlantic Coast Conference championships, ten Final Fours, and three NCAA National Championships in 1991, 1992, and 2001. He was inducted into the Naismith Basketball Hall of Fame in 2001. In addition to his duties with Duke Basketball, Krzyzewski will also serve as head coach of the USA Men's National Team that will compete in the 2008 Olympics. Coach K is an executive-in-residence at Duke's Fuqua School of Business and the Coach K Center for Leadership & Ethics.

JAMIE K. SPATOLA grew up in Durham, North Carolina, and graduated from Duke University with a BA in English in 2003. She currently resides in Lawton, Oklahoma, with her husband, Chris, who is a captain in the United States Army. Jamie is the proud daughter of Mike and Mickie Krzyzewski.

STEINBRENNER'S YANKEES

STEINBRENNER'S YANKEES

BY ED LINN

HOLT, RINEHART AND WINSTON NEW YORK

Library of Congress Cataloging in Publication Data
Linn, Edward.
Steinbrenner's Yankees.
1. New York Yankees (Baseball Club)—History.
2. Steinbrenner, George M. (George Michael), 1930–
3. Jackson, Reggie. 4. Martin, Billy, 1928–
I. Title.
GV875.N4L56   796.357′64′097471   82-1002   AACR2
ISBN: 0-03-060416-8

First Edition

Printed in the United States of America
1 3 5 7 9 10 8 6 4 2

ISBN 0-03-060416-8

To Ruth
my own superstar
my own diamond

ACKNOWLEDGMENTS

I would be remiss here if I did not acknowledge a special debt to Donald Hutter, who not only served as editor for this book but who shaped it into something beyond my original concept. I am still somewhat astonished that what was begun as a newsy catalogue of Yankee conflicts and controversies has ended as a full-blown history of the Steinbrenner era.

And a grateful acknowledgment to Cirillo Ventura Wood, for reasons we well know.

CONTENTS

Foreword   *xi*

1 "I'm Afraid of George"   *1*

2 The Spring of Their Discontent   *15*

3 What George Did   *36*

4 The Best Team Money Can Buy   *57*

5 Bringing Reggie Home and Other Arrivals   *67*

6 The Greening of the Yankees   *91*

7 The Crises Begin   *112*

8 Boston: the Unhandshake and the Brawl   *123*

9 The Seven Commandments   *148*

10 The Bunt   *174*

11 Year of Tragedy   *206*

12 "You Gotta Be a Prick"   *224*

13 Before the Strike   *243*

14 The Second Season   *261*

15 Playoffs   *278*

16 Bam! Zap! Whammo!   *293*

Afterword   *321*

FOREWORD

What I have set out to present in this book is an inside picture of the New York Yankees under George M. Steinbrenner III—from front office dealings and machinations to locker room peccadilloes to dugout disputes and strategies. Since we are dealing with the Yankees, there's an occasional brawl. Since we are also dealing with George Steinbrenner, who can wield a telephone with the best of them, there are a lot of phone conversations. And, oh yes, there are all the various triumphs and travails out on the ballfield.

Not a biography of George Steinbrenner or Reggie Jackson or Billy Martin, then, but an intimate, interwoven group portrait of the most colorful, most successful, and most tormented ballclub in history, set in a time when baseball was entering its own turbulent era of free agency.

From a good many sources, especially one who occupied a vantage point central to the club's main tempests, I have noted the dialogues and epithets, drawn the jealousies and confrontations. We move back and forth over ballfield, dugout, and clubhouse—where we witness such indelicate exchanges as the one between Jackson and Martin in Boston in 1977, or the one between Steinbrenner and Rick Cerone during the playoffs of 1981, along with many others perhaps less notorious but no less visceral. Meanwhile, up in the front office where the Boss is terrorizing his secretaries, we describe why the general managers came and went, and why the trades were made or not made.

Steinbrenner's Yankees are our subject, but the background is the free agency revolution as encapsulated by the five years of Reggie Jackson's $2.93 million contract . . . and the incredibly complicated relationships that developed between Reggie Jackson, Billy Martin, and George Steinbrenner as they were tossed together like three scorpions in a bottle to perform their various pairings and withdrawals in a ritual dance of sting-and-embrace. Much of the time, it is Reggie and Billy, whose private demons turned sportswriters into psychiatrists and, presumably, psychiatrists into sports fans. Nearly all the time, looming over all, it is George Steinbrenner, dominating life in Yankee Stadium, brighter himself than his brightest star, if only because he was never enfeebled by a moment's doubt that he was the Sun-God around whom the players, the ballclub, the stadium, the city, and the rest of the world revolved.

Could any novelist have dreamed up three such characters or—in the light of what they did to each other—orchestrated them more perfectly? Can there be any question that the Yankees of this period transcended baseball, transcended sports? In the era of free agency, athletes became the new super-celebrities, the darlings of the merchandisers, as a quick glance at the nearest soft-drink, designer jeans, or deodorant commercial shows.

Who could have known, as the New Era was being launched, that the salaries themselves would upgrade baseball players to a level where the customers would be storming the ballyards to see what a million dollars looked like on the hoof, and to sit back and let the millionaires entertain them? Or that, as the fan interest escalated, the television money would keep the spiral turning ever onward and upward . . . well, at least for the five years we are covering here.

But, most of all, this is a book coming out of the locker room and the dugout. Not only Reggie and Billy and George, but also Thurman Munson, Graig Nettles, Lou Piniella, Mickey Rivers, Willie Randolph, Bucky Dent, Roy White, Catfish Hunter, Sparky Lyle, Ron Guidry, Cliff Johnson, Goose Gossage, Rick Cerone; the revolving managers—Bob Lemon, Gene Michael, and Dick Howser; the general managers—Gabe Paul and Al Rosen; and all the rest of that whole marvelous crew of malcontents and magnificoes.

We open with a signal moment of the recent past. Let the revels begin. . . .

STEINBRENNER'S YANKEES

1

"I'M AFRAID OF GEORGE"

August 27, 1981. It was the worst of days for Reggie Jackson. It was the best of days for Reggie Jackson.

Having subjected himself to a humiliating physical examination that had been forced upon him by George Steinbrenner, Reggie was on the way to La Guardia airport to catch the six o'clock plane to Chicago when he suddenly told the driver to turn off at the next exit and go back to Yankee Stadium. "I'm going to confront Cedric," he said. That's Cedric Tallis, the Yankee vice-president in charge of operations. There was something that Reggie had to get straightened out with George.

And as the car turned onto the FDR Drive and back toward the stadium he said something which he had clearly never been able to admit to himself before. He said, "I'm scared of George. I don't know why I'm scared of George. But I'm afraid of George."

By making that admission, Reggie not only turned the season around for himself but, by indirection, may very well have set into motion a George Steinbrenner production that brought the Yankee manager, Gene Michael, to the center of the stage.

The events leading up to Reggie's turnaround had begun the previous afternoon with Reggie coming to the ballpark early, as had become his habit during this season of his despair, for a private batting-practice session under the expert eye of batting coach Charlie Lau. Awaiting him in his locker was the notice invoking the right of managership to order the physical examination.

When he came back for the game, he was accompanied by his agent, Matt Merola. "I don't need a physical," Reggie told Cedric Tallis and the other Yankee executives. "My problem is between my ears." As if they didn't know that. George Steinbrenner's refusal to offer Reggie a new contract had put him into an emotional whirl from the first day of spring training. It wasn't George he was complaining about, though, it was the manager, Gene ("Stick") Michael. How could anybody have any respect for Michael, Reggie wanted to know, when he was nothing but a tape recorder for George. (Michael had sent up a pinch hitter for Reggie the previous night, and Reggie had come back to the clubhouse vowing, "They're not going to get the best out of me on this one. Those motherfuckers, they've had their better day out of me. The season's over." Well, he had said that before, too.)

When Michael arrived, Reggie lit into him. They were making him feel like shit, he told him. "Part of the reason I've been playing so horseshit is that you show no confidence in me." He had to be made to feel that he was something special if he was going to produce. "And if that's what I need, that's what you guys should do." If he needed a little pampering, all right, then pamper him a little bit. "But don't make me feel like dirt over here. Don't make me feel like I'm through." Because that's exactly how Michael was making him feel. "Like I'm through."

Well, in fairness to Michael, that was exactly how Reggie had been acting. Like he was through. He had been moping around the clubhouse all season asking everybody what was wrong with him. Dragging himself up to the plate and swinging so feebly that it seemed as if he were resigned to striking out. Before Stick had taken him out of last night's game, Reggie had swung so half-heartedly in two straight appearances that the fans booed. How the hell could he show any confidence in him, Stick very well might have asked, when he was showing so little confidence in himself? But what was the difference? It was George Steinbrenner who made out the lineup, not Gene Michael. Nobody disputed Reggie on that. If it had been up to Michael, Reggie probably wouldn't have been playing at all.

After the game was over, Tallis called Reggie back upstairs to tell him that he had phoned George to let him know how Reggie felt, and George wanted him to fly to Tampa immediately after the physical and spend the day with him. Stay overnight. Miss Thursday's game, and not worry about rejoining the team in Chicago until Friday.

Reggie refused. Cedric kept after him. "George *really* wants you to come down."

"I'm not going down there," Reggie told him. "Forget about it. I'm not going."

Tallis wouldn't give up. George has a very clever way of getting his people to do what he wants them to do. "Do it," he says, "or you're fired."

Reggie wasn't going.

Okay, it's easy to be cynical about George's motives. The first impulse is to say, Yeah, George could see the headlines already: REGGIE FLIES TO TAMPA FOR SHOWDOWN WITH GEORGE.

But let's forget personalities for a moment, and look at the situation. Reggie was batting .212 and hadn't hit a home run in 32 games. A few days earlier George had asked Charlie Lau and Gene Michael whether they thought Reggie was ever going to straighten out. "What's your honest evaluation?" he asked Lau.

Asked by his boss for an honest opinion, Charlie Lau had given it. "Well, George, I think Reggie's through."

Gene Michael had agreed. "I don't think he can do it here," Michael said. "I don't think he can do it anywhere."

Somewhere along the line, George had to come to a decision on whether to offer Reggie a new contract. And it was becoming increasingly clear that he had overplayed his hand. It was one thing to beat Billy Martin into the ground; there was always another manager in the wings. But there was not another Reggie Jackson. Dave Winfield was in a woeful slump, and even when he was hitting he had proved that he was not the kind of a hitter who could carry a team and certainly not the kind of personality who was going to draw people into the Stadium.

What did it profit him to beat Reggie down, if he was spiting himself in the process?

Reggie wanted to be treated special? Reggie wanted to be pampered? What could be more logical than to have Reggie spend the entire day with him, in the intimacy of his home, and have a heart-to-heart talk?

George may have even been ready to make an offer, who knows.

Reggie might have eventually come to that conclusion himself if he hadn't bumped into the club attorney on the way down from Cedric's office and learned about the conversation between Steinbrenner and Charlie Lau. And it shattered him.

Reggie had come to lean heavily upon Charlie Lau for emotional support. No batting coach was going to tell Reggie Jackson, at thirty-five, how to hit, but Lau could keep telling Reggie to hang in there, he was looking great, and pretty soon he'd come out of it. Reggie did look great in batting practice. It was only in the game that his head became unscrewed.

If anyone had reason to know how mixed up Reggie was, it was Charlie Lau. But to Reggie, who sees the world in terms of allies and enemies, one of his allies had betrayed him.

The attorney had made it clear that he hadn't been present during the conversation. He was repeating what George had told him, and George doesn't necessarily tell the truth. But while Reggie was up in the office, talking to Tallis, Michael had been answering the writers' questions the same way he had answered George's. Asked whether he believed that Reggie had lost it as a hitter, he had said, "Maybe he can't do it here. I don't know if he can do it next year. I don't know if he can do it anywhere next year. I think the ability is there but I can't keep waiting and seeing nothing."

"It makes me sick to see somebody like that sitting back and judging my ability," Reggie wailed. "His name should be Gene Michael Steinbrenner."

There you had it. Reggie had been saying all along that the physical examination was part of George's plan to destroy his value on the free agent market, and what better proof than to have his manager state publicly that he could no longer play anywhere.

The physical took place at the New York University Medical Center and, not unexpectedly, Reggie tested out perfectly. His eyesight, which Steinbrenner had expressed particular concern about, was even better than Reggie expected: 20/16 *without* glasses, 20/10 corrected. Not so surprising when you think about it. To be a great hitter, you have to have exceptional eyesight. Reggie wears those glasses to correct for an astigmatic condition.

Having passed with flying colors, he was flying high. Tommy John's two-and-a-half-year-old son, Travis, was in the same hospital, and Reggie went upstairs to entertain him. The boy was recovering from an almost fatal fall out of a third-story window two weeks earlier, and Reggie spent an hour with him. Playing with him, joking around, dancing the disco Robot.

Shortly after he had returned to his apartment, Cedric Tallis called. But it wasn't to ask about the physical. George Steinbrenner had been unwilling to take no for an answer, although that wasn't the way Cedric put it to Reggie. The way Cedric put it was that he had told George that Reggie was coming down, and George was going to have his daughter pick Reggie up at the airport.

Reggie was incredulous. "Cedric," he said, "why did you do that? How could you tell him that? You lied. You lied! I can't believe you could lie to him like that." He said, "I told you last night I wasn't going. I distinctly told you that I was . . . not . . . going."

Cedric pleaded with Reggie to help him out. "You know how George is. This could end up costing me my job."

Reggie said, "I don't owe you anything. I don't think I owe you a damn thing in this town." And, when Cedric persisted in asking him to reconsider, he said, "You better call George right now, Cedric, and you better make sure that you tell him I'm going to Chicago."

When you drive to the airport from Manhattan, you pass very close to Yankee Stadium. And that was probably where Reggie came to the decision that Cedric was simply too frightened of George to tell him anything he didn't want to hear. George would be expecting him, he wouldn't show up, "and it's going to make me look like an asshole with George and with the press."

And maybe why he admitted to himself, as he turned back to confront Cedric, that if he was so concerned that George know the true story, *he* must be afraid of George too.

"You've been lying to everybody long enough," Reggie told the stunned Cedric Tallis as he came bursting into his office. "Let's call George from here right now."

He didn't ask Tallis whether he had called George. He didn't ask George either. "I don't know what's been happening, George," he began. "But I told Cedric last night that I wasn't coming down there. I hope you understand that." He wanted to go back with the ballclub, he explained. "I want to start playing again." And then, apparently realizing how apologetic he sounded, he said, "I'm going to be honest. I'd given up on the season. I had just totally given up. But now with this thing on the physical, I'm not going to give you the satisfaction. This thing makes me look like shit. Makes me look weak. There's five weeks left to the season, and I'm going to get out of this fuckin' town in glory. I don't *need* the glory, I just want to show you guys. I'm going to show you guys and I'm going to show everybody else what I'm made of, and after that you can take your contract and wipe your ass with it."

Steinbrenner apparently wanted to know about the physical, because Reggie gave him a quick rundown, lending special emphasis upon the eye examination.

And then George must have said something like, "But if you're in such great physical shape, why have you been going so bad? What do you think is wrong with you?"

"The only thing I'm doing wrong," said Reggie, "is I'm going out and getting a little pussy."

He had finally told George off, and it was as if he had loosed the shackles of his mind.

The next night, he was in the lineup, playing right field instead of merely DHing, and if you think that wasn't on orders from Steinbrenner you don't know how the Yankees operate. Actually, Reggie had been given the option of sitting the game out against a tough left-hander, Steve Trout. Reggie didn't want that. He was finally ready to bear down and play baseball, he told Michael, and the sooner the better. Whereupon Michael told him to go out there and do whatever it was he had to do, and then called the press into his office and did what he had to do. And what Gene Michael had to do took the headlines away from Reggie and everybody else.

Referring from time to time to written notes, he told the assembled writers that he was sick and tired of Steinbrenner's threats. The final straw had apparently come during a phone conversation that morning, the same phone conversation in which George had undoubtedly given him his instructions to play Reggie:

> He said, "Gene, I think I'm going to have to let you go." He might do it before the game or after the game. He said he was coming to Chicago. He said it was nothing personal but that he was going to have to let me go. I don't know how serious it is, but I don't like the threats. I said, "George, do it right now, don't wait. I can't manage with that hanging over my head."
>
> After we lose a ballgame, I get threats that he's going to let me go. Maybe he thinks that we won the first half because he put pressure on us. But I just get tired of it always being my fault. After we lose a ballgame, it's my fault I made the wrong move. I did this, I did that. You don't hear other managers going through that. The threats and embarrassment, I don't need that. I'm going to be my own manager. I'll listen to his suggestions, but I'm going to do what I think must be done. You can't be second-guessed every time you lose a game.

It wasn't what Michael said that was news but the fact that it was Gene Michael, this man who had always been looked upon as George's wholly owned subsidiary, who was saying it.

The two most obvious questions were:

1. Why had Michael decided to go public at this particular time?
2. Why should any of this have surprised him? Nobody knew better than Stick Michael what Billy Martin and Dick Howser had gone through. Taking George's phone calls and enduring George's threats were as much a part of managing the Yankees as writing out the lineup.

Michael had gone public, he said, to save face. ("Save my face" were his actual words.) "I want people to know how tough it is to manage the way it is right now. . . . He so much as tells you you lost the ballgame."

In his position as general manager last year, he continued, the threats to Howser had been channeled through him, and he hadn't necessarily passed them on. "From him to me it goes on all the time. I can't take it any longer. People said you knew what you were getting into and I did, but I didn't think it would be this direct. You try to manage your way, but if it doesn't work out, you know you're going to hear about it the next day."

With the faultless timing of the born showman, George Steinbrenner entered his box just before game time and, upon being apprised of the press conference, had nothing to say. "He's said enough for everybody already. If he knows he's going to be fired, he knows more than I do. If he thinks that will help, that's his problem."

George remained in Chicago for three days, maintaining his vow of silence all the while, and then rejoined the team for a day in Minnesota.

Reggie hadn't exactly disappeared from sight either. In that first game in Chicago, he had ignited the team in the eighth inning by racing back to first base on a long fly to center field and then sprinting to second after the catch. With a runner in scoring position, Trout was removed from the game, and that had opened the floodgates. With Reggie swinging once again like Reggie, the Yankees were in the process of winning five straight, and when they finally lost to Minnesota, 4–3, Reggie had a double and home run and knocked in all three runs.

In those six games, he hit .400, knocked in 10 runs, scored 7, hit 3 home runs; and had the game-winning hit in four.

Michael was praising him to the skies. Not only for his hitting, but also for his base running and fielding. "He's got something to prove, and he's playing like a madman." Reggie was equally generous in bestowing praise upon Michael for showing so much confidence in him.

On Tuesday, September 1, Reggie and George bumped into each other in the lobby of the Marriott Hotel in Minneapolis, and George drew him into a corner. "What are you giving Stick all the credit for? I'm the one who told him to put you back in the lineup, batting cleanup. He's got no say over here. I'm the one who made all the decisions as far as what's been going on."

Gee, that's funny. Reggie had batted fifth that first game in Chicago, Friday night. It was only in the next game that he'd been moved into the cleanup slot. George hadn't talked to Stick since Friday morning, huh?

"I don't care who put me back out there," Reggie told him. "I should have been there in the first place."

George's uncharacteristic silence with Michael had, in fact, begun to make people wonder whether the whole thing might not have been staged. Why would George want his manager to attack him? Well, let's combine the personalities and the situation this time and make some reasonable surmises:

1. *Dramatis interruptus.* Having prepared himself for the summit meeting with Reggie in Tampa, George was left breathing heavily. The next day Gene Michael calls a press conference, and George is right there when the story breaks, controlling the fallout. There is still another thread running between the non-summit and the press conference. Reggie had told George off. Michael is now telling George off. Maybe it was just something that was going around, but maybe it had given George an idea.

2. *Propping up his manager.* The players had been second-guessing Michael even more than usual because of his ultra-conservative play. "We're tired of playing scared ball," they were saying. No hit-and-run. No stolen bases. Completely opposite to the kind of ball the Yankees had always played. All ballplayers second-guess the manager when they're losing. But Michael had little enough respect even when he was win-

ning, and the players were beginning to grumble openly about Michael's fearful over-the-shoulder looks up to George's box every time one of them made a mistake to see whether George was throwing one of his tantrums.

Under Billy Martin, the Yankees had rallied behind their manager only when they were supporting him against the owner's interference. So why not give them the same opportunity to rally behind Gene Michael?

There is something brilliant in this formulation. The Boss is a great believer in "creative turmoil." If he can save his manager and inspire his team at the same time, he has the best of all possible worlds. If the team keeps losing and Michael has to go, he has built up his personality and character for the day he can bring him back, in still another burst of publicity.

There was even a precedent of sorts going back to 1964 when Johnny Keane, who had just managed the St. Louis Cardinals to a World Series victory over the Yankees, told off the owner, Gussie Busch, and became the hero of all working stiffs everywhere. And as proof that virtue does not always go unrewarded he was promptly hired to manage the Yankees.

A story goes with it. A month before the end of the season, the Cardinals were ten games behind Philadelphia, and Busch had made a deal with Leo Durocher to replace Keane at the end of the year. Having been publicly humiliated, Keane walked into the post-Series press conference that had been called to announce that he was being rehired and handed Busch a letter informing him that he was quitting. Set him up and gave it to him good.

But that isn't the whole story. The 1964 Yankees were a disintegrating ballclub that had just been sold to CBS, and Ralph Houk, in his first year as general manager, had also given up on the season. With the word around that Busch had already lined up Durocher, Houk sent an emissary to sound out Keane. A week later, Houk met with Keane himself and sealed the deal with a handshake.

When Keane gave it to the Beer Baron, in other words, he knew the Yankee job was waiting. But by the time the real story began to leak out, in bits and pieces, everybody had such a heavy investment in the story of the little guy who had told the big guy off that nobody really wanted to spoil it.

Oh yeah, one other thing. The emissary sent to sound Keane out was Bill Bergesch, who was now one of George's trio of top executives. Bergesch just might have told George about it.

3. *National Football League.* The Lords of Baseball had always understood that if the strike didn't end before the opening of the NFL season, they might as well write off the rest of their own season. With the NFL season about to begin, and the Yankees puttering along in their wholly meaningless Second Season (following the Great Baseball Strike), George was faced with the real problem of competing with the Jets and Giants for newspaper space. Reggie and The Contract had become the staple publicity story of the year, and the humiliation of the physical exam had swept the headlines before Reggie aborted it in its second stage by refusing to go to Tampa. That left the Boss with the hardiest publicity staple of them all, the firing of the manager. George had raised the firing (and nonfiring) of the manager into an art form that should become part of the curriculum of any institution of higher learning that presumes to offer a degree in communications. The firing (nonfiring, semifiring, quasifiring) of Billy Martin requires a full semester all by itself—The Leak, The Confirmation, The Confrontation, The Leak of the Confrontation, The Reconciliation, The Aftermath. Good for a week's worth of headlines any old time.

The NFL season began on Sunday, September 6.

The notice for the physical exam was delivered to Reggie on Wednesday, August 26. If Reggie had accepted Steinbrenner's invitation, the Tampa meeting would have taken place on Thursday and Friday, and what George may have hoped to accomplish from there, no man knoweth.

Gene Michael called his press conference on Friday, August 28, and George was able to leave him twisting slowly, slowly in the wind for a full week by the simple expedient of *saying nothing*. A newspaper leak on Thursday, leading up to a TV "Game of the Week" appearance on Friday, dominated the early part of the weekend sports news. Michael was fired on Sunday, September 6. The Yankees came back to New York with their new manager on Monday, September 7. Michael wrapped it up with his own statement on the same day and then went off into the wilds of New Jersey to join a monastery or something. Out of sight, out of touch, and don't bother to call.

The NFL season crept into New York on little cat's feet. . . .

All conjecture, right? A little light fantasizing? Well, not entirely. Three days after Michael had issued what was being called his "Declaration of Independence," the Kansas City Royals hired Dick Howser, and Cedric Tallis was heard to tell Lou Piniella (who had been left behind because of an injury) that with Joe Burke, the current Kansas City general manager, so ill, maybe Dick could open some doors for him to go back there. "When George has to start staging things," Cedric confided to Lou, "that's when I know it's time for me to get the hell out of here. Because then I got to start bullshitting everybody."

Lou's comeback answer to that was, "But, Cedric, you're always bullshitting anyway. So what's one more going to do? You had to know that shit was fixed, because George just ain't the type to stay quiet after someone tells him to fuck off."

All of which doesn't prove that George told Cedric it was staged. Cedric could have been guessing too.

But there was more. One of George's closest friends was saying that George had told him that it had been staged. On Tuesday, the same day George accosted Reggie in the Minneapolis hotel lobby, he was telling his friend that Stick—whom he presumably hadn't been talking to—had become "too cocky"; that all the praise was going to his head to where you just couldn't talk to him. It had got to the point, George was complaining, where Stick was believing it.

The next day he was still talking about Stick being "too cocky," but he was also saying, "It's a double cross," the same expression he would use when he fired Stick, except that in the latter context he was saying that Stick had double-crossed him by calling the press conference. (In the first context, it was being used quite accurately; in the second it didn't really apply. Could it have been that the word had simply stuck in his mind?)

By Thursday he was back in New York and passing the word along that he was going to fire Gene Michael sometime between Friday and Sunday. He preferred to fire him after a loss, he said, but if the team kept winning, it was going to happen on Sunday before the Yankees' last game on the road trip.

In the afternoon edition of Thursday's *New York Post*, a front-page story appeared saying that George had ordered his top executives not to speak to Stick or have anything to do with him. The story was attributed to "an undisclosed source" and carried the by-line of the writer covering the team in Kansas City. That didn't fool George for a minute. George went storming through the offices at the stadium, terrorizing everybody, screaming that he was sick of all the leaks that came out of there and that if it happened again, heads were going to roll.

Do I have to tell you who the "undisclosed source" was? For the slow learners, it was George himself.

On Friday afternoon, he was on NBC's "Game of the Week" via a recorded telephone conversation, confirming the report. He had told Cedric Tallis and Bill Bergesch not to call the manager anymore, he said, because Michael had hung up on them more than once in the past. "I told my top people, who in turn report to me, that if they're getting hung up on and not getting the utmost cooperation, one way to stop that is to communicate through other people."

Did that mean that Michael was on his way out? It was hard to tell what was going to happen, George said. "There are things that have to be decided. I have not made up my mind." To prove how open his mind was, he said, "If you stood up in front of your bosses at NBC like that, I don't know if you would be broadcasting the game tonight."

Let's run this over again. George tells his friend that he can't talk to Stick, and then instructs his top executives not to talk to him. He then tells NBC that Stick has been hanging up on his top officials—which turns out to be one hang-up on Tallis and Bergesch apiece when they called him in the dugout during a game. It's hardly conceivable that Stick would have hung up on George—that's almost too much ecstasy to bear. It's far more likely, if the whole thing had indeed been staged, that George kept berating Stick for taking all that credit for the Yankees' turnaround, and that Michael finally might have said, "Well, what the hell am I supposed to do when you keep telling me to say we haven't been talking? This whole fucking thing was your idea. So why don't you just float with it and fuck off?"

To George, that would be tantamount to hanging up, whether Michael actually slammed the receiver down or not. And, just to go along with the fantasy, maybe *that's* what George wanted him to apologize for.

The Yankees kept on winning.

On Sunday, Michael was fired.

The official version, again, was that Michael called George on Friday evening after hearing the NBC tape, and that George had given him a chance to apologize privately. Not even a public apology. All he had to do was tell him he had made a mistake and he was sorry. Instead, Michael was supposed to have told him, "I have nothing to apologize for."

George's private version, as passed on to his friend, was that he had fired Stick in the course of the Friday call. Since George was going to fire him on Sunday anyway, it didn't matter whether Saturday's game was won or lost, did it?

The public firing was a Steinbrenner production, meaning that George went to superhuman lengths to prove that he was firing Stick for his own good. When he fired Billy Martin the first time, it was out of concern for Billy's health. When he fired Bob Lemon, it was so that Bob could go home to his family after the tragic death of his son. When he fired Dick Howser, it was to let him take advantage of "a fabulous real estate deal" (which like all fables was a figment of the imagination). With Gene Michael, George was able to achieve heights of paternalism previously undreamed of.

Listen, when George gelds one of his stallions in his horse-breeding farm in Florida, you can be sure the horse has been told that it's the best thing that ever happened to him.

For those who were keeping a running score on George's agony, he wanted it on the record that this was the most agonizing decision he had been forced to make since he bought the Yankees. He was also "shocked and hurt."

"I knew what I had to do, and I hoped I wouldn't have to do it, but discipline is the most necessary condition for success. . . . He was like family to me; I nurtured him. All I wanted him to do was come to me and say, 'I meant some of it, but I'm sorry I said it.' I told him, 'All you have to do is see my position and apologize. I'm not saying I want you to stand up publicly and apologize,' and he said, 'I'm not apologizing for anything.'

"Maybe, with the kind of close relationship Gene and I have had, you don't admit you're wrong. I couldn't spank him, but I had to let him know somehow that he was wrong, and I can't teach him by having him just ignore me."

George was a big enough man to admit he was tough to work for. "It's one of the dents in my armor, and I can't remove it."

He also admitted that his silence had been most uncharacteristic. "I agonized for ten days over this, and I was hoping against hope he would apologize. This was the toughest decision I had to make, because he was like my own son."

And then, significantly, "But this parting is on a high level. Stick will have a place with me, and it isn't beyond repair."

Don't apologize to George and you're set for life.

The deposed manager contented himself with issuing a rather mild rebuttal to some of the things George had accused him of. He pointed out that he had never complained about front-office interference, as George had said in his NBC statement (every New York writer reporting on the interview had already pointed that out); that he had specifically stated in his press conference that he would always listen to the owner's suggestions and take them into account; and that he had always cooperated with the front office, except on the two occasions he had hung up on executives who called him in the dugout.

There was not a word in there about the Friday night phone call, nor would he answer any questions about it from the writers who were able to reach him at his home.

His statement was issued by the New York Yankees' public relations department after it had been cleared by George Steinbrenner.

How did the players react? While it was happening, they were divided between those who thought it was staged and those who didn't give a damn. Back in New York, they simply laughed the questions away. Yeah, Michael had been a bad boy, but it wouldn't surprise them at all if he became their manager again.

Bob Lemon, the once and present manager, had already called Michael to tell him, "I'll keep the chair warm for you."

What the hell, Michael was still on a three-year contract, paying him $150,000 a year. Bob Lemon was on the last two years of his managerial contract. It didn't even cost Steinbrenner anything.

2

THE SPRING OF THEIR DISCONTENT

It was clear from the beginning that the 1981 season was going to be critical for both George Steinbrenner and Reggie Jackson. For Steinbrenner, it was critical because he was coming in for the first time with his own handpicked manager and general manager. The manager was Gene Michael, who was looked upon as George's wholly owned subsidiary. The general manager was Lou Saban, who had trained for the job by hiring George as an assistant football coach at Northwestern in 1955. He would be assisted by Cedric Tallis. For the first time both front office and bench would be totally under George's control. If the Yankees won, he could take due credit. If the Yankees failed, there was no way he could escape the blame.

The duties of the front office executives baffled the players all year. "Just exactly what does Saban do?" they would ask. The answer would come back, "He handles the defense." "And what does Cedric do?" There were two answers. The printable one went "He waters the plants."

For Reggie, it was the final year on a five-year $2.93 million contract that had shaken the baseball world and had become, in the rapidly escalating salaries of subsequent years, little more than routine. This year's fabulous contract belonged to Steinbrenner's new magnifico, Dave Winfield: an incredible $20 million-plus over ten years. Forgetting the bonuses, Winfield's $1.4 million annual salary made Reggie's $332,000 look like a paltry sum indeed.

If you are Reggie Jackson, you see the world as entitled to period-

15

ic communiqués on the state of your emotions. Before Winfield was actually signed, Reggie was the neutral observer: "If Winfield gets $2 million or more a year, it's none of my business. I'm not going on record now as saying I should be the highest paid or I want as much as Dave Winfield. I think the Yankees can afford us both." After Winfield signed: "Now it's my turn. I'm not concerned about it."

To show how unconcerned he was, he had already begun to talk about overcoming his "false ego, false pride." As he had to admit, the struggle was not going to be easy. "I don't know if I'm secure enough not to have the largest numbers next to my name. I don't know if I'm secure enough and mature enough not to be the top banana. That's the question I have to ask myself, and I don't know the answer."

The answer was not long in coming. In a testimonial to insecurity that should become mandatory reading for all students of personality development and high finance, Reggie came to the conclusion that "I don't think I'm secure enough to kneel in the on-deck circle knowing I'm hitting cleanup behind a player who is making three or four times more than I am."

Under normal circumstances a superstar in the last year of his contract is sitting pretty. Reggie was coming off one of his best seasons. He had led the league with 41 home runs, and he had hit .300 for the first time in his career. Over the first four months of the 1980 season he had carried the team on his back. He had finished second to George Brett in the MVP voting (and no one will ever be able to convince Reggie that he shouldn't have won).

So what was the problem? Well, Reggie was going to be thirty-five in the first month of the new season, and George Steinbrenner, whom he had once looked upon as a dear friend, would not let him forget that while the Yankees were being swept three straight in the divisional playoffs, the man who had labeled himself "Mr.October" had knocked in exactly no runs.

Reggie wanted to stay in New York, where the bright lights shine, and Steinbrenner knew it. He also knew that he could wait until July or, for that matter, until the season was over to find out whether Reggie could still perform well enough to justify paying him a million-plus for another two or three years. By signing Winfield he had taken the pressure off himself to sign Jackson. It was as simple as that. "If you want to know where the cards are," said a man close to the clubhouse scene, "the cards are in Winfield's bat."

Reggie knew that, too.

Even though Reggie reported to camp two days late, he had called from California the day camp opened to find out how Winfield had looked in batting practice and, more important by far, "Is he putting on a show?"

In other words, "Is he the Dog out there?" "Dog" as in "Hot Dog."

With Reggie himself, it's not just stepping into the cage and hitting the ball far and deep, it's coming out of the batting cage and strutting your stuff for the press. When he approached the batting cage for the first time on his own first day of training camp back in 1977, he had trouble finding a batting helmet that fit. So he took the notebook out of the hands of the man from *The New York Times* and wrote, "Jax shows up in camp, has no helmet, wants to know if he's been forgotten already." Now there is a man who is media-wise. It's a nice little name to fit a headline. It has character, color, and a subliminal message. Jax as in Axe. Nor was it any accident that Jax had taken the notebook from the man from *The Times* instead of the man from the *Newark Ledger*.

Already Reggie knew. Even before coming out on the field that first day he had given a series of wide-ranging interviews that had astonished admirers of the English language and set the tone for his whole turbulent career with the Yankees.

"I am the hunted," he had proclaimed. "I am the hunted on the team of the hunted."

As for his relationship with those lesser prey, his teammates: "Part of what they pay me for is what I have to deal with emotionally, psychologically, and socially. Anybody wants to make money, play out your option. But as soon as I get here, people want to create controversy. Hey, I'm a good dude. But sell your newspapers. If there's a man that can handle it, here he is. I can deal with it like a Big Dog."

The first thing you have to understand is that Reggie writes his own scenario. He is Autobiography in a roomful of Biography. "You never met anyone like me," he told the mass of writers assembled around him that first day. "I'm not just a ballplayer, I'm a multifaceted person, a myriad of personalities. There's lots of stories that you can write about me. I'm a businessman who happens to be an athlete."

No, he wasn't talking about his financial holdings. "I've got my attaché case here," he said, pointing to his equipment bag, his spikes, and his bat. "My files, my tools." Reggie had been using that line for years, except that sometimes he was a surgeon and his bat was his scalpel. Perhaps it would be more accurate to say that for Reggie, the living manuscript, his bat is the pen with which he writes his continuing saga. In his first day in a Yankee uniform, he had set forth the main theme and conflicts, and unquestionably presented the star.

A teammate at Oakland, Darold Knowles, captured him for all time with the immortal line, "There's not enough mustard in the whole world to cover this hot dog."

Upon hearing that Winfield had done little enough with the bat during his first day in a Yankee uniform and, perhaps more importantly, had spoken only when spoken to, Reggie's spirits rose. By the time he got to camp he was saying: "He's going to have a real tough time in New York. I really feel bad for him."

Why did Reggie arrive late? His excuse was that he had been busy completing the voice-over for ABC-TV's "Superteams" and had needed a couple of days to go home and put his affairs in order. (A year earlier it had been "closing down" his home in Carmel, California.) The real reason, of course, was that Winfield was going to be getting all the attention for the first couple of days. Reggie was just going to lay back, as he told a friend, until the spotlight was ready to fall on him.

Having manipulated the spotlight so expertly, he looked upon the array of newspapermen and TV cameras waiting in the clubhouse and couldn't understand what all the fuss was about. You see, he explained, that's why he had wanted to get the contract settled ahead of time. "Because I knew there would be a disproportionate magnitude to any contract negotiations with Reggie Jackson."

The magnitude of Reggie Jackson. How lovingly that phrase falls from his lips. He has used it often over the years. "The disproportionate magnitude of Reggie Jackson being late," he repeated for the hard of hearing, "is ridiculous." Okay, if he were two weeks late and had been spotted cavorting with the Playmate of the Year in Rio de Janeiro, that would be newsworthy. "But when I left home yesterday there were three photographers outside. I was on the front page of the *Oakland Tribune.* That's absurd."

He also thought it absurd that George Steinbrenner had thrown a public fit and fined him $5,000 for his tardiness. (Not quite so publicly, George had also rescinded permission for Reggie to use the Yankees' training camp to shoot a scheduled Jeep commercial.)

The players themselves couldn't have cared less. There were only five left from the team Reggie had joined in that first turbulent year. The others were either brand new or were no longer paying attention. They knew that Reggie was always in perfect shape. They also knew that he would be the hardest worker in camp. And, anyway, as Reggie was quick to point out, he wasn't the only superstar of baseball who had reported late. "Imagine the nerve of that Pete Rose," Reggie said. "He had all winter to have those teeth pulled."

What about the angry words from Steinbrenner? "I've heard so many statements like that from George, I could write a book."

What would he call the book, asked an enterprising columnist.

Nobody has ever accused Reggie of missing a cue. "*On Your Ass,*" he said.

He loved every minute of it. After the training session was over, the photographers got him and Winfield to pose together. "There's only one thing about getting the most money," Reggie advised his new teammate. "You got to have a big fanny. You get whipped." Then he walked behind Winfield and, while Winfield laughed, took a look at his.

Reggie has a way of working himself around the field from player to player during the opening week of spring training, confidentially making unflattering comments about selected teammates. "Boy, he's fat this year," he will say about one guy. Or "That bat's kind of slow, isn't it?"

His line for Winfield at first was "He's not swinging so hot there. He's going to have to make adjustments." Soon enough, however, Winfield had straightened out his swing, and the line had to change. "How . . . a-bout . . . Dave Winfield?" Reggie would ask in a tone so agog with amusement and disbelief as to need no answer. He liked that line so much that he carried it over from the field into the clubhouse, from the players to the writers, and finally to Winfield himself. "How a-bout Dave Winfield?" he would say to Winfield, and the writers gathered around him. Winfield would just smile his pleasant smile and chuckle his pleasant chuckle. For it had become obvious from the beginning that Winfield was going to handle the rivalry by refusing to recognize that any rivalry existed. "Reggie's a strong personality," he would say when the inevitable question came, "and I'm a strong personality. There are a lot of strong personalities on this club."

Winfield understood very clearly that since he was the new guy in town with the megabuck contract, any confrontation with Reggie Jackson was bound to hurt him with the New York fans. And so whenever Reggie would approach him in the clubhouse or behind the batting cage with that look in his eyes, Dave Winfield would just give him a great big smile and say, "Oh-oh, here it comes."

Not that Reggie didn't keep trying.

George had not been backing away from any spotlights either. One thing Reggie and George have in common is that when they walk into a room and find a camera bearing down on them, neither goes running into a closet. George had put things into their proper perspective by warning Reggie "not to embarrass me" by being late. For George embarrassed is George provoked. "I told Reggie's lawyer not to put me into a corner," he growled, "because out of a corner I'm not too easy."

Embarrassing Reggie, on the other hand, is one of the privileges of being a club owner named George Steinbrenner. During a preliminary meeting with Reggie in Fort Lauderdale a week before the opening of camp, there had been talk about Reggie signing a lifetime contract to serve as a high-class spokesman and goodwill ambassador. The way Reggie explained it afterwards in a quickie press conference he would be working for the Yankees and Steinbrenner Enterprises. "He talked to me like a business associate. . . . He really thinks something of my name, my drawing ability, what I mean to the sport. I always thought I had the mental makeup to be an asset to whatever company I was involved with. I always thought I'd like for someone to say, 'We want you to be part of us.' "

Reggie would shortly discover that in talking about everything, George had been talking about nothing. "There has been no invitation into my business," Steinbrenner replied.

What George was talking about now in camp was the need for a would-be businessman like Reggie to straighten out his priorities. "If I wanted to build a lasting relationship, the last thing I would do is show up late. That's common sense."

He had come to camp himself on opening day, he now explained, only to make a contract proposal to Reggie that would have settled the matter once and for all. That, of course, was in the context of explaining why he was not going to sit down with Reggie anytime in the foreseeable future. "Personally I'm very disappointed with Reggie. I'm not going to make a big deal of it because I don't think it's that big a story." And to make absolutely certain that the story would not be overplayed, he dropped a parting sally. "You kind of hope that a guy who is known as Mr. October, who wasn't Mr. October in 1980 and didn't drive in a run in the playoffs, would want to make amends and come in early, wouldn't you?"

The Contract. It preyed on Reggie's mind. Ate at him. Consumed him. Turned his mind upside down. He wasn't being treated with respect, he complained to the writers. "I've done a lot for New York, and now George is treating me like shit."

The change in managers didn't help, either. Last year's skipper, Dick Howser, had not only appreciated Reggie, he had protected him. It was one of the things that had contributed to his demise. For example, before the second game of the divisional playoffs, in Kansas City, George had called down to Howser to order him to tell Reggie to shave. You see, Reggie always starts to let his beard grow out at the close of the regular season. In point of fact, he had gone into a previous playoff series, against Kansas City two years earlier, with a far heavier growth. The difference for George was that Reggie had been hot in 1978, and the Yankees had been handling Kansas City with ease. "I'll tell him," Howser said, "but I'm also going to tell him that as far as I'm concerned, I don't give a shit."

But Reggie responded—he went back and shaved. And with the clubhouse filling up with writers and George himself in attendance, he sat in front of his locker and shouted, "I didn't do it for the Fat Boy. I did it to keep Dick from getting hassled."

So now he had come to camp complaining that with Howser gone, there was nobody to stand between him and George. He found out how right he was when Gene Michael called him and Elliott Maddox into his office before the first exhibition game at the University of Florida and ordered them to shave, whereupon Reggie took sick and retired to the trainer's room to munch potato chips and such other nutritious roots and herbs as were available.

It wasn't Gene Michael, though. It wasn't even Dave Winfield. It was George Steinbrenner and the Contract. The owner's refusal to negotiate troubled Reggie so much that he was attacking George off the record, and that wasn't like Reggie at all. "On the record or off" is what he usually says. "I'm just telling you how I feel." Now, just for their own ears, he was telling the writers that not only didn't George want to sign him, but George was deliberately staying away from camp in order to avoid him. In ridiculing Reggie for not coming to camp on time after saying he wanted a big contract George had accused him of talking out of both sides of his mouth, and that seemed to bother Reggie most of all.

Then, too, he wasn't hitting. Usually for a slugger like Reggie, this means nothing in spring training. With home-run hitters it isn't a matter of mechanics, it's a one-piece swing—*whoosh*—keeping the head in there and whipping the bat. Which is why hitters like Jackson and Nettles are very hot once they've got their groove and timing down, and very cold when they haven't.

But Winfield was beginning to hit, and the more he hit, the more depressed Reggie became. And the more depressed he became, the more convinced he was that Steinbrenner was deliberately messing with his mind in the hope that he'd have a bad season.

Why would George want him to have a bad season when an unproductive Reggie Jackson would hurt George Steinbrenner just as badly? "Because he hates me. He's trying to destroy me."

An explosion was due, and it came after a game against the Atlanta Braves. The catalyst was Al Hrabosky, known popularly as the Mad Hungarian. Hrabosky sent Reggie sprawling, something that a pitcher normally doesn't do in spring training. But there was bad blood between them. Hrabosky has to rely on a fast ball which isn't as fast as it used to be, and that means he has to pitch Reggie especially tight. During the previous season, Reggie had got off the ground a couple of times to hit the next pitch into the seats.

Reggie got up this time and yelled at Hrabosky, "Come on, give me your cheap fast ball." They glared at each other. Reggie shouted out a curse. Hrabosky countered by going into the ritual that had won him his nickname, something else which he normally wouldn't waste on a spring-training audience: stomping off behind the mound, turning his back to the plate, sinking into a period of deep meditation, then slamming the ball into his glove and wheeling back to the mound.

Reggie pantomimed an underhanded throw as if to say, "After all that crap, this is how fast you can throw," and to make his disdain even more emphatic, he tried to catch the pitch with his bare hand.

Everybody knew that it wasn't Hrabosky he was angry with, it was George, and that as soon as the writers descended upon him, it was all going to come pouring out.

But not right away. Reggie stormed into the clubhouse yelling, "I have nothing to say. Nothing to say." As questions were thrown at him, he cried out, almost tearfully, "Leave me alone," and went running into the trainer's room, a retreat out of bounds to writers. He remained there for an hour and a half. Knowing Reggie, the writers waited. They knew him well. "I'm a keg of dynamite," he said upon emerging. "You all know that." And then it all came pouring out of him. Everything he had been saying off the record, and more.

"It's just killing me," he said. "When you don't have Mom and Dad saying, 'How you doing?' you can't deal with it. I so much want to have a confrontation with him, and I can't wait for it to happen. I want to tear this fucking building down, but I know he won't come in here."

The "Mom and Dad" says it all. The emotional deficit. The lack of structure to his life. The damage done. Reggie's parents separated when he was three. The three girls went with the mother, the three boys stayed with the father. Reggie was the youngest of the boys, and so he became the housekeeper. The little boy who returned to an empty house after school. The black kid in a white middle-class neighborhood. He needs to be wanted, to be appreciated, and when you need to be wanted and appreciated that much, you can never be wanted and appreciated enough.

He began to talk longingly about the year he had spent in Baltimore before signing with the Yankees. "The way Earl Weaver treated me, you'd have thought I was the cat's meow. Same way last year with Howser. I loved that man. I played hurt. I played sick." But he didn't want to bring Gene Michael into this. "It's not fair to him. It's that I'm worn out, I guess."

What was killing him most was George's accusation that he talked out of both sides of his mouth. "It's with me every day." Steinbrenner had also said, as Reggie interpreted it, that "I was not the right kind of person he would want to have a lasting relationship with. It has eaten me since I heard it. Tell me I'm no good to my face. I'm tired of the situation."

Would he ever sign another contract with Steinbrenner? "I'm not saying no, and I'm not saying yes. But I've been saying for months that George didn't want to sign me. I can't go wrong leaving."

The one thing he kept coming back to was the need to *talk* to George Steinbrenner. "To have him say those things to my face." And yet, with it all, there was the implicit promise that he was going to be a good boy from now on and that he understood the problem George saw in his advancing age. "The only thing I have on my side is talent, and I won't have that much longer. If I was twenty-eight, somebody would have to kick my ass. I'd come in at twelve-thirty or skip town for three, four days. But I don't do it now." (Just in case you're wondering, he didn't do it when he was twenty-eight, either.)

He went on for a full hour, and when he was all talked out, he thanked the writers for listening to him. "I needed to get my feelings off my chest."

And where was this boss of his who could make it all okay by simply talking to him? Right there off the locker room through it all, as unaware of Reggie as Reggie was of him. While Jackson had been hiding in the trainer's room, George had stepped into the clubhouse and gone right to Michael's office, which was blocked from view.

The writers found the club owner in his car just about to be driven off to the airport for a flight back to his home in Tampa. "I could have predicted it," he told them. "Winfield has looked so good, and you can see it in Reggie's actions. I've known Reggie for four years. I know how he reacts to these things. Winfield looks so good and Reggie's struggling. And I must say it's not very mature."

Then he stuck it in deeper. "One of these years you won't pay that much attention to him." Typical Steinbrenner—he had used the same line about Billy Martin. "But," he added virtuously, "I don't want to say anything critical or detrimental about him. It's not right." Again, typical.

Off goes Steinbrenner. Back to Reggie go the writers, to continue the game of "You Said—He Said," which the writers had been playing for four years. Well, said Reggie, since Winfield looked so good to Steinbrenner, he wanted George to know that the owners of the California Angels and New York Mets were looking better to *him* every day. Now, that was more like the old Reggie. Any time he got depressed, he threatened to take his bat to California, where the sun always shines, or his box office allure to the Mets, the city rival. There was even a Reggie Jackson line coming up. "I can call Federal Express and say I got a big package for them."

With Steinbrenner winging off to Tampa, any further response was going to have to wait until later in the evening. And so it came. This time George likened Jackson's outbursts to that of "a four-year-old kid sitting in a corner and screaming, 'I want my candy.' " Reggie had wailed, "I want my mommy," and that was George's interpretation. And again George seized upon the opportunity to get in a plug for Winfield by commenting that Reggie was troubled "because he sees a young guy come along with all that talent."

After all the sniping, George was back again early the next morning. Overnight, it seemed, he had read what Reggie had said about being eager for a confrontation. A meeting took place in Michael's office between George, Reggie, and Stick.

When the three came out, the building was still standing, and George was proclaiming it "one of the better meetings I've had since I've been in baseball." That didn't sound so good. George normally characterizes any meeting that didn't end with the dog licking the blood off the floor as "the best meeting we've ever had."

George was all muscle and macho. "He knows and I know there's no way I wasn't going to walk into that locker room today. I'm glad I did because we got a lot of stuff straightened out."

"I'm here to play baseball and play very hard," said Jackson. "I'm ready to go. I'm in a better frame of mind now."

It had just been a good old-fashioned bitching session, to hear Steinbrenner talk, with each of them voicing their complaints and concerns. They both maintained that the question of the contract had not come up. And, to all practical purposes, it hadn't. Before, in the pre-camp meeting, they had talked not about the contract but about some lucrative lifetime alliance off there somewhere in the great beyond. This time they talked not about the contract but about Reggie's emotional *need* for a contract.

Over the heads of the writers, Reggie said to the clubhouse man in Spanish: "I asked to be traded."

He had talked to George and got nothing, and the next day he sank right back into his mental slough.

Reggie wasn't the only player in camp looking for a new contract. There were two others, Ron Guidry and Willie Randolph, the two most underpaid players on the club and—could it be only coincidental?—two of the best human beings. Guidry had been paid nearly $30,000 minimum when he pitched the Yankees to a pennant and World Championship in 1977, and was currently on the final year of a three-year contract at $125,000 a year, with bonuses that brought it to something closer to $225,000. And that was after Guidry had pitched the Yankees to a second straight World Championship with one of the greatest seasons in modern baseball history.

Willie Randolph has always been the most underpaid player in baseball. In his rookie year, 1976, he signed for $23,000, little more than the minimum then. A year later, after an operation on his knee, he was so worried about his future that he signed a four-year contract at somewhere around $70,000 a year. Two years later still, in 1979, he got himself a top agent, Dick Moss, who renegotiated an extension that brought him a flat million, $200,000 across the board for five years, plus a $225,000 signing bonus.

Nowhere is the fallout from the constantly escalating pay scale better exemplified. A contract is a contract, right? Willie was happy with the contract when he signed it, wasn't he? On the other hand . . . Here you had the heart and soul of the New York Yankees, an all-star second baseman, the one player whom the other Yankees felt they could least afford to lose over a whole season. In 1980, he hit .294 and led the major leagues with 119 walks. His .429 on base percentage was second only to George Brett's .461. He led the Yankees in runs scored with 99 and stole 30 bases in 35 attempts, the fourth time in five seasons he had stolen 30 or more bases.

And even then Willie's greatest value to the team wasn't on offense but on defense. In point of service, he was the third-oldest player on the team. He never made waves, never caused problems. Played with joy. Until now. Compared to what everybody else was getting, the $200,000, which had seemed like such a fortune two years ago, now looked like a pittance.

One of his problems was that Steinbrenner had never given the slightest indication that he recognized Willie's value. Willie was "a skinny little guy," in George's opinion. Didn't hit home runs, didn't hit .300. Even when he approved the five-year contract that had been negotiated by his general manager, Al Rosen, George bawled Rosen out for being overgenerous.

Willie was determined not to be another Roy White, another quiet man who never made waves and never got paid what he was worth. During the off-season he had suggested that the Yankees buy him a new house to show they respected him as a team leader and recognized that he had always been underpaid. George was willing to do better than that for Willie; George was willing to renegotiate the whole contract so that Willie would be getting paid what he was worth. George then promised that they'd talk about it again during spring training.

George is great at holding forth promises of future discussions that somehow never take place. He's too busy right now, but remind him. Press him, and he'll put on the hard face that frightens people and begin to talk fast and loud. "Now, look, I *told* you we'll talk about it later. You're not the only thing I've got on my mind, you know."

The only one who ever called him on the maneuver was Jeff Torborg, a coach. Torborg had signed with the Yankees in the last couple of months of 1979, after he had been fired as manager of the Cleveland Indians, with the understanding that he would eventually become vested in the pension plan. A major-league club can carry all the coaches it wants to, but only four of them can be vested in the pension

26

plan. The Yankees already had their four coaches listed for 1980, and Torborg signed on the understanding that he would be vested in 1981.

When he tried to talk to George about it, George never seemed to be available. Finally Torborg was able to corner him after the press conference that introduced Winfield to the New York press. "It's not that I've forgotten," George told him. "I'm working on it. You're going to have to be patient. There are other more important things on my mind right now. I'm sure you can understand that."

And Torborg said, "No, I don't understand. You made me a promise, and I want to know if you're going to honor it." Jeff had cornered him at the buffet table directly behind the writers gathered around Winfield, so George whisked him off to a side room. There he put on his tough face and yelled, "You're going to *have* to understand! You're going to *have* to wait!"

And Jeff came back just as loudly. "Don't you use that tone of voice to me, George! Don't talk to me like that!"

George came out of the room looking angry, and Torborg kind of expected to be fired.

But, do you know what? Within a few days George began to talk about Jeff Torborg with great admiration. Some guy! Great fellow! Jim Hegan, the incumbent bullpen coach, was informed that he really was anxious to take off the uniform and begin a fascinating new career as a Yankee scout, and Jeff Torborg's name went on the pension list.

As far as Willie Randolph was concerned, however, George had a new ploy up his sleeve. During the off-season Willie received a call from Steinbrenner informing him that they had decided to name him team captain. The announcement was going to be made in spring training.

Willie was thrilled. He was also, come the third week of training camp, still waiting. Finally, he was called into the trailer that George uses as his office in spring training, and was told that the captaincy was being offered to Graig Nettles. Willie steamed about it for a few days and then went in to see Steinbrenner again. No, he didn't go storming in, that's not Willie. He had asked for an appointment. Face to face, he told George that the only reason he had wanted to be named captain was that he thought he'd be getting the respect that was due him as one of the leaders on the ballclub. "If you're going to make me a promise, don't renege on it, that's all." Just like George seemed to be reneging on the promise to renegotiate the contract.

Listen, George understood exactly how he felt. Willie could take his word for it. As soon as the actual season started, he'd get together with Willie's lawyer and get it done. (You're going to find this hard to believe, but when the season started, Willie's lawyer was never able to get an appointment. And when the team went into a slump, George let out a blast at players who were so worried about "negotiating and re-negotiating their contracts" that their minds weren't on the game. He was talking about Reggie Jackson and Willie Randolph, and he was ab-solutely right. It was affecting Willie's game so much that he finally told George, "Forget about the whole contract. Keep the money, keep the house. All I want to think about now is playing baseball.")

Why had the captaincy been offered to him in the first place? Well, George is a creature of impulse, and it had obviously occurred to him that if Willie wanted a proffer of respect, a title would be a helluva lot cheaper than a house. Why had he changed his mind? Well, there had been only two captains in the entire history of the New York Yankees: Lou Gehrig and Thurman Munson. On sober second thought, George had apparently decided that the gesture, with all its enormous symbol-ic value, would be wasted on the likes of Willie Randolph.

Why was it offered to Nettles? That's easy. Because it had worked so well with Thurman Munson.

In the spring of 1976, with Billy Martin about to begin his first full year as the Yankees' manager, Steinbrenner and Martin had had a long discussion about what to do with Thurman Munson. "Munson's such an arrogant person," George had finally decided. "If we make him captain, maybe he'll at least act differently."

Oh, Thurman had tried to pretend that it didn't mean anything to him, but as the season progressed and it became evident that the Yan-kees were on their way to their first pennant in twelve years, Thur-man began to take his new position so seriously that he could always be handled by appealing to his responsibilities as team captain.

Nettles had been Munson's closest friend. And he was becoming even harder to handle. If Munson's latter-day difficulties with Stein-brenner had been well publicized, at least there had been a closer rela-tionship between them than most people realized. Graig Nettles disliked George Steinbrenner and did nothing at all to hide the fact.

Graig Nettles has a prickly personality, which may have come about at least partly from going through life seeing his first name mis-spelled. He may very well be the only Graig in the world. He'd be Craig—which is how everybody automatically saw the name, heard it, and spelled it until a few years ago—except that his mother had a thing about the letter G.

Nettles's dislike for Steinbrenner went back to 1977 and the first tempestuous training camp after the signing of Reggie Jackson, where half the ballclub was either holding out or demanding to have their contracts renegotiated. Nettles, who had a far better case than anyone else—based on a misunderstanding about a tax situation—finally walked out of camp, and before George would allow him to come back, he had not only humiliated his all-star third baseman but had boasted, publicly, about how he had humiliated him.

Graig Nettles doesn't forget. He has his own arrogance, and it comes with a withering wit. When the Boss came flying in to raise a little hell with the club after they had got off to such an atrocious start that same season, it was Graig Nettles (not Dock Ellis, to whom it was somehow attributed) who said, "The more we lose, the more often Steinbrenner will fly in. And the more he flies, the better the chance will be of the plane crashing."

Whenever George would join the club on the road—which would be when the club was going bad, with George irate to begin with—he would ride with the players on the team bus. The players' repartee on the bus is wildly funny and very rough, and it is understood—by the players, if not necessarily by George—that if he wants to ride with them as one of the boys, he has to take his chances. "Hey, George," Nettles once yelled as some 350-pound man came waddling past, "hurry up and get aboard or we'll have to leave without you."

The stories are endless. Because George's daughter attends the University of North Carolina, he has always scheduled an exhibition game there on the way back to New York. And so, one time when the bus taking the players from the Dallas airport to their hotel got hopelessly lost, Graig yelled out, "Why are we going to North Carolina again? What's the matter with that kid, George. Isn't she ever going to graduate?"

George went running down the aisle of the bus, red-faced. "Who said that?" he screamed. "I want to know who said that."

When George is asked about that incident, he says that Nettles just sat there cowering. More objective observers say that as soon as George realized what a fool he was making of himself, he turned on his heel and went back to his seat.

The point is made. Nettles has an attitude about the organization, and a dislike for George. He also has a temperament so unpredictable that a couple of times a year the word will go around the clubhouse, "Watch out, Graig's on the rag again." You could give odds that it was going to happen in spring training, 1981. Like Reggie, Graig viewed Gene Michael as George's boy. For Reggie, the view was conditioned by a sense of loss of the buffer Howser had provided. For Nettles, who is so ferociously his own man, it was simply a lack of respect for anyone who so conspicuously wasn't.

Michael had Nettles hitting seventh in the lineup, which he didn't particularly like, though he had batted seventh from time to time under other managers. But he had missed the last half of the previous season with a bad case of hepatitis, he was thirty-six years old, and maybe he felt he wasn't the fielder he used to be—which meant he was only one of the best third basemen in baseball instead of indisputably the best. Yup, with one thing and another, Graig was on the rag again.

In the second inning of an exhibition game against Atlanta, he took a ground ball, threw it wild, and when his turn came to bat in the last half of the inning, Graig wasn't in the dugout. He was back in the clubhouse, getting dressed.

For Michael, it was a critical situation. Nettles was a veteran, the oldest player in terms of continuous service on the ballclub. Not only had he been a teammate of Michael's, he had played directly alongside him in the infield. So if Michael needed anyone's support, it was Nettles's. On the opening day of camp, Michael had read off the same rules on dress and deportment that every other Yankee manager had read off. After all, they weren't Gene Michael's rules, they were Steinbrenner's rules. Everybody there knew that. Except, of course, those who chose not to know it. "Boy," they were saying to each other when the meeting broke up, "Stick sure has forgotten what it's like to be a player, hasn't he?"

Thus, Steinbrenner, with his special interest in protecting his handpicked manager, decided to bring Graig around by making him captain.

It was hard to tell who was the more insulted: Randolph for having the promise of the captaincy withdrawn, or Nettles for having it offered to him.

Nettles's answer came a couple of nights later. He was drinking at the Banana Boat Bar, a local watering hole where the players hang out, when another customer started to bother him. Next thing anybody knew, they were going at each other, and both ended up being hauled off to the pokey. Since the job of getting ballplayers out of jail has historically belonged to the club's traveling secretary, the Fort Lauderdale police probably called Bill Kane automatically. It's too much to hope that Nettles could have told the desk sergeant, "Sure, call George Steinbrenner." At any rate, Steinbrenner was in the car with him when Bill Kane drove up to the police station. Kane went in to straighten things out, while Steinbrenner waited in the car. George wanted to impress upon Graig the necessity of covering up what had happened.

Nettles's answer couldn't have been completely satisfactory, because although George did succeed in keeping the story covered up, Graig was kept out of the lineup. The story was given out that his shoulder had become so sore that he couldn't play. Well, Graig always has a sore shoulder in spring training. In fact, Graig's shoulder is always sore, period. The Yankees, it would seem, weren't quite sure that Graig wouldn't throw another ball away, or take another walk, and even less sure what he'd say when the writers asked him about it.

Somewhere in all of this the question of Graig Nettles's captaincy got lost. Nettles was so contrite that he was back in the Banana Boat a couple of nights later. The same guy came over to buy him a drink. "Hey," he said, "we had a pretty good one the other night, didn't we?"

"Yeah," Nettles told him. "Maybe we ought to do it again sometime."

Reggie Jackson was out of the lineup, too. With Reggie it had nothing to do with his attitude, but rather with Steinbrenner's ambition to help the Mets remain one of New York's best-kept secrets. It was bad enough that the Mets never failed to beat the Yankees in St. Petersburg. What made it intolerable was that the Mets would telecast this game from their home park back to New York. The Yankees had always gone to nearby St. Petersburg during their annual sojourn in Tampa. For 1981, George had eliminated the week in Tampa and substituted a three-game trip to New Orleans to take on three different opponents. He thereby gave the Mets the opportunity to play their "home" game under the auspices of the Superdome—with no TV back to New York—unless, of course, they wanted to be churlish about it.

The Yankees' home game in Fort Lauderdale had already been played by then, and of course the Mets had whomped the Yankees badly, so badly that George had thrown his first rookie pitcher (Mike Griffin) out of camp, delivered his first "It's time to screw down the hatches" speech, and given Reggie Jackson, who had hit his first spring home run, an unaccustomed compliment. If you can call "Reggie didn't pack it in today" a compliment.

Two things happened in New Orleans. The Yankees lost to the Mets again, but at least the coverage was at a minimum. And they lost Reggie Jackson for the rest of the spring. The final Superdome game was against Philadelphia, and to Reggie Jackson the Phillies mean Pete Rose. Whenever Reggie is up against one of the superstars from the other league, he gets all hyped up. In the first of the three games against Pittsburgh, he had been out to hit a ball farther in batting practice than the Pirates' Dave Parker. Against Philadelphia, he was going to out-hustle Pete Rose. He ran hard before the game, hustled his butt off while he was in the game and, when he was taken out after seven innings, went to the outfield and ran his sprints through the rest of the game. Now, Reggie does not float gazellelike across the landscape. He went to Arizona State University originally on a football scholarship, and he runs like the fullback that he was. He pounded up and down the hard artificial turf of the Superdome, showing Pete Rose how it was supposed to be done, and woke up the next morning with a pulled Achilles tendon.

Actually, Reggie didn't seem all that unhappy about it. He even seemed kind of relieved. The leg was put in a light Fiberglas cast, and along about the second or third inning of subsequent games, Reggie would come walking out on the ramp and stand there leaning on his crutches while the entire park came to its feet, pointing and applauding. Then, instead of watching the game from the dugout, he would sit out in the open, allowing everybody to watch him eat his hot dog and sip his Coke.

So, when the season started, Reggie was still in Fort Lauderdale working himself back into shape. Away from the team, his mind seemed to clear. In his first game after his return, he lined a double off the center-field wall. After the first six games, he was hitting .333 with 2 home runs and 6 rbi's. He was doing so well that George made an appointment with him to talk about the contract. At least, that's what Reggie thought. It turned out to be an appointment not to actually talk about the contract but to *set up a schedule* for future contract talks. "I owed Reggie that courtesy," said George.

Reggie went right back into his slump.

If Reggie was moaning low at the start of the 1981 season, George Steinbrenner was riding high. By coming into camp late, Reggie had given him the opportunity to play the role he likes best: the Boss.

By 1981, his main adversary, Billy Martin, was long gone. The crash and clamor of Reggie & Billy & George, in which George had been the third man on the seesaw, shifting his weight from one to the other, had faded away. Billy had been broken and discarded (only to rise again in Oakland). Now, Reggie's time was just about played out. Managers had come and gone. Players had come and gone. George remained, bulking larger by the year. The Yankees were no longer a mere property, they had become his fiefdom. And in the spring of 1981, he stood astride his allotted portion of the earth like a colossus.

What did it matter that the Yankees had not been in the World Series for two years? George Steinbrenner had captured the imagination of the media. He was being followed around by the crew of "60 Minutes." There were magazine writers all over the place. Not only was he starring in the Yankees' own commercials, he was being paid to do commercials for other products, and what greater status is there in this great wide television world? There was talk of George having his own panel talk show. He was selected to lead the Florida State University band in the singing of "The Stars and Stripes Forever." And when *Playgirl* selected its ten sexiest men, who was there staring back at us in all his loveliness but good old George III.

To answer the question that is driving America mad, George does not wear a toupee. It is simply that he has used so much hair spray over the years that unless his hair is continuously spray-styled, it comes out looking that way. The secretary who lets the supply run dry is in deep trouble. "Where the hell's the hair spray?" George screams. "What the hell's wrong with you? You know you're supposed to get the hair spray!"

To those who want to delve even further in the mystic springs that go to make a sex symbol, George carries a little comb in his pocket. In the street he'll stop alongside a car, take a quick look around, hunch over and *whish . . . whish . . . whish.* In the elevator he'll reach for the comb, scrunch down to catch his reflection in the shiny steel panel, and *whish . . . whish . . . whish.*

Spring is the time of ultimate activity for George. While he is in camp, he is also taking care of his multifarious business interests, thereby allowing himself almost unlimited opportunity to scream imprecations and threats at vice-presidents and other hirelings and snivelings along the leased lines of AT&T.

Spring is the time for making trades to overcome whatever weaknesses may exist. In the spring of 1981, it was apparent that the Yankees needed a center fielder—what with last year's center fielder, Ruppert Jones, having failed to live up to expectations—a left-handed-hitting first baseman, and a right-handed pitcher. And that involved frequent meetings with his scouts and front office personnel.

And the coaches.

It is almost axiomatic in baseball that the best teams have the worst spring-training records. Exhibition games aren't for winning, they are for getting ready to win. But what is axiomatic for other baseball men is not necessarily axiomatic for George. He cannot stand losing games in spring training. After every loss there is a meeting, sometimes even after a win. Every day he keeps the coaches extra long to find out what the hell is going wrong. Two hours later, you see the coaches coming out of the trailer that George uses for an office, their heads down. "Drills," George calls them. A good football term, one of many George has brought into baseball. Like FUNDAMENTALS! George roars the word. Never mind that the players don't believe that George would know a fundamental if it crawled into bed with him. ("All he knows," they say, "is how to ride his boats!") Whenever George sees a weakness—too many balls getting through the infield, too many errors, sloppy base-running—whether it's during spring training or the regular season, there is going to be a meeting to drill the coaches.

Fundamentals, conditioning, discipline! In former years George would bring his team into Tampa for five or six days and schedule exhibition games against the teams in the immediate area. Why not? George makes his home in Tampa, and he happens to own a hotel there. Only one thing wrong with the arrangement: George would have his friends and family in proud attendance, and the Yankees would invariably lose. The Yankees would lose, lose, lose, and George would throw fits, fits, fits.

In the spring of 1979, the Yankees lost their first six games, and George slapped down a curfew. It didn't matter that the Yankees had just won two straight World Championships, George wanted them to understand that exhibition games were important too. When the team arrived in Tampa, he stationed a guard on every floor and warned the players that anyone who wasn't in his room at the appointed time was going to be fined $250. Well, ballplayers are competitive people—give them a challenge, and they are compelled to meet it. Led by their doughty captain, Thurman Munson, the Yankee players turned the tables.

Munson's room was on the second floor rear, so all he had to do was tie his sheet to the rail of the balcony. The others on higher floors came tiptoeing down the staircase and, as soon as the guard's back was turned, skedoodled down the corridor, through one of the rooms, and out onto the balcony. Five players went down the sheet: Munson, Nettles, two rookie pitchers, and a rookie outfielder. Unfortunately that left nobody to pull the sheet back up. Even more unfortunately, there was a restaurant facing the back of the hotel. When the players came back around three or four in the morning, George was sitting in the restaurant, waiting to catch the culprits. Munson and Nettles may have been fined. Who knows? The Yankees were hardly going to tell the world that their captain was leading an insurrection against law, order, and George Steinbrenner's hereditary right to treat his players like children. The two rookie pitchers, Tim Lollar and Christopher Welsh, were sent back to the minors before another dawn rose. They both went to San Diego two springs later in the Jerry Mumphrey trade. The outfielder is still in the organization.

George Steinbrenner sees all and knows all. The man is everywhere. No question about it, he has become a media spectacular, as merchandisable as Reggie himself. And yet . . .

Is that a snicker in the background? A laugh slipping through? The first faint glimmer of a bad joke?

He has made himself, after all, the ringmaster of the circus, the keeper of the Bronx Zoo. A money machine, a reckless consumer of talent. As the 1981 season was beginning, he was paying two ex-managers, Dick Howser and Bob Lemon, not to manage; and if Billy Martin hadn't signed on with Oakland, George would have been paying three.

And through it all, this one-man temper tantrum—the only businessman convicted of a Watergate offense—lays down his dress codes and his curfews and talks endlessly about the pride and tradition and class of the Yankees.

He is out there, naked and exposed, and he had better win. Because winning overcomes all. Winning you're a human dynamo. Losing you're the Fat Boy in a Freak Show.

3

WHAT GEORGE DID

George M. Steinbrenner III is a businessman, the first to be convicted of breaking the U.S. election laws. He treats his historical role in two ways. He avoids talking about it whenever possible, and when he does talk about it, he portrays himself as a victim of an unscrupulous and vindictive Nixon gang that was out to get him because he was a highly successful fund-raiser for the Democratic Party and a friend and supporter of Teddy Kennedy.

The way George's version goes, these insidious forces zeroed in on him by giving his company, American Ship Building (AmShip), trouble on three separate fronts: a series of antitrust suits and investigations, rejection of a settlement claim on a $5.4 million cost overrun on a Coast Guard vessel, and a $10,000 fine after a fatal fire aboard one of the ships under construction in the AmShip yards.

At a March 1972 meeting with the Committee for the Re-election of the President (CREEP), he says he was led to believe that a $100,000 contribution to the Nixon campaign would go a long way toward solving his problems. On the advice of his lawyer, he raised $25,000 by granting "bogus bonuses" to selected "trustworthy employees," and contributed the other $75,000 out of his own funds. "If I hadn't believed it was legal, I would have been a perfect idiot to give $75,000 of my own money and $25,000 in company money," he has said. "If I hadn't believed it was legal, I'd have given all personal funds."

As time passes and memory recedes, he paints himself as a man who did no more than had to be done in the political climate of the time and was then hounded into court for refusing to betray his friends and employees. The way he puts it, "I can say that I didn't bring anybody down with me." In a latter-day refinement of that statement, he goes so far as to claim that once the Nixon predators had his money, they upped the ante and tried to get him to reveal the darkest secrets he had become privy to in his role as a Democratic fund-raiser.

The only thing wrong with his version is everything. For starters, the Watergate investigators were hardly Nixon people. They were the guys who were out to bury Nixon, remember? The first Special Prosecutor, the man who instituted criminal proceedings against George, was Archibald Cox (you remember the Saturday Night Massacre). Archibald Cox first entered the political arena as one of the original members of John F. Kennedy's Harvard brain trust, back in the days when Kennedy was running for the U.S. Senate. When Kennedy became President, he made Cox his first Solicitor General, the Number Two man in the Justice Department right behind the Attorney General.

And who was the Attorney General? Bobby Kennedy.

So Steinbrenner was targeted because he was so close to Teddy Kennedy? Come on. Archie Cox was such a good and faithful Kennedy-ite that if those mysteriously missing records of the telephone calls Teddy Kennedy made from Chappaquiddick ever arise from the ashes, my bet would be that Archie Cox's number would appear high up on the list. (And I wonder why nobody ever asked him.)

In any case, George's "bogus bonus" scheme was not devised to slip money to CREEP. He had come up with it two years earlier to make campaign contributions to two Republican Congressmen and a Democratic Senator who happened to be on the commerce committees of their respective houses. Congress was voting on a new maritime law that was so vital to American Ship Building that if it hadn't passed you would probably never have heard of George M. Steinbrenner III.

And, finally, it wasn't CREEP who came to George, it was George who went to CREEP.

To believe that George really didn't know he was doing anything illegal, you would also have to believe that the man who had been chairman of two national Democratic fund-raising dinners had never been informed that it was illegal for a corporation to contribute money "directly or indirectly" from corporate funds.

With that background, let us now look into the personal and business background of the martyred George M. Steinbrenner III. We'll get back to what George really did to get himself into all that trouble later.

George came into the world on July 4, 1930, as heir to the Kinsman Marine Transit Co., a five-ship fleet that carried ore and grain on the Great Lakes. His father, Henry Steinbrenner, is a tough old German who was the NCAA hurdle champ at M.I.T. His mother is Irish. By George's account—and we don't have any other—he was brought up very strictly. Every story written about him tells the tale of how he was given a dozen chickens when he was nine years old, in lieu of an allowance, and proceeded to build up an egg route that was so profitable that when he was sent off to Culver Military Academy at the age of thirteen, he was able to sell it to his two younger sisters.

Culver Military Academy is where, most typically, unmanageable or unmanly little rich boys are sent to have some discipline and patriotism knocked into them, or to be made men of, and between the strict father and the military school, a stamp is apparently placed on the boy.

In the one notable departure in his biography, he goes to Williams College. Since George is going to be taking over the shipping business, it means that he either did not have the marks to get into M.I.T. or that for once the old man didn't win out. Williams College is one of the Little Three (Williams, Wesleyan, and Amherst), a lovely institution that is probably every bit as difficult to get into as M.I.T., and considerably more charming.

At Williams, he majors in English Literature and excels in the choir. Like his father, he runs track. He becomes sports editor of the college newspaper. And in his final year he is a halfback on the football team.

From college he goes into the army, and although the Korean War is on—and who can doubt that George wants to go fight for his country?—it's solid stateside duty.

After his discharge, he coaches high school football and basketball for a couple of years. He becomes an assistant football coach at Northwestern and Purdue at a time when the Big Ten is the most powerful football conference in the land. Even when he surrenders to his father and goes into the family business, his main interest seems to be sports. To his father's disgust, he buys a basketball team in an industrial league—the Cleveland Pipers—and you can almost hear the old man telling him, "George, when are you going to grow up?"

Henry Steinbrenner is a tough taskmaster. When George conducts basketball business on the office telephone, the Old Man will come up behind him and clamp his hand down to break the connection. His son, an excellent student, is learning how employees are supposed to be treated. But no, that isn't fair. From all accounts the Old Man is tough but never impulsive or unpredictable. Henry Steinbrenner has the arrogance and self-control of a Prussian. He does not throw temper tantrums. He does not humiliate his employees. When you think about it, George Steinbrenner is not at all like his father.

The Cleveland Pipers win two championships in a row in the industrial league and move into the short-lived American Basketball League. George shows his entrepreneurial instincts by signing the most sought-after college player in the country, Jerry Lucas, to a personal service contract. There's a little confusion about that, in that Lucas already seems to have signed a contract with Cincinnati in the N.B.L. But it doesn't matter. Before the matter can be resolved, the league collapses and the team goes bankrupt. It is both the low and high point of George's life. In addition to his own losses, his friends are out $50,000, and although he is under no legal obligation, he pays them all off. "That's the price I had to pay," he would say later, "for continuing to do business in Cleveland."

There follows a brief period of depression, and when he emerges, he comes out running. A year after going bankrupt with his basketball team, he takes over his father's shipping business. The way the official bio has it, he borrowed money from a New York bank and bought the old man out. The old man had decided, it seems, that there was no future for the shipping industry on the Great Lakes, because the steel companies had their own fleets and carried their own ore. George has other ideas. He goes down to Washington, sells his heart out, and comes back with a briefcase full of orders for carrying grain.

Could be. Actually, great things were about to happen for Great Lakes shipping, centering around the burgeoning ore production in the upper Lakes region and southern Canada, and the inadequacy of the steel companies' fleets.

The Great Lakes maritime fleet had, in fact, been falling apart for thirty years because inland carriers were specifically excluded, under the Merchant Marine Act of 1936, from any kind of subsidization by the government. (Independent old shippers like Henry Steinbrenner had actually *fought against* being subsidized, and then the tax situation killed them.) And—to compound the discrimination—only those lines that were subsidized had the right to set aside profits in tax-deferred reserves for the construction of new ships.

Clearly unfair, thought George. But also an opportunity. If the maritime law could be changed, there would be a lot of shipbuilding going on. George set out to spearhead a massive lobbying effort in Congress and, before he was finished, to make himself its chief beneficiary.

In April 1964, one year after he had taken command of Kinsman Marine, George became one of the six new directors on the board of the Lake Carriers Association.

In April 1965, the featured speaker at the association's annual meeting was Rep. William S. Mailliard (R-Cal.). Mailliard was there to announce that he was drafting legislation for a new maritime bill that would grant Great Lakes shipping companies all the benefits that had been accorded hitherto only to deep sea shippers. The other news item of interest coming out of that meeting was that a new member had been elected to the association's advisory committee: George M. Whatsisname.

It was going to take five years and a change of administration before the Maritime Act of 1970 went through, and by all accounts George did not spend an idle day. He had found his niche as a political operator, and in Cleveland he became an exemplar of that great American phenomenon, the civic booster. In 1966, he formed Group 66, an organization of young Cleveland business leaders dedicated to improving life in the city and, while they were about it, advancing their own careers. ("Every city has its establishment, but the younger men must break with the status quo. Otherwise, they are going to have to wait until they are in their fifties before assuming leadership.") He was chairman of the fund-raising committee for CLEVELAND: NOW, another program for community betterment. He was the first chairman of the Inner Cleveland Urban Coalition. As the youngest member appointed to Cleveland's "Little Hoover Commission," he drew up the long-range plans for the area's harbors and airports. He was director (and eventually vice-chairman) of the Greater Cleveland Growth Corporation.

If civic betterment was the name of the game, George Steinbrenner was going to be there when the roll was called. In 1968, he was cited by *Fortune* magazine as one of the twelve young "Movers and

Shakers" of the nation. He had already been selected by the Ohio Junior Chamber of Commerce as the most outstanding young man in the state.

And all the time he was also running Kinsman Marine and leading the lobbying effort in Washington. If he could get Congress to give the Great Lakes fleets the same benefits as the deep sea fleets, he'd be putting new life into the fleets themselves and setting up a veritable bonanza for the shipbuilders.

The challenge, then, was twofold: Get the new maritime act passed and get yourself a shipbuilding company.

In May 1967, four years after he had bought the Old Man out, George M. Steinbrenner led a takeover of the giant American Ship Building Company. It wasn't a merger, as is frequently suggested in articles about him, it was a classic takeover. Under the aegis of Roulston and Co., a Cleveland brokerage, "the Roulston group" bought up more than $9 million worth of AmShip stock over a six-month period. They asked for fifty percent of the seats on the board of directors, plus the right to install their own president and chief executive officer, George M. Steinbrenner.

Turned aside in May, they were back again in October, and this time they took it over completely—lock, stock, and board of directors.

"In the very immediate future, probably within six months," Steinbrenner told the stockholders, the first of a series of contracts would be given out by U.S. Steel for the construction of a huge new iron-ore hauling vessel, "and the company that gets the first order will be in a dominant position."

George was being overly modest. He had the contract in eighteen days.

Even before that, within just a week of the takeover, the port authority of Lorain, Ohio, where AmShip had its shipyards, had voted an $8- to $10-million bond issue for enlarging and modernizing the dry-dock facilities.

It was a remarkable performance. And what does it tell us? Among other things, it tells us that George Steinbrenner was not a man who came to AmShip as an innocent woolly lamb in the world of politics, ready to be sheared by the hard-eyed Nixonites.

George had every reason to be grateful to the Nixon administration. Once the Maritime Act of 1970 went through, the profits of American Ship Building took a quantum leap. If George himself ever said an unkind word about Nixon, it certainly wasn't in public. On the contrary, he was always lavish with his praise. As in a speech before the Detroit Rotary Club on May 19, 1971: "I am from a family of sailors and shipbuilders, and to me personally the decade of the seventies with the Maritime Act of 1970 will be to the maritime industry what the decade of the sixties was to the aerospace industry—a period of excitement and great activity. . . . The Great Lakes fleet in 1970 had an average age per ship of 43.6 years, and no new ships had been launched for ten years. The fleet had dwindled almost 38 percent in ten years. . . . Then came President Nixon's great Maritime Act which, for the first time in history, included the Great Lakes in the program—despite considerable opposition. . . ."

And in a speech before the Propeller Club of the United States on October 13, 1971: "I am confident that from 1970 to 1980 we will see the largest, most productive era as far as new ship construction and new tonnage is concerned that we have ever seen on the Great Lakes. . . . For that, we owe thanks to the Nixon administration and to the Secretary of Commerce, Maurice Stans. . . ."

It was Maurice Stans whom George contacted, in an attempt to have his brother-in-law appointed ambassador to Denmark after the illegal campaign contribution had failed to win him anything else.

When George says in his own defense that he would hardly have given $25,000 in laundered money along with $75,000 of his own money if he had known that the laundered money was illegal, he is suggesting that no question ever arose as to the legitimacy of the $75,000. And that isn't exactly true, either.

Item: The initial bogus bonuses, which actually totalled $30,000, were given out on September 27, 1970. George got his bonus two weeks later. Why two weeks later? Well, the $75,000 was divided into two bonuses of $37,500, one dated October 9 and the other October 12. Am-Ship's fiscal year ended on October 10. By doing it that way George was able to split the bonus over two separate years on the company's books.

Item: George's bonus and the bogus bonuses were both listed as rewards for meritorious work on the Coast Guard claim.

Item: There were three packets of bogus bonuses given out over three years. Except for George's bonus and those bogus bonuses, no other bonuses were given to anyone.

Item: According to the minutes of the meeting, George's bonus was voted by the board of directors "for effective settlement of the U.S. Coast Guard claim." In April 1973, with the Watergate cover-up under way, Steinbrenner called in the company secretary, Robert E. Bartlome, and had him change the minutes to read: "For effective operation of the company during the year just ended."

Testimony before the Senate Watergate committee:

Question: Mr. Steinbrenner directed you to change the minutes?
Bartlome: Yes.

Why would George doctor the books—a crime in itself—unless he had something to hide? Maybe it was because the Coast Guard claim hadn't been settled satisfactorily at all. Not only didn't AmShip get a cent back, an additional $200,000 penalty was eventually levied against the company. And that was *after* George had made the contribution. The Watergate prosecutors didn't go after George because of the illegal contributions. More than twenty other corporations were found to be, or admitted to, doing the same thing. Nor was he the only one who had attempted to launder the money. He wasn't even the only one to use the bogus bonus scheme. So why, then, did the Watergate prosecutors go after him? Because the chief executives of those other companies came in at Archibald Cox's invitation, made a clean breast of it, and took a fine. True to the spirit of Watergate, George was the only one who tried to cover up what he had done and who then attempted to cover up the cover-up.

As for his difficulties with the government, that would seem to be his own doing.

1. He had a cost overrun on a Coast Guard contract, and he was trying to recover the money from the government? You bid on a contract and don't meet the terms, maybe you should be a man and live with it. That's what George always tells his ballplayers.

2. The government fined AmShip $10,000 for a fire that killed four workers? That hardly seems oppressive. During the 1977 World Series a jury handed down an award of $800,000 to an AmShip worker who had fallen into an open hatch and broken his legs.

3. He had antitrust problems? Well, that was because American Ship had been reaching out and absorbing most of the carriers on the Great Lakes. AmShip was not only building new ships and repairing and renovating old ones, its own fleet had more than doubled. Through other mergers, it was building bridges, barges, tugboats and dredges; selling building materials; building oil-drilling equipment and manufacturing metal products; and it was operating a galvanizing plant.

The antitrust suit involved the proposed takeover of the Litton Industries facilities on Lake Erie. With the revitalization of shipping on the Great Lakes, Litton had built itself a shipyard and bought a ten-ship carrier fleet. In four years it had not only failed to pick up a single order to build a ship, but had also lost its only profitable carrier contract. Get the picture? The old shipbuilding and shipping companies had banded together to push the new maritime law through Congress, and they were not going to let any outsider, no matter how big, come in and take advantage of the new prosperity. That was how it looked to the government, anyway—and that's almost a definition of what the antitrust laws are all about.

Nor had the suit come as any great surprise. In making the announcement, the American Shipyard spokesman had cautioned that the takeover was dependent upon "a favorable review by the Justice Department and other governmental agencies."

No, Steinbrenner's problems with the government would seem to have been earned on merit.

And, finally, the best reading of the evidence is that it wasn't CREEP who came to George, it was George who went to CREEP.

George had a friend in court. Thomas Evans, a classmate at Williams College, was a partner in the law firm of Mudge, Rose, Guthrie and Alexander, the prestigious New York firm that had also carried the names of Richard Nixon and John Mitchell during that period when Nixon was out of office. As national director of Citizens for Nixon-Agnew in 1968, Tom Evans was so high in the councils of the mighty as to be one of the three men who had a key to the vault where the $700,000 that had been left over from the 1968 campaign was being kept. (That was the money that started all the trouble.) In the 1972 campaign, Evans was the Deputy Finance Chairman of the Committee for the Re-election of the President.

Steinbrenner's connection with Tom Evans went beyond the old school tie. In 1970, George had hired Evans to become AmShip's New York attorney and had also put him on the board of directors. They were still so close when George bought the Yankees in January 1973—a time when he knew that he was being investigated—that he listed Thomas Evans as one of his fourteen limited partners.

It was Tom Evans who set up the meeting with Herbert W. Kalmbach, who was both Nixon's personal attorney and the chief honcho of CREEP. As a top official of CREEP himself, Evans was hardly walking into the room as a stranger. Herbert Kalmbach happened to be one of the other two men who had a key to that vault, and the only way it was possible to get to the cash was by having two of the three key-holders there together.

The big daddy of the illegal contributions was the $2 million contributed by the Milk Producers Association. The two CREEP officials the milk producers worked through in making the arrangements for that heartwarming donation were, according to the testimony, Herbert Kalmbach and Thomas Evans.

Question: Do you think George was being blackjacked or that George was trying to see what good he might be able to do for himself?

The message George was given was no different from the message that was given to the chief executives of all the other big companies that were operating under federal regulations:

1. He was expected to kick in $100,000.
2. It would be a swell idea to get the money in before April 7, the date on which the new campaign law requiring that the names of the large contributors be disclosed would be going into effect. Until April 7, they were to remain secret.

The meeting with Kalmbach took place on March 16, 1972. On April 6, George instructed Bartlome to tell the trusted employees that they were playing the bonus game again.

The way that game was played was described by one of the employees, Matthew E. Clark, Jr., in his testimony before the Senate Watergate Committee.

Bartlome informed Clark that he was going to get a bonus of $5,000, and that he was to make out two checks totaling $3,100 to the front organizations whose names had been supplied by the Committee for the Re-election of the President. Thirteen hundred dollars was deducted for income tax, and the remaining $600 went into a slush fund that was kept in the cashier's office as petty cash.

To make sure the checks arrived at the CREEP offices the same day, George had a courier fly to Washington with instructions to deliver the packet to Kalmbach personally. Upon discovering the following morning that Kalmbach hadn't been in the office when the courier arrived, George called Kalmbach to confirm that the checks had indeed been received before the deadline passed.

So how was the contribution that George had gone to all that trouble to conceal discovered? Those damn do-gooders again. And rotten luck. Common Cause, the citizens' lobby, filed a lawsuit in the public interest to force disclosure of the names of those last-day donors. And won. While the case was in the courts, the CREEP folk, being somewhat smarter than Nixon himself was going to be, destroyed their records . . . but Rose Mary Woods, Nixon's overly efficient secretary, didn't. It was "Rose Mary's baby" that brought so many big boys to grief.

For George, the cover-up was about to begin.

In January, around the time he was surfacing as the new owner of the Yankees, George had Bartlome write a fraudulent memo to make it seem as if the company had a legitimate bonus plan. The memo, backdated to April 5, 1972 (the day before the checks had been issued), stated that the bonuses had been approved in the board of directors' meeting of November 11, 1971.

In April, George was one busy guy. In addition to doctoring the minutes on his own $75,000 bonus, he had the company treasurer, Stanley J. Lepkowski, bring the records of the bogus bonuses to him so that he could personally destroy them. Once that had been accomplished, he had the trusted employees sign a statement certifying that the bonus was "in no manner, either directly or indirectly, conditioned upon or subject to the making by me of any contribution, whether charitable, political or otherwise." The statement further certified that at no time had "any director, officer or supervisory employee of the company, directly or indirectedly, directed, requested or suggested that I make contributions to any charitable or religious group or organization or to any political organization or candidate and that any contributions so made by me during the year 1972 were entirely voluntary and of my own choosing."

"You have got to be kidding," Clark told Bartlome when he saw the statement. But he signed it anyway. Backdated to December 30, 1972.

In August, Bartlome and Lepkowski, the two company officers in the Bogus-Bonus Eight, were told that the FBI was going to interview them about their contributions.

Question: Did you discuss this with Mr. Steinbrenner?
Bartlome: We discussed it for a couple of days prior to the interview. . . .

Question: What, if anything, did Mr. Steinbrenner tell you about this interview that you were about to have?

Bartlome: He related a story to us which is the basis of my testimony.

After Bartlome and Lepkowski had been interviewed, the other six loyalists were given copies of their statements and told to read them over so they would know what to say when the FBI interviewed them.

What follows is the cover story that was concocted by Steinbrenner and passed on dutifully by Matthew Clark in his statement to the FBI:

> During the early part of 1972, the exact period of time unrecalled, I discussed the presidential campaign with many of my fellow employees. I felt that I wanted to contribute in some way to the reelection of President Nixon as I felt the shipping industry was profiting more since the passage of the Maritime Act of 1970. I also feel that I hoped indirectly to bring to the attention of Mr. George Steinbrenner . . . that I was personally interested in the future of the shipbuilding industry by backing the Nixon administration. . . .
>
> In particular, I recall speaking more with Mr. Bartlome about making a contribution to assist in the reelection of President Nixon, in which I inquired of Mr. Bartlome how I would go about making a contribution. Mr. Bartlome said he would get a list of organizations connected with Nixon's reelection campaign and that I could choose one of those organizations to contribute to. . . .
>
> I also learned sometime around February 1972 from Mr. Bartlome that I would be receiving a bonus, but I did not know the amount of the bonus or when I would receive it. . . .

Nobody bothered to tell any of these guys, incidentally, that giving a false statement to an FBI agent pursuing an official inquiry is a crime. Almost immediately, however, they were subpoenaed to testify before the grand jury, and for sure nobody had to tell them that lying to a grand jury constitutes perjury.

George certainly didn't tell them. What George told them—and kept on telling them—was that there was not a thing to worry about as long as they all stuck to the same story. He also assured them that they were never actually going to have to appear before the grand jury.

Bartlome, Lepkowski, and Clark met in AmShip's parking lot and decided that they were not going to perjure themselves. When they went back in to break the news to George, he put his head down on the table and wailed, "I'm ruined. The company is ruined. I might as well jump off a bridge."

There were countless meetings during the next few days in which George attempted to force his "recollection of the events" leading to the bonuses upon his co-conspirators, and it was always the same phony story that had been given to the FBI. He also kept telling them that there was nothing to worry about because the company attorney, John H. Melcher, Jr., was in Washington and was going to get their subpoenas quashed. Melcher did succeed in getting the original date pushed back two weeks, but the subpoenas were never withdrawn, and as George was riding to the grand jury with Lepkowski and Bartlome he was, almost to the door of the courthouse, still pressing his "recollection" upon them.

Question: What did he tell you specifically?

Bartlome: He related the same story that he had in the past. He asked us if we could live with this everything would be all right, because we were not going before the grand jury anyway.

With the grand jury hearing definitely on, George hired Edward Bennett Williams to represent him, and at about this time—presumably on Williams's instructions—the employees were told that their interests were so clearly in conflict with Steinbrenner's that the company was going to get them an attorney of their own.

Having done that, George then tried to get them to sign an indemnity agreement whereby they would have to reimburse the company for the legal fees "should improbity or illegality" result from their testimony. In other words, if they told the truth, they were going to have to pay their own legal fees; stick to the FBI story, and they were home free.

You think that's bad? Listen, once the investigation began and the bogus-bonus scheme could no longer be used, he came up with a new one: the old fake expense voucher trick. And using the same guys! The employee signed the expense voucher, a sum was filled in later, and the cash went right into the slush fund.

In July and August, $5,650 was taken out of the slush fund and contributed to the reelection campaign of Senator Dan Inouye (D-Hawaii), a member of the Senate Watergate Committee. According to the indictment, George continued to make contributions from the new slush fund through the month of September, which, if true, would mean that he was still doing it while the grand jury hearings were in session.

On April 5, 1974, Steinbrenner was indicted by a federal grand jury in Cleveland on fourteen counts, including alleged attempts to obstruct investigations by falsifying records and ordering company officers to make false statements. Bartlome and Lepkowski were named as unindicted co-conspirators, which meant that they would be testifying against him.

Two weeks later, John H. Melcher, the company lawyer, pleaded guilty. In his plea, Melcher said that Steinbrenner had "willfully and unlawfully" agreed to make a corporate contribution to the Nixon campaign on behalf of American Ship Building and that Melcher himself "did relieve, comfort, and assist" him in trying to cover it up.

George's secretary, treasurer, and lawyer would be testifying against him, along with the employees who had testified before the grand jury under immunity. The Watergate prosecutors had gone after him as the most horrible example of executive-suite cover-up, and they had him. But you don't get George that easily.

At the time of his indictment, Steinbrenner said, "I am totally innocent, and we will prove it in court," as defendants always say in this great constitutional democracy of ours. But he was not totally innocent, and he did not try to prove anything in court. He did not appear before the Watergate Committee, because the committee had been informed that he would take the Fifth Amendment. He did not take any stand and raise his hand, ever. Instead, he became virtuous. "I feel it very important that I state publicly why I have chosen to fight. . . . There is no way I could plead guilty to a charge involving willful conspiracy to violate Section 610 [illegal contributions] or willful conspiracy or any other charge that may be part of an indictment, because I am not guilty of any such violation."

Section 610 is what he did plead guilty to, also to conspiracy.

And became sanctimonious. "And while the agony of indictment and trial will weigh heavily, I would be less than worthy of my family and a lot of true and loyal friends if I did not fight for what I believe is right."

Also a bit unctuous: "I'm sure that my involvement as chairman of two national Democratic Congressional dinners in 1969 and 1970 has focused much attention on my company and me, but I do not regret that I worked to help preserve the Democratic party at a time when they were desperately in need of help."

And, as it must with all Steinbrenner statements, embarrassing: "I have deep respect for most all of the legislators who serve in Washington, and it is too bad that the nation tends to regard all people in political office today as wrongdoers. It is just not so."

By September he was saying that he had only wanted access to the White House on civic projects to benefit Cleveland. Pure Steinbrenner. He had done it all out of his love for his city. "I was told [the $100,000] would be a good-sized donation, but all of a sudden it was a peanut. I got taken." What a shame. Cleveland sure could have used that new opera house.

George is a man who can never be brought to admit a mistake. It is as if, should he once admit he is not perfect, the whole structure of his life would come toppling down. Even when he pleaded guilty, he gave the court a self-serving statement in which he blamed Melcher for devising the bonus plan, assuring him that it was legal, and then advising him not to go to the Special Prosecutor, as he had always wanted to, to make a clean breast of it. That's funny. On May 9, 1973, John H. Melcher was promoted to executive vice-president of AmShip. In which capacity, Steinbrenner announced, he would be primarily concerned with acquisitions and corporate operations. Sounds like the Number Two man, doesn't it? The promotion came after the books had been doctored and the records destroyed, and the fraudulent memo and fake employee statements had been issued. All of which, incidentally, George also blamed on Melcher in his statement to the court.

He also blamed his old friend and soon-to-be-no-longer partner in the Yankees, Tom Evans, for advising him not to testify before the grand jury. Which would seem to indicate that he had been asked to appear on a waiver of immunity, even before he hired Edward Bennett Williams, and had refused.

George Steinbrenner is a guy who bawls out rookie pitchers and leaves them crying, then defends himself by saying that he wasn't trying to be cruel, he was only trying to make them tough enough to pitch for the New York Yankees. "Pitching in Yankee Stadium is the hardest thing they will ever be called upon to do, and I want them to be ready."

Facing up to the music on the illegal contributions may well have been the toughest thing George was ever called upon to do. You could say that he panicked, but that's too easy. George III isn't a man who panics. George III is a man who believes he can get away with anything.

Here, after all, is a man so arrogant that he could start a new slush fund for illegal political contributions while he was being investigated on the old one, and then dip into the new one to make an illegal contribution to a senator who was on the committee investigating the old one.

Edward Bennett Williams is the best attorney in the country, not because I say so but because his brother attorneys say so. It's all but inconceivable that Ed Williams would have negotiated a plea without a guarantee that his client would not go to jail. Even then, one can only imagine the difficulty he must have had in getting George Steinbrenner to make a public admission of guilt. Can't you just picture Ed Williams telling him, "Listen, keeping you out of jail is one of the great triumphs of my career. But do it your way, and I'll send my bill to you in prison."

George was allowed to plead guilty on Section 610, a felony. But the cover-up charge, which was what the whole thing was really about, was reduced to devising a "false and misleading explanation for the employees to tell the FBI" and then trying to "influence and intimidate" them into lying to the Grand Jury. A misdemeanor. The hardcore obstruction of justice charges were gone, but on the two counts he did plead guilty to, he could have been sentenced to six years in jail. All he got was a $15,000 fine. The company was fined $20,000. The executives who had come in and confessed were generally fined $100,000.

The *Wall Street Journal* report on the sentencing read:

> In Washington, the special prosecutor's office declined comment. However, legal authorities say they are certain that the prosecutor's staff had been confident Steinbrenner would receive a jail term.
>
> Furthermore, these authorities say that they are puzzled

about how quickly sentencing took place. Usually a judge takes up to six weeks studying presentencing material before he announces his decision.

The special prosecutor's office turned over its presentencing report to the Cleveland probation office last week. The prosecutor's office was notified Thursday night that the sentences would be handed down Friday.

To anyone accustomed to deciphering newspaper sources, it was clear that the Special Prosecutor's office believed they had been sold out but weren't going to say so for the record.

George has to live as a convicted felon. But what the hell, George will tell you any old time that he only pleaded guilty to save the time and expense of a trial. And, of course, to protect those loyal employees. What he was protecting them from isn't quite clear since (a) the hounds of justice had never been after them, just George, and (b) they had been granted immunity from the beginning.

It had to end on some fatuous note, though. Before he was sentenced, George, true to form, told the court, "I'm concerned that my leadership failed them."

What a guy! Always thinking about somebody else . . . like the bereaved fans of New York after the Yankees lost the 1981 Series.

So George got away easy, and he kept getting away easy. Because of all that doctoring of the books, he had the honor of becoming the first business executive to be charged by the Securities and Exchange Commission with filing false financial statements to cover up illegal contributions. One wonders why they bothered. Having filed the charge, the SEC entered into an agreement to allow the company to appoint two of its own directors, along with one outsider, to investigate itself.

One of the directors was Jimmy Nederlander, best known for his theatrical productions, who by then was also a partner in Steinbrenner's Yankees and, by the way, is an old, old friend. But don't worry about that, Nederlander himself said it didn't influence him.

The panel found that while some of George's contributions were illegal, the original ones weren't—the difference seemed to depend upon how long the money had remained in the slush fund—and it was clear that the panel believed George's story that he had only been following his lawyer's advice. The one outsider was Allan K. Shaw, a retired executive and vice-president of the Cleveland Trust Company, an institution that George just might have done some business with from time to time. When he was asked how the panel could have found George innocent of something he had pleaded guilty to, Shaw answered cheerfully, "You got me. I don't know."

By this time, as the owner of the New York Yankees, George had already faced the wrath of Bowie Kuhn. The baseball commissioner's investigation was about on a par with the Securities and Exchange Commission's.

There was a time when a club owner who transgressed conventional morality was in for a swift banishment. The examples duly cited are William D. Cox of Philadelphia who, in 1943, was caught gambling on his team's games, and Fred M. Saigh, Jr., of the St. Louis Cardinals, who, in 1953, was convicted of income tax evasion. But those were other times and other commissioners. And, anyway, Cox and Saigh were poor millionaires, and who wants that kind of guy around?

Bowie Kuhn had to do something. He did as little as possible—and then pulled back even on that.

The commissioner has almost unlimited power in protecting the integrity of the game. But before we go any further, let's get off the piety. Baseball's integrity is held inviolate on the presumption that if the customers should ever come to doubt the honesty of the game, the game itself would go under. That's not a moral argument, it's an economic argument. Oh, sure, you can say something here about setting an example for kids, and no one would argue that an enterprise that exerts such a pervasive influence over young people does not have that overriding responsibility. But when you're talking about setting an example for the kids, you're talking about the players and the play on the field, aren't you, not the extracurricular activities of the front office?

Kuhn summarized the issue very nicely. He noted that Steinbrenner had admitted that he had "caused certain of his employees to make false statements to agents of the FBI and attempted to influence these employees to give false testimony to a Federal Grand Jury." He pointed out that, "Ignoring this conduct could easily lead to the suspicion that such conduct may occur with the game itself and affect play on the field. . . . In sum, suspicion of dishonesty can be as corrosive and destructive as dishonesty itself."

All of which has a nice moralistic ring to it, cannot be denied, and does not account for the continued popularity of horse racing, basketball, and professional wrestling. This country is not as naïve as it used to be, and probably never was. Everybody has a pretty good idea that George Steinbrenner is not a model of sterling ethics, and the Yankees have spent the last six years breaking nothing but attendance records.

Bowie Kuhn is a lawyer of no overwhelming distinction who was hired because the Lords of Baseball were well aware that their future problems were going to be fought on the legal front, i.e. in the halls of Congress and in the courts. Steinbrenner was still being represented by Edward Bennett Williams, a legal and political powerhouse. No contest.

On November 27, 1974, the commissioner suspended Steinbrenner for two years and pronounced him "ineligible and incompetent [to engage] in any association whatsoever with any major league club or its personnel."

"Whatsoever," as it turned out, did not mean whatsoever. And when it doesn't, the word means nothing at all.

In summarizing his decision, Kuhn stated, "Any violation of this order will be grounds for further action against Mr. Steinbrenner or any individual who has knowledge of this order."

Steinbrenner was allowed to retain his stock but was to have no say in running the club, a ruling so absurd, so unenforceable, that it strains credulity to believe there was any intention of it being enforced.

Baseball, after all, was already well into its industrial era. The Yankees were a $10-million property, which by any reasonable assessment was closer to $15 million. Why should Steinbrenner be expected to sit back and allow decisions affecting his property to be made by others? And, more to the point, how could anybody with even the most cursory knowledge of his background expect that he would?

The commissioner already had ample evidence that he wouldn't. In September 1974, shortly after his conviction, George had entered into an agreement to refrain from all contacts with the Yankees pending the commissioner's final ruling. That same night he was at the ballpark, rooting for his team. He continued to be in conspicuous attendance for the remainder of the season.

When the Yankees began to falter, he recorded a pep talk and sent it to his manager, Bill Virdon, with instructions to call a team meeting. "George says he wants me to play this," Virdon told them. "So I'm playing it."

Apparently Kuhn didn't think that violated the agreement. As the season was coming to an end, Sparky Lyle was unsigned, and Kuhn gave George permission to go to Milwaukee so that he could sit down with Sparky over a drink, turn on his charm, and sign him.

Two weeks after the season ended, Bobby Murcer, George's highest-paid player, was traded for Bobby Bonds. Nobody believed that Yankee president Gabe Paul, who was presumably handling the affairs of the club, had the authority to make that kind of a deal without—ahem—some elementary contact with George.

Hired to serve as president of the Yankees during George's suspension was Pat Cunningham, the Democratic leader of the Bronx (where Yankee Stadium is located) and, more important, the chairman of the Democratic Committee of the State of New York. That made Cunningham the political boss of the most important state in the country, a man close to the seats of power in the city, state, and country. Exactly what Cunningham did as president of the Yankees remains a mystery.

While George was under suspension, he fired his manager, Bill Virdon (who had been Gabe Paul's selection), and hired Billy Martin (against Paul's advice). Martin himself acknowledges that the deal was clinched by Steinbrenner in a telephone conversation.

Catfish Hunter became available in the first Free Agent Sweepstakes within two months after George had been suspended, and the bidding very quickly ascended into the millions. Happily, Gabe Paul was able to call up the ghostly instructions of the disenfranchised felon and dig deep into the treasury, saying:

> When the Yankee partnership was created . . . George Steinbrenner publicly stated that everything possible would be done to provide a winner. He further told me we were not to back off in any money deals, and when his unfortunate suspension was invoked, he told me, "Anytime you have an opportunity to buy the contract of a player for cash, I want you to go ahead whenever, in your judgment, it would be advantageous to the Yankees."

Not to be hypocritical about this, why shouldn't the man who owned the property have the final say in how much he was willing to pay? But did he really have to make the commissioner's life so difficult by sending his private jet to North Carolina to fly Catfish and his lawyers to

New York? And to then stick his thumb into the commissioner's eye by saying, "If he can prove I did anything wrong, let him."

Evidently Bowie couldn't prove anything. On the contrary, he lifted George's suspension after sixteen months, eight months early—for good behavior, apparently.

Bowie Kuhn's contract had already been renewed by then. Although his term of office wasn't due to expire until July 1976, he had asked to be voted upon a year earlier, as he had a right to do under his contract. Four votes in either League could unseat him, and on July 16, 1975, four owners in the American League joined forces to vote him out: Charles O. Finley of Oakland, Jerry Hoffberger of Baltimore, Brad Corbett of Texas, and Pat Cunningham representing You-know-Who of New York. The National League, whose attorney Kuhn had once been, was able to save him by calling that original vote "a straw vote," tabling the final vote indefinitely, and summoning Walter O'Malley from his sickbed in Los Angeles to plan their strategy. "They can table it forever," Charley Finley said with a laugh. "But the American League absolutely won't change its vote."

Steinbrenner changed his vote the next day. George was in Dallas watching the Yankees play the Texas Rangers. The meeting was in Milwaukee. He called Brad Corbett, the story goes, and told him, "I'm not voting against Kuhn anymore. I'm voting for him." And that was the end of the move to dump Bowie Kuhn.

Welcome home, Bowie.

Nine months later, just in time for the beginning of the 1976 season, Bowie Kuhn lifted George Steinbrenner's suspension.

Welcome home, George.

4
THE BEST TEAM MONEY
CAN BUY

George M. Steinbrenner is a Yankee Doodle Dandy, born on the Fourth of July. He had a Yankee Doodle Sweetheart and he picked up the Yankees for a song.

He bought the team from CBS in 1973 for $10 million. Allowing for inflation, that was less than the $9.4 million Bob Short paid in 1968 for the woebegone, soon-to-be-gone Washington Senators. The Cleveland Indians were sold for $10.8 million in 1971, and the Seattle Pilots were bought in a bankruptcy sale in 1970 for $10.5 million and moved to Milwaukee.

CBS had bought the Yankees in 1964 for $13.2 million and turned the team over to Mike Burke, a one-time Yale halfback, OSS commando, and, briefly, operator of the Barnum & Bailey Circus. The 1964 Yankees were a pennant-winning team on the decline, by which we mean that they had won the pennant for the fourteenth time in sixteen years but had lost their second consecutive World Series.

Under Burke's stewardship, they finished sixth, tenth, ninth, fifth, fifth, second (but fifteen games behind Baltimore), fourth, and fourth. In 1972, Burke's last year, the New York Yankees drew less than a million customers for the first time since World War II. At the bottom line, the operating losses had reached $11 million.

The Yankees had become something of a corporate embarrassment, a mote in the glittering CBS eye. As a reward for serving the corporation so well, William Paley, the master of CBS, gave Burke permission to put together a syndicate to take the team off his hands. What that meant, practically speaking, was that Burke was being given the right to make the best possible deal, not for CBS but for himself.

For some reason, Burke was unable to find a buyer for the New York Yankees for more than a year—only a few "exotics" who climbed out of the woodwork but couldn't really come up with the money. Just couldn't give the club away, until Gabe Paul, general manager of the Cleveland Indians, heard about his difficulties and introduced him to George Steinbrenner. The way Steinbrenner tells the story, he had one quick meeting with Paley. "He said, 'We have a lot of people who seem to be interested, but they are all talking Chinese paper.' I said, 'Mr. Paley, I'm talking cash. I'll make one offer in cold hard cash. If it is acceptable, fine. If not, no hard feelings.' I said, 'Ten million dollars.' He said, 'You got a deal.' " That was what did it, the offer of cash.

A nice story. The only thing wrong with it is that in this kind of deal, the seller *always* gets cash. The buyer doesn't take the money out of his own bank account, he borrows the money from the bank, and it is then conveyed, posthaste, to the seller. Which then leaves the real question for George: "How come you got the club so cheap?"

With Steinbrenner, $10 million would have been no trouble at all. Beyond that, he was the kind of wheeler-dealer who could call upon friends in the world of industry who would be only too happy to be allowed to come in on the deal. The first calls went to Lester Crown of Chicago and Bunker Hunt of Dallas. Lester Crown is merely one of the richest men in the world. He was also the real money behind the takeover of American Ship Building, of which he has owned as much as thirty-one percent. At one time he owned the Empire State Building. Got rid of it at a quick profit because it was cluttering up his books. Bunker Hunt is one of the "As long as we're up, why not corner the silver market?" Hunts of Dallas.

You call any bank and tell them, "This is George Steinbrenner. Me, Lester Crown, Bunker Hunt, and a few of the boys are buying the Yankees for $10 million," and the only thing left to talk about is how low the interest is going to be.

The other partners in the deal were people like John DeLorean of General Motors, Jimmy Nederlander of the Nederlander Theatrical Circuit and Nederlander Theatre on Broadway, Steve O'Neill, retired chairman of Leaseway Transportation Corporation (current owner of the Cleveland Indians), and Jess Bell, president of Bonne Bell Inc.

Mike Burke was a partner too. Mike had been given five percent of the stock as a finder's fee. "A very clandestine operation on Burke's part," Gabe Paul has said, and there is no doubt whatsoever that Mike was sitting on both sides of the table at the same time. (Mike's five percent is in a special category. He, alone among the partners, does not participate in dividends, nor does he have to put up any money when a call goes out. There haven't been any dividends, the profits are ploughed back into the club. Calls did go out for money, however, in the first two years, and if it had not been for that special clause Mike would have had to get up $150,000.)

The original list of partners that was given out unofficially at the time Burke and Steinbrenner made the original announcement of the sale did not list Gabe Paul. Mike Burke didn't find out Gabe had stock until the partners were gathered together at the "21" a week later to be introduced to the press. At which point, that loud noise emanating from backstage was the sound of Mike screaming.

In the original announcement, George had stated that he and Burke were both general partners but that Burke would be running the club because "We're not baseball people. I'm in the shipping business. I'm going to be an absentee owner." It was to prove the most wantonly misapplied promise since Reggie Jackson took his vows of silence.

In the Yankee yearbook that was put out at the beginning of the season, Mike Burke was still being listed as a general partner, and in a limited partnership the general partner runs the business and assumes the financial responsibility. But the partnership agreement made it perfectly clear that there was only one general partner. George Steinbrenner. It stated that Steinbrenner "in his full and exclusive discretion shall manage, control and make all decisions affecting the business and assets of the Yankees." The fiction that Mike was a general partner had obviously been put forth to reassure him. Once he got the word at the "21" that a man with Gabe Paul's imposing baseball credentials had been brought into the deal, he couldn't help but realize that Steinbrenner intended to have his own man at the helm of the club.

At that early stage, Mike still had enough leverage so that he had to be placated. How he was placated is made clear by his remarks to the press after the partners had been introduced. "This is a nice way for Gabe Paul to close out his baseball career," Burke said. "He is sixty-three and intends to retire to Florida in a few years."

The nature of his leverage was explained a few months later by Joe Durso in *The New York Times*:

> Burke's prestige was essential because it provided the outsiders with two essential links: to City Hall, which had agreed to spend $27 million to buy and modernize Yankee Stadium; and to CBS, which spurned an offer of $14 million in order to sell the team to Burke's group for $10 million . . . so when he resisted the move to make Gabe Paul president, things had to wait.

The reconstruction of Yankee Stadium was clearly part of what George was buying. Nobody had believed the original figure put forth by Burke and his great friend, Mayor John V. Lindsay. By the time the rebuilt stadium opened in 1976, it had cost the taxpayers $106 million. Too bad Mike Burke couldn't have stuck around to see it. The 1973 season was barely a month old when Mike decided to relinquish his duties, mostly because those duties had become nonexistent. Gabe was going to be president, and Mike was going to be "Chairman of the Board," a title that came equipped with an office and a yo-yo.

George Steinbrenner suddenly became unavailable to the New York press. When he finally did allow himself to be quoted on the Burke freeze-out, it was by Sid Hartman of the *Minneapolis Tribune*. "When Burke didn't relinquish the business and baseball ends," George said, "we thought it best for him to concentrate on public relations." That's what is known as surgical precision. A slash right across the throat. Until then, Steinbrenner had allowed Burke to get away with the fiction that the Yankees had split even in the CBS era. In the Hartman interview, George not only revealed the $11 million operating loss, he implied very strongly that with all of the CBS expertise behind him, Burke had managed to mess up the radio and TV rights.

He didn't mess up his settlement with George, though. Two weeks later, George and Mike held a joint press conference at Yankee Stadium, which is memorable because Burke quoted from Yeats's "An Irish Airman Foresees His Death," and nobody in his right mind believed a word either of them said.

Never had a more rancorous situation been carried off more amicably. Burke was going to be getting a consultation fee of $25,000 a year for ten years to go with his stock, in return for which he was saying that the whole thing was his own idea and that George was a great guy. "A lot of times making someone a consultant is putting him out to pasture or a settlement," Steinbrenner said. "This isn't the case here. Mike Burke is going to be of great value to the club on a consulting basis."

Burke said, "I hope in this role to make an ongoing constructive contribution to the Yankees' success."

"It may be difficult to believe," George said, "but we are closer personally than ever before. I am pleased Mike will continue with the Yankees."

Whereupon Mike Burke disappeared completely from the Yankee scene.

Sing no sad songs for Mike Burke. Three months after he had settled with the Yankees, Mike became president of Madison Square Garden and was able to spend another eight years tending to the decline of the Knicks and the Rangers. A truly inspirational example of how a man can become fabulously wealthy if he keeps on his toes and his failures are monumental enough.

The improvement of the Yankees under George Steinbrenner proceeded so rapidly that they were able to win a pennant in four years and a World Championship in five.

Before anyone knew there was going to be a Re-entry Draft, George went after everybody who was available. Catfish Hunter was a one-shot deal. A fluke, brought on by Charley Finley's refusal to pay him some money that was due him. In the spring of 1976, there was another free agent, Andy Messersmith. Messersmith had been declared a free agent in the landmark case on the reserve clause and, once again, it was the Yankees who signed him. For four years, at a total of $1.5 million. It didn't matter that Messersmith immediately disclaimed the agreement or that it was eventually nullified by the commissioner. Two players had come on the market, and Steinbrenner had signed both. What did the guy want, you had to ask, everything?

On the June 15, 1976, trading deadline, with the Yankees already ten games out front, Steinbrenner made a deal with Baltimore for Ken Holtzman (and signed him to an expensive contract), then bought Vida Blue from Oakland for $1.5 million. Charley Finley, who was going to lose his star players at the end of the year anyway, had put them all on the market. A regular shopping list. The other star players had a $1 million tag on them. Vida Blue, the jewel of the collection, had been knocked down by Steinbrenner. Wasn't anything going to be enough for this guy?

It didn't matter, again, that the commissioner nullified all the Oakland sales a few days later. "The Best Team Money Can Buy" was what the Yankees were being called because the tag did, in fact, provide the best possible definition of Steinbrenner's philosophy.

When the Yankees then came back from the First Re-entry Draft with Reggie Jackson and Don Gullett, the name was forevermore set in concrete. (Of course, Reggie Jackson was an accident, and we'll get into that in a little while.)

If there is one thing nobody can deny George Steinbrenner, it is that he recognized from the beginning that the free agent revolution was not a challenge to our way of life as we know it but, given George's circumstances and his geography, an incredible opportunity. As a successful industrialist who understood the workings of the marketplace, he understood instantly that the New York Yankees, just by being the New York Yankees, had the ability to recoup almost any amount of money he had to put up. He would build the Yankees into an instant winner, and the increase in revenues would far outrun the increase in expenses.

Still and all . . . "The Best Team Money Can Buy" appellation wasn't really fair. Not when you consider the fact that thirteen of the twenty-five players on the 1976 pennant-winner had been acquired through Gabe Paul trades.

When George Steinbrenner hired Gabe Paul, he wasn't getting any virgin. Gabe had been there before. Gabe Paul started his baseball career in 1919, as the bat boy for Rochester in the International League, and moved on up through the front office as public relations man, club secretary, and director during the days when Rochester was one of the two AAA clubs in the St. Louis Cardinals' farm system, Branch Rickey's noble experiment in peonage. When Warren Giles, the Rochester general manager, moved up to Cincinnati in 1933, Gabe went with him to serve as the Reds' PR man and traveling secretary. He became the Reds' general manager himself in 1951, when Giles succeeded Ford Frick as National League president. Having built the Reds into a pennant contender through a series of excellent trades, he was hired away in 1961 by the new Houston franchise and spent six miserable months as an alien in an alien land, while the team he had built in Cincinnati was winning the pennant. A year later, he was in Cleveland.

Gabe is a survivor. He was with Branch Rickey during the forging of the old Chain Gang, and here he was at George Steinbrenner's side ready to make the opening bids on a whole new era. If you didn't know who he was, you'd think he was a sweet old guy who was kind of out of it. Ready, as Mike Burke was so willing to believe, to go down to Florida and sit on a rock. Not exactly. Among his fellow operators, he has long been known as the Smiling Cobra. Gabe purrs, speaks softly, and walks away with the goods.

Gabe takes care of Gabe. In all his years in baseball, it is impossible to find him saying anything that could hurt himself. Wherever he has operated, he's had stock. Newsmen like him because, as an old PR man, he understands their problems. When it's on the line, he may not give them the whole story, but they know he'll always give them enough to keep their editors happy.

He was not so beloved by ballplayers in the old days, when the grass was green and the roads were dusty and the guy sitting behind the desk held all the power. He was trained, after all, in the Branch Rickey school of management, which held that if you didn't like the salary you were being offered, there were three other guys in the system waiting to take your place.

Gabe adapts. You wouldn't think a seventy-six-year-old man would be able to adapt so quickly to such a total change in his method of operations, but Gabe adapted overnight. He had to take a lot of crap from George. It wasn't easy to take a tongue-lashing from someone young enough to be his son. Gabe would get red in the face, but he'd take it and talk George out of doing something foolish. He took it because after fifty years in the game he was being given the chance to operate in the Big Town, with an unlimited amount of money. And that was irresistible.

In the new era, he still holds to the old Rickey principles. Basic Principle #1: "You ask yourself, is it right or wrong for the team, and then you have to be strong enough to do what you want to do." Basic Principle #2: "If your judgment is good, you'll be proven right, and if it isn't, you'll suffer the consequences." And another one that he had occasion to cite to Billy Martin often: "Thinking of the devil is worse than seeing the devil."

He has a way of remaining so unnaturally calm in the face of dissension, turmoil, and omens of doom that he has been moved to wonder himself whether there isn't a missing "gene" somewhere in his makeup. When Gabe was ready to go back to work after he had suffered what was called a "cerebral spasm," the doctors told him he could get as physical as he wanted to, just so long as he didn't get mad.

"Doctor," Gabe said, "I never get mad."

Lucky for him. Right from the start, George Steinbrenner had been telling everybody how shaky Gabe was. He would belittle him in front of strangers. "Gabe's not what he used to be," he would say. "He's not well. He can't make decisions."

And after Gabe had left, despite George's frantic efforts to hold on to him, George would tell outrageous stories about how poor old Gabe would sit there crying whenever he and Billy got into a screaming match.

Gabe, sitting in Cleveland with more stock than ever, just smiled his Angora smile and purred, "That'll be the day."

Let's take a look at those players Gabe Paul acquired for George that by and large comprised the 1976 Yankee pennant-winning team.

Some accounts include Graig Nettles on that list, which is erroneous. Gabe traded Nettles *to* the Yankees on November 27, 1972, five weeks before the announcement was made that Steinbrenner was at the head of a group that had bought the Yankees. (There are those so cynical as to wonder whether Gabe wasn't delightfully aware that he and Graig would soon be reunited. Naw, that couldn't be. George Steinbrenner has said himself that as a loyal Cleveland fan he had been terribly unhappy to hear that Nettles had been traded away. George wouldn't lie about a thing like that.)

Nettles was either one of Gabe Paul's best trades or one of his worst trades, depending on which side of the fence you see Gabe sitting.

The other Gabe Paul trades . . .

Lou Piniella was acquired for Lindy McDaniel, a thirty-eight-year-old relief pitcher who had been obtained for Bill Monbouquette. Monbouquette had been signed as a free agent.

Oscar Gamble came in the trade for pitcher Pat Dobson (who had been obtained for Frank Tepedino, Wayne Nordhagen, Alan Closter, and Dave Cheadle; only Nordhagen became an established major league ballplayer). Mickey Rivers (along with Figueroa) came for Bobby Bonds (whom Paul had got in the trade for Bobby Murcer). Carlos May (left-handed DH) came for Ken Brett. The other outfielders were Roy White, who was home grown, and Elliott Maddox (who had been purchased at the going rate).

In the infield: Chris Chambliss (along with Dick Tidrow) had come from Cleveland for four pitchers—Fritz Peterson, Steve Kline, Tom Buskey and Fred Beene—in a trade that the Yankee players screamed had wiped out their whole pitching staff. Fred Stanley, the shortstop, had come for the never-to-be-forgotten George Pena. Willie Randolph (and Dock Ellis) came from Pittsburgh for pitcher Doc Medich. Sandy Alomar, the utility infielder, came at little more than the waiver price.

Fran Healy, the backup catcher, came in a trade for Larry Gura, who had been picked up for Duke Sims, Sims having been picked up on waivers. The trade that brought Gura for Sims was a great one, the trade that sent him away was a terrible one. In fairness to Gabe, he had little choice. Billy Martin, by then the manager, disliked Gura and wouldn't use him.

The final 1976 trade was made on the June 15 deadline, as George Steinbrenner moved in to pin down the pennant. The Yankees got three proven pitchers, Ken Holtzman, Grant Jackson, and Doyle Alexander, for three of the top pitching prospects in their organization—Tippy Martinez, Scott McGregor, and Dave Pagan—plus Rudy May (who had been purchased) and catcher Rick Dempsey (who had been obtained for Danny Walton).

The Holtzman deal was made by Steinbrenner, over Gabe's objections, on the advice of his twelve-year-old son. Which may have been one of the reasons that Billy Martin wouldn't use Holtzman either.

The Willie Randolph trade is the best example of why astute old-timers like Gabe do so well. There is, first of all, the ability to judge talent—as Gabe's old boss Branch Rickey liked to say, "putting a dollar sign on a muscle." But it's more than that. Gabe Paul has been around so long that he has contacts all over baseball. He goes back to the days when there were only sixteen major league clubs, which means that he was one of sixteen guys who could hand out jobs.

Gabe had a tip from inside the Pittsburgh organization about a twenty-one-year-old second baseman who was something special. Pittsburgh seemed to be right on the verge of winning a pennant, and Doc Medich, who had been an excellent pitcher for the Yankees in their losing years, looked to be exactly the guy who could put the Pirates over.

The problem was Steinbrenner. George couldn't understand why Gabe wanted to trade a starting pitcher for a skinny little kid who had hit .164 in the thirty games he had played for the Pirates, let alone why he would do it on the word of someone working for the other team.

Willie was playing winter ball in Venezuela, and George wanted a "verification report" from someone in his own organization. Unfortunately Randolph was out with a minor injury. So Gabe sent farm director Pat Gillick to Venezuela, ostensibly to scout Randolph—that's what George was told, anyway—but actually to get a scouting report from Bobby Cox, who was managing another club in the same winter league. During the regular season Cox managed the Syracuse club for the Yankees, he was a favorite of Steinbrenner's, and Gabe knew that Cox would rave about Randolph. The whole thing could have been done over the telephone, but Gillick flew down to Venezuela so Gabe would have his verification report to show Steinbrenner.

The games these people play: A trip to see a player who wasn't playing, in order to get a report to show to an owner who, just incidentally, was under suspension and wasn't supposed to be participating in that kind of a decision to begin with.

It turned out to be perhaps the Yankees' best trade. Randolph went right into the starting lineup. Dock Ellis, who had been little more than a throw-in by the Pirates, won seventeen games for the Yankees. Doc Medich, who came by his nickname honestly—he was attending medical school during the off-season—turned out to be such a flop in Pittsburgh as to inspire Charley Feeney of the *Pittsburgh Post-Gazette* to write "Ellis is probably a better doctor, too." (In all fairness to the Pittsburgh front office, it was generally agreed at the time the trade was made that the Pirates had probably dealt themselves the pennant.)

George has been known to take credit for the Randolph trade. But, then, he's been known to say that he made them all. "Piniella was Gabe's trade," he was saying shortly after Gabe departed at the end of 1977. "I've got to give him credit for Piniella. The rest were mine. But I don't care, let Gabe have credit for all of them. I like Gabe. He had a great career in baseball. Of course, the poor guy was so shaky the last couple of years here that he really couldn't do much of anything."

5

BRINGING REGGIE
HOME AND
OTHER ARRIVALS

The funny thing about the signing of Reggie Jackson was that the Yankees didn't really want him. They got stuck with him. If you want to know how you can get stuck with a $3 million player, hang on.

To begin with, you have to understand that baseball was entering into a wholly uncharted area in 1977. There were two parts to the Reentry Draft:

1. Each team was entitled to sign two free agents or, *in the event that more than two of its own players had played out their options*, as many players as it was going to lose.
2. Each team could draft negotiating rights to as many free agents as it wished, just so long as the player *hadn't already been drafted by twelve other teams*.

Keep both of those italicized provisions firmly in mind. Without either of them, Reggie Jackson would never have become a New York Yankee.

The day after the Yankees were wiped out by Cincinnati in the 1976 World Series, the brain trust met in Steinbrenner's office to map out their strategy. There really wasn't that much strategy to map out. Since a pennant-winning team is reasonably strong to begin with, the Yankees were able to be very selective. George Steinbrenner's opening words were "We are not going to win a championship with Fred

Stanley at shortstop," the same words he had uttered, at a considerably higher decibel level, after Stanley's throwing error, with two out in the ninth inning, had lost Game 2 of the '76 Series.

The other half of selectivity is availability. The only name shortstop on the free agent shopping list was Bert Campaneris, the sparkplug of the Oakland championship team of the seventies. Campaneris, however, was thirty-four years old and had already lost a step or two. Hardly the kind of shortstop you were going to build a dynasty around.

Gabe Paul had another candidate: Bobby Grich. Never mind that Grich's position in Baltimore was second base, he had been a magnificent shortstop in the minor leagues, so good that he had been named Minor League Player of the Year. He had been moved to second base only because Baltimore already had the best defensive shortstop in baseball, Mark Belanger. As a second baseman, Grich had set four all-time fielding records, and Gabe Paul was convinced that he would make an equally magnificent major-league shortstop. In addition to that, Grich would be filling another of the Yankees' needs, a strong right-handed bat to balance off the predominantly left-handed power. With almost no debate, it was agreed that Grich would be the Yankees Number One choice.

The other choice was just as easy. Pitching is, as they say, the name of the game, and the class pitcher on the list was unquestionably Don Gullett, who had just defeated the Yankees in the opening game of the World Series. Gullett was only twenty-five, he was a left-hander (always a welcome commodity in Yankee Stadium), and although he had never been able to get through an entire season without some kind of injury, he had the best winning percentage in baseball.

Manager Billy Martin wasn't there to offer his input. But that's standard in baseball these days. The front office is in charge of player personnel, and it does not welcome interference from the dugout. Nevertheless, Billy had made it known that he wanted Joe Rudi, a solid all-around outfielder who delighted the baseball cognoscenti with all the things he could do that didn't show up in the box score. In Martin's view, Rudi would not only give the Yankees the solid right-handed batter they were looking for, he was a great left fielder with an excellent arm.

Rudi, it was generally agreed, was going to be the most sought-after player on the list, but as Gabe Paul saw it, Rudi was thirty-one years old, he lacked speed, and the Yankees were already loaded with thirtyish outfielders. Having decided upon Grich, the need for additional right-handed power had been satisfied. And anyway, everybody had been saying that Rudi was underrated for so long that in Gabe's view he had become overrated. Joe Rudi's name literally did not come up in the Yankees' discussion.

The outfielder heading the Yankees' list was Don Baylor, who had been traded to Oakland from Baltimore for Reggie Jackson in an exchange of non-signed players. A big right-handed hitter, with great speed. Next on the list was Gary Matthews, who had pretty much the same credentials. Reggie Jackson? Steinbrenner mentioned him, dutifully they put him on their list, but it was there for cosmetic reasons only. Even Steinbrenner understood that Reggie was exactly what the Yankees didn't need—another left-handed power hitter.

As American League pennant-winners, the Yankees drafted last in every round. They selected nine players, in the following order: Bobby Grich, Don Baylor, Don Gullett, Gary Matthews, Wayne Garland, Reggie Jackson, Bert Campaneris, Dave Cash, and Billy Smith.

Baylor was named ahead of Gullett only because four clubs had already selected him by the end of the second round, while only two had named Gullett. Reggie Jackson had been picked so late for the same reason—Matthews had been picked by eight clubs by the end of the fourth round, and Jackson by only two. When the Yankees' fifth turn came around, Wayne Garland, the second-best starting pitcher on the list, had been named by ten clubs, and Jackson still by only four.

"Grich, Gullett, Baylor, and Jackson are the players we're most interested in," Steinbrenner said. Note the order. George still wasn't interested in signing Jackson, but he did want to let the fans know that the Yankees weren't backing away from the player who would be asking for the most money.

They knew who they wanted: Grich and Gullett. And so positive were they that they would get both players, they didn't even bother to open negotiations for Don Baylor even though Baylor was represented by Jerry Kapstein, the same agent they were dealing with for Grich and Gullett. And why shouldn't they be confident? In return for the right to be the last person to talk to Gullett and Grich before they made their final decision, George was guaranteeing that he would top anything anybody else might offer.

With Gullett, he didn't even have to do that. On Wednesday, November 17 (keep your eye on the date), Steinbrenner and Paul went to

Kapstein's office in Providence to meet with Kapstein and Gullett. They closed the deal by making an offer that was evidently too good to refuse.

The screams that followed emanated from St. Louis. Bing Devine, the Cardinals' general manager, had flown out from St. Louis with the Cardinals' lawyer to put their own proposition in front of Kapstein. During the stopover in Boston, they had phoned Kapstein's office and been told that he was out of the office. When they called back, they were told that he had gone to New York.

The Cardinals, who obviously believed that Kapstein had steered his client to the Yankees, vowed that they would never deal with Kapstein again. And they haven't.

Wednesday, November 17, was a hectic day for Kapstein at the end of what must have been a hectic two weeks. Before it was over, he announced the signing of three other clients: Joe Rudi (to California), Bert Campaneris (Texas), and Dave Cash (Montreal). A day earlier he had announced the signing of Baylor (also to California). On other fronts, Atlanta was just about to announce the signing of Gary Matthews, and Cleveland the signing of Wayne Garland. You see what was happening here? Six of the Yankee draft choices (if we include Gullett) were signed within this same forty-eight-hour period.

During that same period, they lost Bobby Grich.

Grich was driving leisurely across the country from Baltimore to his home in Long Beach, California, visiting different American landmarks. He had reached the Indian ruins in New Mexico, the last stop on his itinerary, when he learned from Jerry Kapstein that Don Baylor, his best friend in baseball, had signed with the Angels. Grich and Baylor had roomed together at Rochester in 1971, when they were the two best minor-league players in the country, and had remained together in Baltimore the following year. The chance to rejoin Don Baylor, Grich told Kapstein, certainly made the Angels more attractive to him.

All things being equal, Grich had always preferred to play for the Angels. For one thing, he lived only a few miles from the stadium in Anaheim; for another, he was still very friendly with the Angels' general manager, Harry Dalton, who had signed him to his original contract in baseball.

On the other hand, Grich wanted to be with a winner, which the Yankees certainly were and the Angels certainly were not.

The following morning, Grich had made it to the outskirts of Las Vegas when the news came over the radio that the Angels had called a press conference to announce the signing of Joe Rudi. That got Grich so excited, he drove off the road to place another call to Jerry Kapstein. Bobby knew that California had lost three players to the draft—Lonnie Dade and Billy Smith, two infielders of limited major-league experience, plus Tim Nordbrook, an unsigned utility infielder who had been bought from Baltimore at the end of the season—either in anticipation of replacing the infielders they were going to lose (as California claimed) or to make themselves eligible to sign a third player (as George Steinbrenner would—not without reason—eventually claim).

Kapstein had indeed passed on Grich's expression of interest to Harry Dalton immediately after they had come to an agreement on Rudi, and Dalton's answer was that it had cost so much more than they had expected to sign Baylor and Rudi that they were now out of the market. Bobby couldn't believe it. He knew Gene Autry was loaded, and he knew that California was eligible to sign three players. "I don't understand why they'd drop out. If they wanted to build up their ballclub, it would make sense to me that they'd try to get three free agents. I'm still available. Why would they drop out?"

He asked Kapstein to put Dalton on the phone.

"Listen, Harry," Grich said, "I want very much to play for the California ballclub." So much so that he could assure him that if California made a decent offer, he wouldn't get them involved in any bidding war.

"Well, then, stand by," Harry told him. "I'll talk to Gene Autry and see if there's a chance we can come in with a serious bid for you."

Dalton's call came into the Angels' office just as Autry was entering his staff room for the press conference in which he was going to announce that he had bagged Joe Rudi, the biggest prize of them all. (For $2.09 million over five years, with $1 million of it in the form of a bonus.) A day earlier he had signed Don Baylor ($1.6 million over six years, with $500,000 in the form of a bonus). All pumped up as he was, Autry understood that he could have Grich and become an instant contender, which was, after all—just as Grich had said—what this whole thing was about. After a minimum of thought, Autry gave the word that if Grich was really serious about not getting them involved in another bidding war, he would reach into his own pocket for the money. What the hell, Autry was so rich that he could tuck George Steinbrenner into the southeast corner of his corral. "Any ballplayer who wants to play for us that bad," the Singing Cowboy passed on to Harry Dalton, "let's go get him."

The irony here is that California had put Grich on their list only as an afterthought. They already had an excellent second baseman in Jerry Remy and two excellent young shortstops coming along in the minors. And, most important of all, they had heard through the grapevine that the Yankees were prepared to pay whatever it took to get Bobby. Indeed, the Angels had passed Grich by in the sixth round, even though ten clubs had already selected him, and had picked Reggie Jackson—whom they also had no intention of bidding for—instead. When Grich was still around in the seventh round, they had added him to their list, making themselves the twelfth and last club eligible to draft him. But, as all the clubs were doing by then, they were simply adding a name player who hadn't been closed out yet in order to make their list look as impressive as possible to their fans.

With Grich driving the final leg of his journey home, and Dalton scheduled to fly back to California after the Joe Rudi press conference, Dalton and Kapstein decided that the best way to handle the situation would be for Dalton and Grich to get together in Anaheim the following day and work out the details.

And so the first thing Harry Dalton did when he got home was to call Kapstein and confirm that Jerry had passed the word on to Bobby. "Things have changed," Jerry told him. "Grich is flying back to Providence."

What had happened was this: Kapstein had called the Yankees to pass on the information about Grich's preference for California, and Steinbrenner had presumably reminded him that he had been promised a chance to talk to Bobby before he made up his mind . . . or whatever the agreement was. The least he was entitled to, given this sudden turn of events, was the opportunity to tell Grich what the Yankees and New York City had to offer.

Halfway between Las Vegas and Los Angeles, Grich had called Kapstein again to find out if Dalton had been able to get in touch with Gene Autry and was told that Autry had given Dalton the green light. "But before you make a final decision," Kapstein said, "I want you to talk to Steinbrenner and Gabe Paul."

"I will," Grich said. "I'll talk to them, and I'll listen to them, and I'll see what they have to say before I make up my mind."

The next morning the Yankees held their press conference at the Americana Hotel to announce the signing of Don Gullett. Steinbrenner and Paul thereupon headed for the airport, but not before Steinbrenner had accused Harry Dalton of committing an unethical ploy by buying Tim Nordbrook from Baltimore in the knowledge that they were not going to make any real attempt to sign him.

That evening, Steinbrenner and Paul sat with Grich in Kapstein's office and went all out to change his mind. Steinbrenner spoke of his determination to build the Yankees into a World Championship ballclub, regardless of the cost. Not only did he feel that Bobby's presence in the lineup would guarantee a World Championship, but he also considered him exactly the kind of high-class young man who fit the Yankee mold. Gabe Paul focused upon his confidence in Bobby's ability to do the job for them at shortstop. "In my opinion, Bobby, you're just one heck of a ballplayer. I want nothing more than for you to play for us."

They had him wavering. George was so encouraged at one point that he was advising Bobby to get in all the work he could at shortstop during the winter. While no actual figures were being thrown around, Grich was led to believe that he could pretty much write his own ticket.

Having listened, Bobby reminded them that he was a California boy, that he had always dreamed of playing for the Angels, and that a move to New York would constitute a drastic change for him and his family. "My hopes are leaning strongly toward California," he told them. "But my mind isn't completely made up. I'll think very seriously about what you have said."

That wasn't good enough for Steinbrenner. Go-getter that he is, George was there to nail his man. Having failed to sell Grich on the positive advantages of playing in New York City, he began to bluster and to threaten. Because of the unfair methods Harry Dalton had used, he warned, he didn't think California was entitled to sign a third player. And so if Bobby signed with the Angels, the Yankees were going to ask the commissioner to conduct a full-scale investigation of the legitimacy of the Angels' efforts to sign the three players they had lost, and his contract would quite probably be nullified.

Well, that was a mistake. Bobby Grich had a long-standing relationship with Harry Dalton, and Harry Dalton has an excellent reputation. The first thing Grich did upon meeting with Dalton the next morning, a Friday, was to ask him whether there was any truth to Steinbrenner's charges. "Not only isn't it true," Dalton told him, "it's the very opposite of the truth."

That was good enough for Bobby Grich. An agreement was reached on the money very quickly, and since Dalton had to be in Hawaii on Monday, they agreed to get together again on Saturday morning to wrap the whole thing up.

It wasn't wrapped up Saturday morning. Kapstein had decided that before the negotiations went any further, he wanted something in writing from the commissioner clearing the Angels of Steinbrenner's charge.

During that same day, Steinbrenner leaked word that it was the Yankees who had suddenly "cooled" on Grich. They were now, wrote Murray Chass, the leakee on *The New York Times*, in hot pursuit of Reggie Jackson. "A source close to the free-agent scene said yesterday that the Yankees apparently had backed off in their quest for Grich because they weren't convinced they should pay close to $2 million to find out if he could make the switch back from second base to short-stop. . . . The source said that Steinbrenner has favored signing Jackson from the time the Yankees drafted negotiating rights to him and has slowly brought Paul around to his way of thinking."

On Monday, Kuhn sent a telegram clearing California of any misconduct, and Steinbrenner immediately withdrew his protest. By Monday, Dalton was in Hawaii. The ultimate effect of the delay was to push the announcement of the signing over to Wednesday, November 24, which, by a coincidence that can only be deemed fortuitous, was the same day Steinbrenner was wrapping up Reggie Jackson.

From the moment he had heard that Grich was lost to him, Steinbrenner went after Reggie. And if you have to ask "Why Reggie?" then you haven't been paying attention. *There wasn't anybody else.* Six of the players on the Yankee list had been signed within that hectic forty-eight-hour period. When Grich walked out on George the following day, the Yankees were left with nobody except Reggie Jackson and the utility infielder Billy Smith.

We're talking Ego here, the kind that burns so bright that it can only be looked at through smoked glasses. Steinbrenner had put himself in a position where he had to sign Reggie Jackson or suffer the twin humiliations of (1) admitting to the whole wide world that he had been rejected by Bobby Grich, who now sounded like somebody who went around spoiling Christmas for orphans, and (2) emerging from the First Re-entry Sweepstakes, after all his big talk, with only one player.

Still, Gabe Paul was against it. Only now it wasn't a matter of overbalancing the lineup with left-handed hitting, nor was it a question of weakening the outfield defensively. It was Reggie himself. Now that it had come down to Jackson or nobody, Gabe cast his vote for nobody.

Astonishing. Under normal circumstances, Gabe would be the last man in the world to concern himself about personality conflicts. Dissension? To old baseball hands like Gabe Paul, that's newspaper talk. Gabe had been with the St. Louis Cardinal organization when the members of the Gas House Gang battled each other not with words but with fists—when Ducky Medwick cold-cocked Dizzy Dean in the dugout during the game for daring to complain about his fielding, and Rip Collins cold-cocked Tex Carleton for spending more time in the batting cage than befitted a pitcher. He had seen the St. Louis police batter their way through a mob in the downtown shopping area to rescue Mrs. Sam Breadon, the owner's wife, from her car after Rogers Hornsby had been traded to New York. Dissension meant nothing. Turmoil meant nothing. "The only thing that counts," Gabe had said a thousand times, "is talent. If you have enough talent, you will win; if you don't have enough talent, you will lose."

But every situation turns on its own circumstances. "The only question you have to ask yourself is: What is best for the team? And then you have to be strong enough to do it." Gabe had said that a thousand times, too. With Reggie, they would be imposing a mercurial, wildly articulate, ego-driven player on a pennant-winning team, and they would be paying him far more than they were paying any of the players who had won it for them. "Reggie Jackson," Gabe told Steinbrenner, "will be a destructive force on the New York Yankees."

Steinbrenner's response was to order Paul to find out where Jackson could be reached.

According to one version, which is so perfect as to perhaps be untrue, Steinbrenner's opening line to Reggie the following evening was "I want you more than anything in the world. What do you want more than anything in the world?"

"A Corniche Rolls-Royce," Reggie answers. Top of the line. Went for a tidy little $63,000.

"All I'm asking in return," Steinbrenner is supposed to have said, "is the right to be the last person to talk to you before you make up your mind."

A good story, says Reggie, but not exactly right. The Corniche wasn't the first thing that was mentioned, he says, it was the last. And he wasn't actually given the car, he was given a sum of money which he chose to use to buy the car.

What George really said in that original phone call, according to Reggie, was that although everybody in the organization was after him to sign Grich, George felt that if he was going to spend that kind of money he wanted Reggie. And that Thurman Munson, who had come to New York for the Gullett press conference, agreed with him.

Well, maybe yes . . . maybe no. . . . Munson liked to say that he wished somebody would give *him* a Rolls just for talking to him.

There's probably a bit of truth in both versions. Reggie's package was originally put at $2.93 million. More recently, with Reggie going for the new contract, it became $2.66 million.

The leaves $270,000 kicking around in grants, bequests, and who knows what. The best bet would seem to be that George told Reggie he wanted him so much that he'd pay him $100,000—let's say—up front for the right to be the last person to talk to him. And that when the deal was set, he threw in another $60,000 or so for the Rolls.

During the telephone conversation on Saturday, Reggie had informed George that he was going to be in New York on Monday. At Steinbrenner's invitation, he dropped by George's apartment in the Carlyle Hotel. George immediately asked what it would take to sign him. He wasn't handling that kind of thing himself, Reggie told him. "I just wanted to meet with you and see what kind of money you're talking." The fact was that Reggie had set his price at $3 million, even before the draft took place, and had already been offered far more than that by Montreal and San Diego. George did something very smart. He offered him something around $2 million, undoubtedly with a bit of a wink. "We can't do business," Reggie laughed. They then spent a couple of hours together in the apartment before going off to "21" and, as Reggie likes to say, "We hit it off as people."

George is a charmer, all right. And, might we add, a showman? As they emerged from the hotel, a middle-aged woman carrying an armful of bags recognized Reggie and, to his obvious delight, expressed the hope that he'd be playing in New York. As they stopped for a red light during the stroll to "21," he was hailed by a group of black kids who— could it have only been by a stroke of fortune?—just happened to be hanging around. Guess where they wanted Reggie to play.

It took two more days to lock Jackson up. He had already sent word to those clubs who were still interested in seeing how rich they could make him that he would be taking all bids at the Hyatt Hotel in the Chicago airport on Wednesday, November 24, which, you will remember, is the same day on which the Angels were holding their press conference for Grich.

Steinbrenner was visiting his son that day at the Culver Military Academy in Indiana. He chartered a small plane to Chicago in the early morning hours, laid out his proposition to Reggie's lawyer and agent, flew back to Culver to spend the rest of the day with his son, and was back in Chicago to meet with Reggie and his people in the evening. Whether by prior commitment, gentleman's agreement, or sheer persistence, George was indeed going to be the last person to talk to Reggie before he made up his mind. And as it worked out, Reggie's advisors left the two principals together to work out the final details between themselves.

The next morning, which was Thanksgiving, they had breakfast together. The deal had already been set, Reggie says, when George volunteered to add another sum of money to the contract as a kind of personal gift. (You know how it goes: Here, Reggie, buy something for yourself that you normally wouldn't splurge on with the lousy $2.66 million.) And why not a $63,000 Corniche!

If Reggie had known how desperately Steinbrenner needed him, he could have held out for a DC-10. With all the turmoil and jealousies that were to arise over Reggie's $3 million deal, Steinbrenner got him cheap.

And there you have the final irony: with all the talk about the greed of the modern ballplayer, Jackson, like Grich, went for the locality rather than the money. Four days later—a week to the day after Reggie had come to George's apartment at the Carlyle—he was standing under the crystal chandeliers of the Versailles Terrace Room being introduced to the New York press. On one wrist he wore a gold bracelet upon which the name Reggie shone forth in a dazzlement of diamonds; the other was girded by a glittering gold watch to go with his Oakland World Series ring.

It is part of Reggie's personality that he could not bring himself to admit to the assembled press that coming to New York was so very important to him, even though he had implied it years earlier when he had told a group of New York sportswriters, "If I was playing in New York, they'd name a candy bar after me." (And, of course, they did.)

Asked about that now, he took care to emphasize that he already had so many commercials and merchandising tie-ins that even with the

$3 million contract he would be making more money from his outside activities than from baseball. "I didn't come to New York to become a star," quoth Reggie Jackson. "I brought my star with me."

The New York press knew better. Wouldn't he have been lost if he had signed with Montreal or San Diego? "Fort Knox isn't lost. Everybody knows where Fort Knox is."

The reason he was a Yankee, he affirmed finally, was that George Steinbrenner had out-hustled everybody. "George Steinbrenner dealt with me as a man and a person. . . . Steinbrenner is like me, he's a little crazy and he's a hustler. And there were certain things he expressed to me, and certain ideologies and philosophies we reached an accord on."

Sociology, ideologies, philosophies. Reggie Jackson talks like that when he's on a roll. But you could see how Steinbrenner had dazzled him—the rich man, the big industrialist, the friend of the mighty. "It will be exciting hitting a home run in Yankee Stadium," Reggie said with a glow. "For me to get applause from the crowd or slaps on the back or have George Steinbrenner say to me that he felt he wanted me to play here and always wanted me here, that's something I never had. I never felt wanted like that."

Ah, Reggie, that need to be wanted. And then, as he went on, he revealed something equally acute about George.

The way Steinbrenner had gone after him, he said, it was "like trying to hustle a girl at a bar." Reggie, who can wield an analogy with the best of them, may not have fully understood how aptly he wielded that one. For Reggie never did find out, perhaps because he didn't really want to, that George had come after him only after he had been spurned by the girl of his dreams.

For Reggie, the love affair was to last two years. During that time he viewed his relationship with the Yankees as a partnership, he really did—always ready to make appearances to promote the team, to fly to Florida to speak before one of George's groups, to let everybody know how nice, how generous, how praiseworthy the owner was.

The end of the affair came when he discovered that George owned the property, and he was just a guy drawing a paycheck. Not a friend, but just another employee. And maybe even, for crissake, the house nigger.

As George Steinbrenner was driving his Yankees into and through the 1977 season, lusting after the club's first World Championship in fifteen years, he and Gabe Paul became increasingly aware of some glaring deficiencies on the roster of the Best Team Money Can Buy. Four players came to fill those holes. Three of them—Bucky Dent, Mike Torrez, and Cliff Johnson—came by way of trades. The fourth—Ron Guidry—stands out as a classic example of the old baseball truism that the best trade is usually the one that isn't made.

Bucky Dent represents the one key Yankee trade for which George Steinbrenner can take credit. George's dream of fielding a team of all-stars had not come to an end with the failure to sign Bobby Grich. Far from it. Gabe Paul contacted Chicago White Sox owner Bill Veeck about Bucky Dent almost immediately, and negotiations continued all through spring training. Oscar Gamble, who had become expendable from the moment Reggie Jackson was signed, was to be part of the deal from the beginning. So was money. But since the cash limit Commissioner Kuhn was allowing to change hands was $400,000, the negotiations revolved entirely around who else Veeck was going to get. In the end, Veeck was able to get only two minor-league pitchers. And he almost didn't get any deal at all.

Superscout Birdie Tebbetts had been following Dent all through spring training, and his reports back to the Yankees weren't exactly ecstatic. "The best shortstop available" was as far as Birdie was willing to go. Dent had slightly more range than Fred Stanley, Tebbetts reported, and he hit a little better. But that was all.

Four days before the Yankees were to break camp, Ron Blomberg, who was supposed to become the left-handed DH, ran into a wall and tore up his knee cartilages, and suddenly Gamble had become less expendable. So much less expendable that Gabe Paul recommended that the Dent deal not be made. Billy Martin felt the same way. From a managerial point of view, he had to look at a roster that would have Stanley plus Gamble, or Dent minus Gamble, and he infinitely preferred sticking with Stanley and keeping Gamble.

Steinbrenner asked Paul two questions:

"In your opinion, is Dent better than Stanley?"

The answer was yes.

"In your opinion, can we win the pennant without Gamble?"

The answer, once again, was yes.

Make the deal, George told him.

And he was absolutely right. When you're talking about shortstops, *this much* difference in range can be all the difference in the world.

The Yankees had broken camp and were ready to pull out when Paul called Gamble off the bus to tell him he had been traded to Chicago. "You've made a big mistake," Gamble told him. "You know I'm a better player than Reggie Jackson."

Ron Guidry, whom the Yankees had all along, came close to being handed away in the expansion draft during the winter, and he was very nearly given away early in the 1977 season as a throw-in in a couple of trades. That he wasn't, as we shall see, was due entirely to Gabe Paul's stubbornness, Gabe Paul's patience—and Gabe Paul's faith in Birdie Tebbetts.

As an *Extra Added Attraction* along the way we are going to catch the opening of the ****STEINBRENNER FOLLIES****—the wild and woolly extravaganza that was going to amuse and amaze the world of baseball for the next five years.

The Re-entry Draft was not the only 1976 draft. There was also an expansion draft to stock the new Seattle and Toronto clubs. But unlike previous expansion drafts, in which the new clubs had been allowed to dip into a grab bag of has-beens and rejects, this one was set up on a complicated structure by which each established club was entitled to protect only twenty-five players, and could then add two more names to its protected list every time one of its players was taken.

The twenty-fifth player on the Yankees' protected list was going to be a left-handed relief pitcher—either Grant Jackson or Ron Guidry.

Not unexpectedly, Steinbrenner wanted to protect Grant Jackson, the one good thing to have come out of the Ken Holtzman trade. In the 1976 pennant run, Jackson had stepped in at a time when Sparky Lyle was going bad and had performed so well that he had taken over as the premier relief pitcher through the last two months of the season.

Guidry was a twenty-six-year-old rookie who had been kicking around the Yankee organization for six years before putting it together in Syracuse in 1976, with an almost unbelievable ERA of .068. He had also come up to the Yankees at the end of the season, pitched sixteen innings, and ended with an all too believable ERA of 5.63. And, talk about your skinny little kids, he was 5'11" and weighed 153 pounds. You could see his ribs sticking out.

Steinbrenner has a thing about rookie pitchers. Nobody has ever accused him of taking the loss of any ballgame lightly, but when it's a rookie pitcher getting bombed, George goes bonkers. Tracks them back to the clubhouse, screams at them, ships them back to the minors where they belong. His automatic reaction was that Guidry didn't have the guts to pitch in the major leagues. Lacked the old intestinal fortitude. Wasn't a tough enough competitor to face the rigors of pitching in Yankee Stadium.

Gabe Paul had a report from Birdie Tebbetts that stated, amidst the superlatives, that Guidry had the strongest left arm in baseball. Not just in the organization, not just in the American League, but in all of baseball! Tebbetts had managed for Gabe in Cincinnati, and as far as Gabe is concerned, Tebbetts is the smartest man in the game.

"Stick with Guidry," Paul kept telling Steinbrenner. "He's going to be the best left-handed relief pitcher in baseball within two years."

George gave in, finally, with his usual good grace. "All right," he said. "We'll protect Guidry. But this is on your head, Gabe."

In your life you never saw a worse pitcher than Ron Guidry in the spring of 1977. And George always seemed to be there, usually with a boxful of friends, to see him getting shelled. Against the Red Sox, Guidry entered the game in the ninth inning with the score tied and gave up three hits, capped by a tremendous home run by Carl Yastrzemski. And, while he was about it, pulled a muscle in his right thigh.

Nine days later, in the second of the five games the Yankees were playing out of Tampa, he pitched two innings against Philadelphia and allowed only one run, a massive home run by a weak-hitting infielder named Fred Andrews.

In the last of the five games out of George Steinbrenner's hometown of Tampa, the Yankees were leading Detroit by two runs in the eighth inning. Guidry came into the game, was hammered for four hits, and the Yankees lost again.

Two days later, he pitched the last inning against the Red Sox, and the guy who hit the long two-run homer off him this time was Jim Rice.

You could hardly blame Steinbrenner. The scouting reports said one thing, and his eyes told him something entirely different. "The trouble with you," he screamed at Paul after the Detroit fiasco, "is that you believe everything Tebbetts says. There aren't any geniuses in this business!"

But Gabe wasn't the only one who believed in Tebbetts' report. Everybody wanted to deal for Guidry. In the early stages of the negotiations for Bucky Dent, Bill Veeck asked for either Lyle (who hadn't signed a contract) or Guidry. Paul was willing to let him have Lyle, Martin wasn't, and Steinbrenner absolutely wasn't. (After Guidry's second horrible appearance in spring training, George called Sparky early in the morning and said, "Now, Sparky, we've got to get this thing settled.") Martin and Steinbrenner were willing to let Veeck have Guidry. Paul said, "Over my dead body."

Although Billy Martin had lent his weight to protecting Guidry in the expansion draft, he had become so totally disenchanted by the end of spring training that he told his struggling pitcher, "Show me somebody you can get out, and I'll let you pitch to him." In fact, Martin had so little faith in Guidry that it was the New York writers who practically shamed him into putting Ron into his first regular season game of the 1977 season. The Yankees had just lost a thirteen-inning marathon in Kansas City after Billy left Dick Tidrow in to pitch to the Royals' left-handed slugger John Mayberry, with two men on and two out. Lyle had already been in the game, and when Billy was asked why he hadn't called on Guidry, his answer was that he didn't want to bring a raw rookie kid into a tight spot like that.

Well, hadn't he better find out? he was asked. If not now, when?

Good question. The next night Billy brought Guidry into the game to face George Brett with the score tied and a runner on second. Brett promptly lined a single to center, but the runner on second hesitated just long enough that Mickey Rivers, the worst-throwing center fielder in baseball, was able to throw him out with one of his dying two-bounce throws. Guidry breezed the last two innings, the Yankees scored, and Guidry had his first major-league victory. "If it hadn't been for Mickey's throw," Guidry says to this day, "that might have been the end of me right there."

The next time he pitched, it almost was.

April 18, 1977, a day like all days except that it marked the first performance of Steinbrenner Follies, a spectacle of clashing temperaments and competing egos in which the ballgame becomes less important than the turmoil and confusion that surround it. Before the day was over, we would see the entire playbill clearly.

Act 1, Scene 1. Enter the Boss

In which George comes bombing in to bring some order to his messy domain.

Act 1, Scene 2. The Press Conference
Which is called to lay to rest some foul and dastardly rumor, some affront or attack on the Boss.

Act 1, Scene 3. The Pep Talk
In which the Boss, now as Knute Rockne, reminds the players that they are the proud carriers of the Yankee tradition, and also informs them about all those young fellows in the farm system who are waiting to take their jobs away from them.

Act II. The Ballgame
The Yankees lose. (It was part of the 1977 edition that a Steinbrenner pep talk became the inspirational fodder for a crushing defeat.)

Act III, Scene 1. Billy Martin's Post-game Press Conference.
The great variable.

Act III, Scene 2. The Players' Reaction (On and Off the Record) to George, Billy, etc.
Turmoil and Confusion.

One of the *dramatis personae* of this opening production was Dock Ellis—player representative, team Bizarro, and a festering wound in Steinbrenner's hide. Early in spring training, Dock—one of the Yankees' six unsigned players—had declared war on George Steinbrenner. As the last unsigned player going into the season he had decided that his position as team representative entitled him to order George to stay out of the clubhouse. As in "We don't need him riding in here like the Lone Ranger." Nor had Dock been silent about the Lone Ranger's current descent from the skies. "Steinbrenner had better stay off Billy Martin's back," Dock had said, "because the players are in Billy's corner."

It was to answer this charge that George called a pre-game press conference. "If anybody says I've been on Billy Martin's butt, he's a liar," George roared. "I've had no conversations with Billy Martin about the ballclub since spring training."

Made you wonder what they talked about when George called the clubhouse every day. That's right, every day!

He also wanted to answer the charge that he had made the deal for Bucky Dent only because he wanted a team of all-stars. George let it be known that the Bucky Dent deal had been dead until Billy came to him in a panic, five days before the opening of the season, and wailed that he absolutely had to have him.

The Dent deal, as has been pointed out, was the one deal which Steinbrenner could rightfully claim credit for, and here, in his fervor of denial, he was disclaiming it.

A chronic problem with George Steinbrenner is that once he starts talking, he can't stop, a personality defect he shared with Billy Martin. When George gets defensive, he begins to lose control of what he is saying, and that was another unhappy characteristic he shared with his manager. Each accused the other of being a liar many times in the course of their murderous relationship, and nobody was ever disposed to argue the point with either of them.

Nor, George said, was he going to trade Dock Ellis out of spite. "I like Dock Ellis," he said. "He's a good pitcher."

George couldn't wait to trade him. A Dock Ellis for Mike Torrez deal had been brewing with Oakland since spring training, and the only reason it hadn't already been made was that they had not been able to agree on the other player—the "something more"—the Yankees should put in to equalize the deal. After Ellis had warned George to stay out of the clubhouse, Steinbrenner had personally reactivated the talks. Finley had proposed that they could balance it off very nicely by trading their center fielders as well: the speedy Mickey Rivers for the speedy Billy North. Steinbrenner loved that. The way he looked at it, he'd be getting rid of two pains in the ass in the same deal. If Gabe Paul didn't like it quite so much, it was because Gabe wouldn't have traded Mickey Rivers for Torrez and North, straight up. "Mickey Rivers ignites this team," Gabe had told George. "We cannot win the pennant without him."

When Steinbrenner told the gathering of reporters that he wasn't going to trade Dock Ellis out of spite, it was because Gabe Paul had just talked him out of it.

Not that Steinbrenner denied everything. "I'm not Little Red Riding Hood," he said, "and I didn't just ride into town on a load of pumpkins either. I'm learning . . . I've ridden people both in sports and in business. There are times to exhort; there are times not to exhort. This is one of those times."

Whereupon George went into the clubhouse to do some exhorting.

Having talked to the press at length about his relationship with Billy Martin, he told the players that they should not talk to the press about his relationship with Billy Martin. And then he went into one of his pep talks about the pride of the Yankees. Too bad Dock Ellis didn't stay to be inspired. "I'm not going to listen to that High School Charlie shit," Dock said as he walked out.

No wonder George liked him. Those who remained to listen were so inspired that they went out and lost their fifth straight game.

George wasn't even able to root for Reggie Jackson to hit one. The reason he had flown up from Florida in the first place was to agitate for Reggie, and Billy had responded by benching him again. He was, however, able to see Ron Guidry get plastered again, and this time by the Toronto Blue Jays, an expansion team. The Yankees lost 8–3; Guidry allowed five hits and four runs in 2⅔ innings.

In the newspaper reports of the game you will find no mention of Guidry's performance. You have to go to the box score to find it. There was little enough written, in fact, about the game itself. The ballgame had got lost amidst the pre-game and post-game chaos.

There was, for instance, Billy Martin's own post-game press conference. After the previous day's loss, Billy had taken sanctuary from the press in the players' lounge. Having been informed that George was coming in, Billy had decided, in a rare moment of caution, that it would be a very good idea to keep his mouth shut.

The first thing he had to do, therefore, was explain to the writers why he had ducked out on them yesterday. The rotten stories they had been writing seemed to have something to do with it.

Had the stories affected the team?

"I think they have, yes."

Were the stories the reason the team was losing?

No, he hadn't said that.

Was he worried about the tension on the club?

"There's no tension. No tension! That's just the way it is when you lose."

Was he relaxed right now?

"Oh, yeah. Awful relaxed. Would you be relaxed if your house was on fire?"

Was his house on fire?

"No," said Billy Martin.

There was so little tension in the clubhouse that even Roy White, always the most pleasant of men, snapped at a reporter who had asked about the Toronto pitcher. "You've got eyes. What do you think?"

Dock Ellis was shouting at a TV guy, and then warning the room at large, "The little TV shit is trying to screw someone."

Graig Nettles, who hadn't knocked in a run all year, was screaming at Lou Piniella not to talk to the writer who as official scorer had given him an error the previous day. Then he screamed a vile insult at the writer himself, and, while he was about it, began to yell at another writer who, as that day's official scorer, hadn't given him a hit he thought he deserved.

Up in the Yankee offices, where Steinbrenner was holding a meeting with his top people, it really got tense. Gabe Paul had collapsed. They rushed him to the hospital. The first reports were that Gabe had suffered a mild stroke.

And now we are back to Ron Guidry. With Gabe Paul in the hospital, Charley Finley came up with a new proposition. As his "something more" for Mike Torrez in the Dock Ellis trade, Charley was now willing to accept Ron Guidry and Mickey Klutts. Klutts was a utility infielder who was out for the season with a broken hand, so there was no loss there. George had never been able to understand why everybody was so high on Guidry, and how could you blame him? Every time he had seen him pitch, the skinny little bastard was getting clobbered. And now he had just seen Toronto with all those AAA hitters knock the kid's jock off. Some smart cookie, that Charley Finley. Gabe had told Bill Veeck that he'd get Guidry over his dead body, and now Finley was trying to do just that.

But Gabe hadn't had a stroke. He had suffered a cerebral spasm, a kind of low-level stroke—bad enough to incapacitate him for a couple of weeks and slur his speech for a few weeks more, but that was all. Lying there in the hospital, Gabe was able to talk Steinbrenner into sticking with Guidry for a while longer. "Where do you find an arm like that?" Gabe asked. "Nowhere."

Patience was the name of the trading game, he told him. They had waited out Bill Veeck on Dent, knowing Veeck was going to need the money to start the season, and they had been able to make the deal they wanted. They could wait out Finley, because Finley needed everything and he wanted to get rid of Torrez, for his own reasons, just as badly as George wanted to get rid of Ellis.

A couple of days later, Finley agreed to take an unsigned utility infielder, whom the Yankees wanted to unload anyway, and a minor-league outfielder. And, oh yeah, one other "something more." George

Steinbrenner had a horse running in the Kentucky Derby, and Finley also demanded that George throw in two tickets to his private box and allow Charley to lead the horse into the winner's circle if it should win.

Luck, fortitude, and fate. If Gabe Paul's cerebral spasm had been a stroke, as first feared, Guidry would have been given away as "something more." But that's only the half of it. If Guidry had shown anything at all in spring training, Lyle would have been traded away and Guidry would have remained in the bullpen. Instead, Lyle became the first relief pitcher in the American League to win the Cy Young Award, and Guidry, who was to win the Cy Young Award the following year, became the most overpowering pitcher of his time. And, to close the circle, it was Torrez's tardiness in reporting that gave Guidry his chance.

The Torrez trade had been consummated just before an off day preceding a weekend series against Seattle, so that Torrez would have all the time he needed to get to New York, meet his new teammates, and go out and pitch.

He didn't arrive on the off day. He didn't arrive the next day. Martin, who was flat out of pitchers, waited until the last possible minute, then went over to Guidry's locker and handed him the ball. Guidry hadn't started a game even in the minors in two years. "All I want from you," Billy told him, "is five innings."

In the first inning, Seattle loaded the bases on Guidry with one out, and it looked as if it was going to be the same story again. But then Guidry got his hard slider going, and struck out the next two batters. Martin had asked for five innings. Guidry went to one out in the ninth inning before Sparky Lyle came in to complete a 3–0 shutout.

Okay, so he had shut out an expansion team. Billy Martin was making no effort to mask his delight at having stolen one. "Tomorrow it will be Lyle," he chortled, "and the day after that, Tidrow. All my starters are going into the bullpen."

Cliff Johnson, the final piece in the Yankees' 1977 mosaic, joined the team on the day Ron Guidry pitched the Yankees into first place. His arrival, in the final irony of Yankee acquisitions, was a powerful contributory factor to the departure of Gabe Paul.

Here, at last, was the right-handed designated hitter Gabe had been looking for from the moment the Yankees had overbalanced themselves so badly on the left-handed side with the signing of Reggie Jackson. To indicate the urgency of the situation, the Yankees' record as the trading deadline approached was 10–15 against left-handed pitchers and 25–11 against right-handers. And not only were the Yankees losing to the left-handers, they were facing every left-hander in captivity. The good ones—and there were only a handful of those—were handling them with ease, and the not-so-good ones were holding their own.

Gabe Paul had been trying to pry Cliff Johnson loose from Houston practically from the day he came to the Yankees. A big (6'4") power hitter with a tremendous home run percentage and minimum defensive abilities, Johnson was a natural-born DH displaced in the National League. For five years Gabe had been making periodic calls, the way general managers do, to express his continuing interest and keep abreast of the other management's current thinking. Tal Smith, the Houston general manager, had been on both ends of those calls. As Gabe's assistant in 1974, he had done some of the calling. As Houston's general manager in the subsequent years, he had been on the receiving end of a great many more.

With the trading deadline two weeks away, Gabe automatically touched base with Tal again. Two days later, Tal called back to tell Gabe that with Houston realistically out of the pennant race, Johnson could be had. "But it's going to be expensive." All he wanted were the two best prospects in the Yankee chain.

Not surprisingly, the talks wound down to the final trading day, almost to the final hour. Houston was playing Atlanta on June 15, and then by a coincidence of the schedule was flying up to New York to play the Mets. On the afternoon of June 15, Gabe called Tal to tell him he would split the difference with him. Tal could have Dave Bergman, one of the two players he was after, and in place of the other he would have to take two lesser prospects, Mike Fischlin, a shortstop, and Randy Neimann, a left-handed pitcher.

After the game had ended, Smith called back to tell him he was still mulling it over but would call him from the Houston airport with a definite answer. (He had to come to a decision by then. The trading deadline was going to toll while the plane was in the sky.)

The answer was yes. But there was going to be a slight complication; not from Houston's side, but from New York's.

In order to deliver Bergman, the Yankees would have to clear him through the waiver list, and since that was clearly going to be impossible, the deal would have to be announced as Fischlin, Neimann, and "a player to be named later." It's done all the time—a routine dishonesty which has become accepted through the practice of years. But this time there would be repercussions.

The following day Gabe met with Tal Smith at the hotel where the Astros were staying to draw the memorandum of agreement on Bergman, and once that had been done, he picked up Cliff Johnson to take him to Yankee Stadium and introduce him around. When he was brought into Steinbrenner's office, Johnson said, "In all fairness, I think I should tell you people I have an ankle condition."

"What!" screamed Steinbrenner.

As Johnson went on to explain it, it amounted to nothing. He had two small bone chips in his ankle that affected his maneuverability not at all. Such bone chips are not at all uncommon in professional athletes. As a precautionary measure they are usually removed by a simple operation during the off-season, at the athlete's discretion.

To Steinbrenner, the explanation didn't matter. George was convinced that Tal Smith had palmed Johnson off on him as "damaged goods," and from then on he tried to get the deal called off. But even if George could prove a case, there was nothing the commissioner could do about it. Baseball trades are made on the principle of caveat emptor. If you're stuck, you're stuck. That's the legal position, anyway. In practice, the general managers have always operated on a code of honor by which an equitable accommodation is made. The code of honor works both ways. Cliff Johnson was not damaged goods, and Gabe was not about to press any such claim against Houston.

Two weeks after he joined the club, Johnson hit three home runs in one game, against Toronto, a feat that only eleven other Yankees had accomplished in the team's slugger-laden history. In fact, Cliff Johnson turned out to be everything Gabe Paul had hoped he would be, and more. In 142 times at bat, he hit 12 home runs and knocked in 31 runs. His slugging percentage was better than the league leader's. And, most important of all, the Yankees were no longer patsies against left-handers.

Meant nothing to Steinbrenner. As far as he was concerned, Tal Smith had pulled a fast one by not telling Gabe about the bad ankle. At one point he went to the commissioner's office to try to get the deal canceled on the grounds that the memorandum of agreement was an illegal document. Well, the way things stand, the delivery of a player is guaranteed by the same code of honor as the trading of a player. The memorandum of agreement is made out only to have something in writing in the event that something happens to one of the parties. It was Gabe Paul's word of honor that Steinbrenner was attempting to break, and Gabe told George that if he didn't withdraw his appeal, he would quit.

But George could not leave it alone. His farm people kept telling him what a great prospect Bergman was, and what the hell did he care about Paul's word? "*I* didn't give anybody my word!" When the season came to an end, on the eve of the playoffs, he was still trying to get the commissioner to return Johnson to Houston and Bergman to New York.

And because George couldn't leave it alone, Gabe Paul, having warned him, was left with little alternative except to quit. If it wasn't the only reason, it was certainly the final straw.

After Gabe left, George continued to try to get the deal canceled—all through the next off-season and into spring training. The bone chips were removed from Johnson's ankle in a successful operation, and even then George persisted. The final angle he came up with was so devilishly clever that you have to stand back and look at the man with awe. When you have a player-to-be-named-later, there is always the possibility that something might happen to him, and so it had been stipulated in the memorandum that Houston was to receive $100,000 in lieu of Bergman in the event they didn't care to accept assignment because of an "incapacitating physical injury."

Steinbrenner attempted to take over Houston's option—get this now—and *pay* the Astros the $100,000 in lieu of Bergman, presumably on the grounds that Houston had delivered an incapacitated player to New York, and fair's fair.

And Cliff Johnson wasn't incapacitated. He performed beyond expectations. The Yankees could not have won the 1977 pennant without him.

Thus did Gabe Paul, with some help and a lot of non-help from George Steinbrenner, assemble the team that won the 1977 World Championship. And it is to the progress of that incredible season, with a *Sturm und Drang* like no other in the annals of Steinbrenner's Yankees, to which we now turn.

6

THE GREENING
OF THE
NEW YORK YANKEES

Was there ever such a season? Was there ever such a team? The 1977 Yankees came to camp with the Magnitude of Reggie Jackson and six unsigned players from the 1976 pennant winners. There were two near fistfights—one between Billy Martin and George Steinbrenner in training camp, and one between Martin and Jackson during the season. There were rampant jealousies and hatreds swirling around Reggie, and crises galore falling down upon Billy. By his own count, Billy Martin was fired five times. Four times the crises were resolved with Billy promising to be more obedient. The fifth time he was saved, literally at the last hour, when the man the job was offered to turned it down.

And with all that, Billy still would not have survived the season if it hadn't been for his popularity with the New York fans.

Billy Martin, the eye of the 1977 storm, was George Steinbrenner's third manager, following Ralph Houk (1973) and Bill Virdon (1974–mid-1975). George went after him as soon as he became available, after Billy was fired by the Texas Rangers.

Billy Martin wears a hurt. It's there in the bony, grating look that grips him when he suddenly becomes angry. It's there, coming over him, in repose. His father was a Portuguese musician who took off before Billy was born. His mother was, still is, a pugnacious, feisty little bit of a woman whose great ambition, as Billy tells it, was to attend the funeral of the sonofabitch who left her . . . "And in front of all his friends and relatives, I'm going to pull up my dress and piss on his grave."

Billy grew up in West Berkeley, California, in a neighborhood so poor that he had to sleep with his grandmother until he was fifteen.

He was signed to his first baseball contract by Casey Stengel, who brought him to the Yankees in 1950. When Stengel told him in 1957 that the Yankees were letting him go, Billy went into the dugout toilet and cried. Stengel came in after him, saying, "Billy, I fought to keep you." And Billy said, "But you didn't fight hard enough."

For seven years Billy refused to talk to Stengel. Not a word. "My heart was broke." The Old Man went so far as to send emissaries, but Billy wouldn't relent. He wrote an article for *Sport* magazine entitled "I Love That Old Man." Loved him but wouldn't talk to him.

It is Billy's story, recounted a thousand times, that George Weiss, general manager of the Yankees, hated him. It doesn't matter why, there is always a good reason in Billy's mind, and it is always a reason that holds Martin misunderstood and blameless. In this case, Weiss thought Billy was a bad influence on Mickey Mantle and Whitey Ford. "I had four roomies on the Yankees," Billy will tell you. "DiMaggio, Mantle, Ford, and Rizzuto. Three of them are in the Hall of Fame, and the other should be. How bad an influence could I have been?"

That also tells you something. It tells you that the big men of the Yankees, the superstars, found something appealing in the fresh little kid from West Berkeley. He is, like Reggie, like George, two people. He is Billy the Kid, with a puppy-dog quality about him, and he is a grown man who hits people.

Billy has a good mind and very firm beliefs about the psychology of leadership. He has always had a tremendous empathy with black and Caribbean ballplayers, especially when they are players every other manager has had difficulty with. "I was raised in a ghetto too," he explains. "I grew up Portuguese. When nothing talks to nothing, they understand each other."

From the day he left home to play professional baseball he has carried a Saint Jude medal in his pocket. The Patron Saint of Lost Causes. When answering charges against his methods of dealing with his own causes, he beats his chest and cries, "I swear! I swear! God looks into your heart and knows who's telling the truth."

In 1977, Billy had to do a lot of swearing.

If Billy Martin was the eye of the 1977 storm, the name of that storm was Reggie.

Reggie Jackson came to camp immersed in the vast, brilliantly lighted theater of his mind. Reggie has some kind of apostolic vision of himself as a man destined to perform great feats of leadership for his people in other, vaster arenas. Not just a ballplayer but a leader. Not just Reggie Jackson but Jesse Jackson. And since baseball is the arena in which he operates at the moment, and hitting is what he actually does, his home runs become infused with some mystic power.

"I am the straw that stirs the drink," he would proclaim, and by the mere saying of it, the magic of his words, he would tear the ball-club apart.

The braggadocio, the compulsive boasting, the overriding ego; Reggie knows what the reaction is going to be. It wrecked his marriage, as he will openly admit.

During his first year in Oakland, a cover story appeared about him in *Sports Illustrated,* labeling him the new Babe Ruth. There were a couple of lines in there describing how intelligent and articulate he was, and Reggie went strutting around the house until he became unbearable. His wife was a beautiful and brilliant white woman whom he had met while they were both students at Arizona State. He worshiped her. Their divorce is the great tragedy of his life. He will admit that the fault was his; he will admit he had become impossible to live with. "But she should have been more understanding," he will add wistfully. "She should have recognized that I was immature."

Recognizing all that, he cannot help himself. Just as the first recognition of his intellect in a national magazine had overwhelmed him, so did the $3 million contract. His new compulsion became counting his money, talking about it. On the players' bus to the training field, he would sit up in front, take out his wallet, and count his money, all hundred-dollar bills. Every day. He would do it while he was being interviewed. He would do it while he was talking to his teammates. He would continue to do it all year.

By the end of the first week of spring training, when Robert Ward came down to do the calamitous *Sport* magazine article, Reggie was in an emotional turmoil. What with the furor surrounding the free agency drama, his TV commentating, and his commercial enterprises, he had come into camp overweight. The first time in his life he had ever been out of shape. When he came back from his first workout, his elbow was killing him. The first sore arm he had ever had in his life.

Reggie can get into wildly boastful moods when he is either elated or trying to fight off a fit of depression. And Ward caught him at a time when he was trying to keep from being overwhelmed by the terrible fear that he was going to come into New York with the eyes of the nation upon him and be the greatest flop of all time.

> I've got problems other guys don't have. I've got this big image that comes before me. . . . That's not "me" really, but I've got to deal with it. Also, I used to just be known as a black athlete, now I'm respected as a tremendous intellect.

When Reggie begins to talk about the stupendous encounter between himself and his intellect, you can be sure that he is in an emotional turmoil. And that the words "black athlete" will be somewhere close by.

> You know, this team . . . it all flows from me. I've got to keep it all going. I'm the straw that stirs the drink. It all comes back to me. Maybe I should say me and Munson . . . but really, he doesn't enter into it. He's being so damned insecure about the whole thing.

Ward wanted to know why he didn't just talk it out with him, then.

> No, he's not ready for it yet. He doesn't even know he feels that way. . . . He'd try to cover up, but he ought to know he can't cover up anything from me. Man, there is no way. I can read these guys. No, I'll wait, and eventually he'll be whipped. There will come that moment when he really knows I won, and he'll want to hear everything is all right, and then I'll go to him and we will get it right.

They were drinking in the Banana Boat Bar, and Ward, recognizing what Reggie was letting himself in for, asked, in some astonishment, "Do you want this printed?"
"Print it," said Reggie.

> You see, this is the way I am. I'm a leader, and I can't lie down. But "leader" isn't the right word . . . it's a matter of presence. Let me put it this way: No team I am on will ever be humili-

ated the way the Yankees were by the Reds in the World Series! That's why Munson can't intimidate me. Nobody can. You can't psyche me. You take me one-on-one in the pit and I'll whip you. . . . The way the Yankees were humiliated by the Reds, you think that doesn't bother Billy Martin. He's no fool. He's smart. Very smart. And he's a winner. Munson's tough, too. He is a winner, but there is just nobody who can do for a club what I can do. That's just the way it is. Munson thinks he can be the straw that stirs the drink, but he can only stir it bad.

Once again, Ward gave him a chance to pull back. "Are you sure you want me to print that?" They were, after all, in a drinking situation. Writers always like subjects who give them good quotes, and Reggie was at the top of his form. And why wouldn't he be? This was Reggie putting forth the scenario he had obviously fantasized before he came to camp.

Yes, print it. Reggie rapped his knuckles on the bar. "I *want* to see that in print. I want to *read* that."

He is a man trying to surmount his insecurities by accusing everybody else of being insecure. "I am the situation," he would be saying at the end of the season. Certainly he was a man making the situation, choreographing the coming events by setting up the inevitable reaction. And yet, through it all, there would run a consistent note of deference toward Billy Martin. "He won't have to be 'bad' Billy Martin fighting people anymore," Reggie said. "I'll open the road and let the others come thundering down the path."

It still wasn't over. When Ward went back to the clubhouse the next day to wrap it up, Reggie was eager to find out what the other players had said about him. Reggie always wants to know what people are saying about him. Munson, not unexpectedly, had denied there was any problem, any struggle for leadership, any jealousy.

You see, the guys like Catfish Hunter who are secure, aren't worried about me. But guys like Munson. . . . It's really a comedy, isn't it? I mean, it's hilarious. Listen, I always treat him right. I talk to him all the time, but he is so jealous and nervous and resentful that he can't stand it. If I wanted to I could snap him. Just wait until I get hot and hit a few out, and the reporters start coming around, and I have New York eating out of the palm of my hand . . . he won't be able to stand it.

Perhaps, Ward suggested, it was Reggie's verbal ability that put the other players off. Made them feel inferior.

But you know, the rest of the guys should know that I don't feel that far above them. I mean, nobody can turn people on like I can, or do for a club the things I can do, but we are all still ballplayers. We should be able to get along. . . . I'm not going to allow the team to get divided. I'll do my job, give it all I got, talk to anybody. I think Billy will appreciate that.

Although people were saying that either he or Munson would be gone within two years, Reggie didn't want that. "Because, after all is said and done, Munson is a winner, he's a fighter, a hell of a ballplayer . . . but don't you see . . . don't you see that there is just no way I can play second fiddle to *anybody*? Hah! That's just not in the cards. There ain't no way!"

But the "myriad of personalities" is also an emotional kaleidoscope. Shake him, and he comes out different. Two weeks later the man who couldn't play second fiddle was telling *Newsday*'s Steve Jacobson that it was his job to blend into the team, "not for the club to blend with me."

The way Reggie saw it now, Steinbrenner had pressured him into making the wrong decision. "I didn't have time to consider my personality. Where I'd fit in best socially, what sort of players I'd fit in with."

He longed for the days in Oakland when they had all been young together and where he had had real emotional support from Joe Rudi, a quiet and solid man, as different from Reggie as it is possible for a man to be, but always the good friend to whom he could weep unashamedly. In Oakland, Reggie said, he had been the Big Guy, the accepted leader. "When you have that relationship on a team, it gives you a feeling of being home. It takes a lot of the pressure off you, gives you a feeling of security, of sharing. Sharing—that's what man's all about."

The best clue to his frame of mind was that he began to talk about the existence of a clause in his contract that gave him the right to demand that the Yankees trade him after two years. He hadn't played a game for the Yankees yet, and he was looking for an escape. "If I can't relate to the people off the field, then I'm not going to stay there. I'm

96

not sure I want to play five more years anyhow." There was no escape clause in his contract.

Reggie and Jacobson had driven out to the fishing pier in Fort Lauderdale for the interview, so that Reggie, who is an ardent photographer, could shoot some pictures of the sea gulls taking wing. "Birds have a sense of freedom I admire. They're loners. I'm a loner. Look at me. Watch me."

To most of us, a loner says, "Don't look at me. Don't watch me." But to Reggie, it's standing alone in a pool of light and proving, once again, how great he is. Look at me. Watch me. Love me.

What the sea gulls had at the moment that Reggie most admired was a built-in escape clause. They could fly away.

And still he couldn't bring himself to talk about the fear that was consuming him. What if he had lost it? What if his body failed him, with the whole world looking on?

When he came to New York to start the season, he told his close friends, "The New York press to me is like a cobra in the jungle, always ready to attack."

The six unsigned Yankees at the start of the 1977 season were Sparky Lyle, Chris Chambliss, Dock Ellis, Oscar Gamble, Roy White, and Fred Stanley. There were also two others who wanted their contracts renegotiated—Thurman Munson and Graig Nettles—and there was the shining example of Mickey Rivers, who didn't care what they did about his contract so long as they kept giving him money.

Even before the opening of camp, Gabe Paul had begun announcing that in the new order of things, there were those who gained and those who got hurt. Those who thereby numbered themselves among the injured weren't taking the situation quite so philosophically. In the new order of things, they wanted theirs.

Dock Ellis, that wondrous creature, had it nailed. It had reached the point, Dock confided, where he had found himself cursing his sister for the first time in his life.

Dock had signed for $80,000 upon coming to the Yankees a year earlier, on the understanding that he would be amply rewarded if he performed up to the club's expectations. Dock had performed beyond anybody's expectations, winning 17 games as the Yankees were winning the pennant by 10½ games. But when he informed his sister that they wanted him to sign for a paltry $350,000 over a three-year period, she had squealed, "Get the money, Dock. That's a lot they're offering you."

"I told her she sounded just like them," said Dock. "Hell, they ain't ever gonna run dry."

It's really too bad that Dock had to go early in 1977. Dock would have added that one extra dash of spice that would have made the mixture of that bizarre season perfect. The first day Steinbrenner was in camp, he walked into the clubhouse and spotted Dock in front of his locker wearing his earring. George had never seen a ballplayer wearing an earring before. (But who had? Dock always was a man before his time. Like when he became the first player to appear on a baseball field—well, lolling on the dugout steps, anyway—with his hair in curlers. And that was back in 1971 when he was the star pitcher for the World Champion Pittsburgh Pirates.)

George felt called upon to make a comment reflecting upon the virility of earring-wearers, and Dock snapped back, "Watch it, motherfucker, or I'll wear this earring on the field. The only reason I don't do it now is that I don't want to rock your little boat." When George shouted back that he wouldn't wear it a second time, Dock screamed, "Okay, motherfucker, get ready to trade me. Let's get it on. I'm going to kill you through the papers."

So Dock Ellis went to war. "That's when I became hostile," he later confided. "I will be the hanger, not the hangee."

As his opening shot, Dock informed the press that as much as he loved Billy Martin, he was not going to do any more running in training camp. The Yankees returned fire by announcing they were renewing his contract with a twenty percent pay cut, as they had a right to do under the old option clause. Dock came back with a communiqué that he was withholding diplomatic recognition from any such unilateral action.

Dock and the other recalcitrants just weren't listening to Gabe Paul. "There's a new reserve system," Gabe was informing everyone. "We have taken the bad and realistically understand we must live with it. The players have to do the same thing. They can't have their cake and eat it, too."

Wanna bet?

Sparky Lyle arrived in camp late. But, then, Sparky always arrives late, and with two excellent reasons: he doesn't like training camp, and he does enjoy making an entrance. In 1975, when he chose to arrive on time, he had himself driven out onto the field with his arm and leg in a cast. He had two excellent reasons for doing that, too. The first was that it was the year of Catfish Hunter's highly publicized arrival, so Sparky knew that the field would be swarming with writers and television cameras; the second was that the helicopter he had hired to plop him down on the pitcher's mound, smack in the middle of all those television cameras, had canceled out on him.

Sparky came to the 1977 camp equipped with an ultimatum. There was going to be no nonsense about him playing out his option. He wanted a contract calling for $500,000 over three years, or he wanted to be traded. Until then, he told Gabe, he would not set foot on the ballfield. Paul came back with an offer of $250,000 for two years, and Sparky relented somewhat. He would pitch batting practice, he decided, but he would not work in a game.

A day after Sparky's pronunciamento, Billy sent word to the bullpen for Lyle to warm up. Lyle sent back word that he wasn't going to pitch in any exhibition games until he had a contract. "If they don't make a deal for me, I may not show up for opening day," he said. "I'm serious."

"I'm sick and tired of this bullshit," Paul said. "He's under contract, and we expect him to pitch." He pointed out again that the reserve system had changed and that there were pluses and minuses for the players. "He happens to be in one of the minus categories."

Sparky had an answer for that, too. And it was dead on target. During Steinbrenner's first year as owner of the Yankees he had made a locker room speech extolling the virtues of loyalty. "He told us to be loyal to him and he would be good to us. His loyalty went out the window. We helped him to win. I'm not using any specific player as an example, but as soon as a good player becomes available, there goes $2 million or $3 million to him. But the guys who won for him see very little of it."

A few days later, Sparky signed. Loyalty up or down had nothing to do with it. Guidry had been clobbered again, and Munson had advised George over breakfast that if he wanted to win a pennant he had better sign Sparky fast. George woke Lyle up from a sound sleep. How about $450,000 over three years? Sounded good enough to Sparky. "What the hell," he explained later. "I got a three-year contract and a wake-up call."

Two days after Sparky signed, Graig Nettles walked out of camp.

Nettles was galled. Reggie galled him, Reggie's contract galled him, and Reggie's message to the players who were so critical about all the money he was making must have galled him most of all. "Play out your option and take your chances," Reggie had been advising, "or shut the hell up."

Graig had, in fact, held out through the first half of the previous season before agreeing to a contract that would be paying him $140,000 for the next two years. Independent soul that he is, he had done his own negotiating, and unhappily he had done it all wrong.

To begin with, July is the wrong time to talk contract for a man who always has a terrible first half and a great second half. Worse still, Graig had been colder than usual during the first half of 1976 and hotter than usual the second half—so hot that he ended up leading the league in home runs. But beyond that, he obviously hadn't read the new Player Agreement. If he had waited two more weeks before signing, he would no longer have been bound by the reserve clause. So, in effect, he had bound himself to the Yankees for another year after the contract ran out. Worst of all, the contract was written to allow him to take his deferred payments whenever he wanted instead of setting up a schedule of payments that would have given him a huge tax break. Graig said that he had done it that way on George's advice. George said that Graig had insisted upon doing it his own way in the face of George's advice.

Whatever, Graig got himself a top agent for 1977 and tried to get the contract changed. When you look back on it, he really didn't seem to be asking for much: He wanted the contract extended for the same $140,000 over two more years, and he wanted the clause on the deferred payments rewritten so that he wouldn't get killed on the taxes.

George wouldn't talk to his agent.

"They don't want to take care of some of us who made the Yankees a good team," Nettles complained, as Lyle had. "It seems the guys who make money are the flamboyant, controversial guys. On this club, at least. Maybe I should pull something controversial."

The worst mistake he could have made. What Graig didn't seem to realize is that controversial people are born, not made. Promptly upon Graig's walking out of camp, Gabe Paul announced that he would be fined $500 a day. "We're in a time of reevaluation in baseball," he said, yet again. "Now we're left with the residue. A lot of players benefited. Some didn't." George Steinbrenner leaped at the opportunity to make a test case out of Nettles. "If Graig's not there on opening day, we'll go after damages to our ballclub. A contract is a contract. A player has got to realize that."

None of his teammates expressed the slightest sympathy for Graig. Nor did any of the writers. The prevailing opinion was that, okay, looking back it was a bad contract, but nobody had been holding a gun to his head when he signed it.

Only Billy Martin was willing to speak up for him. "He just wants to talk to the man," Billy reminded everybody. "The man doesn't want to talk to him."

Billy put himself solidly behind both Nettles and Ellis, and in the process he defined the issue that was threatening to wreck his team. "Baseball had better find a cure for how it's going to pay money, because it's getting to be a cancer. The free agent gets it all. One guy they don't want to pay nothing because he's too old; another guy, they don't want to give him nothing because they don't like him."

Nettles was in a no-win situation, and Steinbrenner was eager to stick it to him. "He made a bad business deal," Steinbrenner blared, "and he's going to abide by his contract. He's going to understand the facts of life." If Graig realized he had been wrong, had made a mistake in leaving the team, George was willing to discuss the matter with him, but only within the confines of the contract. "He has to stand up like a man and admit he made a mistake," said Steinbrenner. Otherwise there would be no negotiations at all.

Two days later, Graig was back in camp, and now there was nothing to negotiate except the articles of surrender. "I understand Graig feels badly," George said, and quickly came to the point: "He feels he made a mistake. That's the only positive thing to come out of it, and it will make a better man out of him. When I'm convinced of that, there'll be no fine. I was really itching for this battle, and I really licked their tails. These guys can't go through life walking through obligations."

Later in the day a beaten and subdued Nettles handed out a printed statement in which he apologized for any embarrassment or inconvenience he had caused the Yankees.

Why, the reporters asked, had he come back?

"Because it was the right thing to do."

So leaving had been the wrong thing to do?

That far Graig wasn't willing to go. "I don't think I did the wrong thing in leaving."

Funny thing about how it all worked out. If Graig had got the extension he had walked out of camp to get, he would have been stuck. The next year, the final year of his contract, he got an extension that more than doubled the amount of money he had been asking.

"Does it make sense as a businessman to guarantee anybody $140,000 at the age of thirty-six or thirty-seven?" George had asked after Nettles walked out.

At the age of thirty-seven, in 1980, Graig was making $350,000. And at the end of 1981, Steinbrenner picked up the option for two more years. At the age of forty, Graig Nettles will be paid $500,000.

Mickey Rivers arrived in camp an hour late and didn't bother to put on his uniform, thereby taking a full paragraph away from Reggie Jax. Like Sparky Lyle, Mickey had an excellent excuse. "I didn't feel like coming out early," he said. "I work slow."

Mickey was upset because "they're pressuring me again." Billy Martin, Rivers let it be known, wanted him to take more pitches. Possibly because batting lead-off, Rivers had walked only twelve times in 590 times at bat in 1976. Billy also wanted him to take lessons in drag bunting, possibly because Mickey got down to first base faster than is humanly possible. Because of that speed, things happened when Mickey got on base. That, after all, was why he was batting lead-off, despite his disdain for the base on balls and his reluctance to bunt.

Mickey had no intention of changing. "I got my habits," he explained. "If they don't want my habits, then trade me. I ain't gonna work on my weaknesses because it don't do any good. I'm not gonna do nothing extra to please anybody but myself."

Don't laugh. Swinging at the pitches he swung at, and bunting when he felt like it, Mickey had hit .312 in 1976 and knocked in 67 runs. In the minds of most Yankee players, Mickey was the most valuable player on the team. He probably would have been voted MVP in the American League if he hadn't sat out the last month of the season with a minor shoulder injury. Even then, he had finished third in the voting.

Mickey Rivers doesn't even look like a ballplayer. He has the worst looking throwing motion this side of Vassar—a quick, short-armed jabbing motion. Instead of a follow-through, he has a follow-back, like a rifle's recoil, with his collarbones shooting straight back like wings. He comes up to the plate on the balls of his feet, as if it pains him beyond all endurance to touch the ground. Sparky Lyle always said that if he didn't know who Mickey was, "I'd figure he walked on coals for a living." Old Man Rivers. As he waits for the pitch, he doubles over and pushes the bat forward as if he is about to conk a butterfly upon its noggin. And then he hits the ball and—*whooooosh!*

Either Mickey didn't know how good he was or Mickey didn't care. But, then, Mickey had other problems. "If they want to change my habits," he said, "let them get rid of me. I signed my contract because I thought it would be best at the time, but I didn't really like it. I'm sorry I signed it."

As always, it came back to money with Mickey.

When the announcement of the Bonds-for-Rivers (and Figueroa) trade came into the press room during the winter meeting of 1975, everybody thought that Gabe Paul had gone crazy. A more reasonable explanation, with the passage of years, would seem to be that Gabe got lucky. Bonds had to be traded because Billy Martin wasn't going to play him. Mickey's greatest recommendation at that moment seemed to be that he was available. There was very little in Rivers' record to indicate that he was going to be the player he turned out to be.

Rivers was available because he was in trouble. That is, trouble in Debtor City. Mickey gambled, and Mickey had a fondness for wine, women, and song—not to mention rhinestone socks. Moreover, Mickey was a soft touch. In order to get some money from Mickey, there was only one thing you had to do. Ask for it.

Mickey was so deeply in debt, from so many unsuspected places, that there were cities the Yankees hesitated to bring him into. And now he had come to training camp with deeper problems than ever. His marriage was in trouble, and that's the most expensive trouble you can find. When Mickey dropped the word, first day in camp, that he was in no mood to be cooperative, he was imparting a message.

Gabe had signed him to a three-year contract calling for $100,000 the first year, graduated up to $125,000 the third. Not so great a contract, even though it had been necessary for Gabe to go through the whole routine, including threatening to quit, before George accepted it. But then, with Mickey the contract isn't the whole story. When Mickey gets moody, he loses interest. He doesn't run out hits or chase the ball in the field. Somewhere along the line, somebody decided that the way to get Mickey's mind back on the game was to advance him enough money to meet his more pressing obligations.

Very dangerous. Aha, says Mickey, so that's how it's done. You play your tail off and they say, "Way to go, Mickey." You drag yourself around and they give you money.

On his second day in camp, a happier Mickey Rivers confided that he had met with Billy and Gabe and no longer wanted to be traded. "We talked about things. We came to a conclusion, and I feel a lot better." And, yes, they now seemed to appreciate his habits.

Changing Mickey's habits had certainly not been a part of Gabe Paul's plans. Gabe is an old Branch Rickey man, and like all old Rickey men is forever quoting the Master. Fifty years ago, Gabe was at a meeting where the name of Joe Medwick, a future Hall of Famer who was tearing up the minor leagues, was first brought up. "He swings at bad balls," somebody complained. "Don't change him," Branch Rickey said. "I never forgot that," Gabe has been saying for decades. "A full bat is an empty mind" Rickey would say, and Gabe Paul has never forgotten that, either. People do what they do. People are what they are. The only thing that matters is talent. "Talent is so goddam hard to find that when you find it you handle whatever troubles come along with it. That's what we're getting paid for."

Mickey Rivers could be counted upon to give Yankee management plenty of chances to earn their pay. Two weeks into spring training, the Yankees were playing Los Angeles at Vero Beach. Having risen at dawn and made the 140-mile bus trip, Mickey hit a ground ball to lead off the game, dropped his bat, and walked wearily back to the bench. Immediately, Billy Martin took him out of the game. Mickey thought about that and decided Billy had just wanted to give another center fielder a chance to play.

"Is it possible the man can be punished and not even know it?" Reggie Jackson asked. "I wish I had that going for me."

For Billy Martin, there was the continuing problem of disciplining Mickey Rivers enough to satisfy the rest of the players without disciplining him so much that he lost Mickey. Fining him was out of the question—that would only exacerbate Mickey's financial problems and make him even more rebellious. Benching him wasn't a much better solution—you were losing your most valuable player.

What Billy did was to call Mickey's three best friends on the club together and tell them that Casey Stengel had never faced that kind of problem on the old Yankees, because the players could be counted upon to take an offending teammate out in the alley and handle it themselves. Mickey's buddies gave him a good talking to, and three days later, Billy had to pull him out of a game against the Phillies for loafing on two consecutive fly balls. First, Mickey allowed a line drive to bounce by him and kind of yawned after it. Then, he backed up for a fly ball, lifted his glove up without a great deal of interest, and watched the ball fall out. Martin allowed as how he had better find out whether anything was bothering Mickey. "He's one of the fastest guys in baseball, and he doesn't want to run."

In one of his earlier moods, Mickey had accused Martin of not being able to communicate with him—which was kind of funny in that Martin had been fired at Minnesota for "overcommunicating" (i.e. drinking with his players).

In this instance, Billy communicated with Mickey very well. Keep it up, he told him, and he was going to take him out in the alley himself and beat the hell out of him. The rest of the team, he warned him, couldn't understand why he hadn't done it last year.

"Me and Billy don't have any problems," Mickey said, afterward. "He's taken time to understand."

Maybe then, but not for long. Mickey's lassitude would resurface throughout the year. If Mickey was taken out of one game for loafing during the season, he was taken out of ten.

As much as this infuriated his teammates, they still got a tremendous kick out of him. Mickey was one of the most likable people in the world. And he made them laugh. He had his own highly imaginative names for everybody. Fishface. Gozzlehead. For Munson, the catcher, it was Armpit-Breath. "What's the matter with you, Armpit-Breath?"

Mickey had a mushy, slurred way of speaking that was very difficult to understand. Everything began with "Well-uh." His stock answer for almost anything was "Well-uh, let's not get rid-i-culous." When Luis Tiant joined the Yankees, Mickey appointed himself Tiant's interpreter, a task he carried off with great style by combining his almost unintelligible patter with a wholly undecipherable sign language.

Even Mickey's mood changes tickled his teammates. Mickey would come out of Martin's office after an ass-chewing session with his head down and mumbling to himself . . . *sumbitch* . . . *bastard* . . . while everybody was sneaking looks at him and each other, and grinning.

The Yankees' favorite Mickey Rivers story goes back to the spring of 1976, when Mickey was exchanging insults with Carlos May, clubhouse style, on their comparative dumbness. Mickey finally told him, "Well-uh, I got a higher IQ than you," which as insults go wasn't half bad.

"You can't even spell IQ," said Carlos.

He wasn't topped often, though. While nobody ever accused Mickey of having more intelligence than he really needed, he had a withering street humor and sharp native wit that made him a charter member of the select group that sat in the back of the bus and kept everybody loose. The one time Reggie Jackson decided to lend his own undoubted wit to the exchanges, he made the mistake of tangling with Rivers and discovered that vocabulary had nothing to do with it.

"Reggie fuckin' Martinez Jackson," Mickey said, bringing the first exchange to an end. "You got a white man's first name, a Spanish man's second name, and a black man's third name. No wonder you all fucked up, man. You don't know what the fuck you are."

A few minutes later, a bus with a black driver at the wheel came whizzing past. "There goes Rivers in five years," Jackson said, not about to give up, "driving a truck."

"Yeah," said Rivers, dead on target again. "But at least I'll be a happy truck driver."

"Listen to me," Reggie said, "arguing with a guy who can't read or write."

"You better stop fuckin' reading and writing," Mickey said, "and start fuckin' hitting."

As much as Mickey aggravated George Steinbrenner, George liked him, too. "Mickey is his own worst enemy," George would say. "He's a good person. He's got a good heart." That's what everybody said. The reason everybody said it was that it was true.

Even Mickey's wife must have thought so, inasmuch as their marriage, which was supposed to be breaking up, didn't . . . though clearly Mickey was driving her out of her mind.

There was, for instance, the day she lay in wait for him at the Yankee Stadium parking lot. As Mickey pulled in, Mrs. Rivers came roaring across the lot in her little brown Mercedes, rammed into the side of Mickey's Cadillac, backed off, and kept on ramming him, bouncing him off four other cars, like a regular demolition derby before she piled him up on the bumper of a fifth. Mickey's head was bouncing off the steering wheel every time the car got whacked, but she was still ramming him when Carlos May and Willie Randolph came running out. "You're killing him," May screamed as they reached in to stop her.

They carried Mickey into the trainer's room, and he lay there on the rubbing table holding an ice bag to his head and swallowing aspirin until the game was about to start. As each new player came in and heard the story, he would go back to the trainer's room to sneak a look at Mickey and hear the tale retold by somebody else. And each time Mickey would rise up, look at his chortling teammates and say, "Don't be talking my business, Fishface."

And then—ask anybody on the 1977 Yankees if what I'm about to say isn't true—Mickey went out and had one of his best days in a Yankee uniform. A double, a single, and a home run.

George may well have heard about Mrs. Rivers' rampage, because certain it is that he could not handle her any better than Mickey. (But, then, George may very well be one of those tyrants who can take on the toughest men in the world but goes to pieces in front of a strong woman.) Mrs. Rivers, who is a handsome woman, would come up to the Yankee office and demand to see him. She had bills to pay, she would tell him, and she wanted some of Mickey's money before he could get his hands on it and throw it away. George would tell her he was paying Mickey a handsome salary, and on top of that he had just given him another advance. "I don't care what you gave Mickey," she would say. "I didn't see any of it." And George would run into his office in a panic and have a check sent out to her. Five thousand . . . ten thousand . . . anything. Whatever she wants. Eventually George took to hiding in his office when she came. He seemed to be terrified of her.

After the season was over, George got Mickey an agent, Nick Buonaconti, to help him put his affairs in order.

Buonaconti began by putting Mickey on an allowance, and Mickey promptly fired Buonaconti.

Mickey Rivers was traded to Texas toward the end of the terrible year of 1979, when the whole championship team was unraveling. But George came so close to bringing him back in the spring of '81. . . .

Over the winter Mickey had rented a hall about a mile from Yankee Stadium, turned it into a discotheque, called in the press, and announced that he was throwing a party to let everybody know that he wanted to come back to New York. "This is the only place to play," he said, "and the Yankees are the only club to play for." A sentiment utterly calculated to strum upon the strings of George's heart.

But what Mickey really missed, he confided to his friends, was the New York racetracks. The only thing you could bet on in Texas, he had discovered, were the fuckin' cockfights.

The reports George was getting at the time said that Mrs. Rivers had succeeded in calming Mickey down, and so when it became clear that Ruppert Jones was not going to come back from his shoulder operation, Mickey became George's first choice to replace Jones and reclaim the Yankees' center field. George was right on the edge of closing a deal when Texas informed him that Mickey owed the club $100,000. Now, there is a rule in baseball that a player cannot be traded while he owes his current team money. And while there is no rule that says the team he is being traded to can't pay off the debt, George can be forgiven if he began to wonder just how calm and settled Mickey had become.

In 1977, Steinbrenner showed Thurman Munson a way, too. Only with Thurman they weren't talking about walking-around money.

Contrary to general suspicion, Thurman had not been at all unhappy about the signing of Reggie. He had been on the dais to represent the players when Don Gullett was introduced to New York, and he had answered the call to the colors once again when Reggie came swinging in on his star a couple of weeks later. Cap'n Munson was being such a good soldier that he even went along with the story that it was he who had advised Steinbrenner that if George was going to spend all that money he should be spending it on Reggie Jackson, not Bobby Grich.

But maybe save a little of it for Thurman? Munson had signed his contract for 1977, after the Messersmith decision came down, on the understanding that he would always be the highest-paid Yankee with the exception of Catfish Hunter, who was already under contract. When Ken Holtzman was signed, Thurman's salary was raised from $120,000 to $165,000, on a four-year contract which was going to be paying him $275,000 by the final year. After Jackson came aboard six months later, Munson signed yet another contract, this time for $200,000, with appropriate adjustments up the line. If Thurman had a sneaking suspicion that George wasn't being entirely truthful about what Reggie's salary was, he soon found out that he was right. In addition to the $200,000, Reggie was getting another $132,000 in deferred payments. The only thing that was so surprising was that Thurman hadn't known about it before he signed the new contract. It was in all the papers.

Thurman signed his new contract in January, and promptly went up to Canada, where he dropped word to a sportscaster that he was either going to buy out his contract or ask to be traded if George didn't keep his promise.

George's reaction was to put in a frantic phone call asking Thurman to fly right back to New York and issue a formal press release stating that the story wasn't true. Great little campaigner that he was, Thurman came back, issued no press release, and signed yet another contract. It still wasn't up to Reggie's, but at least Thurman was getting there. It was the third contract he had signed in six months, all with good raises, and this time he was also getting a big chunk of money up front.

Again, as with the other contract signings, Munson stipulated that he was not going to be satisfied until George lived up to his word. And not being satisfied meant that he was going to attack George in the public prints, at every opportunity.

Munson's war was very different from Dock Ellis's war. Munson sniped away at George constantly, both on and off the record, but he maintained a relationship with him too. (Of course, the amount of time George and Thurman spent together just signing contracts constituted a relationship in itself.) Thurman was a budding businessman with holdings in real estate and shopping centers, and he liked to go up to George's office, put his shoes up on the desk, and get the benefit of his advice. George would assure him that he had some great properties, while to others, including any passing writer who might happen to ask, he would chuckle that Thurman was a great baseball player who thought he was a smart businessman but wasn't. "Anybody can buy property. The thing that makes it a good or bad investment is how much of it is mortgaged. Thurman has more debt than the rest of the ballclub put together. If he thinks he can get along without his baseball salary, he's crazy."

There is a chain of command in baseball—or at least there used to be—and when it comes to the privileges of command, Billy Martin is a great believer in the way it used to be. Before a player goes to the front office, he's supposed to let the manager know. Otherwise, it's known as "walking up the back stairs."

Thurman wouldn't exactly ask Billy's permission, but he was always careful to stick his head into his manager's office and call out, "Anything for your pal up there, the Shithead? Anything I should tell him?"

And if, while Thurman was up there, the talk did move to the disarray in the clubhouse, why not? As team captain, he had an official position, and as a ballplayer with a burning desire to win, he could not be insensitive to "the deplorable conditions" that were threatening to keep the Yankees out of another World Series.

There was never any question, however, where Munson's loyalty lay in any confrontation between his manager and his owner. Thurman may have been somewhat disenchanted with Billy Martin, but he hated George Steinbrenner. "He lied to me," Thurman would say. "He made a fool of me." First, George had denied to him that he had ever made the promise to keep him the highest-paid Yankee and, after Thurman went public, he had denied it to the press.

Thurman Munson was a truck driver's son from Canton, Ohio, and he wanted what was his. The only thing worse than to be lied to and made a fool of, in Thurman's view, was to be looked upon as a man who would allow himself to be lied to and made a fool of.

There were strong parallels between Munson and Steinbrenner. Thurman's father had also been a harsh, unyielding German. George's father, Henry Steinbrenner, according to George, was a man incapable of showing love. The elder Steinbrenner had ridiculed his son's preoccupation with sports until he pulled off the coup of the decade with his purchase of the Yankees. "The first smart thing you've ever done," the Old Man told him.

Nothing Thurman had done had ever been able to please his father. It was Thurman's older brother who was supposed to be the athlete of the family, and Thurman was always being compared to him unfavorably. Let Thurman get five hits in a college ballgame and his father would tell him how pitiful he had looked on his one error.

Thurman's father, the long-haul truck driver from Ohio who went off on a long haul one day and never came back, was the other powerful man who had "lied" to him and made a fool of him.

Thurman Munson campaigned for what he thought was his all through 1977, and, as the season was coming to an end, he began to talk about how he wanted to play out his career in Cleveland where he could be close to his wife and three children.

Following the second game of the World Series, Thurman and his wife came into a steak house and found Gabe Paul sitting with a party of about half a dozen people. Gabe invited them over for a drink. "I don't want to drink with you, Gabe," Thurman said. "I love you, but I won't play another year for Steinbrenner. He lied to me, and I won't play for him."

After the Series, Thurman was still saying that he would not be back the following season under the existing conditions. His buddy, Sparky Lyle, would tell writers, "Thurman doesn't want to go to Cleveland, he just wants you guys to write that there's no way Cleveland could give up enough to get him unless they give away their whole ballclub." Well, Sparky had a piece of it there, but only a piece.

There were promises that had been made to Thurman.

Before the '78 season he signed yet another contract, and with another big chunk of money up front. He came into camp, refused to talk to the writers, and was given still *another* contract. Even when, in July of 1978, Munson did finally reveal that he had achieved something like parity with Reggie Jackson, he remained unhappy.

Yes, he growled, the contract was satisfactory. "The way it should have been before I was disgraced for two years." No, he snapped, it didn't help his attitude. "Are material things supposed to help a guy who's had these things eating at him for two years?"

He had been embarrassed. "It was very difficult for me to come back. In the matter of self-respect, it was very difficult. I still don't feel good toward myself."

A very difficult man to satisfy. He had been MVP one year and captain of the World Champions the next. He had forced Steinbrenner to give him the contract he wanted. In the World Championship season he had become the first catcher in the entire history of baseball to hit .300 and knock in 100 runs for three straight years.

And, to top it off, he was a happily married man, who boasted constantly of his beautiful wife and three children.

You look at Thurman and you say: You've got it all. You're in the books, you're rich, you've got a great family, and you beat the bastards down. What the hell more do you want?

And Thurman answers: But what about the way it should have been?

7

THE CRISES BEGIN

Billy Martin was fired for the first time a week before the end of spring training, after the Mets had shut out the Yankees 6–0 in St. Petersburg, in a game that was telecast back to New York.

But it was more than just the loss of the ballgame. Billy's troubles went back through the whole disorganized 1977 training season.

George had been screaming all along that the team wasn't prepared to open the season. And not without reason. Billy had always run a loose training camp, but this camp had been, well-uh, rid-i-cu-lous. And for a great deal of that laxness, George had only himself to blame.

Billy Martin's marriage had broken up, and he was living a bachelor life several miles away in Boca Raton with his buddy Mickey Mantle. So he would drive to the practice field every morning, not always on time and not always without a lady companion. Gabe Paul had told him at the beginning that the team couldn't stand that kind of thing, had in fact instructed him to move back into Fort Lauderdale and stay with the team and ride on the team bus. Whereupon Billy went over Gabe's head to Steinbrenner, and George, being the great guy that he is, told Billy that it was perfectly okay, boys will be boys, enjoy.

With the team going so rotten, George was no longer in a mood to be so indulgent. "Preparation" is a favorite Steinbrenner word. The football man, again. Statistical breakdowns, tendencies, fundamentals. It was time to "tighten the screws." The boatman. But most of all,

112

George wanted Billy on the practice field on time, and he wanted him on the team bus with the players.

Well, it was no great issue. The team was living in Tampa now, and Billy was living with them. But, still, he liked to drive back and forth from the ballpark with his coaches, so he could talk things over while the coaches made notes.

When George came striding toward the clubhouse after the Mets game, he was ripping mad. The Yankees had not only lost, they had been shut out. Instead of starting Reggie, as Billy had promised to, he had sent him in late in the game as a pinch hitter. Instead of playing the starting lineup all the way, as George had instructed him to, he had finished with a team of substitutes.

But if you want to know what George was really furious about, it was that he had discovered during the game that Billy had driven to the ballpark in a rental car.

Half the players were already in the bus when George came striding toward the clubhouse with Gabe. The first thing the players heard was George scream, "I don't give a fuck. This shit has got to stop right now. Do you hear me, Gabe? I've got to stop it right now!"

Into the clubhouse he stormed, a wild man. "I want to talk to you right now!" he shouted at Billy. "You lied to me!"

Billy knew exactly what was coming. "I don't want to hear it," he shouted back. "I don't want to hear that shit anymore."

"You heard what I said! That thing is going to stop right now!"

"You fat bastard, I don't give a shit what you say. I'm going to do it my way."

"You lied to me! You told me you were going to ride on the bus."

"Fuck you, I'm not riding on no fucking buses. Get the fuck out of here."

"Hey," Gabe Paul said, "hey, watch yourself, Billy. . . ." Gabe has lifted a glass or two in his time, and when he gets excited, his nose turns bright red. "Don't," he said, as he placed himself between them. "Billy, don't. . . ."

George was back near the wall, about ten feet away, staring at Billy incredulously. "What did you say?" he muttered, as if he couldn't bring himself to credit what he was hearing. "What did you say?"

"Billy," Gabe was saying, "don't talk to him like that."

"Then *you* can tell that fat bastard to go fuck himself. Hear me? He can go fuck himself!"

This time George heard him. "You don't talk to me like that, god-dammit! You don't ever talk to me like that!"

"I'll talk to anybody like that," Billy said. He turned and went striding into the trainer's room, with George and Gabe right behind him. Everybody was ordered out. The door slammed shut. The screaming went on.

George was yelling that Billy had lied to him. And not only about the bus. He had promised to play the starting team all the way.

"Don't tell me how to manage my ball team, you lying sonofa-bitch," Martin yelled back. "I'm the manager, and I'll manage how I want to manage. It was an *exhibition* game!" An ex-hib-i-tion game. "This is not a game where you leave your blood and guts on the field to win." It was a game where you prepared yourself for a winning season, where you tried things. "There are things I have to find out *now!*"

He should have already found them out, George yelled. That was what he had been telling him all along! The season was beginning in a week, and he didn't have the team ready.

They were on opposite sides of the trainer's table, shuffling back and forth, and as Billy was shouting back that you didn't prepare for a 162-game baseball season the way you prepared for a 10-game football season, his fist went slamming into the big bucket of ice in which the pitchers soaked their elbows, the ice cubes and the water went splashing all over George, and George went into total rage. "I ought to fire you!" he screamed. He was wiping off his face, digging ice cubes out of his pockets.

"You want to fire me, fire me! But leave me the fuck alone."

George sent for Coach Yogi Berra and offered him Billy's job on the spot. "You're the manager," he said.

Yogi is not one of your more excitable men. "Now take it easy, George," he counseled. "Billy's a good manager. You don't want to go doing anything because you're mad now."

"The job is yours!" George yelled.

When they came out of the trainer's room, Billy was very sub-dued. It must have been some drive back to town in the rental car, because as of that moment Billy was fired.

The next morning they got together in Gabe's room for breakfast, and Billy was un-fired. From then on, Billy rode in the bus. And he never yelled at George in public again. But whenever Billy expected to be fired during the season, he would tell the writers that from the moment those ice cubes hit George's face, he knew that his days as the manager of the New York Yankees were numbered.

Be that as it may, it was Gabe Paul who wanted to fire him the next time around and George Steinbrenner who saved him.

Billy Martin had been George Steinbrenner's idea all along. Gabe Paul certainly didn't want him, and indeed there are a lot of reasons baseball men could give for not hiring Billy Martin. "You know, Billy bends an elbow," they would say. Or, "Billy's trouble." Well, Gabe bent an elbow too. And trouble was what Gabe was being paid to handle, right?

But Billy brought a particular kind of trouble with him—the one kind of trouble you were least looking for if you were a general manager. Billy was going to move in on you. Billy wanted a voice in player decisions. Billy wanted a piece of your territory. Or, to look at it through Billy's eyes, Billy thought you had a piece of his territory. There was such an intensity in the way Billy went about asserting his claims as to leave the impression that he had to have a corner of that front office in order to protect himself.

Billy's world was a world of betrayal. Wherever he had been, he had whomped up an enemy for himself in the front office and presented himself as Billy the Blameless. It had happened in Minnesota, it had happened in Detroit, and it had happened in Texas. Bob Short, who hired him in Texas, admired him so much that he gave him what he had always wanted, total control. But Short had been forced to sell, and with the new group Billy was just the manager again. They wanted him to come in every day and talk to the club officials and stockholders. Billy wouldn't do that.

Sooner or later, Billy was going to make a run at Gabe, nothing personal. It happened in May, right after Gabe returned to work following his collapse.

The Yankees had come back from their miserable start in 1977 and gone into first place by beating the weak West Coast teams seven games out of eight at Yankee Stadium. They were heading out to the West Coast for another seven games, with every prospect of building up their lead.

It didn't quite work out that way. The Yankees made only two Western trips all year—one in May and the other in August—and both of them were disasters, particularly for Billy Martin, who just barely managed to escape with his job both times.

The May trip started with Reggie Jackson hitting a two-run

homer in his first time at bat in Seattle's new Kingdome Stadium, making it the eighteenth major-league ballpark in which he had homered. Throughout the rest of the trip he had one infield single in twenty-five times at bat, and suffered the ignominy of being benched upon his return to Oakland, the city in which he had spent the glory years of his career.

For Billy, it was all downhill, too. It just happened to him quicker. His ballclub kicked the first two games away against the terrible Seattle club. On the third day they were in Anaheim, and it was on that day that he was almost fired for the second time.

The first Seattle game was lost on errors, weak throwing arms in the outfield, and a pop fly that fell between Mickey Rivers and Bucky Dent. It was the kind of fly that is usually the responsibility of the center fielder, but Mickey always had a tendency to get moody on the West Coast trips, presumably because he had left a lot of bills behind him. Billy pulled him out of the next game, in Seattle, and again in the next, in Anaheim. "I wanted to use Blair," Billy snapped to the inquisitive writers. "Period. I don't have to explain why I use guys."

To listen to Martin, what really seemed to be bothering him was that he had not had a left-handed pinch hitter to use in Seattle when the Yankees had runners on first and third base with one out in the seventh, and were behind by only a run. "I want Elrod Hendricks brought up," he fumed. "I need three catchers plus a left-handed pinch hitter. I've been asking for Elrod for a week and a half. But George and Gabe think I'm kidding. Why are we going with twenty-four players? Are we that great? It cost us tonight's game as far as I'm concerned."

Elrod Hendricks was at the time playing for the Yankees' farm team, Syracuse—a thirty-six-year-old catcher with a lifetime average of .218. And Billy did have a left-handed hitter on the bench in George Zeber.

No, the issue wasn't a left-handed-hitting pinch hitter, the issue was turf. In addition to being a spare catcher and pinch hitter, Hendricks was, to all practical purposes, another coach. Billy Martin's coach. Hendricks had come to the Yankees as one of the five players in the Holtzman deal after playing on the Baltimore championship teams. In addition to being a sound baseball man, he had a happy, sunny personality that made him extraordinarily valuable as Billy's emissary in the clubhouse. He had served Earl Weaver in that capacity also, and Weaver had advised him to play out his option with the Yankees so that he could come back to Baltimore as a player-coach, a galling reminder to Martin that Weaver, his arch-rival, had privileges in Baltimore that Billy did not have in New York. To make it more galling still, Billy couldn't even lodge a protest against what would seem to be a clear case of tampering by Weaver without hurting Hendricks, and that was something Billy didn't want to do.

The Yankee front office had sent Elrod back to Syracuse to clear a place on the roster for a rookie pitcher named Ed Ricks, on precisely the same day they were trading away Billy's other emissary in the clubhouse, Dock Ellis. Billy had then refused to use Ed Ricks, who had been kept around only so the Yankees wouldn't have to waste one of their regular pitchers in the upcoming Mayor's Trophy Game. That game, as it happened, was to be played on the same day that Gabe Paul was returning to the stadium.

The Mayor's Trophy Game was rained out, so Billy didn't come to the stadium that day. But during a long telephone conversation with Gabe, Martin asked for the return of Hendricks. Gabe had other plans for filling that spot. While he had been recuperating in Tampa, he had opened negotiations with Texas for a 2–1 deal involving the seldom-used Ken Holtzman. The Yankees would be getting Johnny Ellis and Ken Henderson. Ellis would solve the right-handed-DH problem and become the second-string catcher, and Henderson would give Billy a good left-handed bat and another excellent outfielder. (A hell of a deal. It didn't go through in the end, only because Ken Holtzman, who had the right of approval, turned it down.)

The next day was an off-day for travel, and Gabe told Billy to come to the office before he left and they would work out something that would settle the Hendricks matter to Billy's satisfaction.

Billy didn't show up. Instead, he seized upon a situation that arose in the very next game to carry his battle on in the press. On the following day he picked it up again.

The Yankees had lost that one too, on pure merit. Five errors in the first three innings, one of them by Thurman Munson. Munson was hurting. In addition to the error, there had been three stolen bases against him, and he had taken himself out of the game in the seventh inning with a cramp in his calf after a weak effort at running out a double play. "His legs have been bothering him for a week," Martin said. "I need him for the whole year, not for one game."

Billy was back to Elrod Hendricks again, and this time with Munson to help him. "I can't visualize a major-league team without three catchers," Thurman said. "All I know is I'm not thrilled with what's going on. We have so much talent, we ought to go out and just love to play. Sometimes a millionaire will magnify your problems because he's frustrated all the time."

Whether the millionaire he was talking about was George Steinbrenner or Aristotle Onassis, he didn't say.

Since Fran Healy, the second-string catcher, almost never got into a game, the writers wanted to know why was it so important to have a third-string catcher?

Billy Martin had the answer to that one all prepared. A year earlier, when he'd had three catchers, Martin had been able to give Munson a chance to rest his legs by using him as the DH. If he used Munson as DH with only two catchers and then had to pinch-hit for Healy, Munson would have to go back behind the plate and, the way the designated-hitter rule was written, the pitcher would have to bat for himself. Not very persuasive. In the unlikely event that situation ever came up, there was nothing to prevent Billy from using another pinch hitter.

Billy was making an issue. And he was making his stand against the front office as he had throughout his career: over a player of almost no consequence. During the off-season he had fought Gabe Paul over the trading of Sandy Alomar, a utility infielder. Billy's break with Minnesota had come when he attacked the farm director for sending a minor-league pitcher, Dick Woodson, to a AA farm club after Martin had told him he would be going to AAA. He had lost the job at Texas, in the end, over an identical dispute over a third-string catcher, Jack Egan. Billy had told Egan he'd be brought back. The front office wouldn't do it.

What was it about Billy? The conventional wisdom back then was that Billy had a death wish. But that didn't answer it. If you're fighting with the front office for a piece of the turf, who else is there to argue about except the twenty-fifth player? And that isn't the whole of it.

Billy believes that one of the basic tenets of leadership is that you can't have loyalty unless you give loyalty—that's what he says, anyway. What he really believes in is drawing the wagons in a circle. Us against them. He wants his players to know that he will fight for them—on the field, with the press, and with the front office. If he was willing to risk his job by fighting for the least among them, how could any of the others doubt that he would also fight for them?

It wasn't just in popping off about Hendricks that Billy had challenged the front office. He had set up the confrontation a day earlier by breaking the appointment with Paul. Think about this for a second: In talking to Gabe over the phone for two and a half hours, Billy had discovered that there was still a noticeable slur in Gabe's speech. Now, it is not entirely impossible that Billy had interpreted the slur as a sign that Gabe was never going to be able to function at full capacity again. Gabe was, after all, sixty-seven years old and, remember, Steinbrenner had gone out of his way to ridicule him even before he was stricken. If Gabe wasn't going to be able to hack it anymore, there was going to be a power vacuum in the Yankee front office, and Billy may well have been moving in to stake out his claim.

If so, it was a very serious miscalculation, almost a fatal one. Gabe had never believed that the Jackson-Martin-Steinbrenner mix was going to work, and his prediction of disaster had been borne out from the first day of spring training. Since you couldn't fire Jackson, the only thing left was to get rid of Martin, and here Billy Martin had handed them this marvelous opportunity to fire him on the old familiar grounds. No sweat, no repercussions, no recriminations from the press and the fans.

George Steinbrenner, however, saw it somewhat differently. As far as George was concerned, they had anticipated that this kind of thing was going to happen sooner or later, and he saw it as the perfect opportunity to make Billy understand that taking on the front office was going to be a losing proposition in every way. Martin, after all, was Steinbrenner's manager. All through the winter he had been boasting that he, George Steinbrenner, was going to do what nobody else had ever been able to do: lead Billy Martin through a second successful season, "make a man out of him."

The compromise George and Gabe agreed upon was to hit Billy with the stiffest fine ever levied by a ballclub against its manager—if, indeed, any club had ever fined its manager before. But that was only the first part. In order to show Billy and everybody else that Gabe was still firmly in command, George was going to fade into the background and leave the disciplinary process entirely in Gabe's hands.

Gabe Paul's phone call found Billy Martin in the lobby of the hotel in Anaheim, across from the wonderful world of Disneyland. The message Billy got, slurred though it may have been, was blunt enough to bring forth an anguished "Gabe, if you want to have a winner, you've got to leave me alone. You've got to stop harassing me."

Gabe then called publicity man Mickey Morabito, a one-time Yankee bat boy who was catching all this flak in his first year on the job, to dictate a statement for the press. It started as a routine announcement that Dell Alston, a left-handed-hitting outfielder, was being brought up from Syracuse, and went on to make the point that Alston was hitting .338 with 11 stolen bases in 19 games while Hendricks was hitting .105. And then it stopped being routine: "Certain comments directed at Mr. Steinbrenner, the club's principal owner, by manager Billy Martin concerning the alleged failure to add a twenty-fifth player are totally inaccurate and unfounded." And went on to say, in part: "Martin was asked to report to my office on May 10 prior to the club leaving for Seattle, and at such time the determination of the twenty-fifth player was to be made. He agreed to be there. However, Billy failed to show up for the meeting with me. If we had that conversation as scheduled, the twenty-fifth player would have been added and the matter would have been settled then and there. . . . Frankly, if we have to depend on a player batting .105 at Syracuse to enable us to beat an expansion team, with the kind of talent that has been provided, we are indeed in bad trouble. The reason for the two losses in Seattle was strictly a matter of too many errors in the field and inconsistent pitching."

The $2,500 fine was never officially announced, it just kind of leaked out from both coasts. Reggie Jackson, having apparently counted the hundred-dollar bills in his wallet and found them all present and accounted for, said, "I'll pay it for Billy."

Even though Billy's calls to Steinbrenner weren't being returned, he was still being mildly defiant. "I should know what the needs of the ballclub are a lot more than Gabe Paul," he maintained. His principal need, he said again, was to protect Thurman Munson.

"A lot of clubs have gone with two catchers," Paul pointed out. "Cincinnati went with two all last year, and they had a pretty good season." If anything happened to Munson, he said, Hendricks was only twenty-four hours away.

"I've got no recourse," Billy admitted finally. "I'll just accept it. It's their team. I'll manage what they give me." And by the time he had got to the ballpark, he had retreated to "For the good of the Yankees, no comment." By then, of course, he just might have received a call from George Steinbrenner telling him that if he embarrassed the ballclub one more time, he was gone.

But Billy is irrepressible. When Dell Alston arrived the next morning, Billy had his no-comment sharpened to the point of a serpent's tooth. "I'm like a submarine being attacked by depth charges. Complete silence, and I'm cruising on batteries."

No controversy was going to end silent and submerged on the 1977 Yankees, and the Hendricks Flap was no exception. On the very next night, Thurman Munson got hit with not one but two foul tips. The first one slammed down on his foot, leaving it badly swollen, the other left a bruise on his right wrist. To make matters even more uncomfortable for the battered backstop, he had to drag himself back to the park the following morning for a Sunday afternoon game. "They" wanted him to play, he snarled after he had taken a couple of pain-killers. "Don't I always play? But I'm not going to kill myself. If they think I'm going to catch 160 games, they're crazy."

The next day was Billy Martin's forty-ninth birthday, and in honor of the occasion Thurman Munson decided to take the day off. That got him into great shape to play the final game of the road trip, a fifteen-inning pitching duel, as it turned out, between Ron Guidry and Vida Blue. Who do you think scored the winning run in that one, finally? Dell Alston. Billy sent him to the plate as a pinch hitter to open the fifteenth inning, and in his first time at bat in the major leagues Alston doubled.

If that made Gabe Paul look good, Billy said, it was all right with him. He still wasn't backing off on anything he had said about the need for another catcher.

Fine or no fine, the Hendricks issue simply wouldn't die. Having arisen on the first day after the Yankees had left New York, it flared back to life again on the second day of their return. Baltimore's Lee May came barreling into home plate with the go-ahead run just as Munson was reaching for the throw, and there lay Thurman Munson flat on his back with a badly jammed hand and a sliced index finger. Munson remained in the game long enough to come to bat in the last of the inning. He had been on a hitting tear. In the opening game of the home stand, he had knocked in four runs with a homer, triple, and single. In this game, he already had a double and two singles to run his streak to six out of seven. He made it seven out of eight by pounding out another double, and then retired to have three stitches put in his hand.

Fran Healy came in to replace him, and wouldn't you know that Billy's Third Man Theme would come rising out of the orchestra pit with him. The music started when Dell Alston—who else?—came to the plate as a pinch hitter with one out in the bottom of the eighth and promptly got himself another double. The next batter was Willie Randolph, with Mickey Rivers and then Fran Healy waiting in the wings. On the mound for Baltimore was a right-hander.

Randolph grounds out, and the scene is set. Earl Weaver, well aware that Martin cannot pinch-hit for Healy, deliberately violates one of the basic precepts of managing and orders his pitcher to put Rivers on base with the potential winning run. And naturally Fran Healy grounds out.

"I'll tell you this," Weaver said afterwards. "If Elrod Hendricks was sitting there, we would have found out what Rivers could have done."

Billy Martin, dealing with the same question, was as discreet as it was possible for Billy Martin to be. "The last time I said anything about that," he answered, "it cost me money. No, I don't want a third catcher." And then he lifted his eyes to heaven to ask forgiveness for telling such lies.

Gabe Paul had already wired Syracuse for Elrod Hendricks. Elrod was in the clubhouse the next day. "He's not on the roster" was the way Mickey Morabito explained it. "He's in a holding pattern."

If he was needed, he could be activated instantly. In the meantime, he could function as Martin's unofficial coach and emissary to the clubhouse. Which, as it happens, was precisely the solution that Gabe Paul had intended to present to Martin in the meeting Billy hadn't bothered to come to.

Billy had his Elrod Hendricks. Hendricks never had to be activated.

It was the one time during the season where it was Gabe Paul who wanted to fire Billy and Steinbrenner who moved in to save him. On June 20, one month from the day the Hendricks Flap was resolved, George came flying into Detroit determined to fire his manager, and this time it was Gabe who saved Billy. Not because Gabe's opinion had changed, but because he believed that to fire Billy at that particular moment would blow the Yankees apart.

Billy's third crisis had come about as the result of the brawl with Reggie Jackson on the bench in Boston. To fire Billy over that, Gabe felt, would be tantamount to making Reggie Jackson the manager.

8

BOSTON:
THE UNHANDSHAKE AND
THE BRAWL

I'm not going to argue with anybody about this, but there is no rivalry in the great wide world of sports to compare with the Yankees versus the Red Sox. It's the gracious expanse of Yankee Stadium versus the looming Green Monster of Fenway Park. The Power and the Glory of the New York Yankees versus the never-ending Challenge of the Boston Red Sox. There are ghosts on the field when these teams meet, a history that speaks of great deeds and sleeping heroes. And don't think it doesn't communicate itself to the players on the field. The fielding is crisper, the hitting is firmer, the ball comes shooting off the bat with the fresh, clean *poing* of another opening day. Baseball becomes again what baseball is supposed to be, a game of shifting fortunes within a series of steadily rising climaxes—an excitement, an entertainment, an event.

And even if expansion had reduced the games between the two teams from twenty-two to fifteen, it didn't matter. The schedule makers had done their work so well that when the book is written on the Great Yankee–Red Sox Rivalry, the year 1977 will be writ large and bold. And largest and boldest will shine the name and legend of Reggie!

The first ten games were packed into a thirty-four-day period in May and June, and in those ten games the two great dramas of the first half of the season would take place.

The Robert Ward *Sport* magazine article, a time bomb that had been ticking . . . ticking . . . ticking since the first week of spring training, exploded all over Yankee Stadium on the day of their first meeting. The other time bomb, a tension that had been building . . . building . . . building between Billy and Reggie, erupted in Boston three weeks later.

For those who couldn't make it to the ballpark, both games were shown on national television.

The first meeting between the two teams wasn't scheduled until May 23, the thirty-ninth game of the season. And it was on May 23 that the issue of *Sport* magazine containing the Ward piece on Jackson hit the stands. Three or four copies somehow materialized in the clubhouse early in the afternoon, and they were passed around from player to player all through the day. Wherever you found the magazine, you would find a small group of players huddled together, reading—first with curiosity, to see whether Reggie had said anything about them, and then in utter disbelief and fury as they read what he had said about Munson. "That prick," more than one said, glaring over at the culprit at his corner locker. "That dirty sonofabitch." Reggie dressed quickly and went out to the field, but not before a few of his teammates had come wandering by to kick his equipment bag or his shoes.

Munson, who had been kicked in the teeth, went into shock. And when Reggie's pal Fran Healy, who hadn't read the piece, tried to pass it off by saying that Reggie had probably been quoted out of context, Thurman yelped, *"For three pages?"* He then retreated into the sauna in the trainer's room and sat down alongside Ron Blomberg, who had come to the stadium for physical therapy. "All right," Thurman said, "I could see it if he knocked me for one page. But I couldn't find enough adjectives about myself to fill three pages." And, almost as if he were trying to sort it out for himself, "I just go out every day and play. I helped the Yankees win the pennant. I was MVP. What's so bad about that?"

Normally when a player of Reggie's stature takes batting practice, the others automatically stop what they are doing and watch. When Reggie took his early swings before the Boston game, the entire area around the batting cage suddenly became a deserted outpost.

Reggie plunked ball after ball into the right-field stands, while out in the field and along the sidelines his teammates conspicuously ignored him.

Put Reggie in the eye of the hurricane, and he is almost guaranteed to produce. Put him in the eye of ABC-TV's "Monday Night Baseball" at the same time, and you can bet the family jewels on it.

For seven innings, Reggie Jax was the entire Yankee offense. Reggie led off the second inning with a line drive double and scored on an error. On his next turn at bat he hit a scorching ground ball that was turned into a double play. In the seventh, with the Red Sox ahead 2–1, he teed off on one of Bill Lee's sinkers and hit a tremendous home run to tie the score—a ball hit so far and deep that Reggie stood at the plate in awe and reverence to watch it disappear into the stands. And maybe do a little thinking about the magnitude of a Reggie Jackson home run, not to mention the risks of shooting one's mouth off to writers, and the Nielsen ratings. As he rounded the bases and crossed the plate, his teammates gathered in the well of the dugout waiting to shake his hand. Reggie ran right up to them and then, ignoring the outstretched hands, turned away and headed for the other end of the dugout.

You don't do that in professional baseball. Once the game starts, winning is the only thing that counts, and there had been nothing insincere about the proffered handshakes. Everybody on the team knew that without Reggie Jackson's bat they weren't going to win. As professionals, they might even have had a sneaking admiration that the sonofabitch had come through again under enormous pressure.

The Yankees were a shaken team when they took the field. And they showed it. Reggie himself immediately played a Red Sox single into a double by completely overrunning the ball. A bunt went for a base hit when Willie Randolph, who just didn't make mental mistakes, forgot to cover first base on a bunt. Both runners eventually scored.

The Yankees were handed one of the runs back in the last half of the inning, when Boston's George Scott, who happened to be Reggie's closest friend in baseball, dropped the throw to first base on Munson's two-out ground ball. The game came to an end when Munson, the smartest base runner on the team, got picked off first base for perhaps the first time in his life. But then it had been a day of firsts for Munson.

When the writers came into the clubhouse after the game, they found Reggie at the sandwich table. "I had a bad hand," he said.

"He's a fuckin' liar," Munson said. "How's that for a quote?"

Why did Thurman think Reggie had refused to shake his teammates' hands?

"I don't know. I'm just happy to be here. I wish George would buy *me* a Rolls-Royce."

Billy had a possible explanation. "Maybe Reggie was mad at me because I didn't play him a couple of games against left-handers. Go ask him. I'm sure he'll have some answers for you. Ask him about the ball that got away from him at the start of the eighth. He probably forgets about those things."

As for the other players, they had made their feelings known to each other well before the writers got there. "If that's the way he wants it," they had been telling each other, "fuck him."

When Thurman Munson came to the plate the next day, he received the greatest ovation he had ever been given in his life. The same thing could hardly be said about Reggie. And if getting booed wasn't exactly a new experience for him, being ostracized by his teammates was.

There were to be four more days at the stadium before the club went to Boston: a twi-night doubleheader against Texas and three games against Chicago. When Reggie came into the clubhouse before the twilight game of the doubleheader, he was handed a freshly cleaned uniform. He hung it on the hook of his locker, started to unbutton the jacket, and pulled back. There were no pants on the hanger, just a long hunk of adhesive tape hanging down from the crossbar.

SUCK MY ASS, it said.

"This is what I have to put up with," Reggie said to the writer who had come in with him.

Since it was the only twilight game the Yankees would be playing all year, Reggie called over to Willie Randolph to find out what time they were going to hit. Willie, sitting two lockers away, didn't even look at him.

Four times Reggie asked him, each time a little louder. "What time do we hit, Willie?"

Willie just sat there, leaning on his chin and giving not the slightest indication he had heard him.

The writer was Roger Kahn, author of *The Boys of Summer*. "Did you ever see anything like this?" Reggie asked him. "Thank God I'm a Christian. This stuff doesn't bother me."

To prove how little it bothered him, he decided to ask Billy Martin to call a team meeting so that he could apologize to everybody. On his way to Martin's office, he looked back over his shoulder at Kahn. "You know," he said, "I don't have to do this. I'm going to make three million dollars this year."

Billy Martin, who was making $75,000, told him that if he wanted to apologize he was going to have to do it on a man-to-man basis—there was going to be no team meeting. And so, during the twenty-five-minute period before the game when the press was barred from the clubhouse, Reggie went from locker to locker apologizing. "What are you apologizing to me for?" the guys who had been in the bullpen asked. "I wasn't there."

He just wanted to tell everybody he was sorry, Reggie explained.

Munson listened to his apology, said nothing, and turned his back on him. And he wasn't the only one.

It was during Reggie's *tour d'apologia* that the words that were to echo through the clubhouse for the rest of the season were spoken for the first time. They went, "Can you believe this? This is becoming a fuckin' circus."

Now that the Unhandshake had been followed by the Apology, the question became: Was Thurman going to shake Reggie's hand the next time the situation arose?

Well, the easiest way to find out was for Reggie to hit a home run.

First time Reggie came to bat against Chicago, the Yankees were behind 5–0. Believe it or not, Reggie tried to get on with a bunt—the ultimate act of contrition—fouled it off, and hit the next pitch deep into the right-field bleachers, 450 feet away.

Into the dugout he ran, with both hands extended, grabbing every hand in sight. Munson's wasn't among them. Munson had taken it, together with the rest of him, down to the other end of the dugout.

In the final game of the series, Munson was on base when Chris Chambliss hit a home run. Jackson, coming to the on-deck circle, stuck out his hand, and Munson ran right by it.

"I don't think he saw it," Jackson said.

"I saw it," said Munson.

How about that, Reggie? "I'm just trying to be a good Christian," Reggie said.

Under the pressure, Reggie's fielding, which had always been the weakest part of his game, broke down completely. It wasn't only the errors, he wasn't getting any kind of a jump on fly balls—line drives that should have been caught were falling in front of him, and he was battling anything he had to go back for.

The Great Handshake Affair was finally settled in Boston.

During the flight from New York, a couple of the writers had put forth the argument to Munson that no matter what Thurman's personal feelings might be, it was his job as captain to bring the team together, not to pull it further apart. It was something to think about, Thurman had to admit.

One week had passed since the Unhandshake. For the second straight time it was the Yankees versus the Red Sox on "Monday Night Baseball." For the second straight time it was Bill Lee pitching for the Red Sox, and for the second straight time, Reggie hit a home run off him. Last time, Reggie had hit his home run and gone off to a corner to brood. This time Reggie ran around the bases, and when he got to the dugout, Cap'n Munson was there to shake his hand.

Before the game was over, it had turned into a festival of handshaking. Jackson had got things going, but it was Munson who knocked in the winning run. And it was Munson who stood like a block of granite at the plate to make the final out. The final unofficial handshaking tally was: Munson 3, Jackson 2.

Had Munson forgiven Reggie? Like hell he had. For the good of the team, he had been willing to put the best face on it. But he was never going to forgive Reggie. During the next Western trip, Fran Healy was able to bring them together over dinner. "Tell me, Jackson," Thurman said as he sat down, "tell me one thing you have that I'd want. I have three beautiful children and a lovely wife. I have a happy home life. What do you have? You have nothing."

Jackson didn't answer.

The Yankees had set out on that Western trip tied with the Red Sox for second place, 1½ games behind Baltimore. When they came back to Boston, on June 17, they were in first place as the result of Guidry's first complete game. They had won twelve of their last fifteen games. Reggie was on a twelve-game hitting streak. The pitching staff was healthy for the first time all year, and the team had found its stopper in Ron Guidry. Six days later they were five games behind the Red Sox, and the ballclub was in a shambles.

Win or lose, the tension had been building. "I'm the problem," Reggie had said toward the end of spring training. "I cause problems just by being here." Billy Martin had been known to cause problems too. Through his whole career Billy had been hired for being Billy, and he had been fired for being Billy. It was going to happen between Reggie and Billy, everybody knew, because Billy was going to make it happen.

Wouldn't you know that it would happen in Boston? And that it would happen on national TV. Saturday's game was going to be on NBC's "Game of the Week," and so, in natural anticipation, Reggie was in a happy mood. In the five games in which he had been on national television during the season, he had hit .363 with four home runs. By the time the last Boston game was over, Reggie's average was up to .410, and Reggie was on the slippery edge of a mental breakdown.

The scores tell you why the series came to be known as the Boston Massacre: 9–4, 10–4, 11–1. Sixteen Boston home runs, an all-time record for three consecutive games. And they were not Fenway Park home runs, either. Monster shot after monster shot disappeared over the left-field net and into the right-field and center-field bleachers.

The home runs will be forgotten, the record will eventually be broken. The game, the season, the explosive relationship of Billy and Reggie, they all focused down to a checked-swing pop fly off the bat of Jim Rice.

Now, let's be fair about this. Right field is the sun field in Boston, one of the worst in the majors (Ted Williams was moved from right field to left field after his first season to protect his eyes), and it was one of those hot, clear summer days where the air seems to take on a shimmer. It's more than possible that Reggie didn't pick up the ball as it came off Rice's bat; maybe he couldn't have caught it under any circumstances. What there is no doubt about is that he started slowly, that he showed little enthusiasm about going after the ball after it had fallen, and that with Rice, who could see the whole play unfolding in front of him, racing around first base into second, Reggie made a weak, almost uninterested throw in the general direction of the pitcher's mound.

When you look at the reruns of the play today—how many times has it been shown through the years?—it doesn't really seem as if he hesitated that long. What is it that makes the action while it is occurring seem so much slower than when you see it repeated immediately afterwards. Anxiety? Concentration? Anticipation?

How many times have you seen it watching a football game? The quarterback seems trapped, you're sure he's about to be sacked, you're sure he will never be able to get the ball away. He seems to be running around back there forever. In the instant replay, he goes back, looks, runs out of the pocket, pulls away from one guy, turns from another, and throws. It seems to have taken half the time; it appears as if he was never really in danger.

In much the same way, you watch the reruns of Jackson going

after the ball, and he seems to have hesitated for only a second. You saw it while it was happening, and he seemed to be moving in slow motion, like a man in a fog. "Nonchalanting it," as the ballplayers say. You've got to go with the original impression and ignore the evidence that is unfolding in front of your eyes.

There was no question how everybody in the ballpark saw it. As Martin went to the mound to replace pitcher Mike Torrez, the player sitting alongside Paul Blair on the bench said, "Get ready to put your glove on, Paul. He's going to pull Jackson out of there."

He had read Billy right. As Billy was waiting for Sparky Lyle to come in, he told Munson, "I'm going to go get the sonofabitch."

Reggie was leaning against the bullpen fence, away from the sun, chatting with a couple of the players out there, when the roar of the crowd caused him to look up. When he saw Blair running out, he took one step toward him and then rocked back against the fence in dismay and disbelief. Blair had to wave him in, and when Reggie reached him he asked foolishly, "You coming after me?"

"Yeah."

"Why?"

"You got to ask Billy that." As Reggie came running in, clearly determined to do exactly that, the center-field camera was carrying millions of television viewers with him. Billy Martin was leaning forward on the edge of the bench, waiting. When Jackson got to the dugout, he spread his hands wide in an expression of total bewilderment. "What are you doing? What's going on? What did I do?"

Martin came shooting up off the bench. "What do you mean what did you do? You're not hustling. That's what you're not doing."

Reggie continued on down the steps, and it was as if he hadn't heard him. "Why did you take me out? You have to be crazy to embarrass me in front of fifty million people." (That's all he was concerned about, the players on the bench would tell the others afterwards, that he had been embarrassed on national TV.)

"I don't give a shit," Martin barked. "When you decide to play, then you play right field. And not until."

Coach Elston Howard had moved to interpose his body between them. Reggie spat out a curse. Billy spat one back. "You don't know what you're doing, old man," Reggie said. "You showed me up in front of fifty million people." He turned his back and began to walk away.

"What! What! *Old man?*" Howard had tried to pin Billy against the pole, but when he saw the look in his eyes, he let go. "You called me

an old man?" Billy screamed. "I'll show you who's an old man!" Dick
Howser, another coach, stopped Billy's initial charge just long enough
to give Yogi Berra a chance to grab hold of him and wrestle him to the
bench. Reggie had already whipped off his glasses, and he was goading
him on. "Let's go, old man. Come on, *old man!* Well, what are you
doing? Come on. Let's get it over with, *old man!*" And all the while Billy
was screaming, "Let me go! I'm gonna break his fuckin' ass!"

It was already over, though. Jim Wynn had wrapped his arms
around Reggie, and Yogi was holding Martin tight. "You never did like
me," Reggie shouted down at him. "You never did want me on the ballclub. Well, I'm here to stay, so you better start liking me."

He had laid it out for him, the final goad. If one of them went, it
wasn't going to be Reggie Jackson, it was going to be Billy Martin. So
watch it, Billy.

The TV camera in center field had caught it all, and a mobile camera at the end of the dugout had come wheeling in to catch a close-up of
the wrestling match. Before the camera could be activated, Ray Negron, who runs the Betamax (closed-circuit camera) for the Yankees,
had thrown himself in front of and was screaming at the cameraman.
Negron is a former Yankee bat boy and Pittsburgh Pirate farmhand.
He had been hired by Billy Martin at the beginning of spring training,
but he had also become so friendly with Reggie Jackson—they shared
the same locker area, and they both spoke Spanish—that Reggie had
asked him to move into his apartment and become his general facto-
tum. Negron was the one man on the club who had reason to like and
be grateful to both Billy and Reggie, and what was happening was so
painful to him that he found himself throwing a towel over the mobile
camera and threatening to break the radar gun over the cameraman's
head. The mobile cameraman recalled afterwards that it was Martin
who had shouted to Negron to cover the camera. It was exactly the
opposite. The first thing Martin did when Yogi let him up was to pull
the still-hysterical Negron away from the cameraman and shove him
down on the bench.

Elston Howard had already moved to keep the brawl from starting up again—first, by encouraging Reggie to go back to the clubhouse, and then by sending Jim Wynn back to talk him into leaving.
Wynn found Reggie talking to Mike Torrez in front of Torrez's locker.
Mike, who had become one of the "allies" Reggie had been looking for,
had arrived back in the locker room just in time to hear the description
of the brawl coming over the radio. He was trying to find out from

Reggie whether any punches had been thrown, but Reggie was more interested in telling Torrez how he had been humiliated in front of fifty million people. Wynn tried to convince Reggie that the best thing he could do was take a shower, go back to the hotel, and try to forget what had happened. Torrez agreed. Reggie, becoming increasingly emotional by the minute, balked. He was the one who had been humiliated, not Billy. Why should he be the one to run away?

Torrez went into the trainer's room to soak his arm, and Reggie followed him. Wynn left. Almost immediately Fran Healy, who had become Reggie's other close friend and ally, came in. Healy had run all the way down from the bullpen to give Reggie the same advice. "For the good of everybody concerned, don't stay around and give it a chance to start up again."

The relationship between Reggie and Torrez was easy to understand. Torrez hadn't joined the club until a month into the season, they both had the same agent, Gary Walker, and they both spoke Spanish. With Healy, it was more complicated. Initially it was believed by the sportswriters covering the team that Healy, the twenty-fifth man on the team, had been assigned to Reggie by Steinbrenner. Very quickly they changed their minds. Healy was everybody's friend—bright, witty, very intelligent. As the second-string catcher, he was as close to Munson as he was to Reggie. He had compassion for Reggie. When he saw that Reggie, the pariah of the clubhouse, was in desperate need of a sympathetic ear, he became the volunteer listener.

As Healy approached the door of the trainer's room, he saw Bucky Dent, who had been removed for a pinch hitter in the Yankee half of the sixth inning, coming toward him. "Fran," Bucky said, "I can't take any more of this. I'm leaving the club. I'm hooking it."

Bucky had been complaining all year about being removed for a pinch hitter whenever the Yankees were behind late in the game, and now he was being pinch-hit for with the game barely half over. He had come back to the clubhouse, torn off the shirt of his uniform, and gone out to the public telephone in the concourse to make a reservation for a flight to Chicago and to call his wife and tell her to pick him up at the airport. By an accident of timing, he had been on the phone when Jackson and Wynn came back, and had returned just in time to catch Healy.

Although Bucky had heard the Boston announcer describe some kind of shouting match in the dugout, he had been too preoccupied with his own problem to pay any particular attention. As he listened to

Healy and Torrez urging Reggie to leave "for the good of everybody concerned," and heard a distraught and overwrought Reggie Jackson explaining why he had played the ball the way he had, and asking Healy whether he thought he had loafed, Bucky's own problem became increasingly insignificant. By the time Reggie had showered and dressed, Bucky Dent had put his uniform back on, called his wife again, and gone back out to the bench to rejoin the team.

If Bucky Dent hadn't changed his mind—that is, if he hadn't decided to take advantage of Healy's always sympathetic ear—Billy Martin would never have survived the next forty-eight hours.

There was one final visitor to the clubhouse, young Ray Negron. With the game completely out of reach, Billy Martin had been just sitting on the bench. Very quiet. Obviously preoccupied. Seething. There could be so little doubt what he was thinking that Negron had decided it would be a very good idea to make sure Reggie wasn't around when the game ended. He found Reggie in the trainer's room with Torrez, fully dressed but still unwilling to leave. "Come on," Ray said. "Let's go back to the parking lot. There'll be a cop out there, and he'll get you a cab."

George Steinbrenner had left Boston after Friday's game to attend a funeral in Cleveland, but he had seen the whole thing on television. No sooner had the brawl come to an end than a call came to the Fenway Park press box for Phil Rizzuto, a call answered by Bill Crowley, the Red Sox publicity director. Since there is no phone connection between the press box and the radio booth, Crowley decided he had a nut on the line and hung up. Immediately the phone rang again, and this time George Steinbrenner could be heard shouting in the background. When Steinbrenner heard Crowley tell the operator that there was no way of reaching Rizzuto in the radio booth, he asked for Mickey Morabito, the Yankees' publicity man.

The only thing that Morabito (who is now Billy Martin's publicity man in Oakland) will say about that call is that Steinbrenner instructed him to have Gabe Paul call him. Anything else George had to say, Mickey insists, had nothing to do with the dugout brawl. Sure, Mickey.

The inning had come to an end, and Gabe had just exchanged a few words with Billy Martin from his box seat alongside the dugout when Morabito came down and passed the message on to him. Gabe strolled up the aisle and was not seen again for the rest of the game.

Steinbrenner wanted Gabe to fire Billy Martin on the spot. The man had lost control of himself on national TV, an absolute disgrace. "Did you see him? He was ready to kill him. What kind of an example is that to set for American youth?"

It wasn't that easy anymore, Gabe had to tell George. It would have been one thing to fire Billy at the time of the Hendricks incident. It wasn't going to be so easy to fire him over this without making it look as if Reggie were running the team. Sure, it had been bad, Gabe told his boss. It had been awful. He had seen and heard it all. And he would talk to both of them, he told George, and take a reading. Meanwhile, the best thing to do was let things settle down. After the Sunday game the team would be flying to Detroit, and George could meet them there.

Gabe did talk to both Martin and Jackson—Martin in the clubhouse immediately after the game, Jackson shortly afterward in his hotel room. Another three-way meeting was set up in Gabe's suite for that evening, but it didn't take place until the following morning. Jackson may very well have flown the coop that night, because Billy Martin appeared in the hotel lobby around seven o'clock asking whether anybody knew where Reggie was. Or it could have been Steinbrenner. Steinbrenner had talked to Reggie, too—can there be any doubt that one of George's instructions to Gabe Paul was to have Reggie call him?—and George could very well have decided that Reggie was in no condition, emotionally, for any confrontation with Billy Martin.

Clearly, George was taking charge. He talked that Saturday to Morabito, he talked to Gabe a few times, he talked to Reggie. He had tried to get Rizzuto, who was Martin's closest friend on the scene, and if he wasn't able to reach him in the radio booth, he certainly must have reached him later. God knows how many people he talked to before the day was over.

Somewhere around nine o'clock, Paul Montgomery of *The New York Times* came to Reggie's room to hear his version of what had happened. Whether Montgomery had called and found his line open or George had set it up is impossible to say because Montgomery pleads privileged information. Which doesn't make it that impossible to say after all, does it? Having made the decision to fire Billy Martin, Steinbrenner would have a vested interest in taking Reggie out of the line of fire.

At any rate, Montgomery had barely arrived in the room before Phil Pepe of the *Daily News* called Reggie to ask if he could come up and talk to him. Montgomery consented to share the interview.

If George did set it up, it was a mistake. As the interview began, Reggie was sitting on the floor, bare-chested except for a gold cross and two gold medallions. A blonde was in the shower, a local girlfriend. Mike Torrez was sitting in a chair alongside Reggie with a bottle of white wine. Reggie had asked Torrez to sit in (perhaps on George's advice) for a very specific reason. "If I go too far," he told Torrez before he began, "stop me." He was wound so tight that he seemed to have only the most fragmented recollection of the disputed play. He took the position that he had charged the ball the way he thought he could play it best. "If Martin feels I didn't hustle, I'm sorry for him. You know, in this game the manager is always right. I'm just a player."

That refrain seemed stuck in his head, almost as if he had been programed. The phone would ring, a reporter would be on the line, and Reggie would say, "I have nothing to say. The manager is always right."

His memory during the interview was that he hadn't said anything when he came back to the dugout, but had merely held his arms open in that "What did I do wrong?" gesture. "The man took a position today to show me up on national television. Everyone could see that."

He also informed them that he had taken three cortisone shots in the arm since spring training, thereby breaking Martin's inviolable rule about telling the press anything about an injury. "With my bad arm, I'm not going to take a chance throwing to second, so I fired home. I didn't want the run to score."

At one point he became so upset that he retreated to the edge of the bed and began to read the Bible. He was a born-again Christian, he told them, and quite often went to the Bible for solace.

Once he had himself back under control, he resumed his position on the floor and went right back to the company line. "I don't know anything about managing, but I'll take the heat for whatever the manager says." He just did what he was told: played right field when they let him, hit wherever they put him. All he wanted to do was to go out and play to the best of his ability.

And then he began to come apart. "If the press keeps messing with me," he sobbed, "I'll hit thirty homers and maybe ninety ribbys and hit .270. If they leave me alone, I'll have forty homers, one hundred and twenty ribbys, and I'll be hitting .300." And the Yankees would be running away with the pennant.

His eyes filled up, and he began speaking with rising emotion about the way he was being treated on the ballclub. "I'm just a black man to them who doesn't know how to be subservient. I'm a black buck with an IQ of 160, and making $700,000 a year. They've never had anyone like me on their team before." Except for Steinbrenner. "I love that man, he treats me like I'm somebody."

His voice broke, and he came rising up on his haunches. "The rest of them treat me like I'm dirt." There were tears running down his cheeks now. "I'm a Christian," he screamed, "and they're fucking with me because I'm a nigger, and they don't like niggers on this team. The Yankee pinstripes are Ruth and Gehrig, DiMaggio and Mantle. I've got an IQ of 160, they can't mess with me. . . ." He was a man so clearly out of control, a man in such terrible torment, that Mike Torrez stood up and told the writers, "I think you'd better leave."

Reggie himself left soon afterwards to pay a call upon George Scott. The visit with Scott did nothing to restore his equilibrium. Sometime around eleven o'clock he drove back to his hotel in Scott's green Cadillac, called his room to say he'd be up in a few minutes, and then startled the tourists and salesmen sitting around the lobby with a long rambling speech about all the terrible things that had been done to him. He was so far out of it that it was hard to tell whether he was on the edge of sanity or whether he was just stoned out of his mind. "The Yankees have never fucked anybody like I've been fucked," he kept telling them. But, you know, in the end Reggie is still Reggie, and before he left he was going to remind everybody who he was. "It's you people I feel sorry for," were his final words. "You're the ones who are going to miss out when I'm gone next year."

When Billy Martin got on the elevator the next morning to go up to Gabe's suite, he found one other person inside: Reggie Jackson. They could have stopped the elevator between floors and settled it right there. Instead they said absolutely nothing to each other. Maybe it was too early in the morning.

Up in Gabe's room, things got very hairy for about five minutes.

Each of them had told his story many times by then. Billy's was that Reggie had embarrassed the team by not hustling, and anytime Reggie embarrassed the team by not hustling, Billy was going to embarrass him by sitting him down. Reggie insisted that he hadn't loafed on the ball. He had been playing deep for Rice, but once he had seen that Randolph wasn't going to make the catch he had charged the ball. To which Martin said, "Boy, what you think you're doing and what my eyes tell me you're doing are two different things."

In his hypersensitive mood, Reggie chose to take the "boy" as a racial slur, and he came bouncing to his feet, ready to fight. Billy was up and raring to go too. "Nobody's restraining me now, motherfucker. You thought I was an old man yesterday. Let's see how old I am right now."

"Aw, come on, you guys, dammit!" Gabe said. "Let's act like grown men. Billy didn't mean anything, Reggie. And Billy, you sit down and relax." It took a few more "motherfuckers" before they were ready to sit down, but after that the breakfast went about as well as could be expected, if you didn't expect any vows of perpetual friendship to be exchanged.

It had never entered Billy's mind that his job might be in jeopardy. "We went over everything," he announced when he got to the ballpark Sunday, "and everything turned out fine. Yesterday is history."

Long after the game was over, Billy was sitting in the Boston press room, drinking with Gabe Paul and the Boston manager, Don Zimmer. "The way you're drinking," Gabe told him dryly, "you'd think we won."

When Billy woke up in Detroit the next morning, he found that Milton Richman, sports editor of UPI, had a story on the line that he was going to be replaced by Yogi Berra within a couple of days "as a result of the Jackson episode, coupled with the three losses in Boston."

Now Milton Richman has a massive reputation along the sports beat. He has broken more stories than any other writer in the country, including enough Yankee stories to indicate that he has a pipeline. But there were a couple of very intriguing things about the way this particular story broke. Milt Richman was in Tulsa, covering the U.S. Open, which means that he would have been out on the golf course all day Saturday and Sunday. That Sunday in Tulsa there had been constant conferences between the press and USGA officials about making public a death threat against Hubie Green, the ultimate winner. To people who understand how a reporter works, Milt Richman would hardly have had time to concern himself about anything that was happening in Boston.

Add the fact that the story had broken in the early hours of Monday morning, and the only possible conclusion was that somebody had gone to a great deal of effort to have the story break nationally with the authority of Milt Richman's name behind it.

And then there was Yogi Berra. Don't ask me why a man who has won two pennants with two different teams in his three years as a major-league manager is looked upon as a joke, but Yogi Berra's name attached to any rumor had come to be regarded as the surest sign that the rumor being dealt with was a trial balloon.

Still, Richman would never have gone with the story unless he had been given good reason to believe that Billy was through. Instead, he found himself caught up in a classic Catch 22 situation. Because by going with the story, Richman quite probably saved Billy Martin's job.

Billy Martin was nowhere to be found all day, and that gave rise to rumors that he had already been fired. Actually he was out on the golf course with Phil Rizzuto. Now the implication has always been that Rizzuto took him out to get him away from it all. Not so. The match had been set up two weeks earlier with a couple of the golf club's officials. The golf club was normally closed on Monday, and it had to be opened especially for them. They were the only four golfers on the course.

Even as the rumors were spreading that Martin had already left town, the decision was being made to keep him. The first thing George had done upon coming into the hotel was to call Reggie Jackson's room and ask Reggie straight out whether he thought he should fire Billy. When it was put to him like that, Reggie said, perhaps to his own surprise, "No, George, you shouldn't." Thurman Munson's response was both stronger and more predictable. Munson told him that if Martin were fired over this, he and Nettles would walk out with him. And as a result of the Richman story, phone calls were pouring into the Yankee Stadium switchboard in support of Martin.

When Steinbrenner and Paul met later in George's suite, Paul laid it out to him again. Gabe wasn't any more anxious than George was to keep Martin on as manager, but he did feel that the alternative could only be destructive. Fire Martin and you were making Jackson the manager, that's what it always came back to. A new manager would be placed in a wholly untenable position, and Reggie's already precarious relationship with his teammates would become impossible.

And then there was the racial factor, which Steinbrenner always referred to as "the black-white thing" and which frightened him to death. It didn't matter that, in this instance, it wasn't there in reality. The fact remained that it was there because Reggie Jackson, in his personal battle with Reggie Jackson, had put it there.

That's why Bucky Dent's change of mind was so critical. If Dent had jumped the club, they would have been able to say that Billy's loss of control over himself was symptomatic of his loss of control over the whole club.

But Dent hadn't jumped the club, and George probably didn't even know about Dent. All George knew was that he was stuck with Billy Martin.

The meeting with Billy took place, finally, late in the afternoon after Billy had returned from the golf course. If George couldn't fire him, he could be least scare the hell out of him. And the reason he wanted to scare the hell out of him had almost nothing to do with Reggie Jackson.

When Billy is emotional a kind of flailed look comes over him, as of highly spun, tightly drawn nerves. But Billy was far from contrite. He was not going to allow anybody to tell him how to manage, he said immediately, and he was not going to allow anybody to tell him how to handle his players.

Nobody was trying to tell him how to manage, George and Gabe said. They were telling him that he was going to have to meet his responsibilities. How about their responsibility to him? Billy shot back. "You do things without telling me."

"How can we tell you things," Paul said wryly, "when we can't get ahold of you."

That's what this was all about. What was being demanded of him was discipline. "Because you can't have discipline on the ballclub without being disciplined yourself," George pointed out.

"All right," Billy said at last, "what do I have to do?"

He had to maintain contact. Contact and preparation. He was not only going to have to make every meeting that Paul called, he was going to have to come up to the office every day when he came to the park. And he was going to have to work harder on preparation. Preparation meant getting to the park earlier—three hours before the game, not fifteen minutes—and studying the charts and statistics Steinbrenner sent down.

And, finally, there was to be no more bad-mouthing the front office. Nothing that wasn't already in the contract. Already Billy could

139

be fired for acts of insubordination, failure to attend meetings, and publicly criticizing the front office.

But there was also one other thing that was being demanded of him, something that wasn't in the contract. He was going to have to be more "flexible" in the handling of Reggie Jackson.

After Billy had agreed to everything, George told him that the decision on whether he stayed or left was going to be made by Gabe Paul. "I won't lie to you, Billy. As far as I was concerned, you were gone when I came here." What he was going to do now, George told him, was remove himself from the scene. The goddamned ballclub brought him more trouble and aggravation than all his other companies combined. "It's in Gabe's hands now," he told him.

Promises, promises . . .

But George Steinbrenner did not fold his tent and quietly steal away. Far from it. If Reggie and Billy had dominated the scene for forty-eight hours, the next twenty-four hours were to become the private domain of the Boss. He started by instructing Martin and Jackson to go to the ballpark together and put on a display of unity to the world. So they took separate taxis to the ballpark (a *show* of unity was all Reggie had agreed to) and walked into the clubhouse with their arms around each other's shoulders. "We are allies," Jackson announced. He cited a passage from the Bible that admonished servants to obey their masters—the same passage, it is worth noting, that Alvin Dark had quoted when Reggie was at Oakland to explain why he was allowing himself to be humiliated by Charles O. Finley.

During batting practice, George Steinbrenner took command. The Boss didn't have to quote Scripture; the Boss was voting his stock. Thurman Munson was summoned to the manager's office to be lectured on his responsibilities as team captain, while the dispossessed manager hung around outside. Then George called Martin in. Then he sent Lou Piniella to pull Reggie out of the batting cage so that George could talk to Reggie and Billy again.

Having instructed his manager, his captain, and his star as to what was expected of them, the Boss was hardly going to deny himself the pleasure of haranguing the troops. But the occasion called for more than a mere pep talk. Almost to a man the players had come to the park believing that their manager was about to be fired. For once it had been the players going to the writers for information, instead of the other way around. The writers hadn't been told anything either. It was "Monday Night Baseball" with Howard Cosell, and George was holding the announcement for national TV.

"You guys are a finger-snap away from firing your manager," George told the assembled players. "If you love him so much, you guys had better get on the ball." That was how the players learned for certain that Billy Martin was still their manager.

Having given them back their manager, George rebuked them sternly for being prejudiced against Reggie. And then he retreated into his standard pep talk. Everybody in every other city was trying to pull them apart, so they had better stop pulling at each other and stand together. The first pennant was easy, it was the second pennant that was tough. "Because now everybody's looking for you." And, finally, from the Book of Knute came an inspirational sermon on how great they would be if they ever got around to playing ball.

The Detroit fans had been caught up in the drama, too. It was a sellout crowd, and by game time every eye was riveted upon the Yankee dugout to see whether it would be Billy Martin or his successor coming out with the starting lineup. When Billy Martin came running out, the Detroit fans gave him an ovation so ear-splitting as to exceed all the standing ovations he would be receiving in New York. Billy came back to the dugout positively aglow. "Wasn't that super?" he beamed. "I'll bet George just loved to hear that."

It was not so super for Reggie Jax. In Boston, disaster had befallen him over national TV in the sixth inning. In Detroit, disaster almost took his head off in the seventh. Reggie came racing in for a line drive, but just as he reached up for the ball you could see that he had lost it in the glare of the Tiger Stadium lights, indisputably the poorest in the major leagues. The ball went sailing over his shoulder, and the next batter singled in the winning run. At the end of the inning, Reggie ran off the field and right into the clubhouse, looking as if he were about to break into tears.

In Boston, Billy had humiliated Reggie. In Detroit, Billy went back to the clubhouse to commiserate with him and assure him that it wasn't his fault.

That was the good news. The bad news was that it was four straight losses and counting.

After the next night's game, it was five. Neither George Steinbrenner nor Gabe Paul was there to see it. Gabe Paul, driven to the outer limits of his almost inexhaustible patience, had dumped the ballclub back in the Boss's lap and gone home. And George Steinbrenner had gone running after him.

After George had unburdened himself of his pep talk, Gabe Paul had gone up to the press box to read the following statement:

> There will be no change in our organization regardless of what has been said. We don't feel there's a better manager than Billy Martin, and we want the Yankees to have the best.
>
> There were some things that had to be straightened out, and they were straightened out. From the first pitch till the last out, there's no better manager in baseball than Billy, and he's the one we want.

Who had made the decision? Paul was asked.

"This was my decision," he replied.

Steinbrenner had been telling the writers the same thing all day. "The decision is strictly Gabe Paul's. I'll stand behind him either way he goes. He's the guy right now."

George had been saying that from the beginning, even while leading the reporters to believe that it wasn't so. After the Boston episode, he had put forth the line that he had stayed away from the club from the time Dock Ellis called him a Lone Ranger, and in the current crisis had merely told Gabe (you could just barely catch the note of impatience under the chuckle), "Don't come to me now." Although, yes, he was going to meet the club in Detroit to find out what was going on.

For the record, George averred that *everything* was Gabe's decision. Privately and off the record, he let it be known that the tension on the team was beyond anything Gabe seemed to be aware of, and that he, George, was getting annoyed with being called whenever there was even a minor emergency.

After the announcement of Martin's retention, George got a little macho, at the expense of his chastised manager. ("Billy was shook . . . shook . . . shook.") The next day, he came to the ballpark and overdosed on testosterone and pure oxygen.

Question: Who made the decision to keep Billy Martin as manager?

Steinbrenner: I did. It was my decision entirely. We were headed for complete collapse. Dissension on the team was terrible. We were getting no leadership and no fire. Something had to be done quickly.

He said he had never intended to fire Martin, but that Martin *and others among the Yankees* had not been doing their jobs. "Billy was very subdued and has promised to get in touch with me every day. I intend to keep in daily contact with the team." He had told Billy, "The next time you drive me to the wall, I'll throw you over it."

He denied categorically that he had always taken Jackson's side in disputes with Martin. In fact, he said, he had warned Reggie that if he ever mentioned racism again, "I'll beat your head off."

And how had Jackson taken that? "Jackson listened and took it."

He had also taken Munson to task for failing to carry out his duties as captain. According to Steinbrenner, Munson had replied, "I thought Jackson was the captain."

"*You* are the captain," Steinbrenner had said. "When I want Jackson to be the captain, I'll tell him and you, too. You are the captain. Now be the captain."

He said that several players had told him that his pep talk had given them a lift. Some of the others, he said, had told him in the lobby of the hotel, that they wanted him to take a greater part in the running of the club. "We want you around," they had said, "watching things, pulling for us."

Why does George Steinbrenner do such things? Why does the Great Helmsman make these periodic voyages of his between the lands of Flim and Flam?

For the same reason, one supposes, that anybody else does what they do. Like Mickey Rivers, we all have our habits, the nature of the beast. The bane of George's life in those first years was that he knew he needed Gabe Paul and wished that he didn't. And so, from time to time, it made him feel better to make believe that he didn't. Or, at any rate, to try to make everybody else believe that he didn't.

George and Gabe had been through this kind of thing before, and what did Gabe care? But this time it was different. In constantly stating that it was Gabe's decision, and then announcing that he had been forced to step in and save the situation for poor old bumbling Gabe, George was making it look as if Gabe Paul's name was his private property to kick around as he wished.

Gabe walked out of the hotel and caught a plane home to Tampa. George was on a plane that same night. The next morning he went to Gabe, hat in hand, and promised him that if he would come back it would never happen again.

At least Gabe got a three-day respite out of it. He remained in

Tampa while the Yankees were salvaging the final game in Detroit, a wild and woolly 10–8 affair in which Reggie knocked in what proved to be the winning runs with an eighth-inning double; stayed on for another day while the Yankees played the rescheduled Mayor's Trophy Game; and walked back into Yankee Stadium in the second inning of the opening game against Boston to find himself confronted with yet another chapter of the Billy and Reggie Story.

Billy had no way of knowing that his fate was really in Gabe Paul's hands. And even if he had, it wouldn't have mattered. The Yankees had come back to New York trailing Boston by five games. The logic of the situation was that he could not possibly survive another humiliation at the hands of the Red Sox.

If it was to be his last shot, he had some scores to settle. The Red Sox were opening with Bill Lee again, for the very good reason that Lee was the only left-hander they had. And that was score number one.

Bill Lee was a free spirit, a flower child of the pot-and-yoga generation living forever in the green fields of the sixties. Billy called him the Lady, as in "Let's get the Lady out of there. She's finished."

His career had almost come to an end the previous season as the result of a wild brawl which had ended with Graig Nettles throwing him to the ground and breaking his shoulder. Lee had developed a set routine about that fracas—he had a whole repertoire of routines about man's inhumanity to man—to explain why he held Nettles blameless.

"I was assaulted by George Steinbrenner and his Brown Shirts," it began. "He brainwashes those kids over there. They're led by Billy Martin, Herman Goering the Second. . . ." After that, it got rough.

Billy sent the batting-practice pitcher out to the market to buy a mackerel. Then he gave the fish to one of the kids who sometimes worked in the visitors' clubhouse with instructions to put it inside the crotch of Lee's pants. He also gave the kid a note to pin to the locker. When Lee started to put on the pants, the fish came flopping out, and he let out a bloodcurdling scream.

"Why don't you stick this in your pussy," the note read. "You might be able to throw harder."

"Really romantic, huh?" Bill Lee sniffed.

And while Billy was settling scores, who else can you think of? That love feast in Detroit didn't fool you, did it? After Billy had finished expressing all that compassion for Reggie Jackson on the fly ball that had been lost in the lights, he had not been able to resist the temptation of offering him some advice. "Maybe," Billy suggested to the writers, "he ought to get his eyes examined."

Good idea, Reggie decided. Especially since it gave him an excuse to duck the pain-in-the-ass Mayor's Trophy Game.

Reggie arrived at the park only an hour before game time, which meant that he had missed batting practice. Big deal. Most of the players skip batting practice from time to time. Thurman Munson, as battered and bruised as he always was, almost never took it.

Just before Reggie came out of the clubhouse, Billy erased his name from the lineup and replaced him with Roy White. Martin's story, which wasn't exactly corroborated, was that the trainer had told him that Jackson's eyes were still dilated. "I've been worried about his eyes," he confided, "both at bat and in the field."

When Jackson saw the altered lineup, he slammed his bat down and walked out to the outfield without bothering to take his glove with him. Now, whenever Billy benched Jackson, there happened to be a left-hander pitching against the Yankees. But in this case that really didn't apply. In the nine times Reggie had faced Lee during the season, he had five hits, including two home runs. Besides, Reggie was swinging the bat good.

When Gabe Paul arrived at the stadium in the second inning, fresh from his three days of R&R in Tampa, he decided that the club's physician should go down to the clubhouse so that he would have the privilege of witnessing that miracle of modern medicine, a thirty-six-hour dilation. Shortly after the doctor returned, Gabe was able to call the dugout and inform Billy that Jackson was "available."

It turned out to be one of the great games in the Yankee–Red Sox rivalry. The spotlight fell on three men: Carl Yastrzemski, Reggie Jackson, and Roy White.

Yastrzemski, always at his best against the Yankees, picked up right where he had left off in Boston with a solo home run leading off the second inning. In the fourth inning, Paul Blair hit a long fly to the left-field fence, and Yaz went up over the wall, caught the ball, reaching back into the bleachers, but came down empty-handed. Literally. A fan in the left-field bleachers had stripped him clean. Yaz looked up, the glove was thrown back to him, the ball was not.

Somewhere there is a Yankee fan who knows he played an indispensable part in winning the pennant for the 1977 Yankees.

The Yankees came up in the last of the ninth trailing 5–3.

145

The pitcher for the Red Sox was Bill Campbell, the first free agent to be signed in the Re-entry Draft. The unbelievable $2 million that had set the stage for the prices that followed. The Red Sox owed their league lead to him. Over his previous ten appearances, he had two wins and eight saves and an infinitesimal ERA of .094.

After Rivers grounded out, Martin sent the available Reggie Jackson to the plate to pinch-hit for Bucky Dent. It was Jackson's first appearance in New York since the fight in the Boston dugout, and he was booed heavily—both before and after he grounded out. Two out, nobody on, and it was beginning to look as if the Yankees were never going to beat the Red Sox again.

Willie Randolph hit a routine fly ball into left center, something between a line drive and a fly. Yaz went running over to make the catch, the game was . . . but wait a minute, Yaz had been playing Randolph in too close and had misjudged the carry. Instead of slanting back, he had come straight over. The ball went sailing over his frantic leap, rolled to the fence, and Willie Randolph went rolling into third base.

The Yankees were still two runs behind, but the tying run, in the person of Roy White, was at the plate. You'll remember that White, a switch hitter, had been substituted for Jackson to bat right-handed against Lee. Against Campbell, he was batting left-handed. Carlton Fisk called for a screwball, a pitch that Campbell usually saved for a two-strike situation. The screwball stayed up, White's bat lashed out, and the ball went into the upper deck in right field like a cannon shot.

Just like that, the Yankees had climbed back from the dead.

Reggie Jackson came to bat again in the eleventh inning with runners on first and second, and lined the first pitch into right field to win the ball game.

Roy White, the man who had started in Reggie's place, had tied the game. Reggie had won it. But the hit that counted was Roy White's. If it is possible to say that one swing of the bat had turned the season around, that's what Roy White had done. Instead of six games behind and fading, the Yankees were four behind and coming on. The wind had changed. You could feel it in the air.

After the victory in Detroit, Reggie had been ecstatic. This was what he loved—a big team effort, a late charge, and Reggie Jackson coming through in the clutch. "It was unbelievable," he had gloated. "I'm just glad I did my job and didn't let the team down."

So now in New York he was really on a high, right? He had shoved it back down Billy's throat. He had, once again, turned the boos into cheers. Not exactly. The Yankees came pouring out of the dugout toward him, and he accepted their congratulations with a restraint bordering upon indifference. When the newspapermen gathered around him in the clubhouse, he was both unsmiling and uncommunicative.

"Just lucky, I guess," he said.

"Lucky to be a Yankee?" a reporter asked hopefully.

Jackson sat there grinding his teeth. "Mmmmm," he explained.

He answered every other question in a similar brief, dull monotone.

What about his removal from the starting lineup? "I don't want to comment about that."

Were his eyes okay? "My eyes are okay."

How had he felt before the game? "I forget how I felt. I forget a lot of things lately. I can't say anything. If you were in my water for a week, you'd understand why."

What if you were in Roy White's water? With one swing of the bat he had turned the first game around. In the third game he was the consummate pro. The Yankees won 5–4, and White was involved in every run. In the first inning, with Rivers running, White slapped the ball right through the position that had been vacated by the shortstop, and Chambliss singled Rivers home. In the third inning, with Rivers running and the second baseman covering, White lined a hit into right field. Munson singled Rivers home, and Chambliss brought White in with a sacrifice fly. In the seventh inning Rivers led off with his third single, White fouled off a couple of three-two pitches and drew a walk. Munson singled Rivers in again, and White led Munson into a double steal.

After the Red Sox had tied the score in the ninth, Roy White worked Bill Campbell for a walk and came around with the winning run on Paul Blair's hit. Blair had been sent out to right field for Reggie Jackson when the Yankees were ahead. Reggie loved that.

And Roy White's water never changed.

At the end of 1979, the year of tragedy, he cleaned out his locker for the last time. After thirteen years, he had not been offered a new contract, given a pat on the back, or a shake of the hand.

"Most guys get a Day," he said wistfully as he looked around the empty locker room. "Maybe I could have got a Roy White Hour."

9

THE SEVEN
COMMANDMENTS

One-thirty in the morning of July 14, Billy Martin was ambling down the corridor to his suite in Milwaukee's Pfister Hotel when he heard the voices of Thurman Munson and Lou Piniella coming out of George Steinbrenner's suite. Billy rapped on the door, and George came to the door in his pajamas. He told Billy nobody else was there. "Right at the door he lied to me," Billy would say later.

The most critical nine days of Billy Martin's tenure with the Yankees had begun. Firings number four and five of 1977 came only nine days apart, and that's including the three-day break for the All-Star game. The crises were beginning to pile on top of each other; it was becoming a weekly affair. Milwaukee had replaced Boston on the other side of the field, and, as with Boston, the crises were played home and away. The meeting in the Milwaukee hotel remains the most intriguing episode because it came out of something closely resembling a player rebellion, led by the captain himself, Thurman Munson.

The Yankees had come to Milwaukee on July 12 tied for second place with the Red Sox, all of half a game behind Baltimore. Hardly a cause for panic, one would think, but they were also coming off three straight losses to the Orioles, and Steinbrenner wasn't taking that too calmly.

And that wasn't the only thing that had set the Boss on a rampage. Two days earlier, in an interview with Murray Chass of *The Times* and Steve Jacobson of *Newsday*, Thurman Munson, identified only as "a prominent Yankee," had set a new controversy in motion by stating flatly exactly what George Steinbrenner and Billy Martin had always been most obdurate in denying. That George Steinbrenner was dictating the lineup. "George doesn't want competition," Thurman had added. "He wants a slaughter. To win you need nine good players plus some capable utility players and a pitching staff. George wants twenty-five superstars. George doesn't care about anybody's feelings. To him, we're not professionals, we're all employees. He treats everybody like that. He's done something to everybody. He's destroyed Billy. He's made him nothing. Not a single guy on the club is happy, except Willie Randolph."

A remarkable statement that, among other things, defined quite succinctly the difference between the 1976 pennant-winners and the staggering 1977 Superstars.

As Thurman Munson had discovered during his salary dispute, George Steinbrenner was incapable of not responding to a public attack. (Nor could it have taken Thurman completely by surprise that Billy Martin might want to deny that he had been destroyed and turned into nothing. Oh sure, Billy said, George was always sending down statistics. "I don't pay any attention to them!")

"It's a lie!" George howled all the way from Tampa. "And any player who says it is a liar." The only thing he had suggested to Billy, he maintained, was that Lou Piniella be used as a permanent DH against all pitching. After all, Piniella was leading the team in hitting, while Carlos May, the left-handed DH, wasn't hitting at all. "He hasn't had one iota of pressure from me about the lineup," George said, an astounding statement for a man who was attempting to establish himself as a truth-teller.

"Do you believe that?" Thurman shot back, still under his cloak of anonymity. And then proceeded to question the use of the recently arrived Cliff Johnson as DH and to criticize the frequent benching of Mickey Rivers and the failure to bat Rivers and White, the keys to the Yankee running game, at the top of the order.

But that wasn't Steinbrenner's lineup Munson was objecting to, it was Billy's lineup (George was pressuring Billy to use Cliff Johnson?!). Under the guise of attacking Steinbrenner, he was giving Billy the old second-guess. He was speaking for the Old Boys, the inner circle, who had been ridiculing Billy's use of Willie Randolph in the lead-off spot. Willie drew a lot of walks, Willie stole a lot of bases, but Willie was not

Mickey Rivers. It was Mickey Rivers who ignited the team, and it was Roy White who teamed with him so perfectly.

What had set Munson off, according to what Thurman told friends later, was that Billy—in one of the low points of his cycle—had been moaning to him that George's constant pressure to bat Reggie fourth was becoming more than he could take. Unfortunately for Billy, he didn't have as sympathetic an ear on that one as he might have thought. Sure, Munson hated Jackson, but above all he wanted to win. He had always thought it silly to torment Jackson by not letting him bat fourth. "If he hits better batting fourth because he thinks he hits better batting fourth, then let him hit fourth, for crissake. What difference does it make?"

Martin's rationale for batting Chris Chambliss fourth was that Chambliss was a contact hitter, and since the Yankees played a running game, they couldn't afford a cleanup man who struck out as much as Reggie. Well, Chambliss was batting fourth and the Yankees' running game had vanished. Billy Martin had thrown it away, partly with his handling of the top of the order. And that's what Munson's second-round outburst was all about!

Back to George. In his first statement out of Tampa, George had backed Billy all the way. "Billy has done everything we expected of him. The people laying down on him are the pitchers, the infielders, and the outfielders. Especially the pitchers." On his second go-around he began to elaborate on his dissatisfaction with the pitching, and the more he elaborated, the more he zeroed in on Billy Martin. "In my opinion, we have given Billy the five best starters in the league. If this is the way they're pitching, the question is if they're handled right."

Just what the pitchers themselves were saying. Billy believed in the five-day rotation. Three of his starters—Torrez, Figueroa, and Hunter—had been insisting that they had to pitch every fourth day. George was putting himself solidly behind the dissident pitchers.

Billy understood what was going on. Billy always knew what was going on in the clubhouse, because he had his spies. This was no secret, he had stated it openly in his pre-season meeting. "I have to have that kind of information," he told the players, "so that if there is anything brewing I can nip it in the bud."

A very worrisome thing for Billy Martin. The players didn't particularly like Billy, indeed many of them hated him. It was only when the owner interfered in clubhouse affairs that they rallied to his support. If he lost that, he lost everything.

"They know George isn't making out the lineup," Billy said. "What they're thinking, I think, is that the whole club lineup has been changed since we got Reggie." Which, of course, was dead on.

While Billy was in the middle of re-denying any interference from George, he received a telephone message instructing him to call Steinbrenner in Tampa.

More bad news. Steinbrenner had to go to Duluth to see whether he could hit the hull of a ship with a bottle of champagne, and he was going to stop off in Milwaukee to find out what was going on. So what was the first thing he wanted Billy to do when the team got to Milwaukee? He wanted Billy to call a press conference and state for the record that the accusations of front office interference were completely false.

It is perhaps the best indication of Billy's precarious situation that he was willing to read a statement that had been dictated by the Boss, a statement denying that the Boss dictated anything to him. And to then deny it on his own by asking, "Would I have been fired three times if I was a company man?"

Before the July 13 game, George held a meeting with Martin and the coaches, and came out to put the onus back on the players. "Those guys have no one to blame but themselves. They'd better stop complaining and go out and play ball."

The Yankees lost a tough 9–8 ballgame, and at twelve-thirty, Thurman Munson and Lou Piniella came knock-knock-knocking on George's door.

It was this meeting that became the ticking bomb of the second half of the season, and exploded before the final game of the World Series in *Time* magazine's World Series issue. George's version, leaked off the record to every writer covering the team, was that Munson and Piniella had come to his suite to tell him that the clubhouse was a shambles, the team was in chaos, and they would not be able to win the pennant with Martin as the manager.

After the story broke, an angry and embarrassed Munson explained, "What I told Steinbrenner was, 'If you're going to fire the guy, fire him and get it over with. Nobody can live with the kind of pressure you're putting on him.'" Piniella's version: "It was understood that nothing of the meeting could come out. We were not entirely on Billy's side." According to Piniella they had said, "Straighten out his contract and remove the clauses. If not, fire him."

The one thing they were all able to agree upon, you will notice, was that there was a lot of talk going on about firing Billy Martin.

Not at all to Billy's surprise either. When Billy heard Munson's and Piniella's voices, he had reason to believe that whatever they were talking about boded no good for him. Otherwise he wouldn't have banged on the door and shouted, "What the hell's going on here?"

"Nothing," George replied. "I'm going to sleep."

Billy pushed his way in and found Munson and Piniella hiding in the bathroom. "Billy, don't go jumping to any conclusions," Thurman said. "This isn't what it seems to be." Maybe it wasn't, but when two people are found hiding in a toilet, they've been doing something they are not exactly proud of.

There were a couple of variations in the off-the-record stories. George would say that Billy was so drunk that he could hardly stand. He would also say that Billy had cried. Billy would say that he went after Munson and they had to be pulled apart. He would also say that he had eventually discovered that the players were on his side. (If he and Munson did have to be pulled apart, Billy was very lucky. Munson would have broken him in half.)

Let's back up again. In George's off-the-record version, he would say that to prevent a very bad scene from developing, he had invited Billy in and told him the two ballplayers were with him because he had ordered them to come up, although the truth of the matter was that the players had asked to come up. "They had told me earlier that they wanted to see me."

Well, he didn't invite Billy in. And on the crucial question of whether the players had come up there on their own or whether George had invited them, he probably reversed that, too. There is every reason to believe that George had sent word to Munson earlier in the day that he wanted to talk to him. It wouldn't have been very difficult to have figured out that Munson was the "prominent player." One indication that George knew it was Thurman was that he pretended to believe that it was Carlos May. Last guy in the world. Carlos was funny, good-natured, and the butt of much of the clubhouse humor. He would have had absolutely no concern about the lineup except whether he was in it.

In the spring of 1978, Lou Piniella, who also lived in Tampa and had a personal relationship with George, said, "The true story of what happened in that room will never be told. I tried to do a favor and ended up looking bad. And that's the last thing I'm ever going to say about it."

A favor?

It is not unreasonable to deduce that George sent word to Munson through Piniella that he wanted to talk to him in the strictest of confidence about the state of the team.

But it wouldn't have been easy for either of the players to pick him up on it. Munson hated Steinbrenner, and Piniella's personality is the very opposite of conspiratorial. It is not difficult, then, to visualize a scene in which Munson and Piniella are drinking, and Munson finally says, "Aw, what the hell, let's go up and see what the Shithead wants."

What Steinbrenner wanted, if Martin was correct, was to drive a wedge between him and his players. What Munson wanted was a winning lineup. That's what George told Billy they had been talking about before he came in. The personnel. It's what they continued to talk about for another four or five hours, with Billy joining in.

Four days after Thurman Munson had given his first anonymous interview, taking Steinbrenner to task for dictating the lineup and turning the manager into nothing, Thurman was up there with George and Billy working out a new lineup. By the time George had to leave to catch his plane, Martin had agreed that Jackson would bat cleanup, Piniella would become the designated hitter against all pitching, and the three unhappy pitchers would go on a four-day rotation. In return, Steinbrenner agreed to remove the clause in Billy's contract that put him in breach of contract if he violated any of the other clauses.

There was a final game to be played in Milwaukee, and then a three-game series in Kansas City before the All-Star break. George had to run off to Duluth to christen that ship, but he promised Billy that he'd be waiting in Kansas City to tell the players that Billy Martin was running the team without any interference from the front office, and that they had better stop blaming everybody else for their problems and start blaming themselves.

Billy's lineup that night had Piniella in left field and batting fourth. (Billy's little joke? You could almost hear him saying up in the hotel room, "Yeah, if Lou's that great a hitter, maybe we oughta have *him* hitting cleanup.") Jackson was batting sixth, Mickey Rivers was leading off, and Roy White was the DH and batting second. Pretty much the 1976 lineup, plus Jackson. Thurman Munson's lineup.

Batting sixth, Reggie had two home runs, including the game winner, and made a diving, juggling catch in the outfield. For the opening game in Kansas City—with George in town, remember—he was batting fourth for the first time since mid-May. The Yankees lost, and the next day Billy went right back to the pre-Milwaukee lineup—Randolph leading off, Cliff Johnson as designated hitter, and Chris Chambliss batting fourth.

If Billy was going down the drain, he would go down his own way. And going down he was. They lost both games. In the second one, with Billy's job hanging by a thread, a tired Thurman Munson was out of the lineup. He had bruised his chest in a collision at the plate, and the temperature in Kansas City was well over 100 degrees. "Why don't you sit it out?" Billy told him. "Rest up for the All-Star game."

An odd time to rest a guy who always plays hurt . . . unless Billy was telling him, in what could be his final game as manager, that in addition to not playing Munson's lineup he would go down without Munson.

While Billy Martin returned to New York to manage the American League All-Star team, the New York Yankees set out to find another manager.

Billy was through. Period. Well, not period. Semicolon. George Steinbrenner was in North Carolina, calling favored reporters to seek their advice. It was a nice way to keep his hand in, now that he had turned the situation over to Gabe, and also a way of getting the word out that Billy was kaput. Through a reporter, he put out a feeler to Walter Alston on the basis of "If you were offered the job, would you be interested?" Alston wasn't going to buy that kind of approach, and even if he had, it wouldn't have meant anything.

Gabe Paul didn't believe that anybody from outside could come into the chaotic situation that had developed. At least not anybody who was available. The man they really wanted was Dick Williams, but Montreal had refused to let Williams go.

George had a candidate from inside the organization: Gene Michael. Michael was traveling with the team as George's administrative assistant, and his principal duty was to sit up in the press box with a walkie-talkie and tell Elston Howard, who had another walkie-talkie on the bench, how to position the fielders. The players, by and large, viewed Michael—fairly or unfairly—as George's spy.

Gabe Paul had his own candidate from within the organization, Dick Howser. Howser had been with the Yankees as a third-base coach for nine years, through all the manager changes. A good third-base coach is so valuable that Billy Martin (who was considered the best third-base coach of them all at Minnesota) has always said that getting the right man for the job is the first decision he makes when he takes over a club, and the one decision he insists upon making.

Dick Howser had always let it be known that he wanted to manage someday. In the opinion of the more knowledgeable sports writers, the only reason he had not been offered a big-league job already was that being such a tiny man he somehow seemed to lack the necessary stature. Howser knew the situation, he had always been loyal to Billy Martin, and he had an excellent relationship with Reggie and the respect of every player on the club. Dick Howser, said Gabe Paul to George Steinbrenner, was their man.

On Saturday, July 23, Paul called Howser to his apartment and alerted Howard Cosell to hold open a spot on "Wide World of Sports." By making the announcement over national TV, he would be accomplishing two things. He would establish once and for all that the decision had been his; and, by submitting himself to Cosell's questioning, he would be able to get everything out in the open at once.

A couple of hours later he called Cosell back to tell him to forget it. "He didn't want it," Gabe said.

Dick Howser had made it clear that he wouldn't be able to manage the club if he was going to have to put up with all that interference from the owner, and it can be stated with some degree of certitude that not putting up with all that interference from the owner was hardly one of the prime requisites for the job. Besides, Howser told him, nobody was going to do a better job with that ballteam than Billy Martin. "The problem isn't the manager, it's the players."

Billy was safe.

Unfortunately he didn't know it. On Saturday, the word was all over the ballpark that Billy was through. Photographers and reporters were streaming into the stadium to catch the magic moment of the announcement. Billy called a team meeting and, in what amounted to a farewell to the troops, made a tearful speech about the subject that is never far from his heart, Yankee pride. Whereupon Piniella took over and talked about the chaos in the clubhouse and the need for discipline. He also went out and got three hits to help the Yankees even up the series against Milwaukee behind Guidry's 3–0 shutout.

Billy was so sure that he was about to be fired that when he came to the park on Sunday morning he didn't even bother to change into his uniform. "I feel like those guys on death row," he told the writers gathered in his office for the Last Mile. "I need a reprieve from the governor." Just then, the phone rang. He answered it, listened, and hung up. "That was Gabe," he said. "I'm not rushing up there. The first time you get fired, you think nothing can be that bad again. But each time it gets worse. Each time I cry. I guess that shows how weak I am."

Instead of rushing up there to be told he was still the manager of the New York Yankees, he sat in his office for half an hour talking about the perfidy of George Steinbrenner. All the old complaints, including the time he splattered George with the ice cubes in St. Petersburg.

Then he went up to the office. Gabe began to talk about the problems on the ballclub, the very kind of talk that Billy had been saying was driving him crazy. And what about all this talk going around that he was through? Billy wanted to know.

"You're here, aren't you?"

Yeah, but what about tomorrow? Next week? Next month?

"You'll still be here. You're the manager." He didn't believe it? "Time proves all things."

Almost the last thing Gabe told him, as Billy was ready to leave, was that he was only going to hurt himself if he persisted in taking on the front office in the press. He had told Billy that before, too—"If you stir shit, it stinks."

Gabe would only have to pick up the paper in the morning to see that while he had been waiting for Billy to come up so that he could tell him his job was safe, Billy had been sitting down there in his office stirring it up good.

Two days later, George held a press conference. He had read all the nasty things Billy had said about him, and he just wanted to set the record straight. "I don't want to be a no-comment guy," said George M. Steinbrenner III, the greatest off-the-record guy who ever lived. Everything Billy had said, he wanted them to know, had been a lie. When, he wanted to know, were they going to catch on to Billy's martyr act? "He is creating the opinion that people are on him all the time. That's just not the case."

No Steinbrenner performance is ever complete without the faint odor of sanctity. "We have come to a time," he intoned, "when for his own good we must demand an accountability of what Martin does and says."

And still nobody believed him when he said that the decision on Billy was up to Gabe. "Whatever recommendations he makes, I will follow," said George, hastening to add that he didn't mean a decision was about to be made.

Poor George. He wanted desperately to fire his manager, and he couldn't do it without Gabe's permission, at least not without losing Gabe. Moreover, the one guy Gabe would agree to for the job wouldn't take it. And he was paying all these people!

To limit his options even further, the stories of Billy's demise had rallied the press and the fans behind him. The team had won two straight games since Salvation Saturday, and for the previous day's game against Kansas City the largest walk-in crowd of the year had come to the stadium to hold a Billy Martin love-in. "The fans are great," said a glowing Billy. "Now if I can only get George to be a fan."

The next best thing to having George for a fan, as far as Billy's career was concerned, was having him for an enemy. Poor George had never been able to get it through his head that in a public contest between big, bad George, the ravenous industrialist from Cleveland, and Billy the Kid, the fresh little street fighter who had always been Casey Stengel's pet, the entire population of Greater New York (minus Reggie Jackson and a couple of bartenders out in Queens) was going to rally behind Billy. Billy had come to be looked upon as a native son, the bad boy of the family to whom all things are forgiven because he has a good heart and can always be counted upon to come through when you need him. Which, come to think about it, was pretty much how Billy saw himself.

Well, if George couldn't fire him, he could at least humiliate him a little.

Having repeated that the decision on Billy's fate was Gabe's, he reached into his desk and came out with a handwritten list of the qualifications Gabe had supposedly drawn up for judging a manager:

1. Won-lost record.
2. Does he work hard enough?
3. Is he emotionally equipped to lead the men under him?
4. Is he organized?
5. Is he prepared?
6. Does he understand human nature?
7. Is he honorable?

Gabe had actually written out only the last six of the seven qualifications, and he hadn't written them out for judging Billy Martin or any other sitting manager. He had written them out three years earlier when they were looking for a manager to replace Ralph Houk. It wasn't for the purpose of firing, in other words, it was for hiring. Not a shotgun, but a screen.

It had been Steinbrenner who posted the won-lost record at the top of the list to make it applicable to Billy.

Appalled at hearing his list being read off for a purpose he never intended, Gabe tried to make a joke of it by saying, "They're short of the Ten Commandments." Worst thing he could have done. Forever after, the list was going to be known as the Seven Commandments.

It was not a joking matter to George. These were *the* guidelines, he wanted everybody to understand, by which Paul was going to weigh and judge Billy's future performance.

Still in there pitching, Gabe said, "This isn't something new or something we've devised just for Billy. These are questions any baseball man constantly asks himself about the man who's managing his ballclub. It's an evaluation you must continually make."

Nobody believed it, just as nobody believed that Gabe was going to decide Billy's fate. The list sounded too much like Steinbrenner.

In attempting to de-martyrize Billy the Kid, George had turned him into the greatest martyr since the British sent Joan of Arc skyward in a swirl of smoke. The first six items on the list didn't mean anything. They were the same crap George had been throwing at Billy all along. It was the Seventh Commandment that did it.

Was he honorable?

For any man to set himself up as magistrate of another man's honor was bad enough. But for this convicted felon, this suborner of perjury, to dare to set himself up as the arbiter of anybody's honor as a condition for future employment was obscene.

Dick Howser had given Billy Martin a respite by refusing to take the job, and George Steinbrenner had given him a reprieve by coming on like a displaced dictator. It didn't matter whether they came up with an acceptable manager now, George *couldn't* get rid of him anymore. At least not without benefit of a disastrous losing streak.

Reggie Jackson helped out his pal Billy by winning the opening game of the crucial Baltimore series with a tenth inning home run. The Yankees won five of the next six games, went on another trip against the patsies on the Coast, and with the continued help of Thurman Munson, Billy came back in the soup.

The Coast trip almost recapitulated the whole season. It started with Reggie Jackson being benched against left-handers because of his bad elbow or, as Reggie explained it, "They told me I had a bad elbow." Actually, he didn't have a bad elbow, he had a bad knee. He had jammed it sliding into second base a week or so earlier, and the Yankees had been holding off the examination until Reggie could see the West Coast wizard, Dr. Frank Jobe, which kind of made sense because they had already made an appointment for Dr. Jobe to examine Don Gullett and Catfish Hunter.

The Yankees were so obsessed about hiding injuries that they lied about them even while they admitted them. After Gullett and Hunter had been examined, the Yankees announced that Dr. Jobe had pronounced them fit and ready, the exact opposite of what Dr. Jobe had said. As for Reggie, his car was hit by a woman driver on the way to the appointment, and he never did get his "bad elbow" which was really a sore knee examined. Instead, he gave the woman his autograph.

When Reggie found himself benched against Ken Brett, a left-hander whom he murders (the 450-foot drive after the Unhandshake had come off Brett), he talked some more about having an escape clause in his contract. Gabe Paul shot back that there was no escape clause, and why didn't everybody stop the bullshit and play baseball for a change? The next night, Reggie, back in the lineup, hit the three hundredth home run of his career, and nobody congratulated him.

A few other happenings on the Coast:

Ken Holtzman called Steinbrenner a fool for paying him all that money for doing nothing.

Lou Piniella excoriated his teammates in the clubhouse after they had kicked a ballgame away against "as horseshit a club" as the Seattle Mariners.

Steinbrenner apologized to the City of New York.

And, through it all, there was Munson's Beard. In strict defiance of the Boss's edict, Munson was growing a beard and thereby putting Billy Martin under the gun again. I know it sounds silly. It sounded silly to Martin. "Petty shit," he rasped when the writers kept asking him about it. "Worried about beards like babies." And then he broke down, began to cry, and went running back into his office and locked himself in.

The writers couldn't understand why Thurman was making things so difficult for Billy Martin, the man responsible for enforcing the rule. Wasn't he hurting Billy? they asked Thurman. And wasn't Billy his friend?

"If the owner is looking for an alibi to fire him," Thurman said, "he doesn't need me as an excuse."

On another occasion, Thurman made it clear enough that he didn't see why he was expected to observe one particular rule while so many other clubhouse rules were going unobserved and unenforced. "This is the most disorganized effort I've ever seen," he said, not for attribution. "Maybe it all gets back to the manager. A lot of problems may come from the manager."

On their way back to New York the Yankees had to stop off at Syracuse to play their annual exhibition game against their top farm club. Sparky Lyle and Mickey Rivers said they wouldn't go. Lyle didn't go and was fined $500. Munson shaved his beard and announced that he wouldn't talk to the press for the rest of the year, a promise he pretty much kept. Mickey Rivers refused to come out of the clubhouse after a rain delay because Thurman Munson had been given permission to leave early so that he could fly home. Mickey loved Thurman, but he didn't like the idea of anybody getting special privileges after he had been denied the right not to come at all. They fined Mickey Rivers $500, which is a new definition of futility.

Meanwhile, the Red Sox had gone off on another of their winning streaks, so the Yankees were coming home five games behind, matching their previous low point. Gabe Paul, who had come to Syracuse to meet the team, took Billy aside and said, "Why don't you end all this horseshit and bat Jackson fourth?"

He had been thinking of doing that himself, Billy told him. "Reggie's been swinging the bat good."

Marvelous, said Gabe. "Why don't you do it today?"

You know something? That's just what Billy had been thinking of doing.

Actually Reggie hadn't been swinging the bat good. Except for Lou Piniella, nobody had been swinging the bat good. But another confrontation with Steinbrenner wasn't exactly what Billy Martin needed, coming back to Yankee Stadium five full games behind.

The Syracuse farm club beat them 14–5.

On August 10, with the team back in New York, another meeting took place in George's office. Billy was to be given one more last chance. They would have an understanding, and Billy was going to live by it, or else. Reggie would bat fourth. And not for just one day this time, but for the rest of the season. Piniella, whose batting average was now up to .330, would play every day. Torrez and Figueroa would pitch every fourth day.

Martin wanted something too. He wanted Art Fowler as his pitching coach. Fowler was Billy's drinking buddy, his pal. Fowler had always been the pitching coach on other Billy Martin teams, and those teams had always been characterized by sound pitching.

Actually it was Gabe who had been against Fowler. Art had a way of being at Billy's shoulder when Billy got into fights, but then why wouldn't he be? Billy didn't get into fights unless he had been drinking, and when Billy was drinking, Art Fowler was usually at his elbow. But that wasn't it, either. Fowler had pitched for Gabe Paul in Cincinnati and had departed under very hostile circumstances, one of a long list of players who had left Gabe Paul clubs under hostile circumstances.

If having Art Fowler would give Billy a greater feeling of security, George was willing to let him have him. "But," he said with a scowl, "the pitching had better straighten out!"

And to enhance Billy's sense of security George gave him something else: a new two-year contract, with a raise from $75,000 to $90,000. A good move psychologically. On George's payroll, $15,000 meant nothing. And, also good psychologically, Billy would be signing a new contract that contained the same restrictive clauses he had been screaming about.

George was right. Of course Jackson belonged in the cleanup spot. Of course Piniella should have been playing every day. But Billy Martin was right, too. From the day Art Fowler joined the coaching staff, it was as if a weight had been lifted off his shoulders. And the pitching staff, which had been such a problem, performed brilliantly down the stretch.

The Yankees won forty of their final fifty games. They clinched a tie by beating Cleveland 10–0, with their $2 million free agent, Don Gullett, back off the disabled list and pitching the shutout and their $3 million hitter, Reggie Jackson, swatting a grand slam home run. The home run gave Reggie 109 runs batted in, more than any Yankee since Mantle's 111 in 1964. It was also Reggie's twentieth game-winning hit.

George Steinbrenner always claimed that the turning point in the fortunes of the Yankees came on August 10, when Billy finally agreed to bat Reggie Jackson fourth. Billy always said that it came when he pulled Jackson out of the game in Boston "and got my team back."

So how come, George riposted merrily, they didn't start to win after Boston?

While the Yankees were making their drive, there was an almost palpable effort to do nothing that would rock the boat. Munson and Jackson would go out to dinner together on the road (chaperoned by Fran Healy). When Martin was going to bench Jackson against a left-hander, he would call him into the manager's office and give him a whole story about how he was getting him rested for some big series that was coming up. And Reggie would say, "Yeah, that's a great idea, Skip. I need that."

The oddest part of the whole relationship between Martin and Jackson is that, except for the Boston imbroglio, they were never really unpleasant to each other face to face. Jackson respects authority. He would come into the office and groan about his sore elbow and banged-up knee, and Martin would tell him just what he wanted to hear. "We need you, Big Guy," he'd say. Big Guy is the ultimate accolade in baseball. The Big Guy is the player who can be counted upon to do whatever has to be done to win the big games.

But it was all an act. As the year was coming to an end, Billy Martin was asked how he really felt about Jackson. "Off the record? He's a piece of shit." And during the off-season Reggie was equally candid about the way he felt about his manager. "Billy Martin," he would say frequently, distinctly, and with feeling, "is a motherfucking bastard." Sometimes without even being asked.

Same thing with Munson. One writer, rejoining the team after a tour with the Mets, found all that goodwill and fellowship so disconcerting that he asked Munson, just for his own background information, whether he and Jackson had really become friends. "Don't believe everything you see," said Thurman. "How could I ever like that motherfucking sonofabitch after what he said about me?"

And through it all Steinbrenner was feeding the writers the story of how Munson and Piniella had come up to his hotel room to tell him that Billy had lost control of the ballclub, that the clubhouse was a shambles, and they wanted him fired. Or telling them how Reggie's lawyer wanted to renegotiate his contract on the basis of Martin being gone. " 'My guy can't live this way anymore,' " he quoted the lawyer as saying. " 'We're being destroyed here. And you're supposed to be his friend.' "

And don't think Billy Martin wasn't giving them his own version of the same event. Billy was telling them that George had invited the players to his suite to try to create more disruption, and had lied to him by trying to tell him that nobody was there.

The other things they had to say about each other went to character and sexual proclivities, and were scarifying beyond belief.

From the moment the division title was won, the façades were dropped and the enmities began to surface. George didn't even come down to the clubhouse for the victory celebration until Lou Piniella phoned him from out in the concourse to tell him, "You're making a mistake, Boss. You ought to be here." George came down reluctantly, made little more than a ceremonial appearance, and left.

Too bad. If he had stuck around he could have caught the beginning of Billy Martin's campaign to force George to admit publicly that Billy had done such a magnificent job that there was no question that he would be back next season, and with a raise in pay.

For the time being, Billy had to be content with admitting it himself. "If we win everything," he said, "I think it's a must for George to come up with another contract. If he doesn't, I'd have to seriously think about asking permission to talk with other clubs."

Question: Having satisfied the first of the Seven Commandments by winning, wasn't he breaking the Seventh Commandment—about being honorable—by taking on the Boss?

Any time Billy was able to field a question on the Seven Commandments, he was ahead. There was only One Man, he intoned, who was entitled to hand down Commandments. "If I get fired, I'll beat him. If he buys $50 million worth of players, I'll beat him with another club and he knows it. . . . If I come back, I'll make him cry."

To listen to Billy you'd have thought he had won the pennant almost single-handedly by holding a team of snarling, basically incompatible players together on one front, while overcoming Steinbrenner's constant interference on the other. "If he ever gets to working with me," Billy sighed, "it could be a lot easier."

Steinbrenner, still incapable of not answering back, reacted predictably by saying that Billy was acting predictably. "If he's playing this thing out in the press—and this is a form of coercion, in a way—then he's crazy. Because he's taking the credit from the players." As far as a new contract was concerned, he said, that was Billy's pattern:

always coming back, looking for more when he was successful. "We were warned about this when we hired him. So it had to come, sooner or later."

Placed within the dramatic trajectory of the full season, it was marvelous. Just as Reggie Jackson had seized the spotlight on the first day of spring training, Billy Martin was seizing the spotlight at the beginning of post-season play. But with Billy it was more than a matter of pure ego. By forcing the issue he was making himself the running subplot of the post-season: "Is Billy Martin going to be fired, win or lose?" And all George could do was lend credence to what Billy was hinting by saying, "We'll have to wait and see."

The first thing Billy had to do was defeat Kansas City in the five-game playoffs for the American League pennant. And the Yankees were going in as the underdogs. They had won forty of fifty down the stretch, but the Royals had won forty-three out of fifty-three. Three of the five games were going to be played in Kansas City, where the Royals had beaten the Yankees four games out of five during the season. They were supposed to be unbeatable on their Astroturf. And so when the Yankees could get nothing better than a split in the two games at Yankee Stadium, and lost the opener in Kansas City, the odds on their winning two out of two were prohibitive.

With all the criticism that has been leveled against George, nobody has ever accused him of being anything less than one of the world's great fathers. With his ballclub on the edge of being eliminated, George went down to the University of North Carolina to keep his promise to his daughter to be with her on Parents' Day. The Yankees eked out a 5–4 victory, and George returned to Kansas City just in time for his manager to let him be the first to know that he was going to bench Reggie Jackson in the fifth game.

Billy could make a case. Reggie had had one single in fourteen times at bat, and he hadn't exactly distinguished himself on the hard Astroturf outfield. Paul Splittorff, a tough left-hander, was pitching for the Royals, and during the season Reggie had two hits against Splittorff in fifteen times at bat—one home run and one double.

The alternate case was that Reggie wasn't the only left-hander who hadn't been hitting. Neither Chambliss nor Nettles had been doing any better. And since when had Billy Martin become a slave to statistics? It was, after all, Billy's scorn for the Boss's statistics that had brought on so much of the strain between them. "George sent down another batch of statistics, *ditditdahdah*," Billy would say, imitating George's computer. "I threw them in the wastebasket." No, statistics were not for Billy. "My secret of managing," he had said during one of those press conferences when he had expected to be fired, "is in getting to the heart of a player."

We are talking here about Reggie Jackson in the fifth and deciding game of the playoffs. We are talking about the Shoot-out at the OK Corral, the moment of truth, the high pressure ballgame in which Reggie Jackson, off his record of ten years, pumps a richer, finer adrenaline.

But we are also talking about Billy Martin, who off a record of twenty-five years had shown that he does not go gently into that good night. If the Yankees lost, Billy was through, and he was going to be taking Reggie and George with him. Throughout the year Billy had answered the questions about the benching of Jackson by asking back, "What do we need him for? We won the pennant last year without him, didn't we?" And Jackson would reply, "They won the pennant, but not the World Series."

And now, the fear that Reggie had expressed from the first week of spring training was about to become a reality: If, having won the pennant without him, they didn't win it with him, "Everybody will say it's my fault, and Steinbrenner will look like a fool." In his darkest moment had he ever envisioned the possibility that they might lose it while he was suffering the ultimate humiliation of having been benched for non-hitting?

Billy sent Elston Howard, his emissary to black players (Yogi was his emissary to white players), to break the news. And then Fran Healy went in to talk to Reggie, sent by nobody knows who. Reggie remained in the clubhouse until the last few moments of batting practice, and when he emerged, he was prepared to say all the right things. Yes, he had been surprised. "You've got to be down, your pride has got to be hurt. But if a man tells me I'm not playing, I don't play. I sit down and pull for the club. I'm not the boss. I'm the right fielder. Sometimes." Was that the message George had sent in to him?

During the game he led the cheering from the bench. When the Yankees were out on the field, he sat beside Billy, and they chatted pleasantly. Billy was so impressed with his attitude that he promised him he would play all the games in the World Series, regardless of who was pitching. Was that a message he wanted to be relayed to George?

For seven innings it didn't really seem to matter. The Yankees were behind 3–1.

Randolph singled to lead off the eighth, an indispensable ingredient to the emerging Reggie Jackson subplot in that it got Splittorff out of the game. Whitey Herzog, the Royals' manager, had been playing the lefty-righty percentages in the late innings all year long, and with Munson coming to bat he called in his ace right-handed relief pitcher, Doug Bird. Bird struck out Munson, but Piniella singled Randolph to third and, with a right-handed pitcher on the mound, Reggie Jackson was sent up to bat in place of Cliff Johnson.

Reggie didn't do anything all that dramatic. Behind in the count, 1-2, he hit a lazy single into center field to score Randolph. But that's Reggie. It might not have been much of a hit, but it was a hit at the right time, and now it was a 3–2 game.

The Yankees scored two runs in the ninth to win it. A single by Blair, who had started the game in place of Reggie, a walk to pinch hitter Roy White, and then all that bunting practice Mickey Rivers wouldn't take finally paid off. Having failed to bunt, he whistled a line drive over second base to tie the score. Willie Randolph, whose hit had put Splittorff out of the game, drove in what proved to be the winning run with a long fly.

But who wants a Willie Randolph for the hitting hero? The story was Reggie Jackson. Billy Martin had used him to write his own scenario, and now Reggie had taken the scenario back. "All season," he said, clutching at his heart, "I had to eat it in here. Thank God. I can't explain it because I don't understand the magnitude of Reggie Jackson and the magnitude of the event. I am the situation!"

Well, if he was the situation, it was partly because Billy had made him the situation, and partly because Reggie knows when to put another touch on the Autobiography.

What would he have said if he had done it with a home run? What if he had done it with two home runs? Would anybody dare to venture three? Stand by.

There were other echoes from the tumultuous season. Leading off the ninth, Paul Blair had stayed alive to get the key hit by fouling off two perfect sliders, low and away. Just the kind of pitch that had left Blair helpless for five years after he had been hit in the face by a pitched ball. Blair was making everybody aware that it had been Munson's instructions that had enabled him to protect the outside of the plate on those two sliders.

"Yeah," Munson said. "The Beachball [his name for himself] can't stir the fuckin' drink, but he can show you how to hit."

Everybody else was giving a faultless rendition of themselves, too. George Steinbrenner found a moral lesson in Reggie's agony: Reggie had become a man. "When he comes in, he delivers a hit instead of sulking. That shows everyone in New York he's a team man."

Billy Martin, the third man on the seesaw, was not exactly glowing in the reflection of Reggie's triumph. Upon being asked why he himself hadn't told Reggie he was being benched instead of doing it through emissaries, Billy answered, "How do you tell a guy he's been butchering the outfield and not hitting worth a damn? How do you do that diplomatically?"

During the victory celebration, Martin pounced upon Steinbrenner and doused him with champagne. "That's for trying to fire me," he yelled.

"What do you mean try?" George said coldly. "If I want to, I'll fire you."

Yes, he could fire him, but he could no longer humiliate him. A call came through from Billy's buddy Mickey Mantle to congratulate him, and Billy, sitting in his office, told Mickey, "He can't hurt me anymore. He can't touch me now."

If Reggie "I am the Situation" Jackson had so much difficulty understanding the magnitude of himself after a little humpbacked single, it was going to take a lifetime of scholarship and dedication to define the limits of his ever-expanding universe after his performance in the World Series. What is forgotten is that he had a terrible beginning.

After the opening two games against the Dodgers in New York, his total was one single in six times at bat, and he half expected to be benched in the third game against left-hander Tommy John. "All I hear is how I'm making too much money and not hitting enough." Seemed like old times.

When Martin was asked about it, he made Reggie feel a lot better by saying Jackson wasn't going to be benched . . . and then gave the writers a chance to keep it going by adding, "Splittorff isn't pitching, is he?" Reggie snapped back that he didn't have to take that from anybody, let alone Martin. "I know what I can do, and if he knew that, he might be a lot better off." And now that his mouth was rolling he decided to criticize Billy for throwing Catfish Hunter, who hadn't pitched for a month, to the wolves in the second game.

The Yankees flew to California. Their two Western trips during the season had been filled with controversy, and just because this was the World Series, why should it be any different? This time the fun started even before the plane landed, with an in-flight near-riot over the location in the ballpark the players had been allotted for their families and friends. "How many box seats does George have?" Munson wanted to know. Unless the players got more boxes, Munson wasn't going to play in the rest of the Series. "No way!"

Reggie went him one better. " I won't put on my uniform until I get better seats." Reggie was going to sit in the clubhouse until Bowie Kuhn brought them in personally.

Billy Martin couldn't resist that one. "Right after Reggie said it, two of my top pitchers went up to Gabe Paul and told him if he really wanted to help the Yankees, he shouldn't give Reggie any tickets."

That was the plane ride. Soon as the team got to Dodger Stadium for its first workout, Billy was informed of Reggie's comments about Hunter. "He can kiss my Dago ass," he said. To which Reggie responded, "If I had an ethnic origin, I'd tell him what he could kiss."

Billy might have kissed it, too. By criticizing him about Hunter, Jackson had played right into his hands. During the World Series, the reporters cover the field like a carpet, and Billy had something for everybody.

He said, "I told him he would be playing in every game, but if he's going to say things to hurt the ballclub, and if he doesn't hit Tommy John, I may have to think about making a change. He has a little growing up to do."

He said, "Where's his memory? What happened to that 160 IQ he says he has? Why do we have to have all that kind of talk now? Do your job, and if you can't do your job then shut up. He has enough trouble in right field."

Sooner or later he was going to say something about being a true Yankee. "A true Yankee doesn't criticize another Yankee player or the manager. We're all supposed to be working together to win. The way to do that isn't with your mouth but with the bat and glove."

He said, "Did I criticize him the other day when he didn't run after a ball? Mickey Rivers had to come over from center field to get it. If I'm gonna back that prick, why doesn't he back me? What is this, a one-way street?" That's another favorite of Billy's: "What is this, a one-way street?"

The next day, Reggie was rather late coming onto the field. When Catfish Hunter, who found the whole thing hilarious, was asked about Reggie's absence, he said, "I think he's inside waiting for Bowie Kuhn to bring him some tickets."

When Reggie did finally come out, he stationed himself near first base and delivered a statement that could have been written by a public relations man named George M. Cohan, or George M. Steinbrenner:

> In the emotion of wanting to win the World Series, maybe I said something I shouldn't have said that was taken the wrong way. I have no desire to comment on anything Billy Martin does in handling the ballclub because he has won the pennant two years in a row, and I'm pleased to be a member of this club. I've had a good year because of the way he handled me.

Billy the Kid, who was sucking a popsicle under the watchful eye of the flower of the nation's press, was happy to learn how badly he had misinterpreted what Reggie had been saying. "There won't be any more misunderstandings," he promised, "because next time I'll talk to Reggie first and ask him what he meant."

What about the Great Seat Controversy? Oh, the seats were great: one tier up behind home plate. Just to show he was willing to suffer too, George and his guests sat with the players' wives. One of his guests became so excited when the Dodgers' Dusty Baker hit a three-run home run that he leaped up and spilled his beer all over George.

And to think that Thurman Munson had objected to those seats.

Game 3 was won by the Yankees, 5–3, on bloop hits and wrong-way hits.

Game 4 was also won by the Yankees, 4–2, behind a four-hitter by Guidry. Reggie scored the first run after hitting a ground-ball double down the third-base line, where you can be sure he wasn't aiming. He scored the last run in the sixth inning with a home run into the right-field stands, where you can be sure he was aiming. Martin didn't send Paul Blair out to right field until the ninth inning, and when the game was over, Jackson embraced Martin and thanked him for giving him an extra time at bat.

With the Yankees now leading the Series three games to one,

Reggie nominated Billy for the Nobel Prize for Managing. What about himself? "How about the Survivor's Medal?"

"I accept," said Billy Martin. "With deep humility, I accept. Thank you very much." Since one good nomination deserved another, it was suggested that Billy might want to return the favor. Why not? "How about the Good Guy Award?"

How about the MVP award? Unless the Dodgers won Game 5 in Los Angeles, they were not going to be able to go back to New York so that Reggie could hit his three home runs. No need to worry. The Dodgers were leading 10–0 in the seventh inning behind Don Sutton when the Billy Martin Story began to blend into the Reggie Jackson Story. Reggie led off the inning with a single and scored the first Yankee run. A very quiet beginning. With two out in the eighth, Munson and Jackson hit consecutive home runs. Don Sutton, who was a friend of Munson, screamed his congratulations in the form of insults at him while he was running around the bases, which is something you can do when you're holding a 10–2 lead in the eighth inning. Reggie's home run he didn't care for so much. "I object to guys who trot the bases like they have saved the world from utter chaos," Sutton said. A good line. Reggie appreciates good lines. Stick around, Reggie could have told him. If Sutton found Reggie's home-run trot so objectionable, Reggie was going to give him a case he could take to the United Nations.

But first there was the Billy Martin Story to be disposed of. *Time* magazine hit the stands on the off-day between Los Angeles and New York, and the whole Milwaukee hotel room caper was out in the open. Munson and Piniella were outraged at the breaking of the confidence. Actually, they knew that George had been giving it out, off the record, because the New York writers had asked them about it at least a month earlier. The New York writers, however, had been hemmed in by the way Steinbrenner had given it to them. In case you're wondering, he had given it to the *Time* reporter the same way. But that reporter was Bob Ajemian, who happened to be the Washington bureau chief. Ajemian had started out as a sportswriter in Boston, and he was doing the Yankee story as relaxation. Having been managing editor and London bureau chief of *Life* before going to *Time*, he was accustomed to dealing with stories where information came pouring in from many sources, and so when George gave him such a remarkable story and then put it off the record, Ajemian automatically told him that if he heard the story from anybody else, without doing anything on his own to stimulate it, he might want to come back to him. Almost immediately Martin had told him about it. On the record. After that it became a matter of allowing each of them to rebut the other's version.

George knew it was coming. In fact, he had asked if the story could be delayed until the Series was over. Martin knew it was coming. Martin had made sure that it would be coming.

Moving quickly to contain the damage, the Yankees called a press conference on the morning of the sixth game to announce that Billy Martin was going to be back to fulfill his two-year contract. He was also getting a $50,000 bonus, along with a public acknowledgment that he had done the job and remained his own man to the end.

On the morning of the final game, the scenario which Billy Martin had set into motion at the close of the regular season had come to a wholly satisfactory end. The scenario which Reggie Jackson had begun to write on the first day of spring training would achieve a crashing climax that same night.

In the first inning, Reggie walked on four straight pitches. (Four straight pitches, that's important.) The next time up he hit a two-run homer off Burt Hooton's first pitch to give the Yankees a 4–3 lead.

In the fifth inning he hit Elias Sosa's first pitch on a line into the lower right-field stands, a ball hit so hard that it was into the stands before the right fielder could turn around.

You look back and there is always the sense of it-had-to-be. Or whatever the opposite of *déjà vu* is. But it really shouldn't have happened. After the first home run, Reggie shouldn't have been given anything to hit on the first pitch. That's basic—everybody knows Reggie gets himself all charged up. After he had hit two, that ancient rule of baseball known as "knock him on his ass" should most certainly have been brought into play. When Reggie came up to the plate, he was so pumped up that if his feet were touching the ground, it was only because the ground was coming up to meet them. Charlie Hough, who had come in for the Dodgers, was a knuckle-ball pitcher, but knuckle-ball pitchers can knock you on your ass, too. At the very least, you would have expected him to fiddle around with Reggie for a while, let him chase a couple of bad pitches, give him a chance to simmer down a little.

The first pitch was a knuckle ball that didn't knuckle. Instead of darting downward, it just kind of snuggled up to the plate about knee high and rolled over. Right into Reggie's wheelhouse. He had never before in his life been so pumped up, and he could not possibly have got a pitch hung up there for him more perfectly. Up, up, and away it went, a 475-foot drive into the center-field bleachers.

In the first inning of the opening game of the season, Jim Wynn had hit a home run into those center-field bleachers, and when Reggie was told it was the first ball ever hit up there in the new Yankee Stadium, he had given the mob of writers around him his most prophetic look and said, "Stick around." You had to stick around all right—for his final swing on his last time at bat that year.

Records of the tallest timber went toppling: Only Babe Ruth had ever hit three home runs in a single World Series game, and not even the Babe had done it on three consecutive times at bat, let alone on three successive swings.

Add the home run Reggie had hit on his last time at bat against Don Sutton, and it was four home runs on four consecutive swings.

Add the home run off Rick Rhoden in Game 4, and it was five home runs in three consecutive games off five different pitchers. And nobody had ever hit five home runs in a World Series before.

Ah, Reggie . . . With most of us the happy times live on in our memory and the sad times fade away. During the off-season, Reggie looked back on what he called "a season of horrors" and remembered only the abuse he had taken, the insults. "Every member of that team hated and despised me," he would say. In one of his more poetic moods, he put it thusly: "I was in the eye of the storm and had no wind to cast back."

Since you cannot have a season of horrors if it ends in triumph, it did no good at all to suggest that it had, at least, ended well for him. "In many ways," he had decided, "it was the worst day of all. Do you know that after the game was over and I had hit three home runs, only three of my teammates congratulated me."

It's too bad he chose to remember it that way because it just wasn't so. Whatever his teammates thought of him personally, they recognized what he had done, they were thrilled for him, and they let him know it. Back in the clubhouse immediately after the game, led by Thurman Munson, they surrounded him, pounded his back, embraced him. "I stood up for you all year, ya coon ya," Thurman shouted. "I hope you know that."

"I know that," Reggie said. "You did."

"Just remember that, you coon, I stood up for you all year. I was the one who called you Mr. October, and you had to live up to it."

Munson was kind of forgetful there himself. Earl Weaver had started it by saying that Reggie was the best September player he had ever seen, meaning that he was a terror down the stretch. Reggie liked that so much that he had picked it up and, with that finely tuned ear of his, moved it forward to World Series time and labeled himself "Mr. October."

What Munson had said during the snap-and-bite of the practice session at Dodger Stadium was this: "Billy probably just doesn't realize Reggie is Mr. October. If I was hitting .167, I wouldn't be second-guessing the goddamn manager. And I'm going to stop talking because the more I talk, the madder I get."

But never mind. He was calling him Mr. October now, and he was meaning it.

The Yankee locker room was totally schizophrenic anyway. While the players were celebrating the winning of the World Championship, they were also announcing, almost to a man, that they absolutely, positively were not going to return next year if they had to spend another season like this—and, all the while, being honestly and unabashedly happy for the guy they blamed for causing all the trouble.

Like Sparky Lyle. Hours after the game was over, Lyle, who had never hidden his dislike for Reggie—least of all from Reggie himself—was slumped down in a chair in the manager's office watching yet another rerun of the home runs on television. "It was so thrilling," gushed the sportscaster, "I had tears in my eyes." Sparky looked up at the television screen and said, "You're not the only one, sucker."

10

THE BUNT

At 7:30 on the morning of July 18, 1978, three men left Reggie Jackson's penthouse apartment, each carrying a large bag, exited the elevator at the fifth floor, and slipped through the window and onto the fire escape.

There was a mob of sportswriters waiting in the lobby, and for one of those rare times in his life Reggie did not want to be seen or photographed or even hear himself talk.

With Reggie were his agent, Matt Merola, and Ray Negron. After a four-story descent down the fire escape, they stepped onto a precarious cement wall, tight-roped across to the adjoining building—not easy when you're carrying a heavy bag—dropped the bags to the ground four or five feet below them, then jumped down, depositing themselves in front of the garage where Reggie parked his car.

Unfortunately the garage was locked, and Reggie had to kick the door open. With Merola behind the wheel of Reggie's Corniche, they headed for Kennedy Airport and a flight home to Oakland. In Reggie's pocket was a telegram informing him that he had been indefinitely suspended by the New York Yankees.

Billy Martin had won.

Except that he hadn't. Seven days after Ray Negron had accompanied a distraught Reggie to the airport, an even more distraught Billy Martin, having slipped back to New Jersey after self-destructing in Chicago, was handing Negron *his* car keys and asking him to drive the car down to Dallas for him.

Reggie had won.

Except that he hadn't. Two nights later, Billy Martin was calling Ray to tell him to hold off for a while because he was probably going to be around New York for a couple of weeks and would be needing the car. "Don't worry," he told him. "Everything's going to be all right."

Billy had won again. And, as seemed apparent, in an incredible Old Timers' Day ceremony at Yankee Stadium two days later, had won big.

Except that he hadn't.

The only winner in the end, as always, was George.

Was there ever such a season as 1977? we asked some pages back. Was there ever such a team? Well, yes. It's called the 1978 Yankees.

Gabe Paul had left to take over the reins in Cleveland, and Al Rosen was brought in to replace him. Although Gabe was leaving, he was determined to leave the Yankees in the best possible shape. And in the second running of the Re-entry Sweepstakes there was only one player who counted as far as Gabe was concerned. Rich Gossage.

Why, of all things, a relief pitcher? Sparky Lyle had not only won the Cy Young Award as the best pitcher in the American League, he had become the first relief pitcher in the league ever to win the Most Valuable Player award. But Sparky was going to be thirty-four years old, and he had had good years and bad years. "I've got one pitch" was the way Sparky always put it. "And either I get them or they get me."

Goose Gossage, at twenty-six, was simply the most overpowering relief pitcher in baseball, and relief pitching had become so important that Gabe Paul felt Gossage could mean the pennant for any one of four teams in the league.

So the Yankees went for Goose on the first round, and they got him. But by then Gabe had left, and what happened after that was indicative of what everybody in the front office feared was going to happen without Gabe there to talk George out of doing something impulsive. As his second free agent George signed Rawly Eastwick, a middle-inning relief pitcher, for $1.1 million over five years. A lot of money for a fast-ball pitcher who had lost his fast ball.

But, as the season proceeded, it turned out not to matter who was sitting at George's right hand. The Yankees of 1978 were the Yankees of 1977, only more so.

On the grand scale:

- The unhappiness brigade was led by Sparky Lyle. Having won the MVP award, his late-inning relief job was being handed over to Gossage. To compound the insult, both of the new relief pitchers, Gossage and Eastwick, were being paid more than he was.
- Billy teetered on the brink, Reggie was tormented, and George screamed a lot.
- Mickey Rivers continued to have "problems," and they continued to show up in a creeping paralysis on the field of play; and Billy continued to treat the malady with carefully applied dosages of benchings and lectures. Somewhere in the land there had to be a Jonas Salk with a better idea.
- The pitching staff was in a shambles, only more so.
- In compensation, Ron Guidry was the ace of the staff, only more so. He kept getting better and better, and had one of the great seasons of modern history, 24–3, running his streak from the second half of the previous season to 34–5.
- The ballclub came from farther behind over the second half of the season to catch the Red Sox.
- They beat Kansas City again, only this time it took only four games.
- They beat Los Angeles again in the World Series in six games, only this time they had to come back after losing the first two.

On a smaller scale:

- George came out of spring training saying the Yankees weren't ready to start the season. He was right.
- Martin made a run at Rosen's authority with another May flap over a third-string catcher.
- Billy was almost fired again in June after losing in Boston— and was saved again in a meeting in Detroit.
- Having fought to get Art Fowler in 1977, he had to fight to keep him in 1978.
- George announced that he was going to keep a low profile and leave the running of the club to his baseball people.
- George said at every crisis that it would be up to Al Rosen whether Billy Martin stayed or went.

- Just before the All-Star break, Lou Piniella complained about that lack of discipline in the clubhouse. This time the final series before the All-Star game was in Milwaukee itself, and once again the Yankees put Billy's job on the line by losing all three games.
- Instead of looking for a new manager after the All-Star game, George took over control of the ballclub himself.
- A new pitching coach joined the club at the absolute low point of the season. This time it was Clyde King.
- The low point came once again against Kansas City.
- Don Gullett and Catfish Hunter went on and off the disabled list. But then—and here the pattern changes dramatically—in one of the greatest miracles since Lazarus was last seen doing loop-de-loops over Jerusalem, Catfish Hunter came back from the dead.

And speaking of comebacks, the Yankees made the greatest comeback in the history of baseball in 1978, coming from fourth place, fourteen games behind the leader, on July 17, to beat the Red Sox in the second playoff game in American League history.

July 17 was the pivotal date. It was on that date, the above-mentioned low point of the season, that there was another confrontation between Reggie and Billy. And—one of those enormous coincidences—another member of the cast "hooked" it, to use Bucky Dent's colorful term, shortly before the confrontation occurred. And this time with far more serious repercussions for Billy Martin.

It was on July 17 that the demons driving Reggie whispered in his ear that it would be a great idea to bunt, regardless of how the manager felt. It was six days later that the furies whipping around in Billy's psyche gave him a perfectly splendid idea of how to top that.

The year before, Billy had made his move on Gabe Paul with the Hendricks Flap, on May 27. In 1978, he had to wait until May 29 to make a run at Rosen. This was Rosen's first administrative job in baseball, and that alone made him an irresistible target.

As with the Hendricks affair, it was Munson's knee that brought the battle on. During a game against Baltimore, the Orioles were able to score what proved to be the winning run on a terrible Munson throw to second base on a broken hit-and-run play and two wild pitches which Thurman couldn't move quickly enough to block. He had to take himself out of the game, and since the Yankees had no third-string catcher, Rosen immediately called West Haven, a AA farm, for Mike Heath, their excellent twenty-three-year-old prospect. You'd think Billy would be grateful for such prompt attention to his problems. That's what the Hendricks affair had been all about, wasn't it? Another catcher to protect Thurman Munson.

Unhappily, the announcement about Heath had been made in the press box during the game, and when Billy found himself in the position of hearing about it from the writers during a post-game interview, he was incensed. "Yes," he said when Rosen called a few minutes later, "I just heard from the press. Thank you." And slammed down the phone.

Once the press conference was over, he went upstairs and bawled out Rosen for not having consulted him.

He was very lucky that he didn't get fired. Gabe Paul, after all, had been eager to use the Hendricks affair as an excuse to get rid of Billy, on those old familiar grounds, and how many times must George have kicked himself during the rest of that season for not having had the good sense to follow Gabe's advice.

With George, however, there always seemed to be the desire to get rid of Martin without having to pay off his contract. Although, in fairness to George, there can be little doubt, off his track record, that having proved to himself he could do it, he'd have relented somewhere along the line and paid him anyway.

Given Billy's contract, a day didn't pass that didn't provide a reason. And if the day didn't, George did. In a moment of impulsiveness excessive even for him, George had signed Andy Messersmith for $330,000, notwithstanding that Messersmith had come up with a bad elbow in Atlanta and had undergone an operation over the winter. "Eastwick and Messersmith are my gambles," George had proclaimed, not without pride. "I wanted them. I'll take the responsibility." George had returned to New York just in time to read a column about how Billy, taking him at his word, had referred to the two questionable pitchers all through spring training as "George's boys."

Criticizing the front office again? "I'm going to conduct an investigation," harrumphed George, "and if I find out it's true, Billy's gone."

George also had in his possession a letter from league headquarters reprimanding Billy for having given the finger to a heckler in Cleveland. George's very own mother had been in the stands on that infamous occasion, and, according to George, she had been terribly offended. Something had to be done, he said, to stop Billy from doing things that "embarrass all good people who like him."

Not a very imposing bill of indictment, to be sure, but Billy had every reason to believe that the threat itself was real. George's secretary had warned him that very morning to be careful what he said over his office phone, because George was out to set him up and the phone was bugged.

Billy summoned Ray Negron and they tore the phone apart, but were unable to find anything. A friend from the phone company was called in, and he couldn't find anything either. Nor had he expected to. Considering that the stadium had just been rebuilt, he told them, the system could very easily have been set up so that *every* call that went in or out of the stadium was tape-recorded.

Billy had always wondered how George was able to go away for a week or two and still know every little thing he was doing. He was sure George had an informant among the players, and he had his candidates, but even that didn't explain how George managed to be privy to his more personal affairs, such as Billy's meetings with a young girl with whom he was very much in love and whom he intended to marry as soon as his divorce became final. George kept warning him that the girl was underage, and that if he didn't break it off with her he was going to end up in the kind of trouble that would disgrace the Yankees.

So now he knew how George knew.

The Yankees were about to make their final Western trip. After running off a streak of ten wins in thirteen games, they had lost three straight to Baltimore. Before he left to catch the bus to the airport, Billy went upstairs for a conference with Steinbrenner and Rosen. A lot of screaming went on, and although Billy didn't bring up anything about the suspected bug at that time, he did tell them as he was leaving that if they wanted to fire him they should call him in his office before he left for the airport. "Have a good trip," Rosen told him.

When the Yankees returned from the Coast, nine days later, Billy still had his job and George's secretary didn't. George had fired her.

From then on Billy made all his personal calls from a pay phone outside the stadium.

On the June 15 trading deadline, the Yankees made a last-minute trade for Gary Thomasson, a left-handed-hitting outfielder. "I need a starting pitcher," Billy wailed, "and they're loading me down with left-handed DH's." Billy had a point. A day earlier, they had traded for another left-handed hitting outfielder, Jay Johnstone. Billy would have had an even better point if he hadn't been aware that the front office had been trying to put together a package to be passed on to San Francisco for pitcher Jim Barr. So OK, time had run out on them, and they were stuck with exactly what they didn't need. But Billy had lost nothing. Johnstone had come for the unusable Eastwick (with Steinbrenner picking up most of his salary), and Thomasson for two minor leaguers.

On June 19, the Yankees went into Boston trailing by seven games. Not that they had been playing badly. Except for the Red Sox, who never seemed to lose, and the National League leader, the San Francisco Giants, the Yankees had the best record in all of baseball. And this despite a horrific run of injuries. At one time, Gullett, Hunter, Tidrow, Holtzman, and Clay were all out of action. Randolph's leg was in a splint, Rivers's hand was broken, Dent had a pulled hamstring, and Munson's leg was so bad that he shouldn't have been playing. The whole middle defense had been wiped out.

That didn't impress Steinbrenner. If the pitchers were getting hurt, somebody had to be handling them wrong. And if the young pitchers—once his pride and joy—hadn't developed, it could only mean they weren't being handled right.

And who was the pitching coach? Art Fowler was the pitching coach. And what could that mean except that George was reminding Billy that he had been given his drinking buddy Fowler in that August 10, 1977, meeting in return for certain promises about not criticizing the front office.

Billy remembered those promises, too. Billy had wanted Fowler, George had wanted Piniella in the lineup. Martin's 1978 riposte was to keep Piniella, who was only the number-two hitter in the league, on the bench—and in Fenway Park, which is made for a hitter like Lou.

In the final game, with the series tied at one game each, Jim Beattie, a rookie pitcher who had been pitching very well up to then, was blown out of the park in less than three innings.

Beattie left the pitcher's box, and Steinbrenner left his upstairs box at approximately the same time. Both headed for the locker room, with George traveling faster. When the other players came in, Beattie was fully dressed and had tears in his eyes. George had excoriated him, called him a coward, and sent him back to Tacoma.

"He didn't have his good stuff," Martin allowed, "but he has all the guts in the world." Billy also had a few words to say about his own situation. "I don't run scared. My mother didn't raise a quitter. I remember last year I was going to get fired here. I'll show you the ring I got fired with. It says World Champions."

The World Champions were going to Detroit for a weekend series. On Saturday morning, league president Lee MacPhail called Bill Veeck to suggest that it might be a good idea all around if the struggling Yankees and the struggling White Sox exchanged managers. Veeck felt it would be an even better idea—since Steinbrenner was clearly coming to him through MacPhail—if the Yankees threw a player into the deal. MacPhail called again on Sunday morning. Veeck hadn't changed his mind. On that lone demurrer of Veeck's the deal hung.

On Sunday night, George had Rosen tell Billy that Fowler was going to be replaced by Clyde King. "Do you want to tell him?" Rosen asked Billy. "Or shall I?" When you fire the pitching coach, you are getting as close as you can to the manager—like a warning shot across his bow. Billy called his coaches together and told them that he was prepared to fight for Fowler. The old "loyalty is a two-way street" speech. Whether Billy would have quit the job that was his whole life remains a fascinating, but unanswered question, because Rosen, the man who was supposed to do the job, decided against it. Instead he recommended to George that they get together when the team returned to New York in the morning. "One of the best meetings we ever had," George reported afterward. "A real air-clearing session."

Billy stayed. Fowler stayed. And Steinbrenner announced that Billy's job was safe for the rest of the year. From all appearances Billy had surrendered. He took the calls in the dugout and answered every question without complaint. (The one time he did show his displeasure, he did it indirectly. A call had come down asking him to explain why he had called for Piniella, who doesn't steal, to steal. Yogi Berra had picked up the phone. "Please tell Mr. Rosen," Billy said over-sweetly, "that it wasn't supposed to be a steal. Please tell Mr. Rosen that it was supposed to be a hit and run.")

Still, it wasn't a total loss. Reggie Jackson was in one of his slumps, and George was willing to allow Billy to use him as a platooned DH—only against right-handed pitchers—until he came out of it.

The eleven days in 1978 that changed the shape and destiny of the New York Yankees began on the day after the All-Star game, July 13.

An item had come out during the All-Star break that Billy was suffering from a liver condition, and George had immediately leaked out a story that Billy had been offered a settlement if he wanted to resign for health reasons, and had refused. Steinbrenner, the story said, was willing to extend Billy's contract for a few years, retain him as a consultant, and work with him on realizing his "long-range ambition" of opening a camp for boys, an ambition so long range that Billy had never realized it himself. The offer had not been made to get rid of the manager, the story made clear, but as a humane gesture.

To be fair about it, Billy did look terrible. From the time of the meeting that had saved Fowler's job, it had all been downhill. On the day after the All-Star game, George met with Billy in his office, went down to the clubhouse to talk to the players for the first time all season, and after the game was over, held a press conference. Having established that he was doing it for Billy's own good, George was taking over.

The first thing he took over was the lineup. Thurman Munson was going out to right field. Mike Heath was going to be the permanent catcher. Gary Thomasson was the new left fielder. And Reggie Jackson would become the permanent DH against all pitching.

You will note that two of the players Billy had made a stink about, Heath and Thomasson, were in George's lineup. With the injuries to Randolph and Dent, the bottom of the lineup read: Thomasson, Heath, Stanley, and Damaso Garcia (a second baseman just up from the minors).

In addressing the players, George had put the changes forward as the manager's idea. But that's part of his standard locker room speech: "I hire a manager to run the ballclub, and if he thinks that's the way it should be, that's the way it should be."

It was so convincing that when Nettles peered at the lineup, he said, "Oh, I see George has given up again."

In the press conference following a 6–1 loss George made a minimal show of pretense. He had asked Billy to go along, he said, and Billy had agreed.

Had he gone along willingly? Billy was asked.

"Very willingly," said Billy.

Did he have a choice?

"I had a choice," he said. "It sounded reasonable. I'm willing to try it."

Out on the field, he had been somewhat more caustic. "That's a helluva lineup," he had said. "We should win easy today."

In addition to taking over the lineup, George was moving into that always disheveled area of discipline. He had statistical proof that there were players who were breaking the curfew. The Yankees were 32–20 in night games but only 15–9 in day games. "Some of them are staying up all night," George concluded. From now on the curfews were going to be strictly enforced. "Guys who abuse the rules are going to be nailed and nailed good."

Oh, come on! A curfew can only be enforced on the road. At home everybody's scattered. Half the guys are living with their families. You don't know George. He had his people calling the players at home on the night before every day game to make sure they were in.

For Reggie, the new lineup was shattering. He had worked harder over the winter than ever before to come into spring training in top shape, for it had become very important for him to prove that he was a good fielder. And now they were saying that a sore-legged catcher could play right field better than he could.

Munson did look good for the first few days, but then he began to look like, well, like a sore-legged catcher playing right field.

Thomasson played exactly one game, and then Piniella was back in left field and batting fourth.

With or without Thomasson, George's lineup had lost three out of four games before the July 17 ballgame against Kansas City in which George, Billy, and Reggie entered the climactic act of their psychodrama. Although Reggie was supposed to be permanent DH, Billy had benched him against Larry Gura, and then immediately after the game announced that Reggie would be playing the next day and batting fourth. Very curious. Reggie hadn't batted fourth for three weeks. And against whom would he be batting in the cleanup slot? You guessed it: Paul Splittorff. George Steinbrenner's revenge. Billy Martin, the manager who had to control everything, had been turned into a puppet.

Has any man ever been as obsessed with a woman as Billy Martin was obsessed with remaining the manager of the New York Yankees? His features were drained and haggard. He wore a look of utter exhaustion. He had stopped eating. He had not stopped drinking.

Normally Billy likes to go out during batting practice to take a few ground balls and kid around with the fans. He hadn't been doing that for weeks. Since the time of his surrender, he had been staying in his office until game time—just sitting there in his civilian clothes, as if he was trying to summon up the strength to change into his uniform. He looked as if he wanted to pull the blankets over his head and stay in bed. He was a man falling into a deep depression.

A day earlier he had passed out on the bench and had to be helped back to his office by Doc Monahan and Art Fowler.

When Reggie came in on July 17, he went upstairs and talked to George for ninety minutes. Reggie wanted to go back to the outfield. He had gone along with being the platoon DH because he had been promised that it would be temporary, but he certainly didn't intend to play out the rest of his contract as a DH, permanent or otherwise.

George—who was picking up all the chips now—informed him flat out that he agreed with Billy that Reggie wasn't a good fielder. Reggie asked to be traded.

But that didn't take ninety minutes. What else would have been said? Wouldn't George have told him that situations change, that nothing is permanent, that at least Billy Martin wouldn't be around much longer? Hell, the team was thirteen games behind, and Billy looked as if he was at death's door. Wouldn't George have told Reggie that he was doing what he thought was best for the team, have followed up with a little pep talk about showing New York that he was a team man?

On to the game. In the ninth inning, the score is tied 5–5. Reggie is the second batter. Against Splittorff he had grounded out and flied out, and against Marty Pattin, a right-hander, he grounded out and walked. The new pitcher is Al Hrabosky, a left-hander. As Reggie is standing in the batting circle, he tells Thurman Munson, "If you get on, I'm going to bunt you over."

"Don't get ahead of yourself," Munson says. "I've got to get on first."

Curious. Reggie had tried to bunt only once before on his own, and that was when he was in such an apologetic frame of mind after the Unhandshake. On that occasion he had fouled off the pitch and immediately hit a 450-foot home run.

What is a bunt? It's a sacrifice. You are sacrificing yourself for the good of the team. You're a real team man.

Munson promptly singles up the middle, and the stage is set. And now something happens that is even more curious. Billy Martin flashes the bunt sign. Billy had given Reggie the bunt sign only once before, and that had been in the ninth inning of a scoreless game against the Red Sox during the heat of the 1977 stretch run. Reggie's greatest game of the regular season. Up to that point of the game he had been the defensive hero, leaping high against the fence in deep right center to take a home run away from his pal, George Scott, and saving at least one more run later in the game with a brilliant diving catch of a short fly ball.

Heck, they didn't even have a bunt sign for Reggie in 1977. Howser had to come down from the coaching box to tell him. Reggie then fouled off a couple of attempts, and on the 3–2 pitch he hit a towering home run to win the game. Billy Martin was in the center of the mob of players pounding him on the back. He had apologized to Reggie for asking him to bunt.

So here is the second occasion Reggie has decided to bunt on his own and the second occasion Martin has given him the bunt sign, and both are coming at the same time. Well, there are two ways to look at it. Considering the situation, considering the way Reggie had been swinging, it was the logical thing to do. So why should Reggie have been angry at Martin for telling him to do what he already wanted to do anyway? On the other hand, Reggie is Reggie. For him to bunt on his own is one thing. For Martin to order him to bunt is something else.

Jackson squares away to bunt. Hrabosky's pitch comes in high and tight, pushing him away. George Brett immediately moves in at third base, and Martin takes the sign off. For Jackson to bunt successfully, surprise is an important factor. If Jackson had stood up there to hit, Billy may very well have put the bunt sign back again on the next pitch. We'll never know. Jackson tries to bunt again and misses the ball completely.

Dick Howser comes down from the coaching box to talk to him. "Billy wants you to swing the bat."

Reggie says, "I'm gonna bunt."

"Yeah, but Billy wants you to hit."

"I want to bunt."

Reggie squares away to bunt again and fouls it off.

The reaction on the bench was interesting, too. The players had seen the bunt sign and had automatically assumed that it would be taken off, so when Reggie attempted to bunt again, there was a nasty feeling that Billy was out to humiliate him one more time.

"Billy's losing his mind," the more sympathetic among them were saying. Howser's trip down the line had meant nothing to them. On that other occasion in Boston, he had gone in to ask Reggie where he preferred to bunt. ("I don't know," Reggie had told him then. "I've never bunted before.")

It wasn't until Reggie fouled off the pitch for the second strike that Billy shouted, "What the fuck is he *doing* up there? What the fuck does he think he's *doing?*" And even then there were those who thought that Billy was criticizing Reggie's not very graceful bunting form.

Who in their wildest dreams would believe he would try to bunt again with two strikes on him?

He fouls it off, and the ball is caught by the catcher. But it didn't matter; he was out the moment the ball was foul.

To bunt on the third strike is the greatest sacrifice of all. It is also absurd, self-defeating, and irrational. But who says we're dealing with rational people here?

Back in the dugout, Billy Martin turned to Elston Howard and snapped, "Okay, tell him that's his hit for the day."

Reggie came back to the bench, took off his glasses, and laid them on the bench, a clear indication that he was ready if Billy came at him again—an invitation, really. Billy said nothing. There were still two more outs in the inning. When the inning was over, he instructed Gene Michael, who had been out on the first-base coaching line, to tell Reggie that he wanted him to go in, get dressed, and leave.

Jackson remained on the bench for a while longer, and then went back to the locker room. He didn't leave. He showered, shaved, got dressed, and waited for the game to end. As he was to tell the writers afterwards, "I wanted to stay and root for my teammates." The team man.

And what about Billy? The game went on. In the tenth inning, the Royals scored four times. There was a long delay when Gossage got thrown out and a new pitcher had to come in and warm up. The Yankees came to bat and scored two runs themselves. But with two men on base, Cliff Johnson, who represented the winning run, flied deep. Johnson was batting for Reggie Jackson.

Almost an hour had gone by, and Billy had been totally involved in the game. He came back into the clubhouse muttering to himself . . . "Fuckin' errors . . . fuckin' walks . . ." and then, catching sight of Reggie sitting fully dressed at his locker by the door, glared at him, hissed "Goddamn you" under his breath, and went running into his office. The door slammed and you could hear glass breaking. He had heaved his clock radio against the wall, shattering both the radio and the glass on one of his framed photographs of Casey Stengel. When the writers came into the clubhouse, they could hear him screaming and storming around behind the closed door.

Okay, clearly Jackson had defied him. But, you know, so what? Normally the manager fines the sonofabitch, and that's the end of it. Consider something else: Sparky Lyle had come back to the bench in the sixth inning, after pitching 1⅔ innings, and told Martin, "I'm no middle-relief man. I'm going to get dressed and go home." Martin wasn't a bit angry about that.

It was only Reggie. Behind the closed door, Billy called up to Steinbrenner and demanded that Reggie be suspended for the rest of the season. Cedric Tallis came down, and when the door was opened for the press about half an hour later, it could be seen that Billy had been crying. The prepared statement said that Reggie had defied the manager's orders, even after they had been passed on to him verbally by Howser, and that he was suspended indefinitely.

"I have never been angrier in my life," Martin said in a loud, strident voice. "I'm the manager, and if he comes back, he does exactly what I say. Period. I'm not making $3 million. I don't disobey my boss's order. Tell me what to do, and I'll do it."

Ahhh, but of course. Where had he gone, that Billy Martin who had said, "Nobody tells me how to manage"? He had given up a great deal of himself, really his image of himself, and when you do that you have to devise a whole new philosophy. *Tell me what to do and I'll do it.* Having surrendered to the enemy above, he was being defied by the enemy below.

Ray Negron, friend of Billy and friend of Reggie, was in the middle again. Like everyone else on the bench, his first reaction had been that Billy was trying to humiliate Reggie and, just as he had in Boston, Ray had gone running to the end of the dugout to get away from it. When he heard Billy screaming, he thought it was because Reggie had messed up the bunt twice. When he heard Billy's instructions to Elston Howard after the third strike, he believed that Billy, having deliberately humiliated Reggie, was now insulting him.

When he returned to the clubhouse after the game, he went into Billy's office to drop the pitching chart he had been keeping on the manager's desk, and was walking out when Billy came slamming in.

And now came the most curious part of all. When Ray finished his chores and went back to the players' lounge to sulk, he found Reggie sitting there smiling, as if he didn't have a care in the world. "Don't worry about anything," Reggie told him, just as Martin was going to be telling him later. "Everything is going to be all right."

It was only upon hearing Billy read his statement to the press that Ray realized what had actually happened. And just as he was hearing it, he could see Reggie walking out the door. Immediately he went running after him, hoping to get him out of there before the writers got to him. "You've been suspended!" he shouted. "Come on!"

"What!" Reggie couldn't believe it. He was so stunned that Ray took the key to his Rolls from him, yelled that he'd pick him up outside, and went racing off.

It was too late. Four writers were coming out of the clubhouse, and Reggie was still moving like a man in a fog.

He had only been trying to help the team, he insisted. "I can't win. No matter what I do, I come off as the big, greedy money-maker and he's the tough little street fighter."

When he got to the car, there was no pretense. He was in such emotional turmoil that he had Ray pull up to the curb after a couple of blocks so that he could just sit there wailing about how miserable he was and how he couldn't understand why all these terrible things were always happening to him. "Why? Why?" he cried out. "I can't stand it anymore. I won't be back next year, and it's people like you who will have to suffer."

All the way to the airport the next morning, he was still giving voice to the same sad plaint. "Why? . . . Why?"

Billy Martin could have told him why, just as he told the press: "No one is going to defy the manager or management in any way. Nobody's bigger than the team." A stand had to be made. "This is probably the best thing that's happened in a long time. It'll pull the team together."

There was some truth in that. Martin's strength against Reggie was the same as it was against Steinbrenner. His players disliked him less than they disliked Reggie. And in this latest ruckus, the players were solidly behind Billy. Even Lou Piniella, who had always gone out of his way to defend Reggie, thought it would be best if they just paid him off and let him go somewhere else next year.

Chris Chambliss, never a man to be involved in any controversy, openly endorsed the suspension. "He didn't just hurt the manager, he hurt the team. He always wanted to hit fourth, and in that situation we needed him hitting so we could score some runs. His point was not to do what the manager said, that's what I got from it."

Reggie was never going to forgive Chambliss for that. His rationalization was that Chambliss didn't like him. (Which may have been true, but how could you tell? Chambliss had never paid the slightest attention to Reggie before, and he kept right on not paying any attention to him.)

Steinbrenner had no choice but to back up his manager, too. But the backing was minimal. In place of the stiff suspension Billy wanted, Steinbrenner went for only five days, and since the first day would be an off-day for traveling, it was really only four. "There may be mitigating circumstances on Billy's side or Reggie's side," Steinbrenner said, and although he went on to affirm that he was deaf to mitigating circumstances that destroyed discipline, it constituted a remarkably muted criticism.

On the plane to Minnesota, Billy sat with Jack Lang of the *Daily News*, who had just been assigned to the team. Lang is the long-time secretary-treasurer of the Baseball Writers Association and was an old drinking companion of Casey Stengel's. When Reggie came back, Billy told Lang he was going to tell him three things: The first was that he didn't think he could play right field anymore. The second was that he did think he could hit. "And the final point is I'm going to tell him if he ever disobeys me again or ever disregards my signs again, I'm going to fine him and I'm going to suspend him, and he won't play ever for me again."

George read Lang's piece the next day in New York and blew up. It was George Steinbrenner who decided who was going to be fined, who was going to be suspended, and who played on the New York Yankees. Again Billy was being reminded of the limits of his authority.

Even worse, the Sparky Lyle story had broken, and the Yankees were being accused of having a double standard. They tried to cover it over by claiming that Sparky had left because of a tender elbow, but that was a story nobody believed (least of all, it seemed, Sparky himself). So Billy was also catching it for embarrassing the Yankees.

And, to top it all off, while Billy was drinking with Bill Veeck in the Bard Room (combination bar and press room) at Comiskey Park after Saturday's game, Veeck told him about the proposed trade of managers between the Yankees and White Sox.

To Billy, that would constitute the ultimate betrayal. He was drinking heavily, he wasn't eating, and he was popping pills for his liver. A terrible combination.

And the next day was going to be Reggie's first day back.

Reggie wasn't there when the bus was ready to leave for the ballpark, and Billy refused to let it wait for a second. Reggie arrived at Comiskey Park by taxi about fifteen minutes after the bus. There was a mob scene waiting for him—twenty-five or thirty reporters and the TV crews. Here we go again. "The magnitude of me, it's uncomfortable," said Reggie. "I'm not the story. What have I done? The magnitude of me is overemphasized."

As far as the bunt was concerned: "I wasn't hitting the ball good. I didn't realize what the consequences would be. If I had known the consequence, I would have gone out and swung the bat and struck out." He had figured that bunting was the best way to advance the base runner.

The inevitable question: Did he think he should apologize? "For the way they interpret the offense, I guess an apology is in order. The way I interpret it, I haven't done anything wrong."

(What was really incredible was that nobody pointed out to him that he had bunted *on the third strike*. In his whole life he had never laid down a successful bunt. And here he had defied the manager not once but three times.)

Did he plan to apologize?

"No . . . I don't know."

Could he and Billy ever get along?

"I don't know that either."

With all the interviewing, he wasn't able to take any batting practice. And since he hadn't touched a bat in five days, Billy sent Howser over to tell him he wasn't going to play.

The Yankees won their fifth straight game without him. The Red Sox lead had been cut to ten games. Very important for the season. And for the psychodrama, too.

After the game, Billy was in the Bard Room again with Bill Veeck, waiting for the writers to file their stories, while the bus was waiting outside to take the team to the airport. Jack Lang came over. "What did he say?" Billy asked him. He didn't even have to mention who he meant. Lang flipped his copy at him. "Read it for yourself." Billy moved to the next table to read it, then threw it back to Lang with an expression of disgust. "I say 'Shut up, Reggie Jackson, we don't need any more of your crap. We've won five games without you, we don't need you coming in with these comments.' " Well, if Reggie didn't learn to keep his mouth shut, Billy wasn't going to play him, and this time he didn't care what George said.

He'd had a couple more drinks with Veeck, and when it was time to leave, he carried a drink onto the bus with him. As the bus was pulling into the airport, he asked Murray Chass of *The New York Times* if he could talk to him in the terminal.

Billy told Chass pretty much what he had told Lang and in almost exactly the same words. Unless Reggie shut up, he wasn't going to play, and if George didn't like it he could fire him.

Was that off the record? Billy was asked.

"No, sir! It's on."

Frank Brown of the AP listened in on it, and Henry Hecht of the *New York Post* came back from the newsstand to catch the last thirty seconds.

Chass headed for a phone to call *The Times*, Hecht tagging along. Since the *Post* was then an afternoon paper only, and Chass knew he was going to beat him anyway, he had told Hecht he could listen in while he called the quotes into his office.

The call was made from a phone booth in the newsstand area.

Then the flight to Kansas City was announced on the PA, and as the two writers started toward the gate, Billy Martin came walking by. He had been waiting out the delay in the airport bar. Figure two more drinks, for a total of perhaps five drinks in three hours.

"Did you get that in the paper?" Billy asked Chass, and was pleased to hear that he had. On the way to the gate the two writers fell into step with him, one on either side. Both knew Billy well enough that their instincts told them that they didn't want him to get away. Sure enough, he picked up right where he had left off. "I ran him out today," Billy said, "and he'll get the same thing tomorrow." By which he presumably meant that Reggie hadn't played that day and wasn't going to be playing until Billy was good and ready to let him.

And then he picked up a quote from Reggie going back to the bunt incident. Asked at that time whether he and Martin were going to talk about it, Reggie had said, "He hasn't talked to me in a year and a half." It pleased Billy's purposes now to take that statement literally, as proof of what a liar Reggie was. Up to this point he hadn't even mentioned Steinbrenner, and he still didn't use his name. He said, "The two of them deserve each other. One is a born liar and the other's convicted." Chass and Hecht looked at each other, and their eyes went clickety-click.

As soon as Billy left them at the waiting area, they put down their briefcases and typewriters and took out their notebooks. "Can you believe what he said?" they asked each other. "Can you believe it?"

There was no doubt in either of their minds that it was a continuation of the original conversation, and therefore on the record. To show how reckless he was being, Billy had been talking to a writer who he knew didn't like him. Hecht had decided—as he was to write—that Billy had deliberately set out to drive Reggie insane. It was Hecht who had pinned down the Lyle story that had helped get Reggie off the hook and put Martin in the soup. And in Minnesota he had printed a story about Billy coming to the clubhouse so late that the hitters didn't know who was supposed to be taking the extra batting practice. Just the previous night, during a heated exchange in the hotel bar, Billy had accused Hecht of being out to get him.

Hecht was sitting behind Paul Blair on the flight. He tapped him on the shoulder and said, "Paul, I can't tell you what he said, but Billy's gone."

Chass called George as soon as he got to the hotel in Kansas City. And Steinbrenner went into shock. "Was he drinking?" he asked. Chass said that he hadn't seen him drinking, so he didn't know.

When Hecht called an hour later, George was still aghast. "Did he really say it?" he kept asking.

Steinbrenner called Rosen, waking him. Rosen called Tallis, who was with the team in Kansas City. Tallis found Martin in his room, drinking with some of his coaches. He denied that he had said it. As he would later deny it to Steinbrenner and Rosen.

Rosen, who could hardly believe that two reporters could have made up the same quote, called Bob Lemon, who had been fired by the White Sox three weeks earlier, to ask him if he was available to manage the Yankees.

George didn't want to fire Billy and give him a chance to be a martyr again. He wanted him to go quietly, to resign. And he had a powerful inducement. If he fired Billy for being in breach of contract, he probably wouldn't have to pay him. If Billy resigned, he'd be paid. It took a few calls back and forth between Steinbrenner and Doug Newton, Billy's agent, but the deal was set. Billy would resign and be paid in full.

Rosen flew into Chicago with publicity man Mickey Morabito. When Rosen called down to Billy's room, Billy refused to speak to him. Morabito was sent down to get him. He found Billy coming down the corridor, headed for the elevator and carrying a little telephone pad on which he had scribbled out his resignation.

Morabito was able to stop him by offering to write the speech out on a single sheet of paper so that it would be easier to read. Billy went back to his room. Mickey went back to his own room and alerted Al Rosen.

Rosen came to Martin's room just as Billy was preparing to leave. Billy threw his arms around him and said tearfully, "Tell George I didn't say those things."

"If there's anything I can do for you," Rosen said, "give me a call."

The press conference took place on the balcony overlooking the crowded lobby, for no other reason, apparently, than because Billy saw a TV camera there when the elevator door opened. It was a crew from a local station. The regular reporters who were waiting in the lobby had to make a mad dash up the escalators.

Billy Martin was wearing dark glasses. He was gaunt and haggard. He looked like nothing so much as a man in mourning: grief-stricken, shattered. If ever you saw a man attending his own funeral, Billy Martin on the morning of July 24, 1978, was that man. His friend Phil Rizzuto was with him. "I thought he was going to have a heart attack," Rizzuto said later.

Billy's statement:

> I don't want to hurt this team's chances for the pennant with this undue publicity. The team has a shot at the pennant and I hope they win it. I owe it to my health and my mental well-being to resign. At this time I'm also sorry about these things that were written about George Steinbrenner. He does not deserve them nor did I say them. I've had my differences with George, but we've been able to resolve them.

He thanked the Yankee management, the press, the news media, his coaches and players. And when he tried to thank the fans, he broke down.

Before reading the statement, Billy had announced that he would answer no questions afterwards. "That means now and forever," he said, "because I am a Yankee, and Yankees do not talk or throw rocks."

That's what Billy Martin, at the age of fifty, said. And the frightening thing about it is that he probably believed it.

You would have thought Reggie would be happy. Reggie was far from happy. Reggie can be a pain in the ass, but Reggie is not a hater. Even Billy knew that. When Bob Ajemian of *Time* magazine was saying his good-byes after the Kansas City playoffs (that other Splittorff occasion), he said to Billy, "I think Reggie hates you." And Billy had looked up sharply and replied, "Reggie doesn't know how to hate. Vic Raschi and Allie Reynolds [Yankee pitchers of the Martin era], they knew how to hate. *I know how to hate.*"

Taking everything we know about the conditions surrounding the Bunt, you could make a great case that in some deep cavern of his subconscious Reggie was moving to give Billy back the authority which Billy had surrendered. By bunting against orders—*and on the third strike*—he was putting Billy back into a position of authority where Steinbrenner, the players, the press—everybody—would have to support him. What greater sacrifice could any man make than to sacrifice himself? By taking off his glasses, he had invited Billy to come out of his doldrums and be again the Billy Martin of Boston, the Billy Martin of Kansas City and Paul Splittorff. And when Billy didn't take him up on it, he had waited around in the clubhouse to give him another chance.

Why in the deep caverns of his subconscious would he want to do that? How many times must Reggie Jackson have lain in bed and wished that Billy would go away, disappear . . . *die*. A child believes that his wishes can kill, and we know that Reggie lives the rich fantasy life of a child. You only had to look at Billy to see that his surrender was killing him. Billy's health had become a public matter. Hell, he was fainting all over the place. But Reggie is no hater, and he's no killer, either. Reggie comes at you out of guilt and fear.

After Billy had made his resignation speech, Reggie went to the ballpark for early practice. That's where he always feels most comfortable: in the batter's box. But when a photographer from the *Kansas City Star and Times*, John Spink, tried to take some pictures of him, he complained that the clicking of the camera disturbed his concentration, and shooed Spink away. Spink moved down the third-base line, out of earshot, and Reggie started to aim line drives at him, and when that didn't move Spink out, he turned off the pitching machine and began to bat the ball at him from out of his hand.

Guilt and fear.

Five days later, Reggie had something else to worry about. Billy-boy was back.

On the day Billy was fired, George called the stadium to get a tally on phone calls. He phoned again the next day and the next. He could have stopped after the first call. The tally was something like 100 percent for Billy. Which, as any pollster will tell you, constitutes a trend. Little Billy had that hold on the people.

But that always happens when a favorite is fired. The fans phone and they threaten to boycott the park, and two weeks later they're trying to get tickets for the Sunday doubleheader.

There was something else for George to worry about. The New York Mets could have pulled the greatest PR coup in the world of baseball since . . . well, since the New York Mets hired Casey Stengel. The Mets were being run by Larinda de Roullet, for no discernible reason except that her father, who owned the club, let her. When Billy was fired, Arthur Richman, who was in charge of promotion, went in and told her he could guarantee 40,000 to 50,000 people for the next two nights if she would do one thing: "Hire Billy Martin." She looked at him as if he was crazy.

Arthur Richman used to work for the old New York *Mirror*, and he's an old friend and drinking companion of Billy's. He saw Billy within the next day or two and told him about it. (Billy had presumably dropped out of sight in the days immediately following his resignation, but his friends knew exactly what Billy would do: crawl back like a wounded animal into his cave, which in this case was his apartment in New Jersey.) For the next few days there were stories all over the papers that Billy was negotiating with the Mets.

What was George going to do, invoke his contractual rights and refuse to let the Mets have him? You could just hear it: He fired our Billy, and now he won't let him work. It would have been a public relations disaster.

A contact was made. George said that Billy called him. If so, you can bet that the call was arranged. George is great at drawing newspapermen into his web. What do you think? George asks. What would you advise? And soon enough it's: Who can I get to make the contact for me . . .? I can't talk to him. . . . Maybe you could make the contact for me. Irresistible!

Four days after George had negotiated with Doug Newton on the terms of Billy's "retirement," he was negotiating with him on the terms of Billy's return. Billy was going to have to do what he had refused to do in his statement of resignation: Admit publicly that he had said what he had been quoted as saying, and apologize for having said it.

What a show George planned. One of the great extravaganzas in the star-spangled history of sports and show business. Billy would return on Old Timers' Day, to the astonishment and delight of a packed house, his old teammates, and the entire civilized world.

It was amazing how well the secret was kept. Billy was driven to the stadium in a limousine, taken to the auxiliary locker room under the stands, and, when everybody was out of the clubhouse, slipped into the boiler room above the dugout. A few of the secretaries in the front office knew he was going to be there, because it had been necessary to get a uniform for him. But they were under the impression that he was coming back to make an appearance with his old teammates. The only other people who knew were Rod Carew and Ray Negron. Billy had sent for Negron because he wanted him to bring Rod Carew into the auxiliary locker room. Billy and Rod had a close friendship going back to Rod's troubled rookie year when Billy had threatened to take him out into the alley unless he straightened himself out.

Billy wanted Rod to be the first to know. And so, when Rod told him how glad he was that he had decided to make an appearance, Billy told him, "I'm going to be the manager in 1980." And grinned at the shock he saw in Carew's face.

After all the old heroes had been introduced out on the field, including the three Hall of Famers who had once been Billy's roommates, the time had come for the *pièce de résistance*. Bob Sheppard, an announcer of surpassingly dulcet tones, crooned, "Managing the Yankees in the 1980 season, and hopefully for many seasons after that, will be Number One . . ." The rest of it was drowned out by the thunderous cheers which rose from surprise to shock to incredulity and, finally, one suspects, to the sheer delight of being there to witness an event which would be told and retold for generations.

The cheering lasted for seven minutes. Billy doffed his cap again and again. At one point he turned to tip his cap to George Steinbrenner, up in his box.

He looked just great, like the Billy the Kid of old. He looked reborn.

What do you mean *looked*?

In the press conference afterwards—no questions allowed—Steinbrenner said right off the bat that Billy's return had nothing to do with fan reaction. Sure, George. "I told him that in my gut, as much as we had gone both ways, I didn't feel what had happened was right." Billy had said he was sorry for what he had said and "admitted that he had committed an indiscretion in denying it."

As the statement went on, the return of Billy Martin became a testament to the good works of George the Great: "I am probably, undoubtedly, going to be ripped a little for being soft or stupid. But there are times in life when you should be tough and times when you have to be rigid, and there are times when you have to be understanding and have compassion. . . . In my gut, I didn't feel what happened was right."

As for the remark that had got Billy fired, George, the old softy, was willing to live and let live. "What happened in Chicago, I can't hide. I was convicted of an election violation. That's part of life, that's what you live with, and I live with the plaques and few honors that I managed to get the same way I live with that; and it's going to come up again and again, and I should live with it, and that had no real part, and should have no real part, unless I am a pretty selfish individual. . . ."

Election violation, huh? Suborning perjury by any other name is still trying to get people to lie to a jury to protect yourself.

"The event that precipitated it, I think Billy will address himself to, but I will be very small if I said that could mean enough to cause what happened to happen. So I am just saying to you as sincerely as I can, and if you want to knock me, you go right ahead, because I am at peace with myself on the thing. . . ."

How could anybody want to knock George? Billy Martin, having been turned into a charity case, was willing to accept all alms. Said Billy: "I am very proud at this moment of the wonderful thing he has done for me. . . . This is the home where I want to be."

In the elevator after the press conference, Steinbrenner sent a member of his entourage back to stay close to Billy and make sure he didn't say anything more.

The next day George was in North Carolina watching his daughter ride in a horse show and basking in his own rich, crunchy goodness.

"I would be a very selfish guy if I let something like what happened stand in the way of Billy having a chance to improve his life. We're not just talking about baseball. We're talking about something a lot bigger than that. In this picture, baseball is a poor third."

The only shadow on the horizon was that nobody believed it. Not even Billy Martin, once he got his feet back on the ground.

Reggie's reaction when Billy came running out on the field, waving his cap, was "I'll be a sonofabitch. The fuckin' guy should have told me something." Meaning Steinbrenner. Afterwards in the clubhouse, Reggie took his grand tour, going from player to player. "I'll definitely be in Anaheim after this. No question about this, I'm going to be in Anaheim next year. Can you believe this?"

Again he asked to be traded. Reggie always believed himself when he was asking to be traded. But if he had been traded in 1978, he would have missed playing in another World Series.

Bob Lemon came in, posted the lineup, let them alone, and the Yankees won.

Bob Lemon takes a drink, too. If his nose didn't betray him, his honesty would. Lemon is a man of unfailing wit. In his acceptance speech at Cooperstown when he was being inducted into the Hall of Fame, he offered the audience the secret of his success: "I never took the game home with me," he said. "I always left it at a bar along the way."

No demons drove Bob Lemon. He had his own world in perfect perspective. "Baseball is a very simple game for children that we grownups have managed to screw up."

No problems of an undernourished or overnourished ego ate at him. He called a meeting and said, "I hope I don't screw up too bad." That was it.

And when the writers asked him how it had gone, he said, "It went like every other clubhouse meeting. The manager talks and the players don't say a word. At least I wasn't booed."

And when the season was over, and he had led the team through its greatest comeback ever, the first thing he said was "Don't forget that Billy Martin won the last five games he managed. This team was already on its way when I came in."

Give Bob Lemon all due credit. With the Red Sox in a tailspin, they came into the Stadium on August 2 with their lead cut to six and a half games, and in the first game the Yankees took a 5–0 lead, but blew it in the ninth inning, and the game was eventually halted in the fourteenth inning by curfew. The next night the Red Sox scored two runs in the seventeenth inning to win, and went on to beat the Yankees in the regularly scheduled game.

Instead of being four and a half games behind and in it, they were eight and a half behind. After the game, there were coaches and players saying that this was the day on which the Yankees lost the pennant.

Bob Lemon shrugged it off. "There are some games that you are not going to win no matter what you do," he said. "I believe that. There are some games you're not supposed to win."

Ten days later the Yankees scored five runs in the top of the seventh to wipe out a 3–0 Baltimore lead, and then the rains—and Earl Weaver—came around to wipe out the five runs. Weaver's contribution was to stall long enough so that the Orioles wouldn't be able to finish their time at bat. With Billy Martin you would have had to call out the National Guard. All Lemon said was: "That takes away the thrill of victory and gives you the agony of defeat."

And he put the Yankee clubhouse into perspective, too. Mickey Rivers and Roy White arrived late at the park in California, and the writers, sniffing a Yankee-type story, came in to find out how Lemon was going to handle it. "Nothing important. Let's not make a big thing of it. They missed the bus, they were fined, and that's the end of it."

(The writers, by that time, were writers from Long Island and New Jersey papers. That was another thing. If Billy had been able to hold on until August 10, he might have been saved once again by the magic of that date. What happened on August 10, 1978, was that the New York newspapers went on strike, and remained on strike through the rest of the season. Billy Martin should have been so lucky.)

It wasn't that simple, of course.

In the fifth game Lemon managed, the Yankees were able to field their starting lineup for the first time since the first week of May, and they remained healthy for the rest of the year. Concurrently plague, pestilence, and an occasional pulled hamstring struck the Red Sox. The team collapsed, no question about it, but their slide began in the game before the All-Star break, when Rick Burleson, their indispensable shortstop, sprained his ankle sliding into second. It was while he was out that the Yankees were able to pull up to that six and a half games.

Carlton Fisk, their other indispensable, broke a couple of ribs and could hardly breathe. Everybody knew about Fisk's ribs, they didn't know the fact that he also had bone chips in his elbow which made it very difficult for him to throw. The Red Sox were able to keep it a deep secret from everybody except those base runners who were stealing on him almost at will. Dwight Evans, who was possibly the best all-around outfielder playing ball, got beaned badly, and tried to come back too soon. Not only couldn't he hit, he got dizzy when he had to look up at a fly ball. Butch Hobson, the third baseman, had floating bone chips in his elbow which were so big that the elbow would sometimes lock. They kept Hobson in there, and he set a world record for bad throws. Jerry Remy, the second baseman, broke his wrist. The center fielder, Fred Lynn, was playing on two bad ankles.

But what else does that tell you? Well, it tells you that putting together a strong bench is just as important as fielding a strong starting team. Steinbrenner's Yankees had been able to survive their early rash of injuries with their reserves. The Red Sox didn't have a strong enough bench.

And Catfish Hunter, never forget Catfish Hunter. The Cat had suffered through a year and a half of torture. No matter how hard he was hit, and despite an ability to give up home runs by the ton that was almost laughable, he would insist that his arm felt good. "My control must be improving," he would say. "They're hitting them farther than ever."

No matter how badly he was going, the Cat wanted to pitch. He never believed his stats. "Winning isn't everything," he would say, "wanting to win is." Every time he went out there, he thought he was going to win. And, just because he was the Cat, everybody else on the team felt the same way.

Catfish was playing out that first free agent contract. If he couldn't pitch, he would drawl, he'd work it off washing George's boats. But whatever happened, it was his intention to go home to North Carolina when the contract was over, work his farm, and watch his kids grow up. He was the old America, the old southern ballplayer. He knew who he was, and he knew where he came from.

In 1977, he had suffered pain and humiliation. When he was examined by Dr. Jobe in Los Angeles, the club announced that he had been pronounced fit. Actually, Dr. Jobe had found that the rotor cuff on his shoulder was rubbing against the shelf of the shoulder every time he threw. In addition to the arm trouble, he had a pain in his groin. The Yankee doctor diagnosed it as a hernia, and it wasn't until the season was over that Catfish found out he had an inflammation of the bladder glands and that it could be treated medicinally.

In 1978, he reported to camp wearing a silver wristband. On top of everything else, he was a diabetic. And for the first half of the season it was more of 1977. In that game in Boston where Steinbrenner stormed into the locker to ship Jim Beattie back to Tacoma, it was Catfish Hunter, just off the disabled list, who relieved him. The pain that day was so bad that there were tears in his eyes as he sat on the bench. "I'll never pitch with that kind of pain again," he said, and that was the first time anybody had ever heard Catfish Hunter complain.

He had his arm manipulated under hypnosis, came back off the disabled list to pitch the game in which Reggie bunted, didn't look bad, kept pitching, and, miracle of miracles, the Cat was back and throwing shutouts. He won six straight games, really seven, because he was leading 12–0, after four innings in Boston, when the groin kicked up on him one inning short of the distance necessary to be credited with the win.

In all, Catfish won nine games out of ten in 1978, and that was the difference.

The Red Sox didn't collapse over the entire second half of the season, they collapsed in stages. When the Yankees were 14 games behind at their low point, there were 72 games to go. They had reduced it to 6½ with 57 games left, but were 8½ with 40 games remaining. Then they won 13 out of 15, and had knocked the lead down to 4 games when they went into Boston on September 7, with 23 games left.

A visiting club hopes to win two out of four in the home park of a contending ballclub. That's what Bob Lemon was shooting for. The players went into Fenway knowing that they were going to sweep the series. That's right, knowing it. It was what had always characterized the Yankees of the Championship Years. They won the games that had to be won.

So they went in and reversed the Boston Massacre of 1977. Only more so. The scores were 15–3, 13–2, 7–0, 7–4.

The line score on the four games—runs, hits, and errors—was:

Yankees: 42 — 49 — 4
Red Sox: 9 — 16 — 11

That's eleven errors for the Red Sox!

In the first game, Thurman Munson, batting third for the Yankees, had three hits before the Red Sox number-nine batter, Butch Hobson, came to bat for the first time. (That was the game Hunter had to leave with a 12–0 lead.)

In the second game, it was Mickey Rivers, the lead-off man, who had three hits before Hobson came to bat.

Guidry, who had never been allowed to pitch in Fenway Park with its short left-field wall, came into the third game with a 20–2 record and had a no-hitter for 8⅔ innings. He became the first left-hander to shut out the Red Sox at home in four years.

"The Yankees are one game behind," wrote Joe Gergen of *Newsday*, "and pulling away."

They left Boston tied for first place and drew out to a 3½-game lead with fifteen games left.

But it still wasn't that easy. The Red Sox pulled up their sox and, with seven games to play, were only a game behind. The Yankees reeled off six straight wins. The Red Sox matched them win for win. On the last day of the season the Yankees failed to match the Red Sox. Catfish Hunter's streak came to an end against Cleveland, the Red Sox defeated Toronto, and the Yankees had to go back to Fenway Park for a one-game playoff that would settle it all.

Guidry, who needs five days between starts, started with only three days' rest and was not the Guidry who had broken all those pitching records.

Mike Torrez, who had suffered through a miserable second half with the Red Sox after a brilliant first half, was beating Guidry 2–0 in the seventh inning when, with two on and two out, Bucky Dent came to bat. For two years Bucky had been moaning about being taken out in this very situation. It was in this park, you will remember, that he had almost jumped the team.

So why was Bucky Dent batting? He was batting because Willie Randolph was out with a bad leg and Brian Doyle, who had been brought up to replace him, had been taken out for a pinch hitter just before Bucky came to bat. Fred Stanley, the only remaining infielder, was going to be replacing him at second base. Bucky Dent was batting only because there was nobody left to put in the field. He took a ball, fouled the next pitch off his leg, and went hopping up and down in pain. Still, they couldn't put in a pinch hitter for him. Time had to be called while he was ministered to by the trainer.

Best thing Bucky could have done. Because of the delay, Mike Torrez lost his rhythm. His first pitch to Dent after play resumed came in over the plate, instead of down and out. Dent golfed it—a high, lazy fly that dropped into the net above the left-field wall, just along the foul line. Torrez never did get his rhythm back, the Yankees scored another run before he left, and in the top of the eighth Reggie Jackson hit a massive home run into the center-field stands. After he had crossed the plate, he ran over to Steinbrenner's box and exchanged a hand slap with the Boss.

It proved to be the winning run. The Red Sox scored two runs in the eighth off Gossage to make the final score Yankees 5, Red Sox 4.

Reggie's homer? Aw, Reggie said, it hadn't been that important when he hit it. What's this? Had Jax been overcome by a sudden attack of modesty? No, Reggie had a line coming up. "It was an insurance run," he said, "so I hit it to the Prudential Building." The Prudential Building is a modest skyscraper which dominates the skyline beyond the ballpark.

It was Reggie who dominated the championship series against Kansas City. Two home runs and 8 rbi's in four games, and a .462 batting average.

But it was Bucky Dent, whose time seemed finally to have come, who won the MVP in the World Series with a .417 batting average and seven runs batted in.

Graig Nettles may have been the true MVP, with his absolutely incredible fielding, particularly in the third game when, with the Yankees down 2–0 in the Series, Guidry was called upon to pitch again on three days' rest, and had almost nothing. Not that you'd know it from looking at the final score. He won the game 5–1. But that was only because Nettles saved him five times in the first five innings, with leaping, diving, lunging catches. Frequently with the bases loaded.

But, as always, it was Reggie . . . Reggie . . . Reggie who provided the two moments of high drama, one in a classic confrontation in Los Angeles with the Dodgers' twenty-one-year-old fireballer, Bob Welch, and the other in an unclassic confrontation with a thrown ball on the base paths of Yankee Stadium.

The confrontation with Welch came in the second game with two outs in the ninth inning, the Yankees trailing 3–2, two runners on base, and the count down to 3 and 2. Welch was firing nothing but fast balls, and Reggie had taken three mighty cuts, fouling the ball back all three times and finishing with his little *kazatski*-like balancing dance.

And then another flaming fast ball, another mighty cut, and the mighty Reggie had struck out. "Fuck . . . fuck," the mighty Reggie screamed as he started back to the dugout. "Why? . . . Why?" Unable to contain himself, he flung his bat into the dugout, where it whistled past Dick Howser's ear and split in two against the wall. Still livid, he strode past the shaken Howser and into the tunnel, pushing Bob Lemon out of his way.

Lemon ran after him, spun him around, and shoved him against the wall. His fists were raised, he was ready to fight. "You get your shit together, you hear me?" he yelled. "You're not that great!"

Reggie gave him a look, his eyes began to tear up, and then he broke away and ran at full speed into the locker room.

He needed an excuse, and he decided that Bucky Dent had upset his concentration by breaking from first base on the 3–2 pitch.

Ahhh, Reggie. When you're the go-ahead run with two out in the ninth inning, you damn well better be running on the 3–2 pitch. On the plane back, he apologized to Howser and Lemon and Dent.

The next time he faced Welch was in the sixth game, in Yankee Stadium. He hit a home run.

The ability of Reggie to be the Big Man, to do what is necessary to win the big game, was never better demonstrated than in the sixth inning of Game 4. Unquestionably, the pivotal play of the Series. The Yankees were down in the Series two games to one and were losing 3–1 in the ballgame. Jackson was on first base, Munson was on second, and one man was out when Lou Piniella slashed a low line drive to the left of second base. Bill Russell, the Dodger shortstop, moved quickly to make the catch, dropped the ball, picked it up, stepped on second to force Jackson, and threw toward first for what looked to be an easy double play. Jackson, having been frozen by the line drive, was about fifteen feet from first base, and the ball was coming right at him. On such a play, the runner is supposed to get out of the way. If the law of self-preservation doesn't suffice, the rules of the game do. Reggie didn't get out of the way. He held his ground and kind of swiveled his right hip into the ball. The ball caromed into foul territory, Munson scored, and the Yankees went on to win the game in ten innings.

The umpires ruled that it wasn't intentional. There was a feeling that if the game had been in Los Angeles, it would have been.

It was another good Series for Reggie. When he faced Bob Welch in Game 6, he felt that a home run would put him in the running for his third MVP award. When he came back to the dugout, he was floating. He didn't get the award, of course. And of course he thought he should have.

His figures give him a good argument. He knocked in eight runs, matching his total in the 1977 Series, had two home runs, hit .391, and sported one black-and-blue mark on his right hip.

The first two years of the Jackson Era had ended in World Championships for the New York Yankees. They were, as it would turn out, the best two years Steinbrenner's Yankees were going to have.

11

YEAR OF TRAGEDY

Everything went so bad in 1979 that it was as if some kind of perverse law of compensation had taken hold.

- Billy Martin showed up at training camp, haunting the scene like a ghost at a wedding.
- Goose Gossage broke a finger in a wrestling match in the club-house latrine, and the Yankee season went down the latrine with him.
- Billy Martin came back to manage in June, not exactly in triumph, and found that he was returning to nothing.
- Reggie Jackson and George Steinbrenner went pfffftttt.
- Mickey Rivers was traded.
- And over everything else, during the second half of the season, hovered the death of Thurman Munson.

Billy Martin had taken an apartment in Boca Tica, about ten miles from Fort Lauderdale, but he was at the bar of Galt's Ocean Mile Hotel, the Yankees' quarters, almost from the first day. He was drinking heavily, and his arm was in a cast. Billy had got into a fight at Bachelors III, Joe Namath's Florida club. It was supposed to be kept a secret, but George Steinbrenner seemed to know about it.

Billy had his great day on Old Timers' Day to warm his memories, and he had George's public promise that he'd be back as manager in 1980. But for all the hoopla and dazzle surrounding the Old Timers'

Day extravaganza, he did not have anything in writing, and George wasn't returning his agent's calls. Though George had proclaimed his intention to the world and had given Billy a contract running through 1980, he had been careful to insert an escape clause requiring a drastic change in Billy's drinking habits. "I go by a man's word," Billy was saying for publication. "His word was that I would be manager in 1980, and I believe him."

Privately he was saying, "I always said George was a liar! Let's see if he keeps his word about hiring me back!"

Billy had ample cause for concern. In November he had made an appearance at a minor-league basketball game, in Reno, Nevada, and had ended up slugging a sportswriter. The team, the Reno Big Horns, was coached by an old friend from Minnesota. The sportswriter, Roy Hagar, ended up with a black eye and three chipped teeth. As Billy explained it, he had only been defending himself. The guy had made a very threatening gesture: he had taken off his glasses. Hagar's version was that the glasses had gone flying the first time Billy hit him. The one point of agreement seemed to be that after Billy had made a disparaging remark about a sportswriter, Hagar had asked him whether he thought sportswriters lied. Billy (claiming that he had been under the impression until then that he was chatting with a fan) demanded Hagar's notebook, and Hagar wouldn't give it up.

Both criminal charges and a civil suit had been filed against Billy, just the kind of thing guaranteed to turn George all quivery at the knees and bring forth a stream of exhortations about Yankee tradition. George had vowed that Billy could not return to the Yankees unless he cleared himself completely, and he didn't sound as if he was going to call Edward Bennett Williams and ask him whether he wanted to take the case.

On the contrary. George was complaining that Billy's real purpose in coming to camp was to apply pressure on him. "I can't attach enough significance to the Reno case," Steinbrenner kept saying. "It's cut and dried. If he's innocent, he'll be back. If he makes a settlement out of court, that's the same as being guilty."

And then, darkly, George dropped the hint that Billy was still at it. "I don't like some of the stories I've been hearing. He is the manager in 1980 as long as those other things are cleared."

What could Billy have been doing to bring further disgrace upon himself and traduce the name of the New York Yankees? Something, it seemed, about a dinner Billy had appeared at in New Jersey:

"One person called me and said Billy arrived drunk. He said Billy's appearance at the dinner was not worthy of the Yankees. I'm not going to believe a guy like that. I told Al Rosen to check it out."

It turned out to be Gene Michael's scholarship dinner, at which Billy Martin and Mickey Mantle had appeared as a favor. Michael said that Billy's intake had been two drinks (it's always two drinks in these things, as any judge will tell you), and that Billy's behavior had been just fine. Well, Steinbrenner had said he didn't believe the guy.

Nor could George understand why Billy and his agent were so upset that he hadn't been returning their calls. The explanation was simple: George understood that the Hagar trial was coming up any day now, and he didn't want to bother Billy when he had so much on his mind. "What's the rush? He's got my word. I live up to my word."

And he did. As the season moved into summer, George's moral scruples regarding Billy's behavior were overcome by an even more powerful moral imperative. The Yankees were going nowhere under a dispirited Bob Lemon. George's compass pointed to Billy as the man who could do him the most good, and on June 18, 1979, Billy Martin became, once again, the manager of the New York Yankees.

Better for Billy if he hadn't. He returned at the wrong time, under circumstances that left him neither the same manager nor the same man. At the end of a miserable season he was gone for good.

In 1978, Billy had left with the suspicion that George had bugged his phone preparatory to his departure. After he was fired in 1979, Billy thought it more than possible that George had tried to plant something on him after he had departed. No wonder he was so upset that in his first public appearance after his firing, he said that George was a sick man.

A true Yankee doesn't do that.

If Billy Martin wore his hurt out in the open that spring, Bob Lemon was carrying a greater hurt inside. Ten days after the triumph of the World Championship, the worst thing that could have happened to him happened. His younger son, Jerry, twenty-six years old, the one of his two boys everybody had always said was most like him—the apple of his eye, as everyone knew—was killed in a Jeep accident. And while the jokes seemed to come as easily to Bob Lemon's lips as ever, the sparkle, that little pucker of amusement, had gone out of his eyes. Since Lem was one of those rare creatures who had come to a good old middle age without ever having learned to lie, he answered truthfully when reporters asked if the death of his son had changed his attitude about managing. "Yes," he would say. "It isn't as important whether we win or lose."

By June, the Yankees had done their share of losing. The relief pitching, which had been the Yankees' trademark for two years, had disappeared. Sparky Lyle had been granted his fondest wish, to get the hell out of there. He had been traded to Texas. Eleven games into the season, Gossage was lost in the aftermath of a clubhouse scuffle.

It started as a fun thing with Reggie asking Cliff Johnson and Gossage, individually, how he had fared against the other when they were both in the National League.

"I hit him decently," said Johnson.

"He couldn't touch me," said Gossage.

Reggie went back to Cliff to tell him what Gossage had said, and Cliff approached Gossage at the urinal. Yeah, Gossage said, that's what he had said. "Because it was true."

Cliff Johnson has always been like a big friendly lion, a very physical man who is forever coming up to people and clamping them in a friendly hammerlock, or throwing a series of fake punches at them. (Thurman Munson, whom Cliff all but idolized, had warned him away a few times, and when Cliff did it one time too many, Thurman said, "Okay, if you want to play, let's go." Thurman gave him a little feint, a little shove, picked him up over his head in an airplane whirl, and heaved him—all 6'4", 220 pounds of him—about fifteen feet across the room onto a sofa. Thurman was *strong*.)

Cliff gave Gossage a playful push, Gossage pushed back harder, and Johnson, not realizing that the Goose was not being playful, shoved again. Gossage went *whack-whack*, two hard rights to the top of his head, and they went wrestling to the ground with Gossage still swinging, until pitching coach Tom Morgan dove in to break it up.

The next day Goose came in with his right thumb all swollen. He had torn some ligaments on his pitching hand. He was going to be out for a good three months. In 1978, Gossage had saved twenty-seven games and won ten others. In the brief period before his injury in 1979 he had had one win and three saves. From the time of his injury to the time of Lemon's departure, the Yankee relief corps saved exactly two games.

With nobody else around to do the job, Rod Guidry volunteered to go to the bullpen. He wasn't overwhelmingly effective, and the change threw his whole pattern so out of whack that when he went back into the starting rotation, he sprained his back.

Reggie Jackson had already torn a muscle in his lower left leg, just above the Achilles, and he was on the disabled list.

And, on top of everything else, it was becoming increasingly clear that Bob Lemon, with his new detachment and his old easygoing temperament, had lost control of the team.

On June 16, with the Yankees in fourth place, seven games behind Baltimore, George joined the team for the final game in Minnesota. The Yankees blew the game when Mickey Rivers and Roy White let a fly ball drop between them. And if that didn't make him angry enough, there was the fun and frivolity in the clubhouse after the game, on the bus to the airport, and on the plane to Dallas. "I knew right there," he would say later, "that a change had to be made." Well, maybe it confirmed what he had already decided. The truth was that he had met with Billy Martin six days earlier in Columbus, Ohio, and offered him the job.

Billy's legal advisors had come up with a brilliant strategy for covering him on the punch-out in Reno. On May 24, the owner of the Reno Big Horns put up $7,500 to settle with Hagar, on the principle that the basketball team had failed to protect Billy from sportswriters as it had presumably promised. To prove that Billy was indeed the wronged party in the dispute, he gave both Hagar and the basketball club a release waiving his right to sue *them*.

If the New York sportswriters took the curious attitude that Billy had settled out of court, it may have been because Hagar had demanded that Billy fly to Reno and apologize to him publicly. But what did that matter? George Steinbrenner's attitude was the only one that counted, and the Yankees' fortunes had turned so bleak by the end of May that George was beginning to look around for another manager.

George's first choice to replace Lemon was Sparky Anderson, who had been dismissed by Cincinnati at the end of the previous season. Sparky was recognized as a class manager, and he had been extremely popular with the Cincinnati fans. In other words, a perfect offset for Billy Martin. But Sparky signed with Detroit, the June 15 trading deadline was fast approaching, and there were no trades in the works to give the fans somebody new to become excited about. Billy Martin, at the very least, would put some people in the stands. And George would be off the hook on his promise.

Put it all together, and Billy had cleared himself.

During their meeting in Columbus, George had asked Billy whether he wanted to take over the team immediately or have Gene Michael serve as interim manager and take over fresh in 1980. Billy may well have suspected it was now or never. He was signed at the same salary Sparky Anderson had signed for at Detroit, $125,000 for three years, making him and Sparky the highest-paid managers in baseball. He was permitted to bring Art Fowler back with him, and he agreed, absolutely, to the necessity of getting along with Reggie.

Although the story was all over Dallas for three days, the announcement was held off until the Yankees returned to New York.

In one respect, Bob Lemon was still Bob Lemon. At the time of Billy Martin's return on Old Timers' Day, Lemon was awarded a contract, at Al Rosen's insistence, as general manager through 1982. The title meant nothing, but the money was good. And when Steinbrenner advanced the date of his departure as field manager in the middle of the 1979 season, he made it clear that he was permitting Lemon to "general manage" wherever he wished—from an office in the stadium or his home in California. In other words: Go home, do some scouting when you feel like it, and spend as much time with your wife and surviving son as you want to. "You know me," Lem said. "I'm a company man. This is the longest contract I've had since I left the Navy."

Reggie Jackson wasn't that philosophical about it. Reggie had joined the team in Minnesota for treatments for his leg. He had sat with Steinbrenner on the flight to Dallas, and sat with him again through six innings during the opening game against Texas on Friday night. And George hadn't said a word about Billy Martin. At 2:30 in the morning, he called George to ask straight out whether Martin was coming back, and when George answered that he hadn't made up his mind yet, Reggie told him he didn't believe he was leveling with him. "I don't have to tell you anything," George said, and hung up.

For the remaining two days in Texas, Reggie was in a funk. "What am I going to do?" he wailed. "I can't play for that man. He hates me."

By the time the team had returned to New York, it had become known that George had consulted with Munson and Piniella in Dallas. Reggie went to Steinbrenner's office to ask him again whether he shouldn't have been consulted too. "When I think you should have a say in who manages the New York Yankees, I'll call you," George said. "You'd better get your head on straight, boy."

The operative word is "boy." The final affront.

It was at that moment that Reggie must have realized he had been laboring under a wholly unrealistic view of their relationship. Until then, he had never spoken of Steinbrenner in terms less than golden. At the time of the interview in the Boston hotel after the dugout brawl, he had railed about being treated like dirt because they "don't like niggers" on the Yankees. "Except for Steinbrenner," he had said. "I love that man. He treats me like I'm somebody."

Always he had gone out of his way to shower praise and honor upon the Boss. When George had distributed $300 bonuses to all the players at All-Star time, Reggie got into a hassle with his teammates by letting the press know about it—just so he could say, "I mean, how nice can you be?" And in his obligatory defense of Billy Martin, when Billy was on the verge of being fired, he had once said, "The manager doesn't make errors, he doesn't strike out, he doesn't throw up on the mound. You can't ask for a better owner. . . ." Out of nowhere.

The hang-up in Dallas, then the "boy" in New York, must have been shattering. They weren't, as he had supposed, friends and equals—fellow millionaires who lunched together at "21," companions of the night. The Boss owned the property, and Reggie was just another working stiff as far as George was concerned, no more than property himself.

The relationship would never be the same again. Oh, George held such sway over Reggie that he would always be able to bring him running whenever he indicated that he was ready to be his friend. And it was still going to take another two years before Reggie could bring himself to admit that he was afraid of George. George could impress him, George could manipulate him, George knew how to push his buttons and strum his strings. But that "boy" was always there in the back of Reggie's mind, and from that day forward he knew who George Steinbrenner was.

It was as close to hatred as it was possible for Reggie Jackson to come.

One wonders why Billy bothered to come back. He had been rehired for the same reason Lemon had been hired a year earlier: for a 180-degree change of direction. In 1978, the tension had become so great that the team needed a manager who would relax them. Now they were so disorganized and sluggish that they needed an instant injection of spirit. But that wasn't the Billy Martin that George was getting. He had hired Billy Martin because he needed a Billy Martin, but he had also made certain that he would be getting a Billy Martin subservient to George Steinbrenner. It was as if Billy had chased after the job so hard and long that he had forgotten who he was and why he wanted it.

It didn't seem that way at first. In the press conference announcing his return, Steinbrenner talked about the new Billy Martin. And then Billy, with that apparently invincible talent of his for twisting events to suit his own purposes, insisted that he hadn't been forced to resign in Kansas City and that the agony of his final days had been nothing more than what any manager went through when his team was losing.

"I'm the same Billy Martin," he said. "Maybe he sees something in me that I don't see."

George saw somebody who was ready to take orders. It started right away. For his first game back, after he had received a two-minute, ten-second ovation, Billy coached at third base. George wanted him to. Billy said something about third-base coach Mike Ferraro's unfamiliarity with his complex system of signs, but obviously they could have used the old ones for one more day. (Actually Billy does have somewhat complex signs. The signs don't change for each individual player; they change according to the situation.)

Billy had promised George that he would get along with Reggie, and so the first thing he did upon coming to New York was call Ray Negron and ask him to tell Reggie that he'd like to sit down with him and talk things out. It was the first time either Reggie or Billy had ever asked Ray to carry a message to the other, and it put Ray right where he didn't want to be, squarely in the middle. Reggie had already told Ray that he was going to avoid Billy for the rest of the year, and when Ray gave him Billy's message, Reggie blew sky high. So he had already talked to Billy, huh? "How can you be my friend and his friend at the same time?" he screamed. "Don't you know what the man has against me? He hates me because I'm the wrong color. He's fucked me, and he's going to fuck you. Because you're the wrong color, too."

"Boy, are you wrong," Ray said. "You're so goddamn wrong, it's pitiful."

No, Reggie didn't think he was wrong. Reggie wasn't so sure that it was *possible* for Ray to be friends with both of them.

Billy wanted to tell Reggie that he was going to play him in right field, bat him fourth, and play him all the time because he knew the team wasn't going anywhere without him. And with the usual mob of writers already in the clubhouse waiting for Reggie, Billy wanted to be able to get to him before he said anything that might make things more difficult.

There wasn't any immediate danger of that. Although Reggie had just come off the disabled list, he was far from ready to play. He wouldn't be coming in to see the doctor until the game was well underway, and by then the reporters could have been told that he wasn't going to be in until the following day.

Reggie came into the clubhouse with Matt Merola, and because of Merola's presence, Billy wasn't able to say what he wanted. Actually it was against the rules for a non-player to be there at that time, and the old Billy would have kicked Merola the hell out. The new Billy contented himself with telling Reggie that he'd like to sit down with him whenever Reggie felt he was ready so that "you can feel me out a little bit and make up your mind." Reggie nodded, not even looking at him and without saying a word.

It didn't matter that they never had the talk Billy wanted. A silent understanding was reached. Five days later Billy walked over to Reggie in the lounge and said, "Just tell me when and where," meaning when he felt he was ready to play and where he wanted to bat in the lineup.

The relationships between George, Billy, and Reggie had become so scrambled that they no longer made any sense. Billy was deferring to Reggie because that was the way George had wanted it. But the relationship between Reggie and George had changed so much by the very fact of Billy's return that, in short order, it wasn't what George wanted at all.

Al Rosen's resignation a month after Billy Martin's return gave Reggie his chance to let loose at George. And if it wasn't Reggie declaring his own war on George Steinbrenner, it was certainly Reggie calling upon the press to take up arms against the Yankee boss. Nor was it the usual Reggie Jackson outburst, either. "Passionately but coolly purposeful" was the way one writer described it. Said Reggie:

> The guy [Rosen] was a good guy who busted his butt and got tired of taking bullshit from Steinbrenner. You don't know that? Well, somebody has to say something as a human being, say why Al Rosen left.

He's a man and wants to be treated like a man, and he couldn't get along with The Man. The guy wants to be a fuckin' man. He's gone because he didn't want to be subservient. All he asked was to be respected and he wasn't. And, given that, he had to leave.

Al Rosen tried his best to be a good person, good human being, and good president, and he was. But he couldn't get along with a guy who didn't want to yield, didn't want to give in and didn't want to understand. All of a sudden he thought he could change it and it was too late. He couldn't get along with the guy, and you know it; write it! You know what The Man is like; it's your city, your team, your town, your fans. Tell the people what happened. Write it!

As for himself, Reggie said, George Steinbrenner could not do anything to him. "Because I can hit the motherfucking baseball over the wall. When I can't hit it, they'll get me. I know he'll get me one day."

For once the press was unable to rouse Steinbrenner at any of his Tampa numbers. His home phone was off the hook.

Billy Martin heard from him, though. "If you can't control your ballplayers," George raged, "I'll get someone who will."

So Billy went to speak to Reggie. "If you could do me a favor, please, please try to keep it down a little about Al Rosen," he said. "I appreciate that you liked the guy, but George is really on my butt about it, and I just don't want to get it on with George this year."

And Reggie said, "All right, I'll respect your wishes on that."

As it was, Billy was going to have to say something, because George had ordered him to attack Reggie and defend the owner. But he was going to keep it in generalities. He wouldn't even mention Reggie by name. He hoped that Reggie would understand that it was something he had to do.

And he did. He said, "No player on this team gets special treatment. I'm getting tired of hearing people talk about the owner. . . ."

After that, they had an excellent relationship. Billy left Reggie completely alone and played him in right field, and for that reason— and possibly because the Yankees were never in the pennant race— Reggie was more relaxed at the plate for the rest of the season than anybody had ever seen him before.

George, incensed that Reggie would dare to question him on the rehiring of Billy Martin, did not leave him alone. After the "boy" exchange in his office, which must have got heated, Steinbrenner—in his lovely way of speaking not for attribution—called Martin in his office and told him to announce that Reggie, in his role as player representative, had filed a grievance against the club for being forced to play an exhibition game in Columbus, and to then launch an attack on Reggie for refusing to play for him.

"If he doesn't want to come back," Billy dutifully pointed out to the writers, "I don't think any player should be big enough to dictate who the manager should be."

Whereupon a call to Steinbrenner elicited his opinion that Billy had done all that was humanly possible. "You can't ask a manager to crawl on his knees."

Actually Jackson hadn't filed any grievances. He didn't know what they were talking about.

Next, George leaked a story that Reggie's original contract called for a $250,000 loan at six percent interest, and that Reggie had missed several scheduled repayment dates and was probably broke.

That wasn't true, either. As a reward for Reggie's performance in the 1977 World Series and as a token of their magnificent friendship, George had voluntarily spread out the loan repayment schedule on his own.

If he was trying to damage Reggie's standing in the financial community, he evidently didn't succeed. All he did succeed in doing was to win Reggie a congratulatory editorial in the *Wall Street Journal* as a man who "has his finger on a basic economic fact" in making inflation work for him.

And then George and Billy and Reggie, indeed everything and everybody, took a back seat to the events of four terrible days in August.

Thursday, August 2. Thurman Munson was killed at 3 P.M. when his Cessna Citation twin-engine jet crashed while he was attempting to make a landing at the Akron-Canton, Ohio, airport. Thurman had, as always, flown home to be with his family on an off-day in the schedule. What an irony that a man's love for his family killed him. Irony on irony: In his last game in a Yankee uniform, just before the off-day, Thurman's knees were so bad that for the first time in his life he had been forced to turn down a manager's request to play in the game. Billy had wanted him to pinch-hit for rookie catcher Jerry Narron and then to go behind the plate for a couple of innings. After his talk with Billy, Thurman had walked over to Bobby Murcer and had mumbled with a crooked smile on his face, "Billy's trying to get me into the game." The crooked smile said all that had to be said about what it had done to him.

August 3. Ray Negron came in early and removed Thurman's bats from the bat bag. He put Thurman's last game bat aside until he could come to a decision on whether to give it to Graig Nettles, Lou Piniella, Bobby Murcer, or Billy Martin.

The players began to file in but spoke very little, and then in hushed tones. "I can't believe it," were the first words on everybody's lips. Bobby Murcer had gone to Canton to lend support to Thurman's wife, Diane, through the long night. He had flown back for the game and was sound asleep in the lounge.

Billy Martin, whose tears are always so close to the surface, was wearing sunglasses to cover his eyes. George Steinbrenner came into the clubhouse and went into Billy's office. When they came out, George gathered everybody into a tight circle in the center of the clubhouse and gave the players every scrap of information he had about how the accident had occurred, including the fact that Thurman had cracked some ribs and teeth in the crash. When he began to talk about how Thurman always played hurt, his face turned beet-red and he collapsed into tears.

Billy stepped in and talked about how they would now have to pull together both as a team and as brothers. Then he began to cry and asked Bobby Murcer to talk a little about Diane.

Bobby related how he had told her there was no way he would be able to play the next game, and how she had told him that the team should play because that was how Thurman would have wanted it.

Reggie gave an inspirational speech about the lessons to be learned from tragedy, quoting liberally from the Bible.

Steinbrenner promised that he would take care of Diane Munson. His lawyers were already in Canton, he said, sorting things out. He said, "Let's hang tough and stay tougher."

After the meeting broke up, Steinbrenner was in the trainer's room with Reggie, Piniella, Tommy John, Jim Spencer, and Bucky Dent. They were talking about how petty all the arguments, quarrels, and contract disputes seemed now. We can put so much emphasis on the game, George said, that we forget the true meaning of life. And that perhaps a bitter tragedy like this might make better men of all of them.

Thurman had left his car at Teterboro, as always, and Martin asked Ray Negron if he would go pick it up. A grisly assignment. Ray had picked up Thurman dozens of times at Teterboro. It was going to be the first time, Ray reflected, he would ever be driving back from that airport without Thurman in the car.

As game time approached, and the loss of Thurman sank in heavier and deeper, Graig Nettles appeared to be so close to collapse that it didn't seem possible he could play. He had to insist upon being written into the lineup. Munson and Nettles, after all, were the two guys of whom it could always be said: If they can walk, they'll play.

It was a dreadful game. The players were so emotionally drained that they were sleepwalking through the action, just trying to get it over with—the very opposite of what Thurman Munson stood for. Nettles had to go back to the clubhouse between every inning, and when he came back you could see he had been crying.

The game was lost 1–0. And then it was back into the sad and silent clubhouse.

Sunday, August 5. The Yankees won the ballgame on Nettles's first home run in a month. He rounded the bases as if it meant nothing to him. The game itself had no meaning. A cloud of depression had descended upon the stadium.

Billy Martin was so low that Negron decided it would be a good time to present him with Thurman's last game bat. There was more crying.

Nettles went over to Negron's locker to thank him for everything he had done for Thurman and tell him he had done right to give Thurman's last bat to Billy. They started to talk about Thurman and burst into tears.

Monday, August 6. The Yankee contingent left the stadium at 7:05 A.M. to get to the airport at 7:35. The charter landed at Canton Airport about an hour and a half later. Two buses were waiting to take them to the Civic Center where the funeral services were being held. The Civic Center held about 500 people, and there were probably another 2,000 people gathered outside to pay their respects.

Sparky Lyle, Mickey Rivers (who had just been traded), and Bobby Bonds had flown in from Texas. Young Mike Heath had flown in from Oakland at his own expense, a tribute to Thurman's generosity in helping young catchers. After the funeral, Heath would rush back to the airport and fly back across the country.

Lou Piniella and Bobby Murcer, who had come to Canton the day before to help with the funeral arrangements, gave the eulogies. "As long as we're wearing pinstripes," Piniella said in the course of a touching tribute, "we will always be close to Thurman."

Billy Martin had gone into such a deep depression that everybody was worried whether he could make it to the cemetery without falling completely apart.

Lou Piniella confided to some of his teammates that he had visited one of the survivors of the crash and had been told that Thurman had been alive and conscious for three to four minutes before he died. He had been yelling, "Get me out of here. Please get me out." The probability was that he had died from burns and asphyxiation.

And after all that, they had to fly back to New York and get ready to play a ballgame that night. Only about half the players bothered to go home. The others went directly to the stadium and lay down on the sofas in the lounge or on the floor in front of their lockers and went to sleep.

When Billy arrived, Lou Piniella told him that he really didn't want to play. Bobby Murcer went into the lineup for him. Murcer had returned to the Yankees only five weeks earlier. Before he had been traded away in 1974, he and Munson had been the two standouts on a succession of dreadful Yankee teams, and through the years they had kept in close contact, phoning each other frequently. Murcer had played very little since his return and had done very little when he did play. The Yankees, as listless as one might expect, were behind 4–0 in the seventh inning when Bobby Murcer stepped up with two men on base and hit a scorching line drive into the right-field stands. Lou Piniella was waiting for him in the dugout, and they stretched their arms out to each other, fell into each other's arms, and hugged each other with joy.

Murcer was coming up again in the ninth inning with runners on second and third. There was a left-hander pitching for Baltimore now, and Bobby was looking back over his shoulder to see whether Billy was going to send in a pinch hitter. "Come on, Bobby," Billy yelled, "I know you can do the job."

Bobby fouled off the first two pitches. With each pitch, the players in the dugout drew closer together. Bobby swung at a knee-high slider and ripped a line drive down the left-field line to win the game.

In his state of near-exhaustion, Bobby Murcer had knocked in all five runs with two scorching line drives.

The crowd kept chanting for Bobby to take a bow, and after a few pushes from his teammates he responded by going out and tipping his cap.

Steinbrenner was waiting in the clubhouse to shake everybody's hand, from Bobby Murcer's right down to the bat boys'. As the players came in, they began to wander down to Thurman's locker at the far corner of the clubhouse, next to the trainer's room. Just to kind of touch it in a final farewell as they passed by.

When the clubhouse had almost emptied, Bobby Murcer came over to Ray Negron and said, "We're the last ones left now." Ray had started as a bat boy in 1973 when the Yankees were playing in the old Yankee stadium. He had come as a frightened sixteen-year-old kid from the neighborhood. Ray remembered how Thurman Munson and Bill Sudakis would have hunting rifles in their lockers, and how Thurman would swing the rifle around the clubhouse, let it come to rest upon him and say, "You guys ready to go coon hunting tonight?" and how he had been so scared that he'd be shivering in his pants. It had taken Ray a long time before he understood that it had been Thurman's way of initiating him into the clubhouse fraternity. "Yeah," he said as the tears began to roll again, "those were the old Yankee days when we weren't winning but everybody was happy."

Whatever chance the Yankees might have had of coming back under Martin ended with the death of Thurman Munson. It took the heart out of the club and cut the heart out of Billy. The sense of solidarity that had developed between Steinbrenner and the players in the initial impact of Munson's death was shattered almost immediately as the result of George's reaction to an incident that had occurred on the day before the plane crash.

The road trip had ended with a three-day series in Chicago. After the first game, a luscious blonde walked onto the bus looking for autographs, and when one of the players told her what he'd like to sign she obligingly pulled down her pants and got her rear end autographed. Being an ardent autograph collector, she kept doing it through the rest of the stay and on the last day Billy asked Morabito to get someone to take her picture. By the time Billy boarded the bus she had already got off, but she gave them one final "mooning" to remember her by.

More than two weeks later, a story came out of Chicago that had Martin snapping the picture himself outside the bus, in front of a bunch of kids who had been unable to get autographs for themselves.

George blew up and came bombing into the clubhouse to scald everybody. And, of course, he climbed all over Billy. Behavior unfitting the Yankees, he screamed. Wouldn't even listen to Billy.

"Right back to the same old shit again," the players were saying. Not the classiest thing that had ever happened, to be sure. But what had happened, they wanted to know, to all those fine words of George's about the "true meaning of life" and keeping everything in proper perspective?

Back to the original question: Why did Billy come back? He had been diddled and dangled and toyed with. Yet nothing mattered except to become, once again, the only thing he wanted to be, the manager of the New York Yankees.

"Why do they hire me for what I am," he had been wailing through the years, "and then try to make me somebody else?" After all those years, he had finally allowed himself to be made into somebody else. And he didn't even complain. In those first years, even when he was giving in, he'd say in the vernacular of the clubhouse, "I'd like to take George and slap the shit out of him." Now he was taking all those calls in the dugout, and while he might say afterwards, "That stupid sonofabitch, he still hasn't learned the game," that would only be after he had explained that he had brought in Ron Davis to pitch to Don Baylor, in place of Ken Clay, who had been pitching a decent game, because Davis was a sinker-ball pitcher, Clay was a fast-ball pitcher who was starting to tire, and he had been hoping to get Baylor to hit the ball on the ground for a double play.

He took the calls upstairs, downstairs, and in the manager's office. In order to remain the manager of the Yankees, he took more than anyone would have dreamed possible.

At the end of the season, he sent word to Reggie that he really appreciated how much he had put out for the club, both at bat and in the field, and that he was particularly grateful for the way he had exerted leadership with the young players.

The Yankees ended in fourth place, 13½ games behind Baltimore.

George's free agent selection, Tommy John, finished with a record of 21–9. Ron Davis, over the second half of the season, rolled up record figures in relief. The club drew over 2,500,000 in attendance, breaking the old record for the seventh straight year.

But it was a very dull season.

On October 26, Billy brought it to an end. Not willingly, but probably inevitably. It ended for Billy as a result of the fight with the marshmallow man, in a hotel bar in Bloomington, Minnesota. Billy's story was that he had been talking baseball with this guy, until he decided he didn't want to talk anymore and left. "He must have followed me out of the bar because as I was walking in the lobby I turned around and saw this guy lying on the floor. He fell and cut his lip. I then just left and went up to my room."

Sounds reasonable.

"How much can the Yankees take and still command my respect?" cried George Steinbrenner.

Billy settled with the marshmallow man out of court. Reggie sent him a note of support. Billy appreciated that.

On October 28, Steinbrenner fired him and began a noisy campaign to beat Billy down on the remaining two years of his contract. Commissioner Kuhn's role in this sorry affair was, to say the least, puzzling. The Commissioner began by making a special appearance on "Monday Night Football" to tell Howard Cosell that the punishment of Billy Martin hadn't necessarily ended with his firing. Cosell was astonished to hear Kuhn say, "I have several options. I could ban him from baseball. I could suspend him. I could put him on probation, or I could fine him." And then the rather remarkable statement, "It has come to my attention that Billy has financial problems and that he has problems when he drinks. We're going to check on this."

On November 9, Billy and his people went to the Commissioner's office to find out what it was all about. The Commissioner didn't show up. His attorney, Sandy Hadden, told them that the investigation was going to cover Billy's "pattern of behavior" throughout his managerial career.

Four days later, Billy flew back to New York from Dallas. He had received an urgent telephone call from a trusted friend informing him that he had better come in quickly because something might have been planted in the manager's office. Billy went to the stadium with Ray Negron. He emptied out his locker, and there was nothing there. He went to his desk, and in the bottom left drawer was a packaged bottle of J&B—which was kind of funny because J&B was probably the only brand of scotch Billy didn't drink. And then he took out something else—a little plastic vial filled with marijuana.

Was it George who had planted it? "He could have," Billy decided.

"A man who keeps a file on my personal life to use against me is capable of doing anything."

"There will be no more Old Timers' games," he said as he walked out. "I'm sick and tired of being used and lied to."

On December 11, he made his first public appearance as the twice-former manager of the New York Yankees, at the University of Rhode Island. He had a few words to say about his twice-former employer.

"I feel sorry for him. I think the man is sick. I'll be honest with you, I'll only go back if George is gone. I won't even play in an Old Timers' game. I'll never put on a Yankee uniform as long as he is there."

The new manager was Dick Howser, and if his selection came as a complete surprise, nobody was going to be more surprised in the end than George himself. George thought he was hiring a quiet little guy who would do as he was told and discovered, to his consternation, that he had a quiet little guy on his hands who was more than even George M. Steinbrenner III could handle.

12

"YOU GOTTA BE A PRICK"

There is a pillow on the couch in George Steinbrenner's office at Yankee Stadium that bears the noble philosophy, "Give me a bastard with talent." Who can doubt that such a pillow so prominently displayed does not proclaim its owner to be the biggest bastard with the most talent?

In public appearances and interviews, George has another way of saying it. "There's got to be a heavy," he says, with a kind of rueful acceptance of his fate. "And I guess I'm it."

You work for him, and he snarls, "You gotta be a prick!" If you're a big enough prick, apparently, the talent will take care of itself. He says it often. He says it in his loud, angry voice. He means if you're not a prick, he doesn't want you working for him in a position of authority. He tells his executives they gotta be pricks, and proves it by the way he treats them. Yankee Stadium is a self-contained little world, and George prides himself on running a tight ship. "We've got to tighten the screws," he commands, "or, I'm warning you right now, heads are going to roll," a most interesting juxtaposition of expressions in this context.

There is a tension that exists, on many levels, between the players and the stadium management. Pat Kelly and his six or seven assistants. The security people. To the players, and all other stadium employees, they are Steinbrenner's spies and strong-arm men. "Steinbrenner's henchmen," the players call them. Or "Steinbrenner's goons."

Or, "Look out, here come the dildoes."
A dildo is a substitute prick.

But then, there is the other George. The man of charity, civic involvement, and splendid service to mankind. His people talk about "all the
good things he does that nobody knows about," a statement that con-
tains a built-in contradiction. George says it himself if you're willing to
sit around and wait for about 80 seconds. "There are all the good things
I do that nobody knows about."

There is, in George M. Steinbrenner III, a sense of noblesse
oblige. From his early days in Cleveland, he has been sending underprivileged kids, mostly black, to college. He reads about a little girl in
need of a rare and expensive operation, and he gets off the train at the
next stop to call her parents and tell them not to worry, because he is
going to arrange everything and pay for everything. He keeps a
"Thank you" file, which consists of letters attesting to the good
things—the marvelous things, really—he does that nobody knows
about. He can be a man of enormous generosity and feeling toward
people struck by sudden tragedy, which may be why he seems to have
such an affinity toward law and order people. A heroic Brooklyn cop
gets killed, leaving a widow and five children, and George sends a
check of $40,000 to be put away for their future education. In 1982, he
will be donating the entire receipts from a Yankee ballgame to a fund
for the widows and children of firemen.

There is this Jekyll and Hyde allusion written into almost everything that has been done on George. The basic story is that he'll bawl
the hell out of his secretary for the most minor infraction—she didn't
have a sandwich for him, say—and then make up for it by paying her
kid's tuition to college. He really has a heart as big as all outdoors, in
other words, but is incapable of putting it into words, the big lug.

Well, if you've got a kid in college these days, everything helps.
Does it make up for the abuse? Let's you and I make a deal: I'll insult
you, treat you like dirt, and you'll stay with me because I'll pay you for
it. We're all purchasable, aren't we?

Actually George pays his secretaries at the stadium very little. He
hires them through an agency—which is as neutral as you can get—
and fires them on what seem to be whims. But, then again, he may not
want them around too long. Who gets to know more about you than
your secretary? His chauffeurs are retired cops. That means they have
a license to carry a gun. Unofficial bodyguards. From all accounts,

they last an average of about six months. Chauffeurs get to know a lot about you, too.

He is exactly what he says he is, a prick to work for. He intimidates, he frightens, he threatens. He dominates his environment with his voice and presence. It is a voice that demands to be obeyed. Do it again, he screams, and you're fired. Not just fired, banished. Let an underling do anything to displease him, and he (or she) is suddenly inundated by Hurricane George. Fast, loud and angry. Fierce. Asserting dominance, claiming dominion.

First, I am going to give the words, and then I am going to try to approximate the ferocity of the onslaught. The words are: "If you ever do that again, I'll fire you. You'll never be allowed inside Yankee Stadium again . . . ever!"

The onslaught is: "IFYOUEVERDOTHATAGAINI'LLFIRE YOU,YOU'LLNEVERBEALLOWEDINSIDEYANKEESTADIUM AGAIN . . . EVER!"

He asks the farm department guys to prepare a list for him. They prepare the list so that it will be ready when he calls for it. Oh-oh. From this day on, they will know that "prepare" means he wants the list sitting there on his desk the next time he comes in. "IFYOU EVERMAKEAMISTAKELIKETHATWHEREYOUDON'TBRING THELISTWHENIWANTTHELISTDON'TYOUEVERSTEPIN- SIDEYANKEESTADIUMAGAIN.YOUWON'TBEPERMITTED." EVER!

And then, of course, there are times when he has justification for being angry. Let a story be leaked out of the office that he finds embarrassing and a call goes out for all personnel to gather in his office, so that they can stand there like children and be yelled at.

Just before Thanksgiving of 1981, a story was leaked that the Yankees had brought Los Angeles's Reggie Smith, a free agent with a background of injuries, into New York for a physical examination. George demanded to know who had leaked the story, and when the culprit didn't step forward, he screamed that he was going to make them all take lie detector tests; and, furthermore, that he was going to make them come in on Thanksgiving Friday to take them. Then he called Henry Hecht of the *Post* (to whom the story had been leaked and who has always been a prime recipient of George's own leaks) to demand that Hecht tell him where he got it. When Hecht told George that he knew better than to ask, George screamed back, "I know who it was. You don't have to tell me. It was Bergesch, wasn't it?" Bill Bergesch is the old baseball hand in the office, the guy who is running the baseball operation these days. If you don't trust your top guy, who do you trust? The answer would seem to be: If he's the kind of prick I want him to be, how can I trust him?

George's secretaries tend to be thirtyish or fortyish, divorced or widowed, with children. When George wants them, they are not supposed to come at anything less than a brisk trot. "LET'S GO . . . LET'S GO!" he screams.

He's always screaming at them, always making them cry. He had one secretary in the early part of 1980 who left after four or five months because she was on the verge of a nervous breakdown.

His next secretary, who was obviously very fond of him, let it all slide by. "All that yelling didn't bother me," she says. "I always saw the little boy underneath." Her demise was foreshadowed, after a little more than a year, when George came in and saw she had a new hairdo, with bangs in the front. "If you ever wear your hair like that again, you're fired!" he screamed. A week or so later, George's daughter came in from North Carolina with a couple of classmates, and when George called around 6:30 to talk to her, he discovered that the secretary, whose normal departure time was 5:30, had left at 6:00. George fired her for not staying with his daughter and her friends through the ballgame.

He fires people, it sometimes seems, for no other reason than that the time has come to fire somebody. After the 1981 season, he fired the assistant trainer for hanging around too much with the ballplayers. What the hell, the guy was a bachelor, he was entitled to hang around with anybody he pleased. Nicest, quietest guy you'd ever want to meet.

George seems to operate on the principle that periodic applications of punishment are good for the organization. Gotta keep reminding everybody that they're afraid of George. The public relations man was demoted during the 1981 season. He had hit the wrong button and flashed the message on the scoreboard that Kansas City would be in the next night, when it should have been Minnesota. You know how many people noticed that as they were filing out? Or cared? George noticed. George cared. Nothing less than perfection will do. Gotta tighten up the screws.

For a guy who's always telling people that they'll never be allowed in Yankee Stadium again, he has a way of keeping a string on those people who leave. Whether it's out of a sense of loyalty or of possession, he lets few people go. The managers come in and out on a shuttle. When they're out, they are still under contract to him—he owns them, they belong to him. He has only to beckon, and back they come.

With all the stories about his temper tantrums, his boorishness, his blatant contempt for their persons and dignity, the people who leave him rarely have anything bad to say about him. Perhaps, like the former secretary, they see something good underneath the screaming. More likely it's the attraction of the powerful. They see in George a man who has the power to change their lives, for good or ill. Why get on his bad side? Show him you're the kind of guy who can keep his mouth shut, and maybe he'll reach out, pluck you up, and make you rich and famous.

On the other hand, to talk about how you were humiliated is to be humiliated all over again. The first time you allow George to take your dignity away, it becomes necessary to reshuffle your values. When you keep taking his abuse, you have to find excuses for either him or yourself. It's easier to find one for him.

"George is a winner. He brought the Yankees back to their former glory." *That's* the excuse.

George has convinced those who work for him that he is entitled to do anything, because he himself never doubts for one second that he is. But it goes beyond that. He sees himself as the sun around whom the universe revolves. The Yankees lose the World Series, and he apologizes to the City of New York, like the Lord of the Manor apologizing to his tenants for not having provided adequately for their welfare over the winter frost. "I put this team together," he says at the beginning of every clubhouse speech, "and I own this team." It's not the Yankees who win or lose, it's George Steinbrenner. Can anybody doubt, after all this time, that in his mind they are one and the same?

He controls everything because he personalizes everything. Reggie Jackson and Graig Nettles get into a fight during the victory celebration after winning the divisional playoffs. "You're disgracing the Yankees in front of these people," George screams at them. A couple of days later he says, "Reggie apologized to me, which Nettles had already done, which means a lot to me. He said he was awfully sorry and that he felt very bad about it."

Oakland beats New York with the help of a couple of ex-Yankees, and George says, "Cliff Johnson and Chicken Stanley are killing me. And Tommy John is letting them."

Read that over. There is not only the sense that it is George Stein-

228

brenner versus the Oakland Athletics, but that his pitcher, from lack of effort or base cowardice, has betrayed him.

His team is losing, and so he calls them "chokers." After carrying the team on his back through the first half of the season, Reggie Jackson goes into a slump, and George calls him a "tanker." There is always the feeling that losses come from a defect in character, or spite. *I put this team together. I own this team.* He has put together a winning team, and so if they're not winning, it has to be their fault.

The remarkable thing is that he is able to draw everybody else into this world where nobody else counts. The examples are endless. Billy Martin, threatened with the loss of his job, comes out of a long meeting restored. "He asked me what I wanted," Martin says, "and I told him the only thing I wanted was to go out and win the pennant for him. I said, 'I want to bust a gut for you. I'll run through a wall for you.' "

Before the final game of the divisional playoff series against Milwaukee, Reggie goes up to talk to Steinbrenner. "I just wanted him to know that his players were pulling for him. I think he appreciated that."

After the Yankees had played in the 1976 World Series, George handed out World Series rings—which are supposed to go only to the players and top executives—to all his friends. The players just loved to see Bill Fugazy, George's bosom buddy, walking around with the ring on his finger. "What the hell did he do?" they'd say. "How many fuckin' hits did he get?"

They were missing the point, the Steinbrenner equation. Fugazy is George's friend, and George is the Yankees. Therefore, it was George who won the pennant, therefore anybody whom George chooses to award a ring to is as much entitled to wear it as any of George's players.

Similarly, the statements. No controversy involving the New York Yankees can possibly come to a conclusion without George issuing one of his seignorial statements.

During the pennant race of 1977, the Kentucky State Police reported that a marijuana crop had been found on Don Gullett's farm. Funniest thing that happened all that year. If you had lined up every baseball player in the country and asked them to spell "marijuana," Don Gullett would have been the one to ask what it was. It took exactly one day for the Kentucky State Police to clear Gullett. Some opportunist had apparently cultivated the seedlings in a hothouse and transplanted them while Gullett was away. The writers covering the team laughed about it in print, and the players had a lot of fun with Gullett. But that wasn't good enough for George. The official Seal of Approval had to be stamped upon Gullett by George himself:

> In twenty-five years of dealing with athletes as a coach and an owner, I have never met a finer young man than Don Gullett. If there is a modern-day Jack Armstrong Gullett is it. . . .Two years ago, they found marijuana growing in the outfield at Anaheim Stadium, and nobody ever mentioned that Gene Autry was involved in that.

Nobody ever accused Autry of riding to the rescue of a fair damsel who didn't want his goddamn help, either.

Silly? Of course it's silly. But George doesn't make an ass of himself on purpose. He does it because it is his duty. If George's opinion is the only opinion that counts, he has a duty to clear the name of his All-American boy.

When everything is personalized to that degree, there is a need to control everything from the tiniest detail to the grandest strategy. The field manager is an extension of the owner. The players are an extension of the owner. They are all, therefore, subject to his will and caprice, much as children are subject to their parents'.

Exaggeration? Listen, George sends people to their rooms!

Cincinnati. First game of George's first World Series. The Yankees lose the game, and on top of that Cincinnati has protested the Yankees' use of walkie-talkies up in the press box—George's very own innovation—and the commissioner has ruled that the walkie-talkie can only be used from the Yankees' radio booth. George feels that his integrity has been called into question, and it's all because the people who were working the walkie-talkie screwed things up. Plus, he's in near-hysterics because of the loss of the game. So it's everybody up to their rooms to think about how they're going to win tomorrow.

The Yankees weren't even staying downtown; their hotel was to hell and gone out of the city. Everybody had to go back— grown men, many of them older than George—forget about stopping off at the home team's Hospitality Room, and sit in their rooms.

Same thing in Los Angeles in 1981. George brought a tremendous number of people to Los Angeles—everybody in the organization, practically. The Yankees had won the two games in New York, George was happy, and nobody has ever said that a happy George can't be extraordinarily generous or that he doesn't have his people travel first-class. Then they lost two straight and he ordered everybody to be in their rooms by ten o'clock. The players, wives, kids, everybody. The Yankees remained overnight on their off-day, so it was two nights in Los Angeles in their rooms. He had brought three or four security people along, and they were stationed all over the lobby, along with the hotel security, to catch anybody who came in late.

George made his house rules clear on his first opening day, in 1973, before the ballgame had even started, when he called the dugout from his box to demand that Number 15 (Thurman Munson) be fined for not wearing a cap. He didn't know the names of the players yet, so he followed up with a note to his manager, Ralph Houk, listing the numbers of the players who were to get haircuts.

The dress code was promptly established:

> no beards
> no muttonchops
> no long hair
> coats and ties must be worn when club travels as a group
> coats in the lobby of a hotel
> back of neck must be visible.

From the beginning he called his managers constantly. Every failure was a personal affront. A player made out in a game-winning situation: "Drop him in the batting order," George screamed. "That will show him!"

A player made an error: "Fine the sonofabitch."

Statistics and tendencies. Who can't hit whom. Notes, notes, notes. Humorless. This is serious business. Billy Martin once pulled the phone off the wall in utter frustration. George called the trainer's room and told him to get Billy because his phone wasn't working. The trainer said, "That's because he pulled it off the wall."

"Okay," George said. "Tell him I'll call him tomorrow."

Sparky Lyle, knocked out of the box that first year, was booed and gave the fans the finger. Two fingers, both hands. The phone rang in the dugout. "Ralph, you tell Lyle right now that will cost him a thousand dollars."

231

A thousand bucks plus a dressing down from George: "I happen to know that your mother was in the stands." Bad boy!

Periodically he will announce, more in sorrow than in anger, that he is withdrawing completely and is going to leave the team in the hands of "my baseball people." He complains, "This team gives me more trouble than all the rest of my businesses combined. It's more trouble than it's worth." You kids are driving Mama crazy. Mama's going to leave home, and then see what becomes of you. But Mama doesn't leave home; she visits her sister and is back to cook dinner. George is back on the phone the next morning. How could the kids possibly get along without him?

Tal Smith was hired in 1974 to become Gabe Paul's eventual successor, but one year of George was all he could take. During a night game, George asked where he was and was told that Tal had gone home because his daughter was having a birthday party. His work was done for the day, there was nothing for him to do during the ballgame. "You call Smith and you tell him to get his ass over here," George yelled. "If he's not here within the hour, he's fired." They called Tal and told him he'd have to leave his daughter's birthday party or look for a new job.

Here's George, such a ferociously concerned father that he travels thousands of miles to attend every college function where he can be with his own daughter, yet he doesn't respect another father's desire to be with his daughter on her birthday. When you're the center of the universe, nobody else counts. Tal Smith left at the end of the year to become general manager of Houston, and George, unable to understand, was furious.

What about those who stay? Cedric Tallis has a distinguished career behind him. He came into baseball as a builder of ballparks. He was the first general manager of the Kansas City ballclub. George calls him a "fat bastard" and treats him so badly that there is nothing for Tallis to do except make a joke of it. And, to preserve some shred of dignity, talk continually of how he's going to get out of there.

George controls everything and everybody, and has no control over himself, no self-discipline whatever. All that screaming and arm-waving while he's watching a Yankee game, and the near-hysteria that follows a defeat. He fines players for embarrassing the Yankees by making obscene gestures, makes those sanctimonious speeches about offending somebody's mother, but thinks nothing of sitting among the Yankee wives during the post-season games cursing away.

His most memorable performance, perhaps, came in the second game of the 1980 playoffs after Mike Ferraro, the third-base coach, had waved Willie Randolph home with the potential tying run, with two out in the ninth inning. Willie was tagged out, and George was up and screaming. "What the fuck is he doing? . . . We're going to see about this. Sonofabitch, who the fuck is running this ballclub?"

The seats were behind home plate, a few rows up, and as George was walking down to the field gate with Gene Michael, he caught sight of Mike Ferraro's wife, shoved his face into hers and, with the TV cameras catching it all, screamed, "Your husband really fucked this game up for us today!"

The man sends grown men to their rooms, and he himself isn't even toilet-trained.

When you're the center of the universe, you are also indestructible. George Steinbrenner fears no man. Absolutely doesn't. If everybody has been put on earth to be used or abused by you, how can anybody possibly hurt you?

Ralph Houk was the manager of the Yankees when Steinbrenner bought the club. "The Major." As a Ranger in World War II, Houk had been promoted through the ranks, including a battlefield commission. A stupendous war record. Dan Topping held him in such awe that he fired Casey Stengel so that he wouldn't lose Houk to Boston.

Ballplayers held Houk in awe, too. There was the story of how Houk took a gun away from a hoodlum in East St. Louis, booted him in the ass, broke a beer bottle, and held the jagged edge up while he and his fellow Yankee revelers, Billy Martin probably among them, backed out the door. Like a real live Western.

When Mike Burke and Lee MacPhail came into the front office, it was the same thing. The Major was the Major, and nothing he did was to be questioned. Ask him about one of his moves, and the Major took it as second-guessing. Ask him about a player who had kicked the ballgame away, and you were wasting your time. The Major never criticized his troops.

Steinbrenner came in and questioned him: Why, why, why? Called him in the dugout. *Ding-aling-aling.* "Why did you pinch-hit for Horace Clark?" Woke him up at three in the morning—*Ding-aling-aling*—to question him some more. Before that first season ended, Houk "resigned." Actually, he had already arranged to manage the Detroit Tigers.

Al Rosen was brought in to replace Gabe Paul. Rosen had never worked in a front office before, and George Steinbrenner set out to make a prick of him. The Boss's formula for success was no secret. The players said it from the beginning. "It's too bad—they're going to turn a nice guy into a prick."

George Steinbrenner knew Al Rosen from Cleveland. Rosen had been one of the young business leaders he had recruited for Group 66, a baseball hero turned stockbroker. After Steinbrenner had served as chairman for two years, he appointed Al to succeed him.

In 1953, as a tough, gritty third baseman for the Indians, Al Rosen had been the first unanimous choice for the MVP award. He had a nose that had been broken many times, and not always by ground balls. A Jewish kid out of Florida, he was another of those players with a father who had walked away when he was a child. Al had been a professional athlete from the time he was twelve—Florida Military School on an athletic scholarship; all the major sports, plus boxing. As a Jew in the South, he had learned to box early, and he earned such a reputation as a fighter coming up through the minors as to preclude any necessity to fight in the major leagues. In 1953, he had one of the great years in modern history (.336, 43 hr, 145 rbi), then broke an index finger, wouldn't stay out of the lineup, and ended his baseball career with an index finger that wouldn't bend.

By the time he came to the Yankees, he had been battered by life. His first wife, a former Miss Alabama, had suffered a mental breakdown, followed by a long, expensive hospitalization, followed by suicide. His brokerage career had come to an end in Cleveland with his name being tarnished when he was used—innocently on his part—as a front man in a real estate swindle in which George Steinbrenner's bank was also involved. Billy Weinberger, an old friend from the good days in Cleveland, brought him out to Las Vegas as a high-class greeter at Caesars Palace.

On November 5, 1976, George Steinbrenner came to Caesars Palace, accompanied by Lou Piniella, ostensibly to see the Norton-Young fight but actually to offer Rosen the job as general manager of the defending World Champions.

It was painful. As a ballplayer, Rosen had been a stand-up batter and a hard-rock fielder, giving nothing and asking nothing. He had worked hard to improve himself year by year, and he had succeeded. In Boston one afternoon he went into the Red Sox dugout after a big, third-string catcher who had been shouting the Jewboy names at him, and instead of banding together to throw the intruder out, the Boston players turned on their teammate and took care of him themselves.

That was how respected Rosen was as a ballplayer.

"You gotta be a prick," George told him, and Al Rosen didn't know how to be a prick. He had come out of the battering life had given him with a sweet, obliging nature. The sweetest guy in the world, the players were saying. A wonderful person.

Nor did he know how to be yelled at. George would scream at him, and Al's nose would turn brick-red. You could always tell when George was screaming at him on the phone, because he would grab the end of the desk with his free hand and squeeze it until his knuckles turned white.

Like Gabe Paul, Rosen became George's emissary to Billy Martin. He was the guy who had to make the calls to the dugout to ask the silly questions. And after the game was over, George would send him down to the manager's office to do the interminable second guessing. Rosen would walk in and very carefully close the door behind him. Billy would get mad, and if secretly Rosen didn't blame him, George Steinbrenner was still the man who was signing his checks, and Al Rosen had come out of a school that said that if you took a man's money he deserved your loyalty.

Something wouldn't work out on the field (it didn't matter what), George would yell at Rosen, "You better get on Billy about that shit! I don't know what the fuck you're doing, Al. I'm sick and tired of seeing that shit!" Somebody made an error: "That's going to have to stop, Al. I'm telling you right now, or heads are going to roll."

So Al Rosen became a little George. "That shit had better stop," he'd tell the offending player. He was blowing up at anything. Small things, big things, anything. "What the fuck do you think you're doing?" A bad guy to deal with, the players told each other. A player would come to him for permission to do something. "Not the way you've been fucking up! Why should I do anything for you?"

It got to where the players didn't like to see him coming. The sweetest guy in the world, they had said at the beginning, and by the end of the year they were saying, "Talk about an asshole."

Although his hair had begun to turn gray when he was still playing ball, there were a few specks of black left when he came to the Yankees. By the end of the year it was solid gray.

The worst part of it was that he knew what was happening to him. Here he was, the general manager of the team that had made the greatest comeback in baseball history, and over the winter he was looking around desperately for some other job. "One day that guy is just going to say something, and I may pop him," he was telling his friends. "And I'm not going to let that happen."

There wasn't that much in New York for an old-time baseball player from Cleveland, he discovered, and he came back to suffer through the first half of 1979. He looked tired and worn out. For his own good, everybody wanted him to leave.

And, finally, he did. "Hell, he can fire me, and the day after he does, I'll be the worst sonofabitch that ever walked the face of the earth. So I got to get out."

"I'm glad he's gone," one of the players closest to George said. "Now he can become a decent guy again."

Eighteen months later, Al had to have open-heart surgery. George called him as soon as he heard. "Can I send you anything?" After the operation, he wanted to know whether he could help with the bill.

George's treatment of Elston Howard was so execrable as to defy rational explanation.

Elston Howard was the first black player on the Yankees and the third in the line of great Yankee catchers running through Dickey-Berra-Howard-Munson. In 1963, Ellie had one of the greatest clutch years any player ever had, and led a decaying team to a pennant. Five years earlier he had been the World Series MVP as a left fielder. He was an all-star nine times.

There is also a tendency to forget that without Elston Howard there would have been no Red Sox Impossible Dream in 1967. The Red Sox bought the aging Elston from the Yankees at the tag end of the season, and with Ellie behind the plate their pitching improved so much that the Red Sox captured the pennant.

When George took over the club, Ellie was the first-base coach, a living symbol of that great Yankee tradition George waxes so soft and sentimental over. For some inexplicable reason, George didn't want him on the field. When Billy Martin came in, George tried to bring Ellie into the front office as a public relations man. Ellie resisted. "What the hell am I going to do in public relations?" he'd tell his friends. "Answer fan mail?"

He wasn't just being stubborn. Elston was a good baseball man, and his ambition was to manage. He had, in fact, been hired by Bill

Veeck to manage the Washington Senators in 1968, only to see Veeck's deal to buy the Senators called off when the Washington ownership got word from the commissioner's office that Veeck had been blackballed.

Elston knew that he had to remain on the field to have any chance of becoming a manager, and Steinbrenner wasn't prepared to risk the bad publicity that would almost certainly come if he fired an old Yankee hero—and a black one, at that.

The next spring Elston was relegated to the bullpen. To make it worse, he wasn't even being put in charge of the bullpen, he was being sent out there as a bullpen catcher, a nothing.

Elston decided that a front-office job was preferable to that. "I offered it to you last year," Steinbrenner told him. "You told me you didn't want it then."

Obviously, Steinbrenner wasn't going to offer it again, and Howard refused to be a bullpen catcher. So he ended up on the bench, serving as Billy Martin's emissary to the black players. His only other discernible duty was to man a walkie-talkie and relay the information that was coming down on the positioning of outfielders.

But then Elston had a heart attack in 1980, and George lost no time in assigning him to the Public Relations Department, for special projects. When somebody was needed to represent the Yankees at some minor function out of state, Elston would be sent. Other than that, he was never given anything to do. And, as he discovered soon enough, he was not on the payroll.

"George," he'd say, "I have a handicapped child at home. And I'm not getting paid."

"Sure . . . sure. I'll take care of it. Can't you see I'm busy now?"

Elston was talking about his youngest child, a victim of polio. He had another daughter, Cheryl, who was a highly accomplished professional singer, and it was Ellie's great ambition to have her sing "The Star-Spangled Banner" before a ballgame. Somehow, there always seemed to be a reason why they couldn't fit her in.

In December, he had another heart attack and died within the month.

On the night before he died, he was visited in the hospital by two friends, one a former Yankee player and the other a Yankee employee. "You know what got me in here, right?" Elston told them. "George Steinbrenner."

He said, "I never got paid."

Don't worry, though. George made up for it. He paid for the funeral. And on opening day of 1981, Cheryl Howard sang "The Star-Spangled Banner" at Yankee Stadium.

That's only one example of the good things George does that nobody ever hears about.

And then there was Dick Howser, the little man who gave George the surprise of his life. When George hired Dick Howser in 1979, he thought he was getting a nice, quiet little coach. Instead, he found himself with a tough little nut on his hands.

George wasn't the only one who was fooled. After Howser had turned down the manager's job in 1977, the consensus was that when the question had been put to him, Dick had demonstrated that he didn't have the stomach for the job. At the end of the following year he left the Yankees to become the baseball coach at Florida State University, and that would seem to have been the end of Dick Howser.

When you take another look at Howser's response in 1977 with the benefit of hindsight, you can see that what everybody took as weakness was strength. Strength of mind. In that response he hadn't set down terms that he knew would be unacceptable; he had set out the conditions he felt he had to have to do the job.

With the departure of Al Rosen in 1979, Gene Michael became general manager. Michael and Howser had been coaches together, and Gene Michael had been hand-trained. Howser would be a pussycat, and the Boss would sit completely in control.

Those who knew Howser well knew better. Dick Howser took nothing from anybody. On the first trip to Boston in 1980, Dick was sitting at the bar in the Sheraton when a guy alongside him decided to strike up a conversation. "George Steinbrenner runs that club for you," he said. A great way to strike up a conversation.

"You fuckin' shit," said Howser, coming off the chair. He grabbed the guy by the collar. "I'll break your ass."

The fight was broken up in a matter of seconds, but not before Howser, giving away about forty pounds, had worked the guy over pretty good.

Toughness of mind. Howser had stated he would not accept any interference from the owner and, wonder of wonders, he meant it. George would tell him to do something. Howser would listen politely and say, "I'm the manager of this ballclub." There were no screaming matches. He always tried to keep the discussion on a cool, professional level. George would make a suggestion, and Howser's answer would run the gamut from "Okay, but this isn't necessary," to "Okay, but I'm not going to insist on it," to "I'll tell them what you say, but I'm also going to tell them that I'm not going to make it mandatory."

Same thing when George would make his suggestions about playing certain players against certain pitchers, or wanted to make some changes in the pitching rotation. Howser's attitude was that he had not spent ten years as a coach, studying the game, in order to take any crap from an amateur.

Nothing at all like Billy Martin, who had always reacted at an extreme. With Billy, it was either "George, what the hell do you think we're running here? What the hell do you think you're doing?" or he'd hold the phone away from his ear and roll his eyes to the ceiling . . . but do it.

Howser would say, "George, I don't think I can do that because it's not going to work."

And Howser's way was working. The Yankees went into first place on May 19, built up a lead of 9½ games by mid-July, went into a bad slump through mid-August that whittled the lead down to half a game, lifted it back to 6, and won, finally, by 3. Under Howser, the Yankees won 103 games. In each of the championship seasons, they had won 100 games.

Howser pinch-hit for Piniella and Nettles, something that no other manager had ever done. And that takes balls. Not only because of their hitting ability but also because of their position on the ballclub. No manager, certainly not a rookie manager, wants to make an enemy out of a clubhouse leader. Billy Martin had never pinch-hit for Nettles, no matter how deep a slump he was in. Howser pinch-hit for him in three straight games.

Piniella took to calling Howser "That Little Asshole." But that was only clubhouse talk. Actually, Piniella liked Howser. There would even be a note of grudging respect in his voice when he'd say, "That little asshole pinch-hit for me. That little weasel-face."

With George, there is no such thing as grudging respect. All of a sudden, he found himself on the outside looking in, a spectator to his own team. By the end of the season he was just kind of hanging around. If Howser didn't feel like getting into a discussion with him, he'd say, "Yeah . . . yeah . . . yeah. . . ." and then go out and do exactly what he wanted to do. Other times, if he didn't mind getting into a discussion, he'd say, "I think you're wrong, George," and do exactly what he wanted to do.

The Boss was not going to put up with that kind of treatment for another year. Even if the Yankees had won another World Championship, Howser wouldn't have been back. When they lost three straight to Kansas City, it just made it that much easier for George.

Considering all the practice George had had in firing managers by then, his handling of the execution of Dick Howser was remarkably inept.

Howser had defended his coach's decision to send Willie Randolph home on the play that had driven Steinbrenner bananas, and that was the only opening Steinbrenner needed. After a brief pause to whack Mike Ferraro around in the prints another time or two, he announced that Don Zimmer was going to be replacing Ferraro as third-base coach in the coming season, and that he saw no necessity at all to consult his manager about the decision.

The unconsulted manager maintained a discreet silence for a while, but then took on a direct question about whether a manager should have the right to hire his coaches. His answer was that it was an organization decision, but the manager should have an input. Not the most inflammatory statement since the Communist Manifesto, you might think, but then neither is George the most difficult man on this side of the Iron Curtain to inflame. He castigated Howser as a "pop-off," and popped off that he could hire whomever he pleased. "It's almost like he's testing me," the Boss said, flexing his muscles. "I'm the wrong guy to be testing."

It was all over right there, but George managed to keep it going for another three weeks. First came the "source" interviews, in which the source was so clearly Steinbrenner that you could smell the hair spray. George, said the source, liked Gene Michael for the job because "he's tough and he's a battler." As for the untough, non-battling Dick Howser, there were a significant number of players who were dissatisfied with him. Next came the leaked stories that suggested that the job was still Howser's if he wanted it. All he had to do was agree to certain things that, the leak itself confirmed, would be impossible for him to agree to.

Finally, with everybody aware that the manager's job was in serious jeopardy, George stepped forward to express his concern for Dick's future well-being, maintaining stoutly that while the decision was entirely in Howser's hands, he would do everything possible to ensure his financial security if he should decide to leave. "I feel guilty about this because I took him away from a secured job at Florida State."

All the while they were presumably holding meetings to negotiate whether Howser would be back, they were really negotiating the terms of Dick's departure. From what Dick told one of the ballplayers during a trip to New York, George had put it to him bluntly: They just were not going to be able to work together, so why didn't they try to work out a compromise? George would pay off the remaining two years on his contract ($200,000), help him out with the debts he had incurred in starting a real estate company, and if Dick should want to manage somewhere else, George wouldn't stand in his way. "It just isn't going to work out," George had told him. "You know it and I know it. You proved that to me this year. You don't like the way I bothered you. You know I'm not going to change. You know I'm not going to stop. I may say I will, but I'm not. So why don't we just make it easy for each other, and you do your thing and I'll do mine."

The three-week charade fooled nobody. As soon as the Texas Rangers learned that Steinbrenner was going to dump Howser, they asked for permission to talk to him. The Texas job was Howser's if he wanted it. If he didn't want it, the job would go to Don Zimmer.

The press conference that George convened to announce Howser's "retirement" ranks, in the eyes of even his most fervent admirers, as Steinbrenner at his living worst. "What's there to say," one of them says, "except that every life has to have a low point, and that was George's."

By then, George had taken Howser's little real estate company and turned it into an unbelievable real estate venture of such sprawling magnitude as to make the Hunts of Texas wonder how come they hadn't been let in on it. Why George finds it necessary to go through these charades is a mystery whose veil may one day be pierced. Why Howser lent himself to it is explained, presumably, by a desire not to upset the apple cart before the settlement was signed. It became clear very quickly that Howser was setting limits on his cooperation.

George began by announcing that Howser had resigned his position, which was being rather free and easy with the objective truth, though not necessarily with the truth that Steinbrenner had created. And, after all, what other truth is there? Through it all, Howser sat with his chin in his hand and his index finger extended up his cheek, and stared directly ahead.

"At no time," George said, denying his own leak to some of the very people he had leaked it to, "did I lay down rules or commandments that Dick would have to live by if he returned as a manager. The door was open for him to return, but he chose to accept this business opportunity. It took so long because he wanted to make sure he was doing the right thing."

Could he still be manager if he wanted to?

"Yes," said Steinbrenner.

"Dick, why don't you want to be here?"

"I have to be cautious here," Howser said. "But the other thing popped up."

"Were you satisfied that you could have returned without conditions?"

"I'd rather not comment on that."

"Were you fired, Dick?"

"I'm not going to comment on that."

What about that, George?

"He was not fired. If Dick doesn't want to comment, for whatever reason, that's up to him. But he was not fired. I think it's safe to say that Dick Howser wants to be a Florida resident year-round. Right, Dick?"

Maybe that little question explains the press conference. Maybe George wanted to see if just once, under the pressure of public exposure, he could make Dick say, "Right, George."

Dick didn't even bother to answer.

The odor of sanctity, so long in coming, permeated George's closing comments: "I feel morally and contractually obligated to Dick and his wife. I took him out of Florida State, where he could have stayed for life. If it hasn't worked out, maybe it's my fault."

There's nothing like an amicable parting. What advice would Dick give to the new manager, Gene Michael?

"To have a strong stomach," Howser replied, "and a nice contract."

George was back in charge. Nobody challenges him. One sees him getting up in the morning, looking into the mirror, and saying, "Mirror, mirror on the wall, who is the biggest prick of all?" And if the mirror doesn't answer, "You are, George," then it will never be allowed in Yankee Stadium again, EVER!

13

BEFORE THE STRIKE

The 1981 season was divided into two reasonably equal parts separated by the Great American Baseball Strike. The first half was won by the Yankees with an invaluable assist from George Steinbrenner. If you don't want to believe that, ask the Boss. Nobody was quite able to appreciate the extent of his contribution until he was kind enough to explain it.

He may be right. The thing to keep your eye on here is the shifting deadline on the calling of the strike.

Looking back, you find that hardly anybody believed the owners would force a strike over the issue of compensation, least of all the players themselves. Why would they? Over the entire history of the Players' Association, every labor negotiation had amounted to the owners caving in to Marvin Miller.

George knew better. In the last-second agreement that forestalled a strike in 1980, the owners had been given the right to invoke compensation unilaterally on a pre-indicated 1981 date, May 29, with the players then having forty-eight hours to decide whether to accept it or go on strike. In addition to taking out their $20 million worth of strike insurance and building up a multi-million-dollar slush fund, the owners had moved to protect themselves against each other by turning almost total representation and control over to their negotiator, Ray Grebey. How could anybody as experienced in labor negotiations as George doubt that the team that was in the lead on May 29 would have an excellent chance of being declared the pennant winner of a truncated season?

On Sunday, May 24, with the season all of thirty-nine games old, the Yankees were slaughtered by the Cleveland Indians 12–5, before a Jacket Day crowd of 53,874. The Yankees had fallen one and a half games behind Baltimore, the strike deadline was five days away, and George Steinbrenner went into his Irate Mode. "When 53,000 fans spend their hard-earned dough seeing this fiasco," he raged, "I'm embarrassed. It's a crime to ask people to pay their money to see an exhibition like this."

The Boss hadn't been in his Irate Mode since spring training, possibly because the Yankees had spent most of the season in first place. Obviously he was in need of a workout.

In the third inning of the "fiasco," with the score still only 9–3, Reggie hit back to the pitcher to start a double play, and George went into Man Irate, a discolike maneuver in which you leap up from a sitting position, assault the air with a few karate chops, slam your hands into your pockets, and look grim. It's a strenuous number. When it's over, George usually has to take out that comb.

"Reggie is killing us," he groaned. "I don't know what's bothering him." All he had to do was ask. There were 53,000 people in the park who could have told him.

To un-damp Reggie's spirits, George went out of his way to praise Dave Winfield, who was leading the team in hitting with an average of .329. "Without the San Diego Connection [Winfield and Mumphrey]," George added, "we'd be ten games out." Jerry Mumphrey, who was hitting .307, was the center fielder he had extracted from San Diego in an excellent late-spring trade. So George had a point.

To lift Reggie's spirits even further, he informed the press that he had been trying to get Gene Michael to drop Reggie down to fifth place in the lineup. Michael, he said, had been resisting his suggestion.

And while he was about it, he gave them all fair warning. "I'm embarrassed at what's happening, and maybe if some of these guys were a little embarrassed we'd be better off. . . . If we go down to Baltimore and embarrass New York, there'll be hell to pay. I promise you that."

There are two things you have to understand here. When the Yankees lose, George is embarrassed, and when he is embarrassed, he apologizes to the City of New York. Not just to the Yankee fans but to the whole city. To the sewer system, the Empire State Building, the George Washington Bridge. . . .

Example: Back in 1977, the year of the first World Championship, the Yankees lost two straight to Seattle—an expansion team, yet— and George felt compelled to vent his disgust through the ever-ready facilities of the national media. "The thing that disappoints me most is the lack of pride the players have. They don't seem to care if they're known as the team that choked. I'm embarrassed. I apologize to the City of New York." See?

The other thing to remember is that when George is embarrassed, he embarrasses others.

After the Cleveland fiasco, Reggie Jackson, for one, was suitably embarrassed. "I'm playing like a junkyard dog," he conceded. All he could do was hang in there and try not to commit suicide. "I hope," he said, "I get a low-floor room in Baltimore."

The Yankees went to Baltimore, lost three straight, and before George was through he had attacked the following people: the umpires, the supervisor of umpires, the league president, the opposing manager, his own star pitcher, his second baseman, his catcher, his right fielder, his manager, his trainers, and his physical coordinator. While he was about it he delivered a glancing blow in the direction of the Baseball Writers Association of America for writing the scoring rules so loosely that Reggie had been able to escape without an error on a ball he should have caught.

And that was just in his spare time. For the first two days of the series, George was operating from Tampa, where he was closing a deal for a hotel.

During the middle game he became so incensed over a safe call at second base in the fourth inning that he had no choice but to phone the press box and dictate another of those embarrassing statements. George hadn't seen the play, but what difference did that make? He had talked to some of his people who had seen it, and that was enough to convince him of the unfairness of it all: "It's hard enough to win the American League East when your players are hurt and you're struggling, but evidently from all the reports that I received from my staff . . . and from what I personally witnessed during the Cleveland–New York series, the umpiring displayed by this crew has been so bad that not even Gehrig, Ruth, and Lazzeri could have overcome it." *Losers complain about umpiring. That's what Yankee-haters have been doing for years. An umpire's decision in the fourth inning does not determine the outcome of a nine-inning game. As Gehrig, Ruth, and Lazzeri could have told George.*

"The crucial play involved umpire Terry Cooney. It was one of the worst of any season." *It was a close play. The worst decision George ever saw may have come in the first game of the 1977 World Series, when an umpire who had been caught out of position called the Dodgers' Steve Garvey out at the plate. The Yankees went on to win that game in extra innings, and George was able to hide his embarrassment.*

He wasn't questioning the honesty or integrity of the umpiring crew, it seemed, only their intestinal fortitude. "Give credit to [Baltimore manager] Earl Weaver. Every close call went against New York. He's a great manager and intimidator of umpires . . . the last thing they wanna see in front of a partial hometown crowd coming at them from the dugout is Weaver. He just plain scares and intimidates them." *True. Weaver knows the rulebook, puts on a wondrously theatrical performance, and has a scathing tongue. But look who's talking about intimidation.*

"Dick Butler, the American League supervisor of umpires, is the man who assigned this crew to the tough Baltimore series—and why he had them follow the Yankees from New York after all the trouble in the Cleveland series, I will never know.

"I feel Butler should have retired two years ago, but [Lee] MacPhail protects him like a security blanket. My people tell me he was never a ballplayer or an umpire, so naturally MacPhail, in all his wisdom, puts him in the position of supervisor of umpires." *The supervisor had been at the job for twelve years, preceding MacPhail by four years. You'd think George would have known that without his people having to tell him, since MacPhail was president of the Yankees in 1973 when Steinbrenner came riding in from Cleveland.*

Smash ending: "It seems so typical of the wisdom we all too often show in baseball. It makes about as much sense as trying to pay a two-dollar traffic fine with a three-dollar bill." *A non sequitur, but I guess George had been waiting to use that line ever since he . . . but naw, let's not get into that again.*

It was the second time George had been heard from, via telephone communication, in two days. In the opening game, Ron Guidry, pitching with a bone bruise on the ball of his right foot, got blasted 10–1. "Don't give me any BS about a bruised foot," Steinbrenner ranted.

"He pitched lousy against Kansas City in the first game of the playoffs against Kansas City last year, and he's been lousy except for one game this year."

Well, he hadn't been lousy all this year. He may not have been the old unhittable Guidry, but he had been plenty good. But that wasn't what made George's attack so outrageous. George gets an injury report from the trainer before every game. Even when he is out of town, it is a rare day when he doesn't call every official of the ballclub to find out what's going on, to let them know they are being watched (and cross-checked against each other), and to make sure that they don't go forty-eight hours without being reminded how afraid they are of him.

Most pitchers drive off their back foot. Guidry, who weighs at most 165 pounds, gets his power by driving off both feet. When he's right, he finishes with a little hop toward the plate. Everybody in the press box and dugout knew that Guidry shouldn't have been pitching, because there was no hop at the completion of his delivery.

Beyond all that, Steinbrenner was talking about the pitcher who, in the single most unselfish act of the big-money era, had volunteered to go back to the bullpen after Goose Gossage was injured. He was talking about a pitcher who had never balked at starting post-season games with two-day and three-day rests, even though he needed at least four days to be at his best. And, to bring it up to the present, he was talking about a pitcher who had taken the shot against Baltimore with his bad foot only because he knew that the Yankees were out of starting pitchers.

Bullshit, says George. George was engaged in contract negotiations with Guidry's agent, and when he's in salary negotiations, he always seems to view the player as an adversary. But, do you know, there's something odd about that too. George battles his players down to the wire on their contracts, and just when they think they're gone, he gives them what they've been asking for.

After Baltimore, Guidry decided not to pitch again until his foot was completely healed. And where he had previously kept himself apart from the clubhouse turmoil, he adopted the prevailing *Bleep him!* attitude about Steinbrenner for the rest of the year.

When the final game of the series began, George was sitting with Baltimore owner Edward Bennett Williams, the same Edward Bennett Williams who in his capacity as America's foremost criminal attorney plea-bargained Steinbrenner out of what could have been a very embarrassing trial and an even more embarrassing trip to the pokey.

The Yankees lost 6–5.

When the Yankees lose to Seattle, the manager is going to hear about it. When they lose three straight to Baltimore, the whole world is going to hear about it. George started his press conference by announcing that Willie Randolph and Rick Cerone had cost the Yankees the ballgame. What he really meant, it became evident soon enough, was that Gene Michael had cost them the ballgame.

Willie had failed to bunt Bucky Dent to second base in the top of the ninth, and had then hit into a double play. The double play came off a line drive to the shortstop. A couple of feet in either direction, and George might not have been quite so upset. "I've been after Gene since spring training to teach them how to bunt," George ranted. "I don't know why our infielders can't be taught to bunt like other people." There was some truth there, even if it wasn't a truth that applied to Willie Randolph, who happened to be the best bunter on the team.

Cerone had just returned to active duty after being out for most of the season with a broken wrist, and he had bounced into two double plays. "Here's a kid just back off the disabled list," George said. "What's he doing batting second?"

There was some truth there, too. It was a strange spot in the line-up for Cerone. On the other hand, the Yankees were so riddled with injuries that Michael was down to a lineup in which a second-string catcher, Barry Foote, was DHing, and a third baseman, Aurelio Rodriguez, was playing first base. (The team was going bad . . . George was in town . . . why does the thought keep intruding that it was Steinbrenner himself who had dictated that lineup? Maybe because Reggie Jackson was batting fifth?)

So you could make a case that the complaints involving Randolph and Cerone were not unjustified. But then George went on to second-guess Michael for using relief pitcher Ron Davis as early as the sixth inning, a criticism that made no sense at all. With Gossage having just come off the injury list too, Davis's territory was from the sixth inning to the eighth. Of course, the first batter Davis faced hit a home run off him. That might have had something to do with it.

George had a few other things to say about his manager, and they came in typical Steinbrenner doublespeak, in which he appears to blame his manager and, simultaneously, defend him . . . kind of. "He's been snake-bit on a lot of decisions he has made lately. You go back a couple of weeks, and two moves he makes cost us ballgames against Seattle. He brings in Davis tonight and, *bam*, a home run."

The manager had to make those kinds of decisions, George pointed out, and then he had to live or die with them. "But don't get the wrong idea. I'm not yelling at Gene at all. I think he's doing the best he can."

Oh-oh. Did that mean Michael was on his way out? Could be. "If that's the case, I'll take the responsibility. I picked the man. That goes with being the leader. But the won-loss is the bottom line. There's gonna be something happening shortly. I'm going to sit down with my people tomorrow by conference phone, and I wouldn't be surprised if something happened."

It soon turned out that the Yankees, according to their own leak, had already called the California Angels—the previous night, in fact—to find out whether Gene Mauch was available. Mauch, as everyone knew, had been sitting in the wings waiting to take over from the Angels' manager, Jim Fregosi. The Angels, who had been holding off any such move in anticipation of the strike, thereupon found it necessary to make the change immediately, and the Yankees promptly sprung the story of the phone call as preamble to the happy news that Michael was going to keep his job with the Yankees.

How serious was that phone call? For the answer, ask yourself another question: Would an owner who couldn't take any back talk from Dick Howser be looking for a strong manager like Gene Mauch?

So what does this all mean to students of George III? There is a pattern here that is repeated again and again. He seizes the headlines by issuing a shotgun blast at his players, keeps it going for a few days by threatening to fire his manager, and gets another headline by deciding not to. For a while, anyway.

And the damnedest thing is that soon after the dust has settled, the team goes off on a winning streak.

The reconciliation meeting this time around took place in Tampa, immediately following the Baltimore series. George had had several long talks with Stick, he announced. "He understands me. I'm satisfied he knows he's made some mistakes, but who's perfect? He made some decent decisions with pitchers, but they backfired on him. That happened five times, but things happen."

A great vote of confidence.

Still, somebody had to be fired to justify all the commotion, and in this case the fall guy was Stan Williams, the pitching coach. Even though the pitchers had been carrying the team all year. But that, again, is a standard Steinbrenner ploy. George had fired seven pitching coaches a total of ten times. When you fire the pitching coach, you are getting as close as you can to the manager himself. That warning shot fired across his bow. Stan Williams was the one coach Michael had been allowed to bring in with him, and now George was stripping him bare.

The Boss didn't even have the courtesy to inform Williams through official channels. He passed the information on to a columnist in the course of a telephone interview, and told him to spread the word.

Shortly afterwards, during one of his more moving tributes to himself, George was explaining to Milton Richman of UPI how everybody he had ever fired ended up better off. "What did I do so bad about Stan Williams?" In George's new version, Williams had been let go because Gene Nelson, the Yankees' great rookie prospect, had been tipping off his pitches, and Williams hadn't caught it. Actually, George pointed out, Williams had merely changed jobs with Clyde King, the minor-league pitching instructor, and to make the passage more pleasant, he told Richman, George had extended Williams's contract and given him a raise.

Well, that's George for you. A compulsive do-gooder. Stan Williams evidently loved his new job so much that he never went to George to ask about that extended contract and raise he had read about. He may, however, have called his lawyer.

But still. . . . Once you have said all that, you have to admit that the Yankees came back to New York from Baltimore and, with George drilling his coaches every day, started to win. At the stadium they swept Baltimore in three straight games, and ran off a nine-game winning streak before losing the final two games just before the strike.

In the process, they clinched a place in the playoffs by winning what was to become known as the First Season. And George was able to say that in looking forward to the probability that, yes, there was going to be a strike, he had felt it necessary to put the pressure on his team to be in first place in the event that the season did come to an end right there.

There's just one thing wrong with that explanation. When George put the pressure on, the strike was scheduled for May 29, and on that date the Yankees were at their lowest ebb of the season. The story about Michael being retained didn't come until a few hours after the deadline had been extended for two weeks! One wonders what

George's scenario would have been in the event that there had been no extension.

Still and all, you've got to give the Boss credit. The team did start to win after he created all that turmoil. Sure, baseball is cyclical. Sure, it's true that when a team as good as the Yankees is cold, the odds are that it is about to get hot. But since you can't prove it either way, George is entitled to the benefit of the doubt.

Take a bow, George. You got them in first place, you got all that publicity, and you made your manager suffer.

Three out of three ain't bad.

Steinbrenner's rationale for giving Gene Michael another chance was the unprecedented spate of injuries that had hit his team. "I have to be sure Stick has had an ample opportunity with the team we had on our drawing board" was how George put it. "He has not had that team."

The sportswriters had been saying the same thing all along, and they had not been holding the Boss entirely blameless. The average age of his starting lineup—that team on the drawing board—was close to thirty-two. His three top starters averaged nearly thirty-six.

Bob Watson (35), Jerry Mumphrey (30), Tommy John (38), Goose Gossage (30), Dennis Werth (28) had suffered muscle injuries of one kind or another. Lou Piniella (38) was playing with a bad knee. Bobby Murcer (35) had a stiff neck.

"Something's wrong someplace," George had complained. "Either we're not conditioning our guys or they're not conditioning themselves. Hell, they can't even run from first to third without pulling a muscle."

The injuries weren't an excuse to Steinbrenner, they were a personal affront. Every year within memory, he had left training camp complaining about the players' physical condition. But for perhaps the first time in his career as a stern taskmaster he had pronounced this team fit and ready to start the season.

The injuries were a puzzlement, and it is not George's nature to allow puzzles to lie around unsolved. Since he had already dismissed the possibility that they could have been underconditioned, he had to consider the possibility that they were *over*conditioned. Howard (Hopalong) Cassidy, his coordinator on conditioning, was sent winging north from Tampa to make sure the Yankees' aging stars weren't working so hard on the Nautilus equipment at the stadium that their muscles were tightening up on them.

If he had thought to consult his players first, they could have pointed out a basic flaw in that theory, to wit: none of the players works on the Nautilus machines once the season begins. If there is one thing you don't need when you are playing baseball every day, it's a good workout in the gym. During the season, the Nautilus room is used *qua* Nautilus room only by the office staff.

Which isn't to say that for individual players it doesn't have other uses. The Nautilus equipment is in the old storage room right next to the clubhouse. Ron Guidry keeps his drums in there. He will go in from time to time with a stereo, put on a pair of earphones, and set up a *rat-a-tat* to the accompaniment of the music.

It is also used as a barbershop. With Steinbrenner so insistent upon proper grooming, "the haircut man," a friend of bullpen catcher Dom Scala, comes in weekly and sets up shop.

It is used as a meditation room, most notably these days by Bucky Dent. Bucky goes in there with his psychologist-priest, Father Joe, to get his head together before every game. We'll get back to that.

During the game it is used as a trysting place by one of the players and a TV camerawoman. *During the game?* Well, there are six cameras set up around the field, and a goodly number of the frequently changing camerapeople are women. During the game, each cameraperson gets a fifteen-minute break, and when the player we are talking about doesn't happen to be in the game they both head for the Nautilus room. The tryst was discovered when one of the clubhouse men opened the door to get some supplies, and then very gently shut it. "What I can't understand," he confided to some friends afterwards, "is that they were on the leg machine, and their legs were the only part of them that wasn't being exercised."

There are a lot of women working around the ballpark these days, and once this splendid new use for Nautilus equipment became known, George's investment in his players' conditioning finally began to pay off.

The suspicion is that George knows about it and has decided that the best thing to do is not know about it. After all, he has spies in the clubhouse—under the Steinbrenner regime, Yankee Stadium has become a tight little police state—and they are supposed to keep him informed about everything that goes on.

The stag movies are something else. Stag movies were being

shown in the players' lounge in 1980 until George found out and ordered Dick Howser to put a stop to it. So they moved the equipment into the Nautilus room and stationed someone at the door to warn the audience when one of "George's henchmen" came into view.

Stag movies are a Yankee tradition. Back in 1974, the year of George's "voluntary" suspension, the team was making a surprising run at first place when catcher Rick Dempsey, who comes from a show biz family, brought in an X-rated movie to be viewed in lieu of batting practice. The Yankees were getting tense under the unaccustomed pressure, and with Transcendental Meditation running rampant through the clubhouse, Dempsey thought he was on to something. "This is a new form of meditation," he told them. "If this doesn't loosen us up, nothing will."

When the Baltimore Orioles, the defending champions, came into the stadium soon afterwards, somebody brought in a privately made movie, which he had somehow managed to have shot exclusively for the Yankees. The film consisted of one young, unclothed and undeniably talented lady whose props consisted entirely of a Yankee yearbook and an empty champagne bottle. Her act consisted of moaning forth the name of each of the players she encountered in the yearbook while she was doing her thing with the champagne bottle. The film relaxed the club so much that they won three of the four games and were suddenly being looked upon as serious contenders for the first time in ten years.

The first player to use the Nautilus room for meditation was Lenny Randle, whom Billy Martin had brought to the Yankees toward the end of the 1979 season. Randle, one of those highly emotional black players whom Billy Martin has always been able to identify with, had got himself messed up by belting Billy's successor at Texas, Frank Lucchesi. Lenny was deeply into the martial arts. He would go into the Nautilus room, turn the lights off, and settle into a squat position with his head down for almost an hour.

Randle didn't return the next year, but the meditation function was taken over by Eric Soderholm—a very religious young man, very sensitive, a poet. By sheer willpower he had come back after shattering his leg two separate times. And it was Soderholm who introduced Bucky Dent to the therapeutic effects of meditation at a time when Bucky Dent was badly in need of therapy.

Bucky's problems stemmed from those remarkable two weeks in 1978 when he hit the three-run homer that turned around the playoff game against the Red Sox, and then hit .417 in the World Series to win the Most Valuable Player award. Bucky became an overnight celebrity, and it almost destroyed him.

Bucky is the last person you'd think of as insecure. His value as a shortstop is that he is so steady. But Bucky has always been as insecure in his own way as Reggie Jackson. And perhaps for some of the same reasons. His parents were divorced before he was born, his mother gave him up, and he had searched for years to find his father.

In Chicago he had been the one star on a terrible team. In New York he found that Billy Martin was pinch-hitting for him whenever the Yankees were behind in the late innings. Why wouldn't he, with all those good hitters sitting on the bench? But Bucky took it so personally that he would go around from player to player saying, "I hope Billy does like me. . . . I've never done anything that he shouldn't. . . . I'm just trying to play. . . . Gee, I hope he likes me and that we can get along."

When Bob Lemon, who likes everybody, took over, he did the same thing, and Bucky was reduced to saying, "Why does he do that to me when no other shortstop in the league gets it done to them?"

And then, all of a sudden, at the end of the 1978 season, he was a celebrity, a merchandisable quantity. Baby-faced and good-looking, he became the darling of the teenagers, and what had seemed to be a perfect marriage with a beautiful wife went kaput. When the next season started, he was still taking his celebrity status so big that his teammates began to call him "Little Reggie," and his best friend on the club, the good-natured Goose Gossage—who had accepted his own sudden brush with fame and fortune without changing one whit—became pretty much fed up with him.

By the end of the 1979 season, with Bucky having taken a grip on himself and trying desperately to save his marriage, he was thrown into another emotional whirl by Steinbrenner's refusal to see his agent. Bucky's contract was coming to an end, he was sure he wouldn't be back in New York, and that was one more source of instability at a time when he was trying to put his roots back down. Steinbrenner, true to form, gave him what he was asking *after* the season was over, and Bucky has been trying to put his life back together ever since.

For the past two years he has been going into the Nautilus room before every game with Father Joe to get himself mentally prepared to play. They spend an hour together, and then Bucky goes out onto the field and plays the steady brand of shortstop for which he is noted.

The Born-Again movement has become big in baseball these past few years for very much the same reason. The pressure on big-time athletes, and most especially on baseball players with that 162-game schedule, has become so enormous that they find themselves in need of something to get themselves up for the game. With many of the players, it's a conscious choice between greenies (amphetamines) and religion. Most players are wise enough to understand that they're doing themselves no good, in the long run, by "greening up." If religion will serve the same purpose, they're all for it.

Reggie Jackson, unique in all regards, goes to religion, as we know, for solace. And in the first half of this season of his torment he needed all the solace he could get.

First of all, let's put Reggie's torment in perspective. Reggie was tormented because George wouldn't commit himself to a million-plus contract that wasn't going to start until next year anyway. On a scale of one to a billion, that puts him in the .03 percentile of human misery. From a narrower perspective, all the children starving in Bangladesh didn't make Reggie's private torment any less real.

Twice during the season, Reggie suffered the ultimate humiliation of being taken out for a pinch hitter. Once before the strike, and once after. Around these two low points we can pretty well chart his season.

Yankee Stadium, June 4. Reggie comes up to bat in the eleventh inning of a 1–1 game against Baltimore, with one out and Dave Winfield on first base. In four earlier appearances he had struck out twice and walked twice, meaning that he hadn't put his bat on the ball all night. When he strikes out for the third time, he goes storming down the dugout stairs, up the tunnel, through the locker room, and into the players' lounge.

In the middle of the players' lounge sits a thin-legged table with a heavy butcher top. The food hadn't been set out yet, but the Coke-dispensing machine has been put in place on one side of the table, and a huge coffee urn, already filled, is standing on the other. "What the fuck is happening to me?" Reggie screams. In a fury of frustration, he picks up the table—sending the Coke machine and coffee urn flying— and hurls it at the wall.

Anger vented, he becomes again the quiet, almost apologetic figure he has been through this whole dismal season. So apologetic that he waves the clubhouse men away and insists upon cleaning up the mess himself. As Reggie is going for the mop, Bob Watson (6'2", 210 pounds) hefts the butcher top in a struggle to set the table back on its legs, looks at Reggie's departing back, and lets out a long, whistling, "Geeeee. . . ."

The rest of the team is already filing happily into the locker room. Graig Nettles, who follows Reggie in the batting order, had won the game with a home run. Lou Piniella, whose temper tantrums are the stuff of legend, comes into the lounge and sets off a howl of laughter by telling Reggie in all seriousness, "You know what? I think that's really good for you. A person should let out his feelings sometimes."

Reggie is not among the laughers. Reggie is so distraught that he asks Gene Michael to let him sit out the following night's game and try to get his head together. It doesn't help at all. For one thing, the newspapers report—in what can only be taken as a reflection of Michael's thinking—that Reggie will be sitting out the next three or four games. On top of that, the Yankees go on a hitting tear, beating the Orioles 12–3, and Reggie is asking batting coach Charlie Lau, whom he has come to depend upon heavily for emotional support, when he thinks he is going to get back in the lineup.

Lau keeps assuring him that he'll be in the lineup the next night against the Chicago White Sox. Unhappily for Reggie, Charlie Lau is right.

Yankee Stadium, June 6. Before the game, Reggie calls over the White Sox's announcer, Jimmy Piersall, to ask him why he is always getting on his case. Piersall was, of course, one of the best outfielders who ever lived. All Piersall can say is that while he has always been very critical of Reggie's fielding, he has also always given him credit for being the crushing hitter that he is.

"Do you think I'm through?" Reggie asks him. "Do you think I'm too old?"

"I don't know," answers the astonished Piersall. "I've never thought about it."

"Well, I'm not." Reggie lowers his voice and leans toward him. "God told me when I woke up this morning that everything was going to be all right, starting today."

Not today, Reggie. On his first two times at bat he strikes out, bringing his run of strikeouts to five straight. And then it gets worse. In the sixth inning Reggie comes to bat with runners on first and third and one out, and hits into a double play. But not your ordinary double play. Reggie hits a slow ground ball down the first-base line, and the first baseman throws home to get the runner. Jackson has already crossed first base and is jogging back toward the dugout—obviously under the impression that the inning is over—when he is tagged out.

Why the first baseman would throw home for the third out instead of just stepping on the bag defies rational explanation. But nobody is expecting anything rational from Reggie at that point. Except Bobby Brown, maybe. Bobby Brown has been shuffled back and forth between the Yankees and the minor leagues with such regularity that he is being called the Designated Yo-Yo, and he feels that it has been Reggie's unwillingness to accept the role of permanent DH that has deprived him of his chance to be the regular right fielder. "Reggie knew what he was doing," Brown says. "He just decided to walk off the base." The other players know better. Reggie's mind is so befogged that he doesn't know what is going on.

Before the game has run its course, many of his teammates are upset with him for a wholly different reason.

With Reggie due to bat again in the ninth inning, Gene Michael calls him over. "I don't want the fans to get on you," he tells him. "I'm going to pinch-hit for you." And instead of shouting, "Goddammit, nobody pinch-hits for Reggie Jackson. Give me the goddamn bat!" Reggie accepts it with a calm bordering on relief, goes back into the clubhouse, eats his meal, watches the rest of the game on the TV set, and goes home.

A hitter of Reggie Jackson's stature is not supposed to take that kind of insult so lightly. When Piniella and Nettles were taken out for pinch hitters the previous season, they had thrown massive temper tantrums. Nettles went rampaging down the tunnel, smashing every overhead fluorescent light with his bat. And Piniella . . . my God. Piniella came into the clubhouse screaming, "How could they pinch-hit for me! I'm the best player on the ballclub! Goddammit, how can they pinch-hit for me!" He yanked his shoes off without bothering to untie the laces and then tried to rip off his uniform. Literally ripped it off his body. The buttons came popping off the shirt, and the shirt went flying, and then he went after the pants. Unfortunately for Lou, he was so wrought up that he had forgotten that the double-knit material is guaranteed not to rip, tear, or even give. He fell to the floor, writhing and straining (Awwwrrr) at the unyielding pants for a full five minutes before he wore himself out.

But that's all right. That's the way a Lou Piniella and a Graig Nettles are expected to react. That's part of what makes them what they are.

Reggie Jackson meant even more to the Yankees. Reggie was respected for his hitting ability, for his ability to rise to the occasion, for being a winner.

His sudden decline had touched off something else in them. All big-league ballplayers live with the specter of "the little death," the decline of their physical powers. Reggie had been moping around the clubhouse all season, looking for sympathy. "I don't know what it is," he'd say, just as he had said to Piersall. "Maybe I'm through. Maybe I'm just getting too old."

It wasn't a question they wanted to deal with. "Naw, Reggie," they would say, "it's just a slump. You'll get out of it." And as soon as Reggie left, they would say to each other, "He's fuckin' through. He can't play anymore. His mind is so messed up, he'll never get out of it."

That was the mental state of Reggie Jackson a week before the Great American Baseball Strike.

With the kind of season Reggie was having, wouldn't you know he'd screw up his role in the strike, too.

None of the players on the club had been expecting a strike. Nobody was even paying that much attention. In all of baseball, there were probably not ten players who were intimately involved in union affairs. For the vast majority, labor relations meant that Marvin Miller told you what he was going to get for you, and you got it. This year's deadline had already been pushed back from May. With the new June 12 deadline approaching, the players assumed that they'd put some more things on the table and move it back to August 28 or whatever.

But when the players came back to the clubhouse after the June 11 game in Chicago, and learned that nothing had been happening, they became so uptight that Goose Gossage was screaming at the writers to hurry up and leave so that a union meeting could begin.

Reggie Jackson was the player representative. Never mind that he achieved that exalted position only because nobody else wanted it, he was the player rep at Oakland, too. He likes to conduct meetings because he enjoys being in charge.

When he returned from a midnight phone conversation with Marvin Miller with the word that the strike was on, there were moans of dismay and groans of disbelief.

"What the hell happened?" they moaned. "Awww, shit," they groaned.

Reggie was all business. Technically the owners had merely invoked compensation, and it would be up to the players to decide whether to strike. Reggie wasn't waiting. "The strike is on as of now," he announced. "I suggest we not go to Minnesota [next stop on the schedule]." With everybody else in too much of a state of shock to say anything, he went out to inform traveling secretary Bill Kane of their decision.

A few minutes later, Kane was knocking at the door to relay the owner's response. You're on strike? Fine. Go get your own hotel accommodations and transportation.

"Okay," Reggie announced. "We're all on our own. We've got to get our bags off the truck and take it from there." But what he was saying didn't really seem to be sinking in. "My feelings are that this is going to be a very long strike," he advised. "So all you guys who are only making about $200,000 apiece, it's going to be rough for you so you'd better save everything you got."

That sunk in. Especially among the $200,000-a-year men who until that very moment had been laboring under the incredible delusion that they were doing pretty well for themselves. Like beyond their wildest dreams. "What's this fuckin' guy talking about," they were muttering to each other. "What's the matter with that idiot."

They didn't fully realize what Reggie had done to them until they went outside and saw their bags being heaved off the truck. The bus, which was now going back to the hotel instead of to the airport, had already been boarded by most of the writers and club officials. As the first players picked up their bags and headed toward it, Bill Kane flung himself in front of the door with his arms outstretched. "Nobody's getting on this bus!" he warned. Boss's orders.

Comiskey Park is on the South Side of Chicago. Once the postgame crowd disappears, you have to phone for a cab and hope for the best. There was, moreover, a partial taxi strike in Chicago. Picture a dozen or so prosperous ballplayers, most of whom hadn't carried their own bags since the rookie leagues, trudging down the street, trying to hitch a ride, and denied even the minor satisfaction of being able to curse their comrades of the international labor movement, the striking taxi drivers.

The only person they could curse was that goddamn Reggie and his bright ideas. Couldn't wait, huh? They were, we might as well add, cursing him *in absentia*. Reggie, as so frequently happens, had a couple of friends waiting outside the locker room, and when the meeting ended, he had hopped into the car with them and sped away.

14

THE SECOND SEASON

Immediately it was called the Second Season. The Seconal Season would have been more like it. By the time the playoff system had been worked out—and reworked—the Yankees, as winners of what had now become the First Season, were in the playoffs for the Eastern Division title regardless. If they didn't win another game, they would be in a five-game playoff with the winner of the Second Season. If they finished first, they would be in a five-game playoff with the team that finished second. And thrown in somewhere along the line, it was decided that a team winning both halves would be playing four of the five games at home. That was put in for the fans. The fans didn't think it mattered, either.

There is a rhythm to a baseball season, and it is that of the long-distance runner. Within this rhythm, each team finds its character and each season writes its plot. The Yankee rhythm in the championship years had been to sputter through 100 games, surviving crises and stress, gather together for the final 50 games, and drive on through to the pennant.

For the New York Yankees of 1981, the Second Season became a fifty-game journey from *ho* to *hum*. The best thing that could be said for the team was that they didn't play any worse than two of the other certified winners, Los Angeles and Philadelphia.

The only excitement—if that's the word for it—was provided by the psychodrama Reggie Jackson was playing for himself in the theater of his mind, and the steady diet of confections and concoctions served up by that incomparable song-and-dance man up in the owner's box, Mr. Yankee Doodle Dandy himself.

With the Yankees playing .500 ball, the clubhouse capers were far more interesting than anything happening on the field. What follows is the background music to the Yankees' fifty-game journey to nowhere.

August 2. The strike having been settled, there is a week to get ready. Gene Michael and Reggie Jackson have both called meetings. Michael's club meeting is just a matter of making sure that everybody has remembered the signs. Reggie's union meeting is to bring the players up to date on the settlement. Of particular interest is a directive from the Players' Association that states that because the players lost so much money during the strike, the players' share of the receipts from the mini-playoffs is to be divided only among the players themselves. That means that the coaches, ground crew, clubhouse personnel—in other words, the people who suffered most from the strike that the players themselves had called—are going to get stiffed.

A few of the players have the ill grace to cheer. Most notably Ron Davis. "We shouldn't be tipping those clubhouse bastards anyway," he yells. "They get too much money as it is."

Not for nothing is Ron Davis known around the club as the Jack Benny of baseball. Ron worked as a waiter during the strike and has been bragging that he made $150–$200 in tips. The bat boys are paid $17.50 per game, and are every bit as dependent upon tips as waiters.

Reggie is saying quite openly that the strike was the best thing that could have happened to him. First, because he was able to "get a new start," and, second, because he can now see the light at the end of the tunnel. "Sixty days and I'm a free man. I've got sixty days," he proclaims, falling pointedly into the jargon of prisoners. "And I can do that standing on my head."

August 3. Steinbrenner is sitting up in the executive box with Tallis, Bergesch, and Saban, overseeing the workout. George has a pair of binoculars trained on the players. A holdover, perhaps, from checking the workouts of his horses. Feeling the glasses on them, some of the players begin to lower their heads before they speak. "Boy," says Nettles, "that fat bastard, if he'd go as far as putting binoculars on us, he's liable to have taken up lip-reading during the strike."

Yesterday, in his first workout, Reggie hadn't hit the ball well at all, and he responded to the ungentle jibes and insults of the handful of fans gathered behind home plate by giving them the finger and a sampling of his own more colorful vocabulary. Today, he is hitting everything out of sight in a breathtaking display of power. Ball after ball plunks into the upper deck, the bullpen, the center-field bleachers. But that isn't unusual. Even on days when Reggie appears at his most helpless during the game, he has been tremendous in batting practice. Still, this is such an awesome demonstration that it picks up everybody's spirits. The players are rooting for him to come out of it. Whether they like him or not, he is Reggie Jackson, and they want him to go out in style.

August 4. In strict contradiction to his reputation, Ron Davis is throwing a barbecue for the players in the press room after the workout. Even has his father, who once owned a barbecue restaurant, there to do the barbecuing. To make everybody realize where they are, a phone call comes down to Gene Michael from George. There is no hiding. "You haven't heard from that asshole in seven weeks," Piniella tells him. "Now you got to hear from him seven times a day. Poor sucker."

Michael does not disagree.

August 6. To help the players get back into shape, George is going to have them play a couple of exhibition games against the kids from his Bradenton rookie-league team. An excellent idea. It will give the kids a chance to play in the big ballpark, and it will give the fans a chance to see the Yankees of the future. Pay no attention to the ugly rumor that George rejected the Mets' offer to play a couple of games for charity. Take George's word for it that the offer came too late. The Mets had only been asking for almost a month.

August 7. The Bradenton kids came into the stadium so nervous that you had to wonder whether the game wasn't going to turn into a (heaven forbid) embarrassment. Far from it. When the kids take the field, they are so relaxed and confident that they actually beat the Yankees, 2–0. To put that in somewhat better focus, George spiked the team with a couple of veteran pitchers who had been working steadily at the AAA club in Columbus. George is so happy that he comes on TV after the game, all full of vim and vindication, to brag about how the Bradenton kids were able to keep their composure like true Yankees. "This," he pronounces, "is what Yankee tradition and Yankee pride is all about."

Yessiree. Yankee tradition, Yankee pride, and an abundance of greenies. Before the game one of the players stationed himself at the toilet door and passed them out to all comers. You never saw such confidence and composure.

Rich Gossage had come in to pitch the ninth, and when one kid came up, he started to laugh. The kid had been drafted from the University of North Carolina. During the Yankees' stopover in spring training, he had lined a base hit off Goose, and then after the game had very respectfully asked Goose to autograph the ball for him. "Get out of here!" the Goose roared. And there's the same kid up there waving a bat at him, as a fellow member of the Yankee organization. The Goose laughs, throws him a fast ball, and damned if the kid doesn't hit another shot off him. Only this time it is a hard ground ball right at the shortstop.

August 8. Gossage isn't laughing today, and neither is George. Goose has come up with a sore shoulder, as is normal for him in spring training. You throw as hard as Gossage does, and you get sore. But this isn't spring training. The season resumes in two days.

George is so furious he calls a meeting of his pitching coaches and trainers. "I got more coaches than anybody in baseball," he yells. "Couldn't you tell he was going to get hurt?"

You've got to say this for George, he never ceases to amaze his people with his keen understanding of the game.

"Torborg," he barks, "you're in the bullpen. Can't you watch over these guys?"

Torborg is the wrong man to ask. "What do you want me to do," he barks back, "throw for him, too?"

Clyde King, the pitching coach, is not going to disappoint him. George looks upon King as something of a genius at handling pitchers, and King has never gone out of his way to disabuse George. "Clyde, what the hell's going on? I got two pitching coaches. Aren't you looking over these guys?"

"Yeah," King says. "I don't know what happened this time. I guess it just slipped by me. I'm sorry."

Jerry Walker, the assistant pitching coach, is sitting behind the other coaches, his hand cupped over his mouth. Whether Walker is trying to hide a smile or muffle a cough, who can say?

George skips over Walker and turns to Doc Monahan, the trainer. "Monahan," he snaps, "you've got an assistant. There're two trainers here, there're two pitching coaches. What the fuck do you think you're doing? You've been here long enough! You should know by now when somebody is about to go."

Monahan might have said that if he could tell when an arm was going to get sore ahead of time, he could hire himself out as a witch doctor and get rich. But only if he didn't need the job. Yet he doesn't buckle under completely either. "I'm doing the best that I can, George. That's all I can give."

"Well," says George in a loud, threatening voice, "you'd better start giving a little more, big fellow."

August 9. Ron Davis is happy. Ron had been so upset at not being picked for the All-Star game that he'd been going around whacking the clubhouse kids on the arm. "I should have made it," he'd say, and whack away, accidentally-on-purpose hard. The way Ron had been pitching, he wasn't wrong. Ron Davis was the throw-in, the player to be named later, in the Ken Holtzman trade, and somebody on the Yankee scouting staff deserved a bonus. As a breaking-ball pitcher in the Cubs' minor-league chain, Davis enjoyed no particular success as a starter (19–18 with a 4.50 ERA). The Yankees converted him into a hard-throwing sinker-ball pitcher, and faced with the necessity of finding a relief pitcher after Gossage's injury, they brought him up in 1979. From nowhere, he compiled an incredible 14–2 record (along with 9 saves) to break the American League record of 13 set by Wilcy Moore of the 1927 Yankees. In 1980 he was just as effective, and this year he changed again. Instead of having his fast ball sink, he was just letting it rip. He throws almost as fast as Gossage—92–93 mph—and from his sidearm motion the ball has an explosive hop. The batters were still expecting the ball to go down, and it had been strikeout, strikeout, strikeout.

When Gossage was withdrawn from the All-Star game, Davis replaced him, and that changed his whole demeanor. For an hour or so. And then he was going around asking what gift the players were going to be getting for making the All-Star team. "Do we get a ring?" Yes, they do. They get a ring for themselves and a pendant for their wives. "When do we get the gift? Do they give it to us right there?"

Davis goes to the game with instructions from the Boss. He is to tell Jim Frey, the American League manager, that he is to pitch only one inning.

August 11. It's only the second day of the Second Season, and Reggie has sunk right back into his mental slough. He went hitless on opening day, bringing his average down to .191, and he was booed. The first time at bat today against the Texas Rangers' Rick Honeycutt, he went to the plate and gave himself up, looking as if he were swinging just to get it over with, and when he came back to the dugout he went over to Charlie Lau. "Maybe I should take myself out of the game. Maybe you should tell Gene to pull me out."

Charlie told him to hang in there and try to work it out. "If you pull yourself out, it's not going to do anything for anyone. Especially for yourself."

The Yankees could have used his bat. Or anybody's. They lost the game 1–0. And having surrendered at the plate, wouldn't you know that Reggie would be around the clubhouse afterwards looking for sympathy? "Boy, I'm not really doing the job. I don't know what's wrong. I wonder if I'll get out of it. What do you think? Think I'll ever get out of it?"

Everybody has just about had it with him. "Why doesn't he just try?" one player says. "Why doesn't he at least make it look good?"

Especially Bobby Brown, who has been fighting to get into the lineup. "So that's fuckin'-the-great Reggie Jackson. The *great* Reggie Jackson. What does he want from me? He's got everything there is in life, and I'm just trying to make it."

August 12. George has Michael phone Bucky Dent and Graig Nettles at nine in the morning to tell them to be at the ballpark at three o'clock for bunting practice. Both of them failed to bunt successfully the previous night in a bunting situation. Dent is a good bunter. Nettles hasn't been called upon to bunt for a long time, because why should you have one of your big RBI men bunt? Nettles shows up at three sharp, and Michael tells him, "I'm glad you could make it."

"I made it," Nettles tells him, "but the next time you call me at nine o'clock in the morning and I get the bunt sign in a ballgame, I'm just going to miss the sign."

Michael laughs, and Graig says, "You think I'm playing, right? Just give me the sign again."

Sure enough, Bobby Brown is told when he comes in that he is going down again to make room for a minor-league pitcher who is going to fill in until Gossage is ready to pitch again. Bobby throws a fit. They had brought him up the day before the strike was called, which had kept him from both playing and receiving his salary, and now they are shipping him back *three days* into the Second Season.

When Bobby comes back down from the front office to pack his stuff, Willie Randolph, who is really concerned about him, asks whether everything is all right. B.B. pulls out an envelope. "What's in this envelope makes it all right," he says. George has given him a sum of cash and the promise that he'll be back before the September 1 deadline. B.B. has been down six times—was even traded away once—and George has brought him back five times.

Lou Piniella, who has begun to worry about Reggie, is going around asking the people who know him best what's wrong with him. Reggie himself isn't much of a help. "I don't know, I just go up there. I can't really put it together."

"You know what I think?" Lou says. "I think it's probably your being DH. That's probably the thing that's bothering you. Yeah, maybe that's it." And then Piniella does something extraordinary. He says, "I'm going to Stick, and I'm going to tell him to let you play right field and let me DH."

Well, it's too late to make that kind of a change for tonight's game. The man upstairs has to be consulted. Reggie does get his first hit, though, a bloop single into center field in the sixth inning. The fans give him a standing ovation, and it isn't sarcastic. The fans don't want to see him go out in abject humiliation, either. It proves to be an important hit. Nettles strokes a home run right behind him, and the Yankees win the game 6–5.

August 13–15. You think Piniella doesn't have influence on this club? When the lineup is posted before the first game in Detroit, Reggie Jackson is in right field and Piniella is DHing. And it turns Reggie around. In the first three games he has four hits in eleven at-bats, and while they are all singles, he is really smoking the ball. In the final game of the series he has two ripping doubles and knocks in what looks like the winning run, until Kirk Gibson pulls it out for the Tigers with a pinch-hit home run in the ninth.

August 16. There is a delay in the flight back to New York, and while the players are sitting in the VIP area, Gene Michael is checking to make sure they are observing Steinbrenner's dress code. If a player isn't wearing a tie, Michael is supposed to fine him. And Michael does fine them. "Hey, Lou," he says, his roving eye having fallen on Piniella, "where the hell's your socks? You know the dress code."

Where did the dress code say he had to wear socks? Lou wants to know. "I got my tie on, Stick. Why don't you take my socks and shove them up your ass."

All around the area the players are grumbling. First it's ties, and now it's socks. Next he'd be checking to see whether they were wearing their dick inside their underwear or out.

August 17. Reggie steps in against Chicago's tough young lefty, Britt Burns, with confidence, pounding his feet up and down in the batter's box as if he can't wait to get at him. He's not going to get much of a chance. After being called out on a questionable third strike, he tenders the bat to the umpire and says, "Here, you take the bat. Maybe you can do better with it." That gets him thrown out of the game. Doesn't bother him at all. "Thirty-five more days," he says, "and I'll be free."

August 18. Dave Winfield, who has been hitless in seventeen times at bat during the Second Season, comes back to the players' lounge during the seventh inning to take a look at his last couple of at-bats on the Betamax. Also, Ron Guidry has come out of the game after pitching six innings of shutout ball, to go with five shutout innings in Detroit. The foot injury has healed very nicely during the strike, but Guidry wants to look at his form, too.

The Betamax is connected to a Panasonic that the whole team has always used, though actually it was installed in the clubhouse for Reggie.

Just as it is being set up, Reggie comes back. "What are you doing?" he screams. "Put the game on."

"Winfield wanted to see his last at-bats," Ray Negron tells him.

"It's my machine," Reggie says. "Put the game on."

Negron throws the switch and the game comes on. "I'm sorry," he tells Winfield.

"Sorry?" Reggie says. "It's . . . my . . . machine! Furthermore, I'm taking it home in October. Let George buy you a fucking video machine."

It *is* his machine, no doubt about it. And he probably doesn't have more than four or five others just like it at home.

Winfield has watched the whole performance with a disbelief not entirely unmixed with amusement. Guidry, over in the corner, has been grinning broadly.

Little Reginald was not going to let David use his ball and bat. Little Reginald is going to take his ball and bat and go home.

The game proceeds. With the Yankees leading 3–0, the White Sox put in a right-hander and Michael sends up Oscar Gamble to pinch-hit for Piniella, and Lou goes berserk. A spread has already been laid out in the clubhouse, and when Lou enters he grabs the hamburgers and the trays and flings them into the lockers. Absolutely berserk. The whole thing of tearing off his uniform as he goes from locker room to lounge to trainer's room and then back into the lounge to send Charlie Lau's projection screen flying. "This is it," he yells. At the end of the year he'll be through. If it weren't for the contract, he'd leave right now. The pants still don't give, and rolling around on the floor still doesn't help him tear them off. Nobody says a word, nobody dares look at him, except out of the corners of their eyes.

When Stick comes back after the game and sees the hamburgers all over the floor, he immediately asks, "Where's Lou?"

"No," Lou tells him. "Just get away from me. I don't want to talk about it."

"Try to understand the circumstances," Stick pleads. "I'm trying to do the best I can for the team."

"Don't worry about it," Lou says wearily, "because I'm quitting at the end of the year anyway. As a matter of fact, I don't even want to play anymore. Why don't you just put me on the disabled list or something for the rest of the year? I've lost my fun over here. I don't want to play anymore."

Michael keeps trying to placate him. "You get a good rest tonight, and everything will look all right tomorrow."

"Sure, sure, Stick."

Bobby Murcer comes in to get a drink, looks around at the carnage, and says brightly, "Oh, I see Lou quit again."

Lou is going to have to get used to it. For the rest of the season the Yankees play righty-lefty with the DH's whenever there is a change of pitchers. When Bob Lemon does it, too, there's no longer any question where the policy comes from.

August 19. Bad day at Yankee Stadium, all around. Tommy John was pitching for the Yankees, his first appearance since his little boy was hurt. George has been very classy, very supportive of John during his ordeal. Home or away, Tommy does not have to be in the ballpark except on the day he is scheduled to pitch.

Maybe the Yankees were trying too hard for Tommy. Whatever the reason, it was the most dreadfully played ballgame of the season. Four infield errors, two botched double plays, and Tommy is out of the game in the fourth inning.

George comes down to the clubhouse to commiserate with him.

The trainer's room and the players' lounge are on opposite corners at the rear of the clubhouse. On his way to the trainer's room, George sticks his head in to see why the television is going. The rule is that the players are not supposed to be in the lounge during the game, although there is an understanding that the DH can do anything he feels like between times at bat.

The lounge has four couches, three tables, and a pool table in the main area, but there is also a kitchen area behind a high partition. The players have a refrigerator there for cold cuts and soft drinks, and a small stove for cooking hamburgers or heating up the TV dinners some of them bring in. All the comforts, a home away from home. George isn't supposed to drop in—in the fourth inning, for crissake—without warning.

Okay, so George sticks his head in and sees five of his players there, watching the game on TV, two of them laid out on the couches.

"What the fuck is going on here?" he howls. "Half the team is in the goddamn lounge. I don't pay you guys to lay around and eat popcorn. I pay you guys to play ball. Piniella, Gamble, what the hell are you two doing in here?"

Piniella:	"Well, we're the DH's."
Gamble:	"Yeah, we're the DH's."
George:	"What does that mean? The game's outside. And there's only one DH in the game. Oscar."
Piniella:	"Yeah, but with this fuckin' Stick, you don't know when you're in or out."
George:	"Get out of here! Both of you. Get out of here!"
Piniella:	"But George, we got to size up the pitchers from in here. We get a better angle on the TV set."
George (screaming):	"And from now on the TV's not going to be in the lounge, it's going to be in the main clubhouse area. You hear that? You've fuckin' lost your lounge."

George leaves to walk across to the trainer's room, while Piniella and Gamble make suitable commentary on his retreating backside. As soon as he disappears into the trainer's room, seven guys come racing out of the lounge. Seven of them? Well yeah? Four others had been fixing themselves up a little snack when George stuck his head in, and they had flattened themselves, spread-eagled, against the wall behind the door so that George wouldn't be able to see them. There's Gossage and Davis, who aren't due in the bullpen for another inning or so, and Rodriguez and Milbourne, who aren't playing.

After the game, there is a meeting. George has ordered Stick to call a practice session for the next day, a scheduled day off.

August 24. Having fouled a pitch off his ankle two days earlier, Piniella is temporarily hobbled. Steinbrenner puts him on the disabled list so that he can make good his promise to bring Bobby Brown back.

Lou becomes more serious than ever about retiring. "I don't need the money anymore. I've got my money put away, and I've got great investments. I don't need any more of this bullshit. There's only one manager, and he's always in Tampa. I've got to get out of this."

He's been saying that for five years, and he means it every year. Until October.

August 26. This is the day that Reggie's physical is ordered. Reggie is benched, and Dave Winfield is dropped to the sixth slot on the lineup. Nobody tells Winfield about it, and since he has been batting third all year, he goes to the on-deck circle at the usual time. Oscar Gamble comes out right behind him, but Winfield thinks Gamble is hitting fourth and has come out, as Gamble sometimes will, to talk. Gamble explains the situation. "Why doesn't anybody tell me when they're making a change like this?" Winfield asks plaintively. Later, some of the guys start riding him a little. Winfield laughs it off. Embarrassed or not embarrassed, hitting or not hitting, his attitude is always the same.

August 30. Bobby Murcer, fed up by his lack of activity, calls Billy Martin to ask him to try to make a deal for him before September 1, when the rosters will be frozen. Bobby first came to the Yankees in the fall of 1965, in time to catch their demise, and was traded away in 1975, just in time to miss their resurgence. But Oakland has won the first half of the season, they are playing better ball than the Yankees in the second half, and Billy Martin is badly in need of a left-handed designated hitter.

Billy tries to work out something with the Yankees, but it's no go. Murcer's feeling is that the Yankees could have done him the favor for the little he was being used. But, then, Murcer has been saying all along that George is one of the biggest liars he has ever met. "He's been lying to me ever since he bought the Yankees, beginning with when he told me I'd never leave the Yankees."

August 31. Despite all the turmoil on the road over Gene Michael's status, George hasn't forgotten the sight of all those players lying around in the lounge. Back in Yankee Stadium, workmen are trying to install a TV set in the main clubhouse. The reception is terrible. They are going to have to work out a special antenna system. And then—heh, heh—the lounge is going to be closed during the game.

September 1. Now that Reggie Jackson has told George off and is hitting the ball with authority, he is his old vocal, exuberant self again in the clubhouse. But the other players, having suffered through his bouts of self-pity and teeth-grinding, suddenly realize that they are tired of being jacked around by his moods. Even somewhat sympathetic players like Willie Randolph and Aurelio Rodriguez and Bobby Murcer are asking each other why the atmosphere always has to revolve around Reggie. "We got to be up when he's up, and when he's down, we have to be down? Fuck him."

Back in New York, Lou Piniella, who was so understanding and helpful during Reggie's days of travail, has had the same kind of awakening. "What the hell is this Reggie Jackson bullshit? We got six fuckin' guys on this ballclub whose contracts run out at the end of the year. I mean, Reggie's a great player. A *great* player. But we still got . . . six . . . fuckin' . . . guys . . . on the club without a contract. *I don't have a contract!* Now, goddammit, I've got sixteen years in the game, and when are they going to give me one? Well, they can keep it. I'm retiring at the end of the year anyway."

September 5–7. Dave Winfield has returned to his hometown of Minneapolis for the first time as a major-league ballplayer, and it has been an emotional experience. On the first day he conducted a free clinic for 1,500 underprivileged kids through his Winfield Foundation. Free medical examinations, a picnic supper, and tickets to the game. The next night, roaming left field, he dropped a fly ball to lose the ballgame 4–3, after Reggie had knocked in all three Yankee runs with a pair of doubles.

Winfield threw a party for his teammates at his mother's home, and he did it in style, sending limousines to pick them up. Reggie took over the party, with his well-known rendition of the Robot.

Before the final game, Reggie is standing behind the batting cage as Winfield is taking his final swings. "Okay," Dave says after the swings have produced nothing spectacular, "I'm going to take two more."

"What are you going to take two more for?" Reggie hoots. "You're just going to hit bouncing balls down the middle."

As Winfield leaves the batting cage, he gives Reggie a vicious look. The kind of look whose meaning is so clear that the other players around the cage get into it. "I don't know, Reggie," is the gist of what they're saying. "I may have to go with Winfield if you guys ever get into it. That's one big dude."

September 7. The Yankees have returned to New York with their new manager, Bob Lemon. Reggie is very subdued, very quiet. Morose. "I need to be left alone" is all he will say. He seems to feel guilty over the firing of Michael, just as he seemed to feel guilty when Billy Martin was fired. He and Michael had become very friendly following Stick's press conference. Whether it was an act—the same kind of act he and Martin indulged in so frequently—or whether Michael's words of praise were all that it took to turn him around is more than even the most fervent Reggie-watcher could tell . . . probably because Reggie—the most fervent Reggie-watcher of all—couldn't have told them himself.

But if he started the day incommunicado, he is going to end it by stalking off the ballfield after Randy Lerch, Milwaukee's left-hander, has knocked him down three times. In between, he did a lot of screaming about not being protected by his own pitcher, Ron Guidry.

Actually the first time wasn't that close. Reggie leans his upper body into the pitch, and he will sometimes go down on a pitch that's very close to being a strike. The next two at-bats, though, the pitches were close enough to hit his bat as he was falling, and what can be more infuriating than to end up on the ground, with a strike? And then strike out. Both times.

"I can't see why my guys won't protect me," he begins to scream when he returns to the dugout. "I thought there was more guts on this team than this."

He didn't say anything directly to Guidry. In the infinitely calibrated code of baseball, that's not the way it's done. As Bob Lemon says afterwards: "I've never asked a pitcher to throw at anyone. On the clubs I've had, I've never had to. There's been enough talk on the bench for a pitcher to know. That's the pitcher's prerogative. If he wants to knock someone down, that's okay."

Guidry has his own sense of values. He doesn't believe in throwing at a batter, and he just won't do it.

Reggie goes to the outfield for the seventh inning and stands there with his arms crossed, as if to say that if Guidry won't protect him, he isn't going out of his way to help Guidry. By the time he gets back to the bench, he has worked himself into such a lather that he announces, "If we're not going to knock somebody down, I'm leaving." And that's what he does. He leaves.

Lemon ducks the issue by claiming that he took Reggie out. The truth is that by the time Lemon came back to look for him, Reggie was already undressed. "It's all right," Lem tells him. "I've sent Brown out there."

September 8. Game called on account of rain. Andre Robertson, a sweet-fielding shortstop brought up to fill in for Bucky Dent, who had broken his hand on the road trip, leaves Yankee Stadium early to get himself settled. Andre is young, slightly built, and black. As he heads for the players' parking lot, George's security cops mistake him for one of the neighborhood kids, and Andre's plans have to be called off on account of blood. He doesn't get out of the hospital until 2:30 the next morning. With a couple of stitches in his head.

September 9. The Yankees had returned to the stadium with their new manager to find the new TV set in the main clubhouse. The antenna system had been installed at a cost of $3,500, and it was being made very clear that there was no longer any need for any player to be in the lounge while a game is in progress. During the second game of the double-header following the rainout, Charley Lau comes in, finds nobody at all in the main clubhouse, and nine players watching the game on the old small set in the lounge. Well, not necessarily watching. Two of them are sound asleep. "I give up," Lau says. "It's not going to work."

September 19. A cool, wet Saturday afternoon in Boston. The policy since the strike has been to let Guidry go six or seven innings and then bring on Davis and Gossage. With the Yankees leading 5–1 in the fifth inning, Lemon wants Ron Davis to warm up. Davis is nowhere to be found. So Lemon has Frazier warm up instead, and sends Yogi back to the clubhouse to look for Davis. Yogi finds him there watching a college football game. "Geez," said Yogi, "I thought it was bad enough in New York."

Davis goes in in the eighth inning, with the score still 5–1, gets the first two batters, then has trouble with his control, then has trouble with everything. By the time he is back in the clubhouse, the Red Sox have scored seven runs and Guidry has lost his victory.

September 23. Back in New York, and it's a great day for Reggie Jackson. His greatest day of the year. It begins, for Reggie, in the second inning, when he's sent sprawling by Cleveland's John Denny, who has come into town as the hottest pitcher in the league, with six straight wins.

Reggie has two ways of describing his reaction to knockdown pitches, depending upon his mood, his audience, and the phase of the moon. Also upon whether he has struck back or struck out.

1. Post-success: "I get knocked down more than anybody in baseball. You have to back out of the batter's box. You have to slow everything down, take hold, and really concentrate." And, just coincidentally, build the drama toward the moment when he steps back in and—will he or won't he?—hits the next pitch downtown.
2. Post-failure: "I get knocked down more than anybody in baseball. I kind of take it as a compliment. But remember, I'm an egomaniac, so I can turn anything into a compliment."

This time, Reggie backs out of the batter's box, slowing everything down, takes hold, really concentrates, takes two mighty swings, and strikes out.

And then he decides to get mad about it. He has taken a couple of steps toward the bench before he turns, points the bony finger of indignation at Denny, and sets up one of those charming exchanges in which the word "asshole" plays the most prominent role. Like: "Don't you throw at me again, you asshole."

"You asshole, the ball wasn't close to you."

Whereupon Reggie goes after him. Bobby Brown wraps his arms around him, swings him around and lugs him away, while Reggie—never a man to go quietly—puts his final signature on the silliness by flinging his batting helmet in Denny's general direction.

"I wasn't mad at being thrown at," Reggie admits later. "I was mad at myself for striking out."

Between innings, he goes back to the clubhouse to find out how it looked on television. The other DH's are there with Gossage, who is injured again, and Charley Lau.

Reggie holds his hands about three inches apart. "That guy missed me by that much, didn't he?"

Gossage and Piniella speak at the same time.

"Yes," says Gossage, who likes to keep the peace.

"No," says Piniella, who always tells it the way it is. He holds his hands about a foot apart. "It was more like this."

"He missed me by this much," Reggie insists, pointing to his chin. "It was right here."

Piniella holds his hands about ten inches apart. "It was like *this*."

Reggie is indignant. "I don't know what game you were watching. I was right up there. You were watching on TV."

They both had a point. The instant replay again. When you see a batter hit the dirt on an inside fast ball, your eyes tell you that the pitch was at his head. When you see it played back, in slow motion, it isn't that close. But the pitch didn't come at him in slow motion. The pitch came at him at better than 90 mph, and at that speed it's reflex action.

Reggie does tend to be on his way down on those inside pitches. And why shouldn't he be? Willie Mays, who *was* thrown at more than anybody in baseball, used to go down on anything within whispering distance of his head. There's an intimidation factor, sure. But the intimidation works both ways. The way Reggie leans into the pitch, he's almost asking to be pushed back. The book on Reggie has always been that he can be pitched to, tight across the letters. It also says that if you miss an inch or two toward the plate, it's Good-bye, Charlie. Which is exactly what kept happening to the Los Angeles pitchers in the 1977 World Series. In other words, if you're going to miss, you had better miss inside. What's the pitcher supposed to do, change his whole style of pitching so that Reggie won't get mad?

Comes the fourth inning, and the drama that has been building from the time Bobby Brown carried him away is ready to play itself out. The fans are screaming "Reggie . . . Reggie . . . Reggie. . . ." The moment he has created for himself has arrived. John Denny, who has not been in good form anyway, runs the count to 2–2, and *whoosh!* up, up, and away . . . a monster home run going halfway up into the right-center-field bleachers. As soon as he hits it, Reggie knows. He drops his bat, and a Fu Manchu grin splits his features as he follows the ball's flight. He starts to first, chug-chugging his fists toward the ground in a gleeful dance of self-approbation. As he rounds third to complete the last leg of his triumphant tour, he takes off his batting helmet and holds it aloft.

It isn't until he crosses the plate that he seems to pay any attention to Denny. The Cleveland pitcher has come off the mound toward him and is yelling that next time he really will knock him on his ass.

What has Denny so incensed is that Reggie has manufactured a drama out of coming back off a knockdown pitch—which really wasn't a knockdown pitch—and is now strutting his triumph for all to see, at Denny's expense.

And he still isn't through. Pumped up as he is, Reggie goes charging out at Denny, hands upraised as if he were going for the throat (watch out, George). Instead, he clamps his arms around Denny's head, they topple to the ground, and a dozen guys from both teams flop on top of them.

At length Reggie is plucked out of the heap by Bobby Brown and Oscar Gamble and is again lugged away, with Brown holding him around the chest and Gamble holding onto one leg, while the other dangles free. In that awkward semi-recumbent position, Reggie is laughing and clapping his hands maniacally.

Set down in front of the dugout, he takes off his shirt, which has ripped, and throws it away. And stands there yet another moment, looking back at the scene, not wanting his moment to end, obviously ready to get back into it. Except that now there is no longer any "it" to get back into.

With the Yankees, no "it" ends until George has been heard from, and George isn't going to let a headline slip away without claiming a piece of it for himself. From Tampa, the enraged owner unleashes a statement threatening to file a lawsuit against any pitcher who throws at one of his hitters, concluding after six paragraphs of nicely vented anger with the solemn pronouncement that "Reggie may well have been thrown at intentionally."

Nor did it end there. When Denny pitched against the Yankees in Cleveland a week later, George had his lawyers there, briefcases at the ready.

As always happens in these things, nothing happened.

15

PLAYOFFS

The Division mini-series aroused more intense interest, I suspect, than the critics of a three-tiered playoff season would admit. Too many people wanted it to be a joke, and therefore it was a joke. But for the Yankees it was the most competitive, the most dramatic, and perhaps the most controversial of the three October series.

The Yankees versus Milwaukee had a lot of things going for it, primarily the match-up between the two dominant relief pitchers of our time, Goose Gossage and Rollie Fingers (and could you make up two better names than that?). Fingers had the best record and would be winning the Fireman of the Year awards. Gossage was the best because everybody knew he was the best. And he was going to prove it.

Finally, the Yankees were going to be tested. No longer would it be possible to make excuses about meaningless games.

The Yankees took the first two games in Milwaukee, and you could see the difference from the beginning in the tension of the moment and the intensity of the play. And, most of all, you could see it in Gossage. Not so much in the way he blew the ball past the Brewers in the eighth and ninth innings as in the wild stalking look that was back in his eyes after the game was over.

You saw the difference, too, in Oscar Gamble and Bob Watson.

Oscar Gamble had gone 0 for 27 at the end of the "regular" season. Which was unbelievable. Up to then Oscar, the Good Humor Man, had never been thrown out of a game. In September he was thrown out of two consecutive games for arguing a called third strike.

Oscar had become unhappy about the way he wasn't being played. Bobby Murcer had come through with a couple of game-winning pinch hits and was getting some starts as the left-handed DH. When Murcer was in the lineup, he batted third. And then when Gamble did get back into the lineup, they dropped him down to seventh.

Oscar went up to see George. George told him not to worry. George certainly knew what he could do and had every confidence that Oscar would continue to produce in the future as he had in the past. He even suggested that maybe they ought to start talking about a three-year extension of Oscar's contract.

The next day, Oscar was in the lineup but still batting seventh. He felt he had been lied to. "I'm batting seventh and playing the sun field," he was saying. "I really get a lot of respect on this club."

So when he took a pitch right down the middle for a third strike, he laid out his frustrations on the umpire. Called him everything. The umpire was so astonished that he didn't remember a player was supposed to be thrown out for saying such things until Oscar was on his way to the clubhouse. "Oscar," Gamble was told as he settled down in front of the TV screen, "you're out of the game."

"Damn," said Oscar. "I'm going so bad that I don't even get thrown out of the game right. Aren't they supposed to give you a chance to stand around and argue?"

The next night he got thrown out again, and this time discovered that he really didn't have anything to say after all. Oscar doesn't really want to argue with anyone. Maybe he just wanted to send a message to George Steinbrenner.

Bob Watson doesn't have it in him to go 0 for 27, but he did end a poor season with only 2 hits in his last 15 times at bat.

So, when the real thing started, the first game of the Milwaukee series, they each had three hits. Oscar had homered in the opening game of the season and also in the first game of the Second Season. He singled on his first at-bat in the playoff season to break the hitless streak, then hit a home run the next time he was up to keep the first-game home-run streak going. That hit tied the ballgame 2–2. His third hit was a double, and it won the game.

Having taken the first two games in Milwaukee, the Yankees came home and lost the next two in Yankee Stadium. The second of those two was the one that brought on all the controversy.

It was a game that was lost on the bases. In the sixth inning, Dave Winfield, the $20 million man, committed the most basic error of base-running: he attempted to advance from second to third on a ground ball that was hit in front of him. In the seventh inning, Rick Cerone lined a single to left, sending Milbourne to third. Cerone rounded first, and Sal Bando—the wise old head at third—whipped the ball to first. With Cerone trapped between the bases, Milbourne made a weak, tentative move toward the plate, tried to scramble back, and was an easy out. No glory there for anybody. Instead of having runners on first and third with one out, there was a runner on first with two out. The Yankees failed to score in the inning, and Milwaukee remained ahead 2–1. That was still the score after eight innings.

George Steinbrenner must have left his box as the Brewers were going out in the ninth because he arrived in the Yankee clubhouse just as the Yankees were coming to bat. Instead of watching the clubhouse TV he had installed at such great expense, he went back to the lounge where he could agonize in privacy. "We're just not hitting the ball," he screamed as the old pros, Piniella and Nettles, made out. "We're not waiting back on pitches." And then some righty-lefty switches were made. Barry Foote was sent up for Dave Revering, and that brought in Rollie Fingers, which brought on Bobby Murcer to bat for Foote. Murcer waited out a walk. Milbourne looped a single over third. Suddenly, the winning runs were on base. And then, just like it had to be—"Aw, shit, what the fuck we doing?"—Rick Cerone struck out on a bad pitch to end the game.

Visualize the scene now, because the way it happened was not precisely the way it was reported:

With the game over, the players are filing in, and the clubhouse man is shouting that there is going to be a meeting ("Meeting here. . . . Meeting right here.") As the last of the players come in—and Cerone is one of the last—Reggie Jackson, from his corner locker, is screaming at the press that they can't come in. And for reasons that have to be pure Reggie, he launches a personal attack on one of the guys who regularly covers the team.

As the door slams shut, Cerone, who is still carrying his catcher's mitt, is headed for his locker at the far end of the room. Steinbrenner is coming from the lounge. In the middle of the room their paths cross, and George, being George, shouts, "There's no place on this ballclub for guys who make mental errors!"

Cerone turns back to him, eyeball to eyeball, and shouts, "FUCK YOU!"

"You're gone next year, Cerone. YOU'RE GONE."

"Fuck that," screams Cerone. "And FUCK YOU!" Cerone keeps on walking, slams his mitt into his locker, and goes into the lounge, while Bobby Murcer, who had been moving toward them during the yelling, says, "The kid feels bad enough, George."

"There's just no room for that shit here," George screams, glaring at Murcer for daring to come to Cerone's support.

"I'm gone next year, anyway," Murcer tells him. "So what the heck. . . ."

Cerone has emerged from the lounge, chewing on a candy bar. He flings the jacket of his uniform toward his locker, turns to George and yells, "What the fuck do you know about it? You never played this game!"

That was the whole thing.

The meeting wasn't that much. Just another pep talk. George stood in the middle of the room, one hand in his pocket, the other stabbing the air, and did his Knute Rockne routine in his toughest give-'em-hell voice. There had been too many mental mistakes. Physical mistakes were understandable, but not mental mistakes.

But, no, there *was* a difference. . . . This was a no-tomorrow speech. They were in the same position, he emphasized, as the 1978 team had been in before the playoff game in Boston. A good point. Just one more game for the Division championship. *And they were making too many mental mistakes.* "The great team of 1978 never did that," he said. "Not once." That great 1978 team was behind by fourteen games at one point, so somebody must have been doing something wrong. But distance lends charm to memory, and George sure did seem to love that 1978 team, the last championship team he had.

"I put this team together," he told them. "It's not the team I thought it was." That's what was so embarrassing. George had been sitting with Bud Selig, the Milwaukee owner. "Do you have any idea how embarrassing it's going to be for me to go upstairs now and face Bud Selig?"

From beginning to end, nobody else said a word. The players just sat there, waiting for it to run down. Bob Lemon was sitting almost alongside Steinbrenner, with that little pucker of amusement that never leaves his eyes. For the first time, with the reference to Selig, there was some murmuring from the outlying lockers.

"I have friends on this ballclub," George went on. "But I'm willing to break it up. Tomorrow's the most important game of your lives. You're playing for your jobs tomorrow. If we don't win it, there are a lot of veterans on this club can forget about it."

He warned them that he had better not hear that any of them were out nightclubbing. "If I do, you're in a lot of trouble because it's going to cost you a lot of money."

The final words fell with that old Rockne rhythm. "Let's think about this ballclub. Stay home and think about the ballgame. Let's try it tomorrow."

If it had been a movie, they would have gone running out to the music of the stirring Notre Dame fight song, and a tearful halfback would have looked up to heaven and said, "I'd run through a wall for that man."

When George departed, he left a clubhouse filled with disgust and loathing. After the kind of game they had played, the disgust would have been there anyway. But George sure helped with the loathing.

"So it's embarrassing for him to face Bud Selig, huh? How about us, how about fucking us? We're the ones with the uniform on."

George had set it up, as they very well knew, so that if they won it would be because George had refused to let them die, and if they lost, it would be because they were an aging, dispirited ballclub.

The doors had remained closed on the reporters for seven minutes, so the meeting couldn't have taken more than five.

Cerone emerged from the showers badly shaken. Murcer told the press to leave him alone. "I was overaggressive" was all Cerone wanted to say, and kept walking.

Guess who was there to fill the vacuum?

Fifteen minutes after he had slammed the door on them, there were close to a hundred reporters gathered around Reggie's locker. A mob.

The players who wanted to duck the press had retreated to the lounge and the trainer's room. Most notable among them was Larry Milbourne, who was inconsolable. Milbourne, who is very quiet and very religious, felt that he had cost the club the game by not staying on third.

But there was going to be no way to outwait the press. When Reggie is holding court, he talks on and on. For two hours this time. *Two hours.*

You realized then what you had always known and had somehow forgotten during the painful early part of the season. Controversy is mother's milk to Reggie Jackson. He breathes it, he wants it, he needs it. If he's suffering, his suffering has to be greater than all other suffering. If he's triumphant, it is a triumph of a magnitude hitherto undreamed of. "I am the situation," he had said after the final playoff game against Kansas City in 1977. And if he had anything to say about it, he was going to make himself the situation again.

As you listened to Reggie now, you were somehow left with the impression that it was he who had taken the brunt of Steinbrenner's abuse. "What I got out of it," he said, "was that if we lost tomorrow, I was gone."

George hadn't said a word to Reggie. Reggie had been off in his corner, more out of it than anyone else. But Reggie wasn't really *saying* that George had. It just sounded that way. And he kept inserting himself into it, if not as one of the principals, then, at least, as the principal peacemaker.

The way the press put the Cerone story together, the exchange between George and Rick had occurred while George was giving his speech, with Cerone—feeling that the talk about "mental mistakes" was directed at him—shouting out his insults. Which made him seem like either a wiseguy or a gutty kid—maybe even a culture hero—but not a tense, downhearted kid who had been spoken to directly from no more than a foot or two away.

During the telecast of the final game, Howard Cosell announced that Steinbrenner would be coming on to talk about the clubhouse meeting, and when word reached the dugout, Cerone and Murcer were among those who asked to be alerted as soon as George appeared.

Steinbrenner stuck pretty much with the newspaper version. He had been talking about fundamentals and mental mistakes, and Cerone, believing it all to be directed at him, had taken it to heart. Cerone had said something, George had said something, and maybe he had raised his voice a couple of times. "I can't believe it," the players were saying. "Why would he want to go on like that if he's going to lie?"

Still, "the situation" had to come back to Reggie Jackson.

Nothing Reggie does surprises his teammates anymore. A day earlier, little Travis John had been brought to the park to throw out the first ball. As Travis and his mother left the dugout to go out on the field, Reggie grabbed the boy and went with them. The fans immediately began to chant, "Reggie . . . Reggie . . . Reggie . . ." and the players were incensed. What the hell was he doing, they asked each other, trying to steal the show from the kid? "Je-sus Christ, the man is sick." Which wasn't necessarily fair. A fairer reading might have been that he had enhanced the moment for the boy.

Nobody could question, though, that Reggie had moved in from the beginning to carve out a role for himself in the Cerone-Steinbrenner confrontation. On the night of the clubhouse meeting, he phoned Cerone to tell him not to worry, the whole team was behind him. ("I told Reggie I appreciated the support. But I also told him not to worry, I'd show up for the game tonight.") The following morning, Reggie went to George's office to tell him he was definitely going to find out what he was worth on the free agent market, and then it would be up to George to decide what he wanted to do. When he came back down, he was carrying a letter from Steinbrenner to Cerone. It said, roughly:

> Your strikeout to end the game with a man on carries little weight with me. Stupid mental errors like rounding first too far does. Your vulgarity to me in the clubhouse afterward is water off a duck's back. It was said out of frustration just as my response to you was said out of anger. It had no bearing at all and I want you to know that.

Vulgarity? "Fuck"s abound in the clubhouse, with George using the word at least as often as anybody else. But the "bleep yous" had appeared in the press, and George had to go on record as forgiving the affront while also informing the world that such vulgarities do not fall inoffensively upon his tender ears. And, while he was about it, keeping as much of the publicity pie as possible for himself.

Cerone, who had baked it, didn't want to take it (will he ever have the recipe again?), so the rights reverted to the original copyright owner, Reggie.

Don't mistake what is being said here. The only reason the exchange was newsworthy was that the events surrounding the clubhouse meeting were so newsworthy. The Yankees at the crossroads, the Boss's tirade, the Boss told off, and the final resolution taking place on the ballfield in the next few hours. By seizing center stage, Reggie was putting the pressure solidly upon himself. Lest anybody have any misconception about that, he said it straight out:

"I'm interested in finding out how much of this Reggie Jackson crap is true. Everybody is always saying I come through in the big game. Well, if I'm ever gonna do anything, it'll be tonight."

In the first inning, he hit a long, towering drive that looked as if it might clear the fence in right center but then died at the warning track and was caught. In the fourth inning, with the Yankees trailing 2–0, he hit a shot that went into the first row of the second deck, *on the rise*, to tie up the game. Right there you knew the game was over. You could see it in Reggie's Fu Manchu smile as he stopped to admire the ball in its flight. Oh, Oscar Gamble hit another home run, right behind him, to put the Yankees ahead to stay, but that was just a matter of bookkeeping. Rick Cerone hit a home run in the seventh, to make the score 5–3, but that was just a matter of *his* bookkeeping. When Reggie's drive went crashing into the stands, it was over.

"Reggie's the best," said Rich Gossage, who had proved again that he was the best at what he did by earning his third save of the series. "Years ago, they [*sic*] said he was the straw that stirred the drink around here. He definitely is. When he stinks, we stink. When he's great, we're great."

And where did that leave that other little old drink-stirrer, George III?

Bob Watson probably spoke for most of the players when he said, "The sad part of it is that George will come down here and get all the credit."

On the whole, the veterans treated George's attempt to motivate them as a joke. Bobby Murcer had come to the park proclaiming Veterans' Day. Graig Nettles had talked about organizing a Save the Veterans movement. Now Lou Piniella was saying, "People keep trying to find a winning combination, and George keeps talking about breaking us up."

As for Rick Cerone, he wasn't backing off one step. Asked whether he thought Steinbrenner's outbursts had helped, he said, "I was thinking about that last night, and I was thinking that I bet what I said would have the same effect on the team, pull us together. It seemed like we pulled together."

Well, wasn't that what Steinbrenner was after? Come on, let's give the guy his due. From the beginning he had said that he believed in "creative turmoil." His ultimatums and tirades had become the subject of controversy, and the controversies had become a source of energy.

Viewing the ballclub as an extension of himself, he finds some mystical connection in the tension flowing between him and the players. In Steinbrennerian physics, $E = MC^2$ stands for Energy = Me × Controversy, Squared.

The counter-formulation, inside and outside the ballclub, goes: Who needs him?

There was no champagne to celebrate the victory. When George finally came down he was accompanied, for the first time within memory, by a security cop. Normally George will go from player to player and throw his arms around them. This time he merely went from locker to locker and shook hands, with the cop never more than a few yards away.

"The trouble with you," George had once told Billy Martin, "is that you want to be loved by your players. That's wrong. That's weakness. They respect you as a manager because they know you're a hell of a manager. Whether they like you or not, they'll screw you just as soon as look at you, the first time they think it's to their advantage. Every one of them."

That same Billy Martin was now the manager, general manager, and acknowledged wizard of the Oakland A's. The sole operator, purveyor, and disciple of Billyball. And he was about to come to town with a team of young and rambunctious players who, after two years, still loved him.

The best indication of George's success in making himself the embodiment of the New York Yankees is that it wasn't the Yankees against the A's, it was Billy versus George. And not just on the sports pages, either, but on the front page. With the biggest, blackest headlines imaginable. The headline on the *Daily News* read:

GEORGE'S GALL
VS. BILLYBALL

On the front page of the *New York Post*, alongside a huge picture of George and Billy drinking to each other's health:

WHO ARE THEY KIDDING?

Billy came riding into town proclaiming that it had not mattered at all to him whether he faced the Yankees or the Brewers. "Why should I want to get back at George?" he asked. George was his friend. He loved George.

No sooner had the interviewers left than he turned to the friends who had gathered in his visiting-team office. "I want to beat George in the worst way," he told them. "I want to see George *down*. I was rooting my ass off for the Yankees to come back in that final game. I was happier than Reggie when I saw him hit that home run."

Yeah, Billy, what about Reggie? "Reggie's a great hitter. He's Mr. October, isn't he?"

Hey, Reggie (across the stadium). Got anything to say about Billy? "Looking for Reggie-Billy remarks that antagonize is degrading to me, and I'm sure to him. I don't want that." Behind him, in his locker, Reggie's cassette recorder was playing "Family Reunion."

Every once in a while somebody solicited the views of one of the spear-carriers. From the Oakland side, Cliff Johnson, who had been caught before in the Billy-George contretemps, offered, "Maybe they should both get guns, go out to the outfield, and settle it that way. As a soap opera, they're better than J.R. and 'Dallas.'"

And from Goose Gossage, who while the fiercest of competitors on the mound is anything but that off: "It's not life or death, is it? There are things more important than winning or losing a baseball game and whether Billy or George wins or loses. Who cares?"

Billy and George, both of whom could be numbered high among those who cared, were in agreement on two things. The first was that their love, affection, and admiration for each other would never die. The second was that too much attention was being paid to them, and not enough to the players. To prove it they held a joint press conference.

The lines were drawn. "The last time we were here," Billy said, "George intimidated the umpires with his comments about my pitchers throwing spitballs. I won't tolerate it this time. I know how George tries to manipulate the media. He's my friend, but his power, influence, and dollars stop right here. This is between my players and his players."

To put that into perspective, you have to understand that when Billy runs out to intimidate an umpire he just keeps screaming at him, "Don't you try to intimidate me! Don't be intimidating me!" Won't even let the poor guy get in a word edgewise.

On the other side of the battlements Big George, who has been known to get in a word edgewise, acknowledged having raised the specter of the dreaded spitball. "We took movies of the A's pitchers," he explained. "I do not want to comment on anything we may have learned, but I do think this shapes up to being a focal point of this season."

He had already met with league president Lee MacPhail, he told the press conference, to warn him that he expected the rule against the spitball to be rigidly enforced. "I'm out to protect my hitters, and I know Billy feels the same way. If they get caught, they have to suffer the consequences, and if it's upsetting to them, that's too bad. This has got to be a championship series to decide within the rules who is the best team to represent the American League in the World Series."

For those with long memories, there was, as George's remarks implied, a history involved. The last time the A's had been in New York, back in May, Steinbrenner had stationed a movie cameraman up in the photographer's box behind home plate to catch Billy's star pitcher, Mike Norris, in action. Norris was thereupon knocked out of the box for the first time all year, and Martin screamed that the camera had been placed there to intimidate the umpires into upsetting his young pitcher by continually asking to examine the ball. To make his displeasure even more emphatic, he lodged an official protest at league headquarters.

In other words, counter-intimidation. Billy had built his ballclub around four great young starting pitchers, all of whom were suspected of throwing spitballs. And at this point we had better define our terms:

Spitball: A generic term going back to the Roaring Twenties. Due to the advances made in the pharmaceutical industry—and a rule against going to the mouth—the modern spitball pitcher loads up by applying some kind of greasy substance to the fingers.

Suspected: A spitball is characterized by a sudden dip downward in any of several eccentric directions. A pitcher is suspected of throwing it within seconds after the batter and other knowledgeable observers have seen it thrown. Seeing it and finding out how the pitcher does it are two different things.

Nobody knew better than Billy that you couldn't catch a spitball pitcher with a movie camera, because it was Billy himself who had first sent that very same cameraman—Ray Negron—up to that very same box back in 1977, to take moving pictures of the Baltimore Orioles' Ross Grimsley. He did discover how Grimsley did it, all right, but the camera had nothing to do with it. A Baltimore cap was left behind in the trainer's room and, son of a gun, inside a little flap in the netting, just above the ear, was a tiny—almost microscopic—syringe. So tiny that it couldn't have held more than a squirt or two of ointment. But that's all you need. In between innings, you go back to the clubhouse, tuck a new syringe in some other flap or fold of your uniform, and all you have to do is brush your hand against it so that your thumb hits the little plunger and delivers a squirt of ointment onto your fingertip. Every inning, you're getting it from a different place, so how is a camera going to spot anything?

Billy hadn't been able to do anything with that. Ross Grimsley had only pitched against the Yankees one more time that season, and had been knocked out early. He had then become a free agent and gone over to the other league. Still, some people around the Yankee clubhouse wondered whether Steve Stone might not have been doing something similar when he joined the Orioles in 1980 and suddenly emerged as a Cy Young Award winner. Possibly because Rudy May, who had come to the Yankees from Baltimore in the same free agent draft, was doing so well. Not that Rudy was doing anything so fancy. The standard operational procedure is to put a blob of ointment on your undershirt; as you work up a sweat, the ointment soaks through your uniform; between innings, you change undershirts and put the ointment in an entirely different place. Rudy was so effective in 1980, working both as a starter and in relief, that he led the league in ERA. But that was last year. After a good start this year, he had got so fouled up that he hadn't been lasting long enough to work up a good sweat.

Do you want to hear gall? Pure Steinbrenner gall. The Yankee pitcher for Game 2 was Rudy May, and George came to the ballpark early and closeted himself with Rudy for forty-five minutes. There had been another meeting with Billy, this time in the commissioner's office, and the talk had apparently gone from the poor quality of umpiring—which was what George wanted to talk about—to the vile and nefarious spitball. "Try not to use it," George told Rudy May. "Billy knows where you're getting your stuff from." And so did Chicken Stanley and Jim Spencer, who had played for the Yankees last year. For forty-five minutes they talked about finding another location. Maybe even putting the stuff inside Cerone's chest protectors and having Cerone load it up for Rudy. But, in the end, George decided that Rudy had better not use it at all. And you can't blame the guy. After all his loose talk about playing according to the rules, it would have been embarrassing to have his guy caught. Some of those bleeping writers who were always looking for a chance to serenade him on his felony conviction might even accuse him of knowing about it.

There's poor Rudy May, given a chance to salvage a terrible season by performing well in the playoffs, and the Boss takes his "out" pitch away from him. And to really grate him, there was Steve McCatty out there for the A's, loading up on practically every pitch.

Rudy didn't do that badly. He was only trailing 2–1 when he was removed with a couple of men on base in the fourth inning.

Reggie had removed himself an inning earlier. Running out to right field, he had felt his Achilles tendon begin to go.

Lou Piniella took his place, but not gladly. Lou had played in the outfield very little after volunteering to give up his right-field position to Reggie. Since coming off the disabled list, he hadn't been out there at all.

In fact, when "the Wild Bunch"—as Lou's lounge group watching inside on television had dubbed themselves—saw Reggie coming back to the bench, Lou yelled over to Bobby Brown that he would be going in. And when Mike Ferraro, the coach who makes the defensive changes, came into the clubhouse, Lou did his best to remain invisible. They wanted *him* out there? "What for?" asked Lou.

"To play right field," said the astonished Ferraro.

"Okay," Lou said, being reasonable about it. "I'll be right on."

Before the inning was over, Dwayne Murphy hit a long fly ball to right field, Lou went back, leaped, and the ball went over his glove and hit the fence. When Lou got back to the bench he was very upset. If he had gone all the way back, he said, he could have caught the ball without even jumping. It had been so long since he had been out there, he had thought he was back as far as he could go. "I still had another foot to go," he said. "I was jumping, trying to keep the ball in the park, and it came back and almost hit me in the ass."

It didn't matter. Lou came up in the fourth and capped the seven-run inning with a three-run home run into the left-field stands.

Reggie's injury was announced as a knot in the calf. It was the abductor muscle again. Just above the Achilles. With the abductor, you have to wait until the next day to find out how badly it is going to tighten up on you. And that gave Reggie something new to worry about. This was the third time it had gone on him, the second time in a year. He'd had it at the start of the season, and here it was again at the end.

To complete his gloom, they were going to play the World Series under National League rules. No designated hitter. Reggie could see the World Series, the showcase he had been waiting for, disappear.

And even if it didn't turn out to be that bad, George knew the true significance of the injury. It was what George was most concerned about, wasn't it? Age.

The meeting between Billy's young, running ballclub and the Yankees' corps of solid veterans promised to be so electrifying, conventional wisdom proclaimed, that no matter which of them won, the World Series was going to be an anticlimax.

And then, suddenly, the Oakland series became the anticlimax. It was no contest, no comparison. Billyball had been built around four pitchers, three great young outfielders, and Cliff Johnson's power as DH. And that was it: pitching, daring base-running, and four home-run hitters. Everybody had been saying all year that Billy had no infield, no relief pitching, and no bench. When Billyball got its bubble burst, you had to sit back and wonder how he had been able to win so many games with such a flawed ballclub.

But let's not completely overlook the Curse of Steinbrenner. George had broken Billy at one time and turned him into a supplicant. It's just possible that Billy will never again be able to handle Big George, one on one.

From the beginning, everything went wrong. Nothing Billy attempted, strategically or tactically, seemed to work.

In the first inning of the first game, the Yankees loaded the bases with two out. Mike Norris, who was throwing nothing except screwballs to the left-handed hitters, got two quick strikes on Graig Nettles. Nettles and Martin had been together for so long that each knew how the other thought. And among the many things Martin had taught Nettles was to take a quick, punch swing at a screwball.

With an 0–2 count, Billy pulled his left-fielder, Rickey Henderson, in and moved him away over toward the line—a very odd positioning. But the 0–2 pitch wasn't supposed to be a good pitch to hit, it was supposed to be something for Nettles to chase. Norris hung it, and Nettles punched it to left, just as Billy had taught him. It wasn't hit particularly hard. If Henderson hadn't been moved, he probably would have made the catch. As it was, the ball plopped into left-center, trickled past Henderson for a double, and three runs scored. That was the game.

In the second game, Billy did something uncharacteristic. He went against Billyball. With no bullpen, Billy's pitchers were supposed to pitch complete games. Steve McCatty had won fourteen games in the abbreviated season and was the leading candidate for the Cy Young Award. Unaccountably, Billy removed him from the game in the fourth inning, with a 3–2 lead, and brought in a relief pitcher, Dave Beard, who had joined the team late in the year and performed very well. But not today. When the inning was finally over, seven runs had crossed the plate, and the game—and to all practical purposes, the series—had come to an end.

Before the first game, Billy had received his basic standing ovation. As the 13–3 slaughter of the second game was coming to an end the next day, the stadium fans were singing, "Good-bye, Billy, good-bye, Billy, good-bye Billy, we hate to see you go."

And, speaking of the Curse of Steinbrenner, whatever chance the A's might have had of sweeping the three games in Oakland came to an end when Billy's two best players somehow managed to disable themselves while swinging at the ball. Won't happen again in ten thousand years. Dwayne Murphy, the center fielder, pulled some muscles in his ribcage (the way Murphy swings it's a wonder it hadn't happened before). And Rickey Henderson, who is only the heart of the offense, suffered a badly bruised *wrist* by hitting himself with his own bat. You figure out how that can be done.

At that, the Yankees were only ahead 1–0 on Willie Randolph's sixth inning home run until Rick Bosetti, who was playing center field in place of Murphy, butchered Graig Nettles's long fly ball with the bases loaded and two out in the ninth to allow three more runs to score.

16

BAM! ZAP! WHAMMO!

They came into Los Angeles like the conquistadors of old, leading the World Series two games to none, and confident of returning home with caravans of loot and plunder. They left four days later like Napoleon's troops retreating from Moscow. Napoleon's troops may have left more equipment behind, but George's left more men on base.

Artistically, it had to rank with the worst World Series ever played. The Yankees had finished the Second Season with a record of 25–26, the Dodgers had finished with 27–26. Los Angeles came into the Series with an aging team they were already planning to break up. The second baseman, Davey Lopes, was on the last year of his contract, and the Dodgers weren't interested in re-signing him. The shortstop, Bill Russell, had never been more than adequate, and the Dodgers had finally come to the conclusion that he never would be. As for the center fielder, they didn't have one. The center fielder was whoever they put out there.

As for the hitting, the Dodgers had been in a team slump for a month. Through the twelve post-season games, including the two losses to the Yankees, Steve Garvey was hitting .340 and the rest of the team was hitting .185.

How, you ask, had such a raggedy ballclub come through the play-offs? Pitching. And a kind of gritty determination to rise from the dead. Down two games to none against Houston, the best team in the National League, they had battled back to win the last three. Down two games to one against Montreal, the second-best team in the National League, they had squeaked through the next two, in Montreal.

Down two games to none against the Yankees as they came back to Los Angeles, they would win the last four. And when it was over, their manager, Tommy Lasorda, would say, "Hey, the Yankees didn't lose the World Series, we won it."

Sorry, Tommy. The Yankees lost it. You just happened to be there. In the ninth inning of Game 6, with the Series irretrievably gone, Bobby Murcer, having retired to the clubhouse along with the other players who were not in the game, was asked who was going to get the MVP award for Los Angeles. The answer came back swift and sure: "It will be either George or Lemon. Whichever of them was making those moves."

In the continuing saga of unauthorized TV-watching, George had opened the World Series festivities by warning his players to stay out of the clubhouse during the game. When the TV cameras scanned the bench, George wanted the nation to see a full complement of Yankees rooting for their teammates.

As for that other continuing saga, the long-running soap opera of that star-crossed couple, Reggie and George, the scenario that had been started on the first day of spring training was finally—mercifully—coming to an end. Life in these soap operas is hard to believe. The guy writing this one was actually trying to get us to believe that the relationship between George and Reggie had come around, here at the end, to where George, who as Reggie's one true friend had railed against Billy for benching Reggie against left-handers, had become the new Billy in Reggie's life except that he (George) was benching Reggie against right-handers too, while he (Reggie) was maintaining a low profile.

Back in Yankee Stadium, Reggie had been taking heat treatments, rubdowns, and massages in order to have the calf muscle ready for the opening game of the Series. Reggie thought he had an understanding that he would test the leg just before game time and tell Lemon whether or not he could play. Returning from a light jog around the outfield, he informed Lemon he was ready. Too late, said Lemon. The lineup had already been made out with Lou Piniella in right field.

And everybody knows that you can't change a lineup.

Burt Hooton, the only right-hander on the Dodgers' Big Three, was pitching the second game, and when Reggie came to the park, he asked Lemon if he was going to play. Nope. This time it was going to be Gamble. To Reggie, who is somewhat paranoid, overly suspicious, and no fool, the message was clear. For as long as the Yankees kept winning, George was going to be using the former DH's in right field.

As Reggie saw it, Steinbrenner was out to reduce his marketability by showing that the Yankees could sweep the Series without him. And for Reggie to make a fuss over not playing while the Yankees were winning would be playing right into George's hands. A classic no-win situation.

After the first game he had gone along with the official word that he wasn't quite ready. After the second game he was still choosing his words with care. "If there were a DH or it was the seventh game of the World Series, I could have played," he said. He also said that he expected to play in the third game.

After the two relatively easy victories in Yankee Stadium, a sweep seemed to be not only likely but imminent. And yet, viewing those two games in retrospect, some of the elements of the impending breakdown had already begun to emerge. The performance of the right fielder was not among them.

Game 1. With two out in the first inning and Mumphrey on first, Piniella hit a ground-rule double down the right-field line. Bob Watson, in his first World Series, hit a long drive that carried over the fence in right center and, just like that, the Yankees had a 3–0 lead.

Dave Winfield, in his first time at bat, struck out on three pitches. Normally a controlled and selective hitter, Winfield had gone down chasing a low curve ball, well out of the strike zone.

With one out in the third inning, Mumphrey got his second straight single, stole second, and scored on Piniella's single. Winfield followed with a 400-foot fly to the warning track in left center, a home run in most other parks.

In the fifth inning, Dodger relief pitcher Bob Castillo walked four straight batters to force in the fifth run. The last walk went to Dave Winfield. It was going to be the only run he would bat in through the entire Series.

The Yankees were rolling right along. Ron Guidry, pitching his allotted seven innings, allowed four hits, struck out six, and walked two. The only run off him came on a long home run into the right-center-field stands by Steve Yeager, the Dodger catcher. Yeager, used very little during the season, had hit only .207 and knocked in a minuscule seven runs. Never a percentage hitter, he carried a .326 average over three World Series. For some reason, he has always hit particularly well against Guidry.

All in all, a neat and tidy performance by Guidry. As he left the field after the seventh inning, the Yankees were leading 5–1, and the game seemed well in hand. Ron Davis would hold the Dodgers in the eighth, and Gossage would throttle them in the ninth.

Not quite. Davis pitched to two batters, walked them both, and looked tight doing it. A disconcerting performance by Davis, which was followed by a not exactly vintage performance by Gossage.

Jay Johnstone, who had been with the Yankees in 1978, greeted Gossage with a pinch single to bring in a run. Dusty Baker, on his way to being the flop of the Series for the Dodgers, hit a long fly to bring in another. Then, with a man on first and two out, Steve Garvey rocketed a fast ball down the third-base line, and it took one of those flat-out, diving catches by Graig Nettles—reminiscent of the 1978 Series—to save the day.

In the previous 33⅓ innings of post-season play, the Yankee relief pitchers had allowed exactly one earned run, and in the first inning they had been called upon to pitch in the World Series, they had allowed two. And were very lucky to get away that cheaply.

But never mind. In the ninth inning, Gossage struck out two of the three batters. Yankee fans breathed easier.

Game 2. The final score was 3–0. The first Yankee run came in the fifth inning, unearned. Willie Randolph reached on an error by Davey Lopes, on his way to setting a Series record for errors by a second baseman. Tommy John sacrificed him to second, and Milbourne doubled him home. With a chance to bring Milbourne in, Winfield grounded out.

In the seventh inning, they loaded the bases with one out, and, with a golden opportunity to build up a cushion, Milbourne hit into a double play.

The pattern that was emerging was not a new one. Throughout the year the Yankees had been singularly unable to score in the late innings. When they were ahead in the seventh inning, the relief pitchers would hold the lead. Almost never had the Yankees come from behind.

The two runs came in, finally, in the eighth inning. Piniella batted for Gamble (who had one walk to show for his three times at bat) and singled, then took second when the center fielder for the day, Ken

Landreau, let Graig Nettles's checked-swing pop fly drop in front of him for a hit. Bob Watson drove in one run with a single, and Willie Randolph brought in the other with a sacrifice fly.

Not a particularly imposing display of power, but what did it matter? If you wanted to be an optimist, you could say that the Yankees had been able to win both games while playing at something less than the top of their form. If you wanted to be a pessimist, you could have made yourself a fortune.

By the time the Yankees boarded the plane for Los Angeles the next morning, they had become aware of a far more serious breakdown. In diving for a ball in the sixth inning, Graig Nettles had fractured his left thumb. Which kind of explains the checked swing.

Nettles made the trip anyway, with the thumb encased in a light plastic splint and packed with ice. From the airport he was taken to a Los Angeles hospital and, true to their long tradition of lying about injuries, the Yankees reported that the X-rays did not show any break.

In this instance, there was an excellent reason for the charade. The thumb, which was up like a balloon, had actually been examined back in New York, the X-rays had shown a hairline fracture, and the doctors had wanted to put the hand in a cast. But Nettles has a high tolerance for pain. He had managed to play the entire 1977 World Series with a shoulder so sore that he couldn't throw except when he had to throw in the actual game. "Let's hold off," he had told the doctors. The swelling might go down enough for him to play. And, after all, if Nettles was to go out to play third base with a broken thumb, it would be just as well if the other side didn't know about it.

Dodger Stadium is built to order for a home-run hitter. With Nettles out, you would have thought that Jackson would go right into the lineup. Unless, of course, the lineup was being made up by George Steinbrenner. Before the game, Reggie again went to Lemon to find out whether he was going to play. "No," said Lemon. "I got a hunch on Piniella today. I'm going to go with Piniella."

Whatever lingering doubts Reggie might have had disappeared right there. "Those motherfuckers want to win it without me."

But having said all along that he wouldn't get into a game until the Yankees had lost one, he still wasn't going to go public. That's what George wanted him to do, he had decided, and he wasn't going to give George the satisfaction. Even when he admitted to the writers that he had told Lemon he was ready to play, he was careful to add, "I'll play tomorrow, I guess." Still, he wasn't able to hide his feelings completely. Asked why he was taking it so calmly, he said, "Why create anything now? You know what would happen if I started complaining. I don't want that, I'm too close to freedom."

Bob Lemon, the man who had to come up with the excuses, could only say, "Yes, he is available to hit, but I don't want to start him against the best left-handed pitcher in the National League." He was talking about Fernando Valenzuela.

Come on, this is Reggie Jackson in the World Series. Reggie in October. Showtime. Which was just how Reggie had been putting it to his friends. "I want to get into the show." Reggie Jackson stepping in against Fernando Valenzuela, in the year of Fernando, that would be a showstopper.

And Valenzuela? Valenzuela's best pitch, the pitch that makes him what he is, is his screwball. A left-hander's screwball is a right-hander's curve. It breaks in on left-handers, away from right-handers. His next best pitch is his fast ball. A good left-handed hitter has a better chance to hit Fernando Valenzuela than a good right-handed hitter.

Of course, every day was Showtime for George Steinbrenner. He had come into Los Angeles riding high. The Yankees had won six straight since the clubhouse explosion with Cerone, and there was every reason to believe that they were going to make it eight straight. And then let's see anybody deny all due credit to that master builder, master psychologist, master strategist, Michelangelo Steinbrenner.

During the season George rarely goes into the clubhouse; once the post-season games begin, he is rarely out of it. Before the third game, with its match-up of the two great rookies, the twenty-year-old Valenzuela against the fireballing twenty-two-year-old Dave Righetti, he was so psyched up that he went rattling around the clubhouse like one of the guys, shaking everybody's hand, waiting until Righetti was ready to go out so that he could give him a final, "Go get 'em, Dave."

It was, for a fact, a dream match-up.

Here was the twenty-year-old Mexican who had become a phenomenon of marketability in Southern California beyond the wildest dreams of even a Reggie Jax, and still had the ability to captivate baseball fans everywhere with a suddenly boyish smile that let you know it was still the joy of the game for him. The wise old head—where had he learned it all?—on the odd-shaped Ruthian body. Leading the National

League with a 2.49 Earned Run Average. A major-league record for a rookie of eight shutouts in two-thirds of a season.

As for his opposite number. . . . If the Yankees had come to Los Angeles abrim with confidence, it was because the players, almost to a man, considered Dave Righetti of the 95 mph fast ball to be the best pitcher on the club. Righetti's 2.05 ERA would have led the American League if he hadn't fallen five outs short of the required minimum. He had finished the regular season with fourteen shut-out innings and had then allowed only one run in fifteen innings of post-season play. One run in his last twenty-nine innings.

Valenzuela's screwball against Righetti's heat.

As so frequently happens, the match-up fizzled. Valenzuela was pitching on three days' rest, which wasn't enough for him. Righetti was starting after six days' rest, too much for him.

Game 3. Fernando struggled. His screwball hung up there to be hit. His fast ball wasn't his fast ball. All day he was there for the Yankees to take. Time and again they let him get away. The key hit wasn't there. The mental lapses were.

It started, almost unnoticed, in the first inning when Valenzuela, without his normally excellent control, walked Randolph and Winfield. Piniella hit into a double play.

After Lopes had greeted Righetti with a double in the Dodger half of the inning, Russell pushed a bunt to the right of the mound. Righetti always falls off the mound toward third base at the end of his delivery, but he was a good enough fielding pitcher to have wheeled back and pounced on Russell's bunt. If not, Randolph, who had broken to cover first base, should have reversed himself and made the play, while Watson, who had broken toward the plate with the pitch, was retreating back to take the throw. It's possible that they wouldn't have been able to get Lopes anyway, because Lopes can fly. What mattered was that *nobody did anything.* It was as if they hadn't actually practiced that play a hundred times during spring training.

The next two batters went out on a pop-up and a strikeout, and, just as it seemed that Righetti had pitched his way out of it, Ron Cey hit a three-run homer. The opening game at Yankee Stadium in reverse.

The Yankees came right back. Bob Watson opened the second inning by driving the ball into the center-field bleachers, giving him a home run in his first time at bat in both parks. Rick Cerone barely missed making it two home runs in a row when his line drive hit the top of the railing a few feet from the foul screen and bounced back onto the field for a double. Aurelio Rodriguez, playing in place of Nettles, sent Cerone to third with a line drive to deep right field, and Milbourne lined a single to score him. A bunt and a walk to Randolph followed before Mumphrey hit back to Valenzuela.

Two runs in and two men left on base. And Fernando was getting racked.

Valenzuela struck out the non-hitting Winfield to start the third inning, but Piniella singled, and Cerone hit a home run, and as quickly as that the Yankees were leading 4–3.

But Righetti had nothing either, and when the first two batters got on in the Los Angeles half of the inning, he was replaced by George Frazier.

Frazier, in his last appearance, had pitched 5⅔ innings of scoreless ball to beat the Oakland A's in the 13–3 game. He looked just as good now, striking out the first batter he faced and getting out of the inning easily.

The fifth inning was crucial. With Watson on third base, Valenzuela walked Milbourne intentionally to bring up the pitcher. With that, the whipsawing of Bob Lemon began.

Frazier had pitched two good innings, but that's all an early relief pitcher is supposed to do. The Yankees had Valenzuela on the ropes. A base hit here and he was probably out of the game, and the fourth game would have become little more than a formality. Any team gets a psychological lift from knocking the starting pitcher out in the middle innings, and with Fernando it would have gone both ways. For Fernando to have been knocked out that early would have taken the heart out of the Dodgers. Sitting on the bench was a hitter who has been known to put pitchers away. But let's not kid ourselves, Lemon understood that he was not to use Reggie Jax.

Lemon allowed Frazier to go up for the automatic strikeout, and Frazier, returning to the mound, never got another man out. Through no fault of his own, either. He got chopped to death on the rock-hard Dodger infield. Garvey started it off with a high chop that Rodriguez had to leap for behind third base. Ron Cey walked, Guerrero faked a bunt, and then, with Rodriguez coming in, hit a high chop over his head for a double. His first hit of the World Series, and it knocked in the tying run. Nor was it a matter of Nettles not being there. ChiChi

Rodriguez is a great fielder, the only third baseman other than Brooks Robinson to win a Golden Glove during the Brooks Robinson era.

Rick Monday was walked intentionally to load the bases. The next two hitters were Mike Scioscia, the Dodgers' left-handed-hitting catcher, and Valenzuela. The key moment of the ball game. Lasorda couldn't pinch-hit for Scioscia because Steve Yeager, the only other Dodger catcher, was already out of the game. And so when Rudy May came in to pitch to Scioscia, Lasorda sent Reggie Smith to the on-deck circle to bat for Valenzuela in the event that Scioscia didn't do anything. As if to show what kind of World Series this was going to be, Scioscia won the game, as it turned out, by hitting into a double play. The Dodgers were back in the lead, 5–4, and since there were now two outs, Lasorda called Smith back to the bench and sent Valenzuela up to hit for himself.

The Yankees went into their late-inning doldrums. Fernando settled down. Great pitchers are able to win without their best stuff because they have the one thing that can never be taken away from them: themselves. The Yankees had another chance to put Valenzuela away in the eighth and turned it into a comedy of base-running. Rodriguez and Milbourne opened with singles, and Murcer was sent up to bunt. Murcer always bunts down the third-base line. He had sacrificed successfully in the second game. His instructions were to bunt for a base hit on the first pitch and, if that failed, to square around and make sure he advanced the runners. The first pitch was right there, but he popped it up, slightly foul, and Cey came racing in to make a great diving catch, barely getting his glove under the ball. As Cey scrambled to his knees, he saw that Milbourne was almost halfway down to second, and doubled him up easily.

A double play on a foul bunt. Great. But there was still a man on second base. Willie Randolph hit a slow ground ball toward third base. Cey had no chance to get him at first, but he didn't have to. Rodriguez, coming down from second base, ran right into his tag.

Can you say the Yankees gave the game away? Valenzuela had thrown 145 pitches, a game and a half. (Normally, 120 pitches is considered a hard day's work.) He had allowed 9 hits and walked 7 batters. The best way to answer the question, I suppose, is to say that with all those opportunities, the Yankees did not score a run after the third inning.

There is no question at all about whether the Yankees gave away the next game. If the brickyard of the Los Angeles infield had defeated the Yankees in Game 3, Saturday got in their eyes in Game 4.

The final two games in Los Angeles were being played over the weekend, and when that happens the television people allow the game to be played under the sun. In Los Angeles, where the sun is mixed with a low, drifting smog, that's no bargain.

For George, the Saturday meetings with his baseball people started early. Write, write, write; scribble, scribble, scribble. Managing isn't easy work for George Steinbrenner, not even when you let somebody else wear the uniform. In certain ways, that makes it even more difficult. From time to time a manager forgets what you tell him. Maybe even thinks he knows better. Such failures of communication can really be embarrassing. Before you know it, there you are again, apologizing to the City of New York.

Cedric Tallis, Bill Bergesch, and Lou Saban went trooping up to George's suite wearing the hangdog Oh-God-another-meeting look that had become their trademark. The urgency of this particular Saturday morning was attested to by the fact that Cedric Tallis was carrying George's breakfast up with him on a tray.

Now that the Yankees had lost a game, Reggie was going back into the lineup. All those runners left on base were very disturbing to George, he wanted all the production he could get. And now that the Dodgers had won a game, Lasorda was going to give his three weary starters an extra day of rest by starting Reggie's old friend Bob Welch, a right-hander, instead of Jerry Reuss, a left-hander.

With Nettles out, George wanted Gamble's bat in there along with Reggie's. Makes sense. Who, then, was to come out? The prime candidate was Dave Winfield, batting 0 for 9 in the Series. Winfield had been tight from the beginning—as the other players were saying in the clubhouse, Winfield had the tight ass, "the tight boody"—and the hitless streak had him pressing. But there was also Jerry Mumphrey, 2 for 10 so far, hitless in his last eight. Yet Mumphrey was the center fielder, and World Series games are won on defense. Plus: he's a switch hitter, a .307 hitter during the regular season, and the steadiest player on the club. Also the fastest.

Just what was finally decided in George's suite only the participants know. All decisions are George's in the end, and his decision was, evidently, to bench Winfield. And a good, tough-minded decision at that. If you can sit Reggie down for three games, you can sit Winfield down for one.

But Winfield wasn't having it.

Way back in spring training, Winfield had said, "Hey, I'm a nice guy, but if you're going to fuck with me, I'm going to fuck you right back."

As soon as he got the word from Lemon, Winfield went upstairs to tell George that he was not going to allow himself to be embarrassed this way. Now, when you tell somebody you're not going to allow them to do something, there is a threat involved. The explicit threat here almost had to be that Winfield would kick up a hell of a storm about it; the implicit threat was in the poisoning of a relationship that had nine more years to run.

Since George is not the kind of man who will give in that readily to a threat, nothing had been resolved when Winfield left. Winfield had been back in the clubhouse for a while—still very upset—before George called down to Lemon to tell him that Mumphrey was going to be the odd man out.

How George put it to him is crucial here, because Lemon was very clearly under the impression that he was not supposed to use Mumphrey at all. He may have simply misunderstood what George was saying—a failure of communication that has always been a risk in George's mode of operation. It's also possible that Lemon did not misinterpret what he was told. Would George admit that Winfield had forced a change upon him? Or would he be more likely to say something like, "I've changed my mind. Mumphrey's been horseshit. Play Winfield, and don't use Mumphrey again until I tell you."

There's also a third possibility, one that takes us into uncharted realms of the subconscious. Somewhere beneath his placid exterior, Bob Lemon, Hall of Fame pitcher, manager of a World Championship team, had to know that he was giving up too much of himself.

Whatever the case, from this point on Bob Lemon, to whom the word "unflappable" had always been attached, managed like a man in a fog. Or like a man who was out to prove something.

Nobody had ever said that Lemon wasn't a good manager. What everybody had always said was that he was a good manager for the Yankees because he wrote out the lineup and left them alone. Suddenly he was about to become a virtuoso of overmanaging. He was going to be making moves to try to force things to happen, against all the percentages, all the odds. He was going to be managing with a divided mind—Bob Lemonbrenner—and it was going to be painful to watch.

The first thing Lemon had to do was break the news to Mumphrey. Just before the players were about to go out for batting practice, he walked over to Mumphrey's locker and said, "Hey, Meat, I want to make some changes in the lineup." That's all. Mumphrey didn't know for sure that he wasn't playing until he saw the lineup posted on the dugout wall.

On the other hand, Mumphrey knew very well what had been going on with Dave Winfield. Probably from the moment Winfield came back from his talk with George. Mumphrey had been Winfield's teammate at San Diego, and a locker room is its own little world. When a player is upset, he has to talk to somebody, and who better than another ballplayer. "Don't tell anybody," he will say, "but . . ." And pretty soon that player is telling the next player, "Don't tell anybody, but . . ."

"Goddammit," Mumphrey said when he saw the lineup, "if I had more of a voice, I could go up and veto it, too. But that's not my style." He knew about Winfield, all right.

When you bench Mumphrey, Winfield becomes your center fielder. But Winfield did not remain in center field through the whole game. Who would have thought that the ballgame—and the World Series—was going to turn upon having the wrong man in center field at the wrong time?

Game 4. The Yankees were beaten 8–7 in a game that was exciting in the way that only a badly played ballgame, full of incident and open to unlimited second-guessing, can be exciting. George had wanted more hitting, and nobody could say he didn't get it. The Yankees held a 4–0 lead in the third inning, and a 6–3 lead in the sixth inning, and still managed to blow the game without getting to call upon Gossage.

- Reggie had three hits, including a home run and two walks. Oscar Gamble had two singles, scored a run, and knocked in a run. Winfield did nothing.
- The Yankees left twelve more runners stranded on the bases.
- The Yankees committed two more blunders running the bases.
- The Yankees messed up two fly balls in the outfield.
- The Dodgers continued to play bouncy-ball on the hard infield.
- Ron Davis failed again.
- The Yankees' middle reliever, George Frazier, in a carbon copy of the previous day's agony, became the first pitcher to lose two straight World Series games in forty years.

And Jerry Mumphrey became the most conspicuously absent player in the history of the World Series.

Bob Welch pitched to four batters and got nobody out. Willie Randolph opened with a triple, Milbourne doubled, Winfield walked, and Reggie—in his first appearance—lined a single to left field. One run was in, the bases were loaded, and nobody was out. Dave Goltz, a million-dollar free agent who had done nothing for the Dodgers in two years, replaced Welch, and the game should have been blown open right there. It wasn't. Only one more run came in, and the Dodgers were still in it.

Randolph's home run in the second inning made it 3–0. Cerone singled in another run in the third.

Fourth inning: Willie Randolph was on second, with one out. Dave Winfield hit a slow chopper to deep short, which he would have beaten out easily for his first—hurray!—World Series hit, except that Willie Randolph—oy!—was running and got thrown out at third. Beyond belief! It was the third time in a week the Yankees had made this most basic of base-running blunders.

Fifth inning: Rick Reuschel, a thirty-two-year-old pitcher who had been bought from the Chicago Cubs on the day the strike was called, had been slowly giving back the lead. Between the sweep of Oakland and the three-day wait for the National League race to be settled, Reuschel hadn't pitched for two weeks, and he looked it. Ron Davis was called upon, with the score 4–3, and struck out two batters to hold the lead.

Sixth inning: The Yankees scored two more runs and were leading 6–3, with Davis pitching. Just the way it was supposed to be. With the three-run lead, Bob Lemon made a defensive change. He sent Bobby Brown to center field and moved Winfield back to left field.

For defensive purposes, you send out your best defensive player. Where's Mumphrey? everybody wants to know. They are asking the question in the press box, they're asking it over radio and TV, they're asking it on the Yankee bench. A couple of the players go over to ask Mumphrey. "Are you all right, Mumph? Are you hurt?"

"I'm fine," Mumphrey says grimly. "I'm perfect."

There had always been a question about Bobby Brown, as he went bouncing back and forth between the Yankees and Columbus. At Columbus, he would tear the league apart, hitting .340 and fielding fabulously. Back with the Yankees, he'd stop hitting and be inconsistent in the field. He had a way of making a bad error at the worst possible time. Like in the ninth inning when it cost the ball game.

Davis walks Mike Scioscia, the number-eight hitter, and Jay Johnstone, pinch-hitting for the pitcher, hits a huge home run into the right-field stands. It's not 6–3 any more, it's 6–5.

And now comes another of those countless turning points. Davey Lopes hits a fly to short right field, Reggie Jackson races over, and you can see by the zigzag course he's running that he's having trouble with the sun. The ball caroms off his shoulder for a two-base error. Since it is Jackson, everybody smirks: "There's Reggie again." Notwithstanding that he has been playing great defense for two months.

Just what poor Ron Davis, who has been trying to collect himself, needs. Davis is so rattled that he forgets about Lopes, and Lopes steals third.

Willie Randolph is screaming at him. "Get it together, Davis. Stop giving us the scare shit. Get your act together, everything is going to be cool."

Anything will now bring in Lopes with the tying run. Anything is an 0–2 line single into left field.

George Frazier comes in for Davis. Frazier is going to be part of the second-guessing. Frazier was picked up early in the season in a low-level minor-league trade. George brought him in to pitch for the Bradenton kids, and he looked so good that the Yankees kept him.

Seventh inning: Aurelio Rodriguez leads off with a drive into left center, and for about eight seconds it looks as if the Yankees are coming right back. That's how long it takes for the thirty-four-year-old Rodriguez to go roaring around first base and get cut down at second.

Dusty Baker leads off for the Dodgers by chopping a ball to the shortstop and beating the throw. And now, just like it has to be, the benching of Mumphrey is going to play itself out. Rick Monday hits a sinking line drive to center field, a routine out. And, suddenly, there is nobody there. Bobby Brown has taken a step backward, comes in not too confidently, dives for the ball, and doesn't get it. There are runners on second and third, and nobody out. Guerrero is intentionally walked to load the bases, and Lemon brings in Tommy John.

Since it is Tommy John's day to throw anyway, he volunteered to go down to the bullpen and be ready if Lemon needed him to pitch to a batter or two.

Second-guess: Tommy John is a sinker-ball pitcher. Nobody throws more ground balls. But it's not one out, it's nobody out. What you need with the bases loaded and nobody out is a strikeout. Gossage, who has been warming up alongside Tommy John, strikes people out. Gossage hasn't worked in a couple of days anyway. Get him in there.

There is still another consideration. By bringing in the left-handed John, you were going to get Steve Yeager batting in place of Scioscia, and Yeager has been rough on the Yankees. He was also Tommy John's catcher in Los Angeles. He goes with the pitch to right field, just as you are supposed to do with Tommy John—a deep fly ball that sends the tie-breaking run across. Another run comes in—the winning run, as it turns out—on yet another of those high-bouncing balls off the infield.

Eighth inning: Steve Howe, a young left-handed relief pitcher, has come in to pitch for Los Angeles, and Jackson hits a home run off him, bringing the score to 8–7.

Reggie Jackson, who hasn't been used for three games, has two singles, a home run, and two walks.

Jerry Mumphrey, who isn't being used today, is going to continue not to be used in the face of what can almost be called extreme provocation. Starting immediately when Lemon sends Lou Piniella up to bat for Bobby Brown. Piniella hits back to the pitcher and goes out to play left field, with Winfield moving back to center.

Ninth inning: Last chance. Rick Cerone singles up the middle with one out, and Lemon sends Barry Foote up to bat for Rodriguez. Rodriguez has four hits in eight times at bat in the Series. One of the outs was a long fly to right field, with nobody out, to advance a base runner to third. In the bookkeeping of the dugout, that isn't a minus, it's a plus. In limited appearances during the season, Rodriguez has hit .346.

"I want to see if I can get a long ball, Meat," Lemon tells him. Well, that's obvious. Foote is a slow-footed substitute catcher who will occasionally hit a home run, but not lately. If they were two runs behind, it might have made some sense—not much, but it could have been defended. But the Yankees are one run behind, the tying run is already on base, and Rodriguez has a much better chance of moving it along than Foote.

On the bench, the players are bewildered again. "Why is he taking out ChiChi?" they are asking. They're not even asking about Mumphrey anymore. The Mumphrey situation has become so clear that their feelings can be communicated with a look.

And that's what makes Lemon's move even more inexplicable. By pinch-hitting Foote, who has been to bat exactly one time in the past month, Lemon has once again turned everybody's attention to the benching of Mumphrey. It is not unfair to say that everybody expected Foote to strike out. It took three pitches.

Murcer pinch-hits for Tommy John and reaches base when Howe misses first after Steve Garvey momentarily bobbles the ball. Once again, the door has been opened. Willie Randolph, who had a triple and home run on the day, backs Derrel Thomas almost to the fence, and that's it for the ball game.

Bob Lemon's explanations afterwards were as confusing as his actions. What else could they be when he was trying to explain why he hadn't used a player whom he would have used if he had been able to use him?

Mumphrey had been benched, he explained, because he had wanted the left-handed-hitting Gamble in the lineup against Welch.

Why hadn't he put Mumphrey into center field for defensive purposes instead of Brown?

"I was saving him," said Lem. "I was going to wait until Jackson batted again, and then move Brown to right and bring Mumphrey in to play center."

Then why not use him to pinch-hit, instead of Barry Foote?

Because there was a left-handed pitcher in the game, and Mumphrey wasn't swinging the bat well right-handed.

Nobody bothered to point out that Mumphrey's two hits in the opening game had come when he was batting right-handed. Or that he had been benched originally when he would have been batting left-handed.

What, after all, could the poor man say?

Considering the exhibition he had just witnessed, George Steinbrenner was astonishingly calm.

"I'm not going to second-guess my manager," he said, "but in the box we thought Mumphrey was coming in."

Uh-huh.

As for the multitude of mental errors: "I'm not lambasting anybody. I want to make that clear. It's out there for seventy million people to see."

Uh-huh.

George denied absolutely that he had ordered the benching of Mumphrey. What did they think he was, the manager or something?

The next day he acknowledged that he had. But, he added (in case you thought he was about to come clean), that Bob Lemon, the coaches, and the scouts had all agreed that the move was necessary. Talk about an organizational decision. The *scouts*?

Since the banishment of Mumphrey could not be explained on any logical basis, there was speculation—amounting to universal agreement—that George was using it as a negotiating gambit to hold down Mumphrey's price. Another glowing tribute to George's negotiating tactics.

Immediately a story was leaked by an unimpeachable source that the terms of Mumphrey's contract had already been agreed to on the day the Series began. And, oddly enough, it was true. Not only was it true, it was even truer than they were saying. The contract had actually been drawn up three weeks earlier; it hadn't been signed only because George had not wanted to get Reggie so upset that he would sulk through the World Series. Mumphrey had actually *signed* the contract on the first day of the Series, and even though he had once again been pledged to silence, it was clear that George no longer cared what Reggie's mood was while he was sitting on the bench.

Mumphrey's contract called for $4.5 million over six years. If the guy ever learns how to swing right-handed, there's no telling how much he could make.

Game 5. Lemon had already indicated that Mumphrey wouldn't be playing against Jerry Reuss. If you're saying Mumphrey isn't swinging the bat right-handed on Saturday, why should he have improved that much by Sunday? And, to show the box they had got themselves in, what if he should embarrass them by getting 3 or 4 hits.

The players were disgusted. "If you're wrong, you're wrong," one of them said. "Shit. Today's another day. Let's go and try to *win* this thing." Lemon snuck Mumphrey into the game in the eighth inning, as a defensive replacement for Reggie in a batting-order flip-flop that would have brought him to the plate in the ninth inning, in the pitcher's slot, if the Yankees had been able to put a couple of runners on base. Batting right-handed against Jerry Reuss.

The Yankees lost 2–1, with Reuss outpitching Guidry. They left six men on base in the first four innings, almost all of them by Rick Cerone.

Over the last five innings, they gave their incomparable imitation of *rigor mortis* setting in.

Dave Winfield finally had a base hit, a soft single into left field.

George knew exactly where to place the blame. "Their catcher had the game-winning hit. Our catcher took us out of two game-winning rallies. He crucified us offensively. That's the difference. Their catcher versus our catcher, and their pitcher versus our pitcher."

The Yankees had scored first. Reggie lined a double down the left-field line to open the second inning and scored on a single by Piniella. For Reggie it was four straight hits, and six straight times on base. It was also the end of the line. From here on he would go out eight straight times.

Guidry was rolling along on a two-hitter at the end of six innings. In the seventh inning he allowed two more hits. Unfortunately both were home runs. Guerrero, who had tied Game 3 with the chopper over Rodriguez's head, tied this one with a long home run into the left-center-field bleachers. Yeager, who had tied Game 4 with the long fly, put the Dodgers ahead in this one with a home run to almost the same spot.

Steinbrenner, seeing the Series slip away, wanted everyone to understand that it wasn't his fault. He had gone over statistics with Lemon before the game, he told the writers, and they showed that Guidry had a 10-plus ERA over the last three innings. "We had discussed going six innings with Guidry and then giving it to Gossage. We had a strategy. Lem chose not to go with it."

Outrageous! Guidry had been pitching his most overpowering game of the year, striking out eight batters in six innings. He had also struck out the lead-off batter in the seventh. No six-inning limit had been set for Guidry. He had, after all, pitched seven innings in the first game. "It's a case where you can't win," Lemon said. "Bring in Goose and he gets rapped, and people say, 'How can you take out a guy pitching a two-hitter?' "

So Guidry had become a seven-inning pitcher? If so, it was because they had turned him into one. They had turned all their starters into seven-inning pitchers. Want a statistic: Over the full season, Yankee pitchers had thirteen shutouts, and in not a single one did the starting pitcher go the whole way. Under those conditions, the 10-plus ERA in the last three innings means nothing. When you have a policy of removing your starter as soon as a runner gets on base in the final innings, it merely indicates that the relief pitcher has allowed a few of those runners to score. If, for instance, Guidry had been taken out three times in the seventh inning with a runner on first and one out, and the relief pitcher had allowed only one of those runners to score, it would have given Guidry a 9.00 ERA in the seventh inning.

It's a good arguing point in contract negotiations, that's all. Like being able to say, "How can a seven-inning pitcher ask for a $7.5 million contract over five years?"

Nor was George going to forgo the opportunity of taking one more shot at Cerone. In the second inning, Cerone had come up with runners on first and second, nobody out, and hit into a double play. In the fourth inning he came up with runners on second and third and nobody out, and hit the first pitch to Bill Russell at short. Russell seemed to be conceding the run, except that Bob Watson, the runner on third, wasn't running. ("The ground ball was the same as a strikeout," Reuss said after the game.)

"There are things I cannot tolerate," said George. "Before the game I told them don't be overanxious. Then Cerone goes after the first pitch in the fourth inning and again in the ninth. Lem and I discussed the take sign for Cerone before the game."

Cerone is a notorious first-ball hitter, and certainly he should have been more selective in those two situations. With men on second and third and nobody out, he should have been trying to hit to right. But if in fact they had discussed giving him the take sign just before the game (it is truly astonishing how George always seems to have the gift of prophecy after the fact), you have to wonder why they didn't give it to him.

All right, since they weren't listening to George, he wasn't going to give them the benefit of his wisdom anymore. "I'm through. I've said all I'm going to say. They understand what they have to do. I don't think they want to be an embarrassment to New York. That's why I'm so cocksure we're going to win. But some guys are going to have to start doing it instead of talking about it."

George wasn't through yet, though, not by a long shot. Do you know what that cocksure little rascal did? He got into an elevator and decked two youthful Dodger rooters. And, boy, did he talk about that.

There was even an A story and a B story. The A version came across the wires to a tense and waiting nation something like this:

George was alone going down from his eleventh floor suite shortly after eight o'clock when the elevator stopped on an intermediate floor, the door opened to let on a couple of bearded young guys (you know the sort) wearing L.A. caps. One of them held the door open while the other, with a beer bottle in his hand, stepped in. Recognizing Steinbrenner, the man with the beer bottle insulted him and his team. "Steinbrenner, why don't you take that team of choke-asses of yours back to New York with the rest of the animals?" Steinbrenner replied in kind, thereby breaking one of the elementary laws of the L.A. jungle; to wit, if you're all alone in an elevator, do not curse a drunk holding a beer bottle. Whereupon the guy with the beer bottle broke an elementary law of a Steinbrenner story: to wit, if you are wearing a beard and an L.A. cap, do not ever come at George with a beer bottle in your hand and an unkind word about New York City on your lips. *Pow! Zap!* And George had flattened him. ("I could feel his teeth cave in under my fist.") When the guy who had been holding the elevator door threw a punch, Steinbrenner unloaded on him. *Whammo!* A thunderous left hook that left the dastard stone cold on the floor.

As anybody in the newspaper game can tell you, first reports on a fast-breaking story are always confusing. This one left open such tantalizing questions as:

- Where was the blood?
- Where were the teeth?
- Where, to get right down to it, were the two anonymous desperadoes of shed blood and shattered denture?
- If there were two bodies lying on the elevator floor, how come nobody had seen them when the door opened? Why hadn't George started yelling for hotel security as soon as the elevator opened (if only to display his handiwork)?
- Where was George's own security man? George doesn't often move around without a guard, especially when he is out of town.

As the questions proliferated, an unhealthy skepticism pervaded the land. Was there nobody in the two largest cities in the country, no one on either side of the Continental Divide, ready to give credence to this surpassingly strange yet wondrous narrative?

It is a testimonial to George's reputation for honesty, rectitude, and the old one-two-three that those who knew him best, the sportswriters and ballplayers, believed him the least. The consensus among his players was that George had either hit the elevator wall with his fist out of sheer frustration or had swung at a Ceronian heckler and missed.

By the time he had returned to New York, these rude questions had been swept away. George, as you will see, is a master of the Authenticating Detail:

He had been riding down from his eleventh floor suite to join his wife and associates for dinner at the hotel restaurant on the second floor when the elevator stopped at the seventh floor and the two young men came aboard. One was wearing a Dodger hat. Not the solid blue you generally see, but blue in the front and white around the back. George had thrown three punches, two right-handers that cut his knuckles, and the left-hand cruncher that injured the knuckles of his other hand. "I clocked them. There are two guys in that town looking for their teeth and two guys who will probably sue me." (If you want to get Freudian about this: The Dodgers had zapped the Yankees three times, and George had belted the insolent beer-swillers three times. *Pow! Zap! Crrrrunch!*)

He had left the chastened louts on the floor of the corridor—"one prone and the other sitting"—continued down to the second floor, and stopped off in the men's room to wash his bloodied face before joining his friends for dinner.

Apparently there was nobody else around to see the bloodied warrior as he made his way from the elevator to the men's room. The men's room itself would seem to have been barren of credible witnesses. (No traffic around the restaurant of a completely booked hotel at dinner time?) Fortunately Cedric Tallis, one of his dinner companions of the evening, was there to testify to the terrible shape George was in. "There was blood on his teeth, and I said, 'What the hell happened to you?' He said, 'You won't believe what just happened!' [that gift of prophecy] His hand was swelling, and he couldn't get the ring off."

Having left his appetite in the elevator, George had only a bowl of won ton soup. He summoned Dr. John Bonamo, the Yankees' orthopedist. Bonamo sent for medical supplies and set Steinbrenner's hand in a plaster cast. The doctor was virtually certain that the left hand was broken near the knuckles. He gave him some codeine for the pain and advised him to go to sleep.

At 11:30, George had summoned the reporters to his suite to describe what had happened and display his wounds. The bump on his head, the swollen lip, the bandaged right hand, and the apparently broken left hand with a bandage over the cast.

And still nobody believed him. The players didn't believe him, the press didn't believe him, the fourteen-year-old kid who delivers my newspaper didn't believe him. Wouldn't it be great if it were true?

And yet it showed the hold the man had taken on the news. In the same way that any great event wires the country together, George had brought the country together in a moment of high hilarity. There was an air of grotesquerie about the encounter in the elevator that was not wholly unconnected with the Yankees' performance on the ball-field. A final, futile thrashing around in the face of the inevitable. The Emperor was finally perceived, not unclothed but clad in the garb of a clown. Was there ever, in the crowded history of big-time sports, an event that lent itself so readily to jollity, cheap humor and crass badinage? The press of New York and Los Angeles and, we can assume, the vast wasteland in between, roared with laughter. If George was not yet the Fat Man in the Freak Show, he was the Fat Clown in the Elevator, and that is coming dangerously close.

As the players boarded the bus for the airport, you'd have thought they had won three straight. "I'd have given half my salary to have been in that elevator and seen that one," said Gossage. To add to the merriment, they had drawn a singing bus driver (this is Los Angeles, the Gateway to the Stars) who announced that he was going to croon a few numbers for his celebrated passengers. "How about dedicating a song to those two guys on the elevator who George punched out?" Bobby Murcer shouted. Bob Lemon had been watching "Good Morning, America" when the story came on the news. "I laughed like hell," he said. "How couldn't you? George is going to get at least two telegrams tomorrow. One from Billy and one from Rosen."

Steinbrenner was kind of sheepish about it himself. He had run into Nettles in the lobby, he said, and asked him, "Where the hell were you last night when I needed you?" To which Nettles had answered, "I was in bed where you told me to be."

Reggie Jackson, who does a great imitation of Howard Cosell, strolled up and down the aisles of the chartered DC-10. "You say you're invulnerable to a left, George. And rightly so. You say you are possessed of a thunderous right. Tell it to us like it happened, George. Perspicaciously and straight from the hip."

Once the plane got off the ground, however, everybody became quiet. Rick Cerone, usually the hell-raiser on the plane trips, was somber and reflective. George was sitting up front, away from everybody. A couple of the players suggested to Reggie that it might be an excellent time for him to ask George's permission for them to appear on ABC-TV's "Superstars!" for which Reggie, of course, does the commentary.

Reggie approached George but turned around and came back

laughing. "I'm sorry, fellows," he said. "As soon as I see that fat lip, I just start to laugh, and I don't want to laugh in his face and embarrass him."

The telegram from Billy Martin came the next day. It said, "Sorry to hear about the bad news. You're fired."

Remember what I said about the *New York Post* trotting out their biggest, blackest type for the "Who are they kidding?" headline on George and Billy? Forget it. They trotted out their Second Coming type for this one. Front page, from top to bottom:

GIVE 'EM
HELL
GEORGE!

In the space under the top line there was a cartoon of Fat George in a boxer's robe, clasping his gloves above his head in the traditional sign of victory.

In the space alongside the second line:

Quote:
"I may have a
broken hand, but
one of them isn't
smiling too well"

And bannered across the bottom of the page:

Yankees' battling Boss ready to
boot Dodgers back to California
Page three

Page three, where the *Post* runs its two-headed-baby stories, was the headline

THE BRONX BOMBER READIES FOR ROUND 2,

over a highly fanciful account of a Yankee fan who had witnessed "The Great Steinbrenner Punch-out" and was there to tell us that the Yankee boss threw punches "like a pro."

The New York fan, who wishes to remain anonymous because his wife was not aware he went to LA to see the game, is a 54-year-old former professional fighter from Long Island.

Aha. An expert, albeit a permanently unidentifiable one. Who better to critique the Bomber's fighting style? "What a punch he threw," the expert confided in describing how George had decked the guy who came at him with the beer bottle.

By this time, the second Dodger fan was at the elevator and saw his friend lying on the elevator floor.

"The guy jumped on George and tried to throw a headlock around him," our witness said. "It was great. George threw the guy off him and connected with a one-two combination. It was real professional! Reminded me of my own boxing days.

"With that, George threw both rowdies off the elevator and continued downstairs to dinner."

The sports pages were a riot.

Henry Hecht had the real scoop on Billy Martin's Lite beer commercial in which Billy insists he didn't punch that dogie. "It turns out he didn't. This spot starts out with Martin turning from a bar and saying, 'I didn't punch that dogie, George did.' "

Phil Pepe: "Duke Steinbrenner wears a cast on his left hand to heal a broken bone that might never have happened if his players had followed the script over the weekend . . . Duke can only hope and pray that his pain and discomfort will not be for naught and that his blood was not spilled in vain."

Dick Young: "He is King Arthur. He rides forth on his mighty steed to challenge the world. Right now, King Arthur has his hand in a cast. These things happen when you challenge the world. . . .

"There are unveiled smiles on the faces of Yankee ballplayers and front office workers, although I have been unable to track down the rumor that the players have voted the two assailants full shares of the World Series money."

Mike Lupica: "The only thing George Steinbrenner could hit with any degree of consistency would be the ocean, if he fell out of a boat. . . . Of all the shameless things Steinbrenner has done—the man is beyond embarrassment—this may be the best. Was there some kind of altercation on that elevator? Probably. Did George hurt his hand and cut his lip? That seems to be the case, though I would like to look at the X-rays of the hand. Did it happen the way he said it did? C'mon . . .

"If George quickly decided to use his injured hand as a motivator, fine. He can occasionally be a good amateur psychologist. But spare us the fairy tales, okay, big fella? If not, I'll have to tell about the night I knocked out Sugar Ray Leonard in that bar in Vegas."

Game 6. If the whole thing was psychological, as Lupica suggested, rather than pathological, as he suspected, it didn't work. George had already played so many bongo games on the head of his manager that poor Bob Lemon no longer knew where he was. Worse luck, neither did his pitcher for the night, Tommy John.

The off-day for travel was followed by a rainout, and that was a contributory factor, too, in that it gave the two wounded third basemen, Graig Nettles and Ron Cey, an extra twenty-four hours to get back into the lineup. Cey had taken a Gossage fast ball on the helmet in Game 5 and was still experiencing a hardly unexpected light-headedness and dizziness. Nettles still had some swelling around the fracture. Given your normal I-score-you-score World Series game, the play of the gallant third basemen would have been the story. Each of them had two hits. Each of them had to take himself out of the game in the sixth inning. Cey's second hit was the game-winner.

Other human dramas were playing themselves out, too.

Ron Davis completed his week of agony with another atrocious performance. In this one, he started by walking the pitcher.

George Frazier, who had started the season in the minor leagues, completed his journey toward dubious immortality. Frazier already had two losses in the Series, and both he and his voodoo lady were ready when Bob Lemon asked brightly, "Want to try for three?"

George Steinbrenner finally got a victory in his battle of the clubhouse TV. Having disregarded his admonition against TV-watching during the first two games at Yankee Stadium, the players arrived in the clubhouse to discover that George had sent an electrician down to remove the fuses from both TV sets.

Reggie was displaying a telegram he had received from one of his fans: "If you're the straw that stirs the drink," it said, "why don't you give Winfield a sip." There was going to be no drink-stirring by either of them, alas. The only contribution the two big guys were going to make was toward the record for most runners left on base (single club) in a six-game Series.

But all of it was overshadowed by the most incomprehensible managerial decision ever made in a final World Series game, when Bob Lemon removed Tommy John for a pinch hitter in the fourth inning with the score tied 1–1.

Otherwise, the spotlight might have fallen, once again, upon Graig Nettles. The swelling had gone down enough before the game so that Nettles decided to give it a try. That's all it was, a try. It was a cold night, you could see him wince when he swung, and still he refused to take anything to kill the pain. In the field he wore a batting glove under his regular glove to protect the thumb, plus a special pad to absorb the shock. After his first hit, a line drive down the right-field line, the thumb started to blow up again so badly that they had to find a larger batter's glove. He was still diving for balls the same as ever, but that was just reflex action. What had everybody on the bench so frightened was the thought of what would happen if he had to catch a line drive hit right at him.

In the sixth inning, he had to field two ground balls in a row, and that was one too many. The first one turned into the best play of the game. With the bases loaded and nobody out, he made an excellent backhanded stop going over the bag, touched third, and made a whirling, very accurate throw to first. With most runners, he would have had a double play. But the runner was the very swift Derrel Thomas (batting, poetically, for Ron Cey), and Thomas was just able to beat the throw. The second one was a bouncing ball that was hit right at him, and he couldn't handle it. In the bottom half of the inning he stroked a line single to center field, and when he reached first base, the pain had become so overwhelming that he took himself out.

It was Nettles's first hit, that line double down the right-field line in the fourth inning, that led—bitter irony—to the removal of Tommy John. For Graig was still standing there on second, with two out, when Milbourne was intentionally passed to bring the pitcher to bat.

Tommy John is a good hitter for a pitcher. Used to be, anyway. In his younger days with the White Sox, he had been used as a pinch hitter. On his first time at bat, he had lined a ball just foul down the right-field line before flying out. This time, Bob Lemon stopped him as he was going to the bat rack. "I'm going to take you out," he said. "I need to get a run over here."

There were two men out. He wasn't asking for a fly ball. It was going to take a base hit to get the run over.

Tommy John was stunned. "I can't believe it, I just can't believe it."

He started to pull off his batting gloves, then turned back to Lemon. "I can't believe it," he said again. "I've never seen anything like it." He walked down to the end of the dugout, turned back again, and said for all of them, "Everybody gets the tight ass here."

The other players couldn't believe it either. By some common impulse, perhaps the need to speak freely, they drifted back into the TV-less clubhouse, eight or nine of them, to talk it over. "What's going on?" they asked each other in dismay. What was Lemon doing? Why was he doing it?

Lou Piniella was perhaps more upset than any of them—his face expressed his utter disapproval, and yet he kept shaking his head and saying, "That move takes balls. That move takes unbelievable balls."

The second-guessing is easy. What if Bobby Murcer, who had batted for John, had hit a home run? Murcer hit the hell out of the ball. A long line drive with just enough top spin on it so that it died at the warning track.

Lemon's explanation was just as easy. He had wanted to get some runs so that he would be able to turn over a lead to Goose Gossage in the seventh. Okay, but what's so terrible about turning a tie game over to Gossage in the seventh?

Tommy John, Lemon pointed out, had allowed six hits in four innings. In the top half of the inning, he had allowed three hits and one run. Okay, but ask any ballplayer about Tommy John, and he will probably tell you, "He's the strongest guy you'll ever see on a ballfield." What that means, in the jargon of the players, is that nothing bothers him. Going good or going bad, he never loses his composure. If the Dodgers were putting runners on base in the early innings against him and not scoring, it was the Dodgers who were in trouble, not Tommy John.

What else can you say: Bob Lemon panicked. It was the residue of those countless meetings of George's.

Steinbrenner's statistical breakdown had undoubtedly shown a disproportionate number of men left on base by the pitcher as, time and again, Tommy Lasorda had walked the number-eight batter in the early innings and, time and again, Lemon had allowed the pitcher to hit for himself, with disastrous results—Righetti in the fourth inning of Game 3 with two men on, just before he got knocked out; Frazier again in Game 4, just before he got knocked out again; Guidry with the bases loaded and one man out in the fourth inning of Game 5. Imagine what those meetings must have been like while the Yankees were losing those three games in Los Angeles. They were going to have to get more production out of the number-nine slot; they were going to have to make better use of their DH's. (Cedric Tallis was always there, poor fellow. As Cedric was leaving the hotel restaurant on their last day in Los Angeles, he was heard to say, "He gave Gabe a heart attack, and he gave Rosen a rash, but he's not going to get me.")

Sure, you'd like to be able to turn a lead over to Gossage. But it was primarily because of the failure of the middle relievers that they hadn't been able to. And here, in what could be the final game of the World Series, Bob Lemon was removing Tommy John and turning the fortunes of the New York Yankees over to George Frazier.

George Frazier was about to become one of the immortals, the only pitcher ever to lose three World Series games while he was trying to win. (The only other pitcher to lose three games was Claude Williams of the 1919 Chicago Black Sox, but Williams was trying to lose.)

Each time, it was happening to Frazier faster—in his third inning the first time, in his second inning the second. This time, with two outs, a man on second, Ron Cey hit an easy ground ball up the middle. No hard-baked infield here at Yankee Stadium; Frazier's voodoo lady had to come up with something else. The ball hit the edge of the grass in front of the dirt infield, took a wicked hop over Willie Randolph's glove, and the Dodgers were ahead 2–1. Dusty Baker, whose chopper had begun Frazier's demise in Game 4, broke his bat and hit a little blooper that just dropped over Randolph's desperate leap. But then came the real crusher, a long triple into left center, and the score was 4–1.

The final score was 9–2, but that's just the arithmetic. To all practical purposes, the game was lost when Tommy John was taken out of the game. It ended, for scorekeeping purposes, on Cey's single.

It ended, symbolically, in the ninth inning, when Reggie Jackson, with two outs, hit a hard ground ball, which Lopes bobbled for his sixth error, as Reggie, digging hard, beat the throw to first. Reggie turned back and walked toward the base, limping just a little on his heavily taped left leg, looking tired and beat. It wasn't only the World Series that was coming to an end. It was the final curtain of the Reggie Jackson era.

AFTERWORD

It will never be the same.

The first impulse is to say that it shouldn't have ended like that, on a whimper. But how could it have been any other way? Sooner or later George was going to foul things up, and what better setting could a man of such gargantuan presence have chosen than the greatest stage of all, the World Series.

As for Reggie, after all his protestations of never playing for George Steinbrenner again, he limped out of New York, not wanting to leave, never wanting it to end. Willing to the very last to come back on any terms George dictated. Reggie is always on trial, and in George he had found the judge he had always been searching for.

Billy is out there somewhere, he will always be out there somewhere—not quite the Billy Martin we knew in those first bombastic days, but far more than we saw at the end. Billy had to find a father he could honor ("I want to honor that man," he has said of each of his owners, "if he'd only let me") and test and defy so that he could come back ("I'll bust my ass for you if you'll let me") to be forgiven and loved. And in George he had found the Biggest Mother . . . sorry, Biggest Father of them all.

Don't discount the possibility that George understood these troubled children of his. Never doubt that while he was playing to his own ego, he was also playing to their needs. Never underestimate George Steinbrenner.

George remains. There will always be George. The Reggie Jackson era has come to an end, and George has set about to build another. For above all, George is a great administrator. There is no business he couldn't run. So although he was forced to turn certain technical functions over to "my baseball people" while he was learning, he is ready now to take it all upon himself, and with his own people. The season wasn't over more than a week before the way was being prepared for Gene Michael to return. Gee, what a surprise.

George believes in statistics, and statistics show the National League to be superior, and so George has opted for the National League brand of ball. He has gone after National Leaguers. To Dave Winfield and Jerry Mumphrey, he has added Ken Griffey and Dave Collins. He'll get his bunting, finally, and he'll get his running, and he'll get his hit-and-run.

But, you know, that won't really matter. It will never be the same for us. And, we can suspect, it will never be the same for George.

You can win another championship, George, you can win ten championships ten times over, but it will never be the same as when Billy was going after Reggie in the Boston dugout. Or on that great Hallelujah Day when Billy came running out of the dugout on Old Timers' Day, waving his cap. Or Reggie standing there at home plate contemplating the sheer majesty of a Reggie Jackson home run before punching the air and riding the wind around the basepaths. Jerry Mumphrey can be counted upon to never loaf in center field, but who else but Mickey Rivers could be Mickey Rivers? And who will crawl back to the dugout with his tongue hanging out, George, now that there is no more Sparky Lyle?

You are building a good, gray New York Yankees, it seems, filled with all those nice guys you could meet any Sunday morning in church. Is it possible that we are going to end up with a good, gray George M. Steinbrenner III?

Say it ain't so, Boss.